Historical and Critical Dictionary

SELECTIONS

St. Louis Community College
at Meramec
Library

ISBN 0-87220-104-X (cloth)
ISBN 0-87220-103-1 (paper)
Originally published in 1965 by The Library of Liberal Arts
Original Library of Congress Catalog Card Number 64-16703

Pierre
BAYLE
Historical and Critical
DICTIONARY

SELECTIONS

Translated, with an Introduction and Notes, by
Richard H. Popkin
Washington University, St. Louis,
and
UCLA

With the Assistance of Craig Brush
Fordham University

Hackett Publishing Company, Inc.

Indianapolis/Cambridge

Pierre Bayle: 1647–1706
Dictionnaire historique et critique was first published in 1697.

Copyright © 1991 by Hackett Publishing Company, Inc.
All rights reserved
Printed in the United States of America

99 98 97 96 95 94 93 92 91   1 2 3 4 5 6 7 8 9 10

Cover Design by Dan Kirklin
Text Design by Stefan Salter Associates

For further information please address
  Hackett Publishing Company, Inc.
  P.O. Box 44937
  Indianapolis, Indiana 46244-0937

Library of Congress Cataloging-in-Publication Data

Bayle, Pierre, 1647–1706.
    [Dictionnaire historique et critique.   English.   Selections]
    Historical and critical dictionary: selections/Pierre Bayle:
translated, with an introduction and notes, by Richard H. Popkin,
with assistance of Craig Brush.
        p.   cm.
    Translation of: Dictionnaire historique et critique.
    Includes bibliographical references and index.
    ISBN 0-87220-104-X (cloth)—ISBN 0-87220-103-1 (pbk.)
    1. Biography—Dictionaries.   2. Philosophy—Dictionaries.
3. Theology—Dictionaries.   4. Science—Dictionaries.
5. Skepticism—Dictionaries.   I. Popkin, Richard Henry, 1923–
II. Brush, Craig.   III. Title.
B1825.D53213B39   1991
190—dc20   90-5246
                                                                CIP

The paper used in this publication meets the minimum requirements
American National Standard for Information Sciences—Permanence
Paper for Printed Library Materials, ANSI Z39.48-1984.

∞

Acknowledgments

I should like to take this opportunity to thank those with whom I have discussed Bayle over the years, and who have given me valuable suggestions about the preparation of this volume. First of all, I should like to thank my good friend Professor Paul Edwards of New York University [now of Brooklyn College, CUNY] for having suggested that I undertake this venture. Next, I should like to thank *la première bayliste du monde*, Dr. Elisabeth Labrousse, for all of the invaluable interchanges we have had about our mutual friend Pierre Bayle. Then I should like to thank my collaborators in other ventures, Professor Paul Dibon of Nijmegen [now retired from the École pratique des hautes études of Paris] and the late Dr. C. Louise Thijssen-Schoute, who have helped me over the years to gain a perspective and understanding of Bayle. I should like to thank my students past and present, whose enthusiasm for the Bayle to whom I introduced them has helped to stimulate and develop my present picture of him. Among these gentlemen, I should especially like to mention Professor Harry M. Bracken of Arizona State University [now of McGill University and Erasmus University, Rotterdam], Professor Richard A. Watson of Washington University, St. Louis, Professor Philip Cummins of the University of Iowa, and Professor David Fate Norton of the University of California, San Diego [now of McGill University]. I should also like to thank Professor Craig Brush of Columbia University [now of Fordham University] for all of his helpful criticism of the manuscript and his efforts in getting it into final form. In addition, discussions with him and with Professor Walter Rex of the University of Califor-

nia, Berkeley, have aided me in formulating more clearly
some of my interpretations of Bayle. And I wish to thank Mr.
Jack Ornstein for helping to prepare the index.

Lastly, and with sincere gratitude, I should like to thank
my family for encouraging me throughout this venture.
They have had to live with the four folio volumes of the
French 1740 edition, the ten folio volumes of the English
1734–1740 translation (the *last* complete one, and not a very
accurate one at that), the five folio volumes of Bayle's *Œuvres
diverses*, as well as assorted reference works. My wife, Juliet,
has labored as an invaluable consultant and proofreader,
Jeremy and Margaret [now a professor and a lawyer respec-
tively], have labored at sorting and arranging the bits and
pieces as they piled up everywhere. And I am also grateful to
my infant daughter, Susan [now a Ph.D. and a post-doctoral
researcher], who has crawled over the volumes, peeked in
them hoping to find pictures, and who in all this time has not
damaged or marked a single page! I want to thank the entire
family for their patience and fortitude, hoping that we will all
feel that the effort has been worth while.

R.H.P.
LaJolla, California, 1965
Pacific Palisades, California, 1990

Contents

Historical and Critical Dictionary (Selections)

Introduction

In this day and age, can we still imagine that a biographical dictionary, a *Who's Who,* could be one of the most exciting works of an age; that such a work could have summed up and exposed the Century of Genius and could have launched the Enlightenment? There has never been another work like Pierre Bayle's *Historical and Critical Dictionary,* and it is almost impossible to imagine today that there ever might be another such accomplishment. One man, Pierre Bayle, working in Rotterdam in the 1690's, was able to wander hither and yonder through the world of man's intellectual and moral thought, from the beginning of written history to yesterday's newspapers and café gossip, and could portray enough of it from *A* to *Z* to encompass all that his age had to offer, and to reveal so many of its failings in such sharp relief. One man's portrayal of the ancient sages, the Biblical heroes and heroines, the kings and queens, the courtiers and the courtesans, the theologians, the philosophers, the crackpots of all times, could fascinate such men as Leibniz, Voltaire, Bishop Berkeley, David Hume, Thomas Jefferson, and Herman Melville. Bayle had roamed from seductions to perversions to murders to massacres to visions to paradoxes, in dazzling fashion, as he marched from "Aaron" to "Zuylichem." He had provided a wondrous body of lore and food for thought. He had provided a marvelous suite of themes and variations, on such problems as those of cuckoldry, and castration fears, and religious intolerance, and historical accuracy, and of finding certitude in philosophy, science, and religion. These themes flash back and forth and interplay through the columns of folio footnotes. A point raised in "Rorarius," or in "Pyrrho," or in "Helen of Troy," or in "Bolsec" could suddenly focus upon some of the most burning issues men have tried to resolve. Bayle wove his themes round and round into an incredible fabric of historical information, lewd anecdotes, moral musings, philosophical and theological analysis, and doubts and super-doubts. The work is really a *Summa Sceptica* that deftly undermined all the foundations of the seventeenth-century intellectual world.

The *Dictionary*, first published in 1697, and enlarged in the second edition of 1702, continued to grow and grow. Subsequent editions and translations added what had been omitted, and refuted or corrected some of Bayle's odd or eccentric views. But the headlong rush of the Enlightenment for enlightenment soon outstripped the confines of any emendations of Bayle's *Dictionary*. Diderot's *Encyclopédie*, the *Encyclopaedia Britannica*, the *Biographie Universelle*, and then in our century the *Dictionary of National Biography*, and *Who's Who* followed. No one man could do it by himself. Teams of experts were needed who would report the facts and would have no time or space for digressions or reflections. A dictionary could no longer amuse or cause philosophical and moral reflection; it had to inform, and only inform. Bayle was too incomplete, too inaccurate, too outdated, too digressive, too lewd, too obscure, too obscene. Hence, he was relegated to oblivion. Library reference shelves needed the space for *Who's Who in American Photography* and *Who's Who in European Bridge Playing*. No one would or could use Bayle for his children's homework, or for cribbing term papers. Hence, the monumental opus has disappeared, a victim of one of its offspring, "scientific" scholarship. The libraries moved their sets to storage, the owners sold them secondhand, to get new reference works. So, Bayle disappeared from intellectual history almost as completely as he had once dominated it. All that was left was a name, appearing and reappearing in almost all discussions of the eighteenth century.

We are now far enough removed so that we can rediscover Bayle, without worrying about what he has omitted, or whether his facts are accurate, or whether more complete studies exist on Aaron, or Beza, or Dicaearchus, or Flora, or. . . . We can now

go back and see how the world looked to an amazing man at
the end of the seventeenth century, before everyone became
"enlightened." We can recover the moment that the Newtonian
age dawned, and see the first signs of what was to come. We can
see the ingenious skeptical arguments that were to excite the
young George Berkeley, the young David Hume, the young
François Marie Arouet (Voltaire), the young Denis Diderot. We
can see the brilliant dialectic that was to bother and badger
Gottfried Wilhelm Leibniz, the Earl of Shaftesbury, Bernard
Mandeville, Bishop King, and unnumbered German and Dutch
professors.

A few years ago, Ernest C. Mossner wrote in his biography of
Hume, "What treasures are to be found in Bayle, but what an
effort to dig them up! Proper source for a twenty-one-year-old
burning with intellectual curiosity, Bayle is definitely to be
avoided by the middle-aged who have little spare time on their
hands."[1] The forbidding look of Bayle's text, with its folio columns of footnotes, and footnotes to footnotes, and its biogra-
phies of totally unknown figures, certainly suggests Mossner's
judgment is right. But the rewards of recapturing the world
Bayle lived in, and of recapturing the force of his skeptical criticisms of his age, can easily justify the effort involved. The character of the issues—the problems and hopes of the seventeenth
century—becomes clear in a most amazing way; and the inner
dialectic that unfolded in the struggles of religion, of science,
of the quest for philosophical certainty, comes alive again. Bayle
seized on every weakness and inconsistency of the intellectual
giants of his time. He claimed he knew too much to be a skeptic
and too little to be a dogmatist. And, as he fought and exposed
and ridiculed up and down his folio columns, and chased from
remark B in "Nicolle" to D in "Pellison" to . . . , he laid bare
every tension and discord in the republic of letters. The intellectuals around him and those who were to follow found that his
footnotes were their battlegrounds. It was only by countering

---

[1] Ernest C. Mossner, *The Life of David Hume* (Austin: University of
Texas Press, 1954), pp. 78–79.

or building on his points that a new intellectual world could be erected.

Pierre Bayle was born in 1647 in the tiny town of Carla (now Carla-Bayle), near the Spanish border south of Toulouse, where his father was a Protestant minister. He lived in the troubled atmosphere of the persecuted Huguenots, whose status as a powerful minority was being undermined by Louis XIV. Throughout the seventeenth century, from the time of Richelieu's capture of La Rochelle onward, Protestant power and rights were being eroded. The situation grew worse and worse in the second half of the century, with severe governmental pressure to force the Calvinists to convert to Catholicism, resulting in the closing of Protestant schools and churches, the quartering of unruly dragoons in Protestant homes, and finally culminating in 1685 with the Revocation of the Edict of Nantes, which withdrew all legal rights and privileges from the Protestant minority. Throughout this period hundreds of thousands of people fled their native land to the freer atmosphere of the Netherlands, England, Germany, Denmark, the New World, and elsewhere, while others suffered terrible hardships and oppressions in France. Young Pierre Bayle, a member of a staunch Protestant family, was sent first to a Calvinist school at Puylaurens and then to the Jesuit college at Toulouse for his education. The problems raised in the controversial literature of the time and the dialectical prodding of the skilled disputants at Toulouse led him to abandon Protestantism for Catholicism on the basis of intellectual considerations. Having committed the most horrendous sin possible for the son of an embattled Calvinist minister, he then redeemed himself, in the family's eyes, by his second conversion, again apparently on the basis of intellectual considerations, this time abandoning Catholicism to return to the faith of his family. (The intellectual journey from Protestantism to Catholicism to Protestantism was undergone by Chillingworth before Bayle, and Gibbon after him, with equally fascinating results.) By this second change of religion, Bayle became, technically, a *relaps*, that is, one who has returned to heresy after having once abjured it, and who, hence, was subject to severe penalties, such as banishment or imprisonment, in the France of Louis XIV. For his protection and reintegration into the Calvinist world, he was sent in 1670 to the University of Geneva to complete his studies in philosophy and theology. He then returned to France, in 1674, in disguise, and was a tutor in Paris and Rouen. We find him visiting with the Basnages, a prominent Protestant family in Rouen; he was also known at Justel's salon in Paris. In 1675 he competed for the post of professor of philosophy at the Calvinist academy of Sedan, which he won as the protégé of the fanatically orthodox theologian, who was later to become his bitterest enemy, Pierre Jurieu. Bayle and Jurieu remained at Sedan until the institution was closed by the state in 1681, which was acting to close the Protestant universities. They each left Sedan separately for the free air of Holland and were reunited as faculty members of a new academy in Rotterdam, the *Ecole Illustre*, and as members of the French Reformed Church of that city. Bayle brought the manuscript of his first book with him, the *Lettre sur la comète (Letter on the Comet)*, reissued later as *Pensées diverses sur la comète (Miscellaneous Thoughts on the Comet)*, in which he began his public attack on superstition, intolerance, bad philosophy, and bad history. The success of this first entry into the intellectual world was soon followed by other publications: *Critique générale de l'histoire du Calvinisme du P. Maimbourg*, a critical attack on the former Jesuit Father Maimbourg's history of Calvinism; *Recueil de quelques pièces curieuses concernant la philosophie de M. Descartes*, a collection of articles on Cartesianism (in answer to Jesuit attacks) by Malebranche, the Abbé Lanion, Bayle, and others. (In this latter work Bayle was already developing a view that was to appear in the *Dictionary*, namely, that the basic concepts of physics—place, time, and motion—have not yet been comprehended in an adequate or coherent manner by any of the schools of philosophy, be they Scholastic, Cartesian, or any other.)

During this period, some personal events and decisions seem to have taken place that greatly affected certain aspects of Bayle's life. The first was the decision not to marry a young lady whose hand was offered to him by the Jurieu family. The theme, which occurs and recurs throughout the *Dictionary*, of whether the scholar should marry, seems to have been a live problem for him at this time; Bayle apparently made his life commitment, that his work was more important than any personal satisfaction or gain he might have obtained by becoming a family man. He dedicated himself to the lonely monastic life of the seeker after truth from then on. He also refused the offer of a professorship at Franeker, seeming to prefer staying in Rotterdam, where he was committed to writing a monthly journal, to pursuing a larger public career in the academic world. The deaths of his brothers and father in France in 1684–1685 as a result of the religious persecutions (his brother Jacob died in prison), seems to have been decisive in committing Bayle to a lifetime allegiance both to Calvinism and to toleration.

During 1684–1687, Bayle published and edited the *Nouvelles de la République des Lettres (News of the Republic of Letters)*, in which he reviewed and commented on books of all kinds. His acute judgment soon made him one of the central figures in the intellectual community and put him in contact with many of its leading figures—Leibniz, Malebranche, Arnauld, Boyle, and Locke. In 1686, Bayle published one of his most masterful works, his *Commentaire philosophique sur ces paroles de Jesus-Christ, Contrain-les d'entrer (Philosophical Commentary on the Words of Jesus, "Constrain them to come in")*. This essay, directed against the persecutions of the Protestants by Louis XIV, was perhaps *the* most outspoken argument of its time for complete toleration, extending the case to Moslems, Jews, Socinians (Unitarians), and Catholics, and hence, going further than Locke's *Essay on Toleration* that was to appear two years later.

In this period Bayle's relations with Jurieu became more and more strained. Jurieu grew more and more fanatical and saw himself as the leader of and spokesman for orthodoxy, fighting against all sorts of heresies and backsliding tendencies, and leading the struggle for political justice and revenge against Louis XIV. His political views became more and more radical while his theological ones became more and more intolerant. His erstwhile protégé, Bayle, found himself often disagreeing with Jurieu's views and policies, and he dissociated himself often from the latter's doctrines, politics and actions. Bayle's letters from 1684 onward indicate that they saw less and less of each other and became more and more critical of one another, while Bayle moved more and more into the circle of Jurieu's enemies. From Jurieu's point of view, the publication of the *Commentaire philosophique* was the last straw. Though Bayle tried to hide his authorship of the work, Jurieu quickly guessed that it was by him and saw that they were in complete and total ideological disagreement. As the fanatical defender of orthodoxy against the incursions of liberalism and rationalism, Jurieu announced that his protégé, his colleague and fellow parishioner, was a menace to true religion, a secret atheist, and so on.[2] Bayle kept making matters worse, with his ridicule of Jurieu, his attacks on intolerance, his attacks on Jurieu's hopes for regaining control of France, and then with the *Dictionary*, where Jurieu was to turn up in the most unlikely places as the villain, while Bayle was to insist until his dying day that he, Bayle, was in the direct line of John Calvin, due to the lessons he learned from Jurieu's thoroughly antirational theology. At first, the liberals—Jacquelot, Saurin, and others—whose theology Jurieu attacked, saw in Bayle an ally in their struggles against rigid Calvinism and intolerance. They were soon to be as disillusioned as Jurieu was. Bayle used all his brilliant critical faculties to decimate their rationalism about theology, and to drive home

---

[2] Jurieu's views about the *Commentaire philosophique* and its role in the Bayle-Jurieu quarrel appear in the latter's *Apologie du Sr. Jurieu . . .* (La Haye, 1691), *Courte revue des maximes de morale et principes de religion de l'auteur des pensées diverses sur les comètes, & de la critique generale sur l'histoire du Calvinisme du Maimbourg* (n.p., n.d., apparently 1691), and *Le philosophe de Rotterdam* (Amsterdam, 1706).

his contention that there could be no reconciliation between the world of rational and "scientific" ideas, and several articles of the Christian faith. The bewildered liberals then found themselves committed to a lifetime of defense of their views from the furious barrage unleashed from the critical, skeptical mind of Pierre Bayle. From 1686 until his death in 1706 (when he died working on his last onslaught against the liberal Protestant theologians, Le Clerc, Bernard, and Jacquelot), Bayle fought Jurieu on the one hand, and the liberals on the other, piling one controversial work upon the other. The Bayle-Jurieu controversies, covertly starting in 1686–1687, often went far beyond the genteel level of polite dispute, especially in the furious pamphlet exchange of 1690–1692, centering around the authorship and the content of the notorious *Avis important aux réfugiez sur leur prochain retour en France (Important Advice to the Refugees on Their Next Return to France)*, concerning which Bayle managed to befuddle the evidence so much that even twentieth-century scholars are not willing to attribute the work definitely to him. In 1693 Bayle's academic career ended with the dismissal from his post at Rotterdam, and this, fortunately, left him with time enough for the *Dictionary*, and all his later controversies.

The spirit that pervades the *Dictionary* was alive and active long before its writing. Bayle had been collecting errors he had found in various historical works for years. His letter of 1675 to Minutoli shows he was already seriously interested in skepticism by then. His Rotterdam lectures show that he was devoted to analyzing and attacking all sorts of theories. The critical and the skeptical attitudes fused in the *Dictionary*. Bayle's original intention in 1690 was to publish a critical dictionary that would contain a list of all the errors in other available dictionaries, especially the earlier one of Louis Moreri.[3] The fights with Jurieu delayed this project until 1692, when a sample appeared

---

[3] Louis Moreri, *Le Grand Dictionnaire Historique, ou le Mélange Curieux de l'Histoire Sainte et Profane* (1674).

to ascertain whether the public was actually interested in such a work. In the Preface, addressed to Bayle's friend Du Rondel, who was professor at Maastricht, the author described the work as "a book filled with the sins of the Latin country [i.e., the learned world], and a heap of the filth of the republic of letters."

The lack of public interest led to a change of plans, that is, a historical and critical dictionary that would offer factual accounts, criticisms of errors, plus commentary, and philosophical discussions. Originally Bayle had planned to deal with persons and things. The final version became almost exclusively devoted to persons, with a few articles on places, as "Japan" and "Rotterdam." Those persons who were adequately dealt with elsewhere, especially in Moreri, were omitted, and many, perhaps far too many, people who had been ignored either through ignorance or insignificance were to find their place in the *Dictionary*. On Plato, St. Thomas Aquinas, Descartes, Richelieu, Charlemagne, Columbus, and Shakespeare, Bayle wrote no articles, while on such obscure figures as Jean Fernel, Armand de Gontaut, Pierre Jarrige, Acidalius, Hermolaüs Barbarus, Dejotarus, René le Pays, Rorarius, and Zueris, Bayle wrote fairly substantial ones.

Despite the ever-constant problem of fighting back against Jurieu's violent attacks, and despite his migraine headaches, Bayle worked feverishly preparing his magnum opus. In 1696 he wrote a friend: "You would excuse my silence, if you knew how overwhelmed I am with work for the printing of my *Historical and Critical Dictionary*. The publisher wants to get it done this year, no matter what the cost, so that I have to furnish him incessantly with new copy and have to correct proofs every day, in which there are hundreds of faults to eliminate, because my original, full of erasures, and footnoting, does not allow either the printers or the proofreaders to extricate themselves from such a labyrinth. And what delays me much is that since I do not have all the books at hand that I have to consult, I am obliged to wait until I have them sought after, if someone in this city possesses them. . . . I am happy that your migraines have left you. Mine would have given me the same pleasure, if I had been able to live without studying; but stubborn work keeps them going and makes them return very often. I lose several days each month on account of this, which then requires me to work harder to make up for lost time."[4]

In spite of all the difficulties, the first edition appeared in 1697 and was a great success. It appeared with Bayle's name on it, because of legal problems caused by the publishers of Moreri's *Dictionary*. The work was attacked by Jurieu and was brought to the attention of the Consistory of the French Reformed Church of Rotterdam by his coterie. It was also banned in France. Both of these events no doubt helped to make the work notorious and more popular. Bayle was grateful for the ban in his homeland, since it saved him from the charge of not having been sufficiently pro-Protestant and anti-Catholic. The examination by the Consistory of his church led to his agreement to remove certain parts of the text, especially in the article "David" (see p. 45), and to explain his meaning more clearly in the second edition on what he had said about the possibility that atheists might be moral, about the inability of orthodox Christianity to answer rationally the Manichean objections concerning the problem of evil, about the relationship of skepticism and faith, and to explain why so much obscene material appeared in his work. These matters are dealt with in the famous four Clarifications, appended to the second edition, in which Bayle makes his case even more striking than it was at first.

Bayle began working on the second edition as soon as the first was finished, adding many additional articles and remarks, answering such critics as Leibniz, Locke's friend Jean Le Clerc, Jurieu, and a host of others, thereby enlarging the text by a couple of million words. This second edition, almost as complete as the work was ever to be, wore Bayle out. For relaxation, he followed this with his *Réponse aux questions d'un provincial*

---

4 Letter to David Constant de Rebecque, May 31, 1696, in Bayle, *Œuvres Diverses* (The Hague, 1727), IV, 724–726.

(Reply to the Questions of a Country Gentleman), in which he defended his views and attacked his opponents of the right, like Jurieu, and those of the left, like Le Clerc, Bernard, Jacquelot, and Leibniz. His polemical activities continued until the day of his death, December 28, 1706, when he put the final touches to his last work, the *Entretiens de Maxime et de Themiste (Conversations Between Maxime and Themiste)*.

Bayle had fought long and hard "against everything that is said, and everything that is done."[5] Despite all his destructive efforts, his good friend, Anthony Ashley Cooper, the third Earl of Shaftesbury, could say in tribute, "Whatever he might be in speculation, he was in practice one of the best of Christians, and almost the only man I ever knew who, professing philosophy, lived truly as a philosopher; with that innocence, virtue, temperance, humility, contempt of the world and interest which might be called exemplary. Nor was there ever a fairer reasoner, or a civiler, politer, wittier man in conversation."[6] His fanatical enemy, Pierre Jurieu, launched another attack entitled *Le Philosophe de Rotterdam, accusé, atteint, et convaincu (The Philospher of Rotterdam, Accused, Indicted, and Convicted)*. The Catholic *Mémoires de Trévoux* observed sadly, "What a good fortune for the literary world it would be if all those who have read much knew how to give their compilations the charming turn he gave to his! What a misfortune it is that, having possessed in the highest degree the precious talent to embellish what is most dry and arid in the sciences, he was content to cul-

---

5 In De Boze's "Eloge de M. le Cardinal de Polignac," the Preface to De Polignac's *L'Anti-Lucrece* (Paris, 1749), Vol. I, Bayle is quoted as having told the cardinal, when the latter stopped by to visit him in Holland and asked what religion he belonged to, "Oui, Monsieur, je suis bon protestant, et dans toute la force du mot, car au fond de mon âme, je proteste contre tout ce qui se dit et tout ce qui se fait." ("Yes, Sir, I am a good Protestant and in the full sense of the term, for, from the bottom of my soul, I protest against everything that is said, and everything that is done.")

6 Letter to Mr. Darby, February 2, 1708, in *The Life, Unpublished Letters and Philosophical Regimen of Anthony, Earl of Shaftesbury*, ed. Benjamin Rand (London, 1900), pp. 385–386.

tivate it only on the edges of precipices, where he could not be followed without danger."[7] And Locke's friend Le Clerc, after piously announcing that he would not argue with a dead man who could not defend himself any more, could only express dismay when Bayle's posthumous attack appeared, showing that, even with the author resting in his grave, his pen could still do its damage.

The writers of the eighteenth century used the endless arguments of Bayle as "The Arsenal of the Enlightenment" and thereby wrought monumental changes in the intellectual world. Many of the *philosophes* and nineteenth-century figures concerned with intellectual history assumed that, since Bayle had provided the Age of Reason with so much critical ammunition to be employed against unenlightened theologians and metaphysicians, he must also have shared the avant-garde views of the Enlightenment. They interpreted him as a precursor of the irreligious, empirical, and scientific tendencies that were to destroy the ideology of the *ancien régime*.

But, regardless of the effects of Bayle's work, we can ask if this was what the author was actually trying to accomplish. From Jurieu and Voltaire, to Feuerbach, down to the present, there has been a wide range of interpretation. Bayle has been seen as an atheist, as the critic of traditional religion, the enlightened skeptic, the advocate of complete toleration, the fideist, the true believer, the man of faith. The task of reading the heart and soul of Bayle has intrigued and baffled many, and I would be foolish if I pretended to be ready with *the* answer. I shall briefly offer my own answer as a possibility. It is obviously at variance with a long tradition and is closer to a relatively new view, expressed by some of the contributors to the recent commemoration volume for the 250th anniversary of Bayle's death, *Pierre Bayle, Le Philosophe de Rotterdam,* edited by P. Dibon. My interpretation is based on the overall argument that

---

[7] *Memoires pour l'histoire des sciences et des beaux-arts (Mémoires de Trévoux;* April 1707), p. 706.

appears throughout the *Dictionary,* and in all the subsequent defenses of this work by its author.

Prior to Bayle there had been a century-long tradition of Catholic thinkers who labeled themselves "Christian skeptics." This group, starting with Montaigne and Pierre Charron, and ending with Bayle's contemporary, Pierre-Daniel Huet, Bishop of Avranches, had combined the classical skeptical arguments questioning the possibility of gaining absolutely certain knowledge of the real world, with an advocacy of pure fideism, that is, the acceptance of fundamental truths solely on faith and not on the basis of any rational evidence. They had employed the materials in the rediscovered treasury of Greek Pyrrhonism, the writings of Sextus Empiricus, to undermine the claims of knowledge by the Calvinists, Scholastics, Platonists, Renaissance naturalists, and so on. They argued in old Pyrrhonian style about the unreliability of our senses and reason in the search for truth, and about our inability to discover or employ any indisputable criterion of truth. This humiliation of human reason, by showing its total and complete inadequacy for acquiring any truths in science, philosophy, or theology, was taken as the preparation for receiving the faith from God (at least this is what the Christian skeptics stated, whether they were sincere or not). With the appearance of Descartes on the intellectual stage, they refurbished the epistemological weapons of Sextus Empiricus to attack the new dogmatism of Descartes, and to show that he also had not managed to find absolutely certain and indubitable truths.

Bayle, however, was not content just to restate the classical skeptical problem of knowledge and to continue the tradition of Montaigne against the latest dogmatic opponents—Descartes, Hobbes, Spinoza, Malebranche, Leibniz, Locke. His over-all tactic was to analyze and dissolve any theory on its own terms, be it metaphysical, theological, or scientific. In so doing, he relied much more on the antimetaphysical sections of Sextus' writings than on the earlier epistemological ones. No matter what subject is being discussed—the souls of beasts, the nature of matter,

Newtonian physics, the nature of truth—the same dismaying results ensues: Each time Bayle takes a different theory and examines it in order to point out the logical consequences entailed by its assumptions, problems, questions, doubts arise everywhere. In the style of one of his heroes, "the subtle Arriaga," the last of the great Spanish Scholastics, Bayle employed the critical technique he learned at the Jesuit college in Toulouse to show *le fort et le faible,* the strength and the weakness, of every human effort to make sense out of any aspect of human experience. Pursued long enough, this approach exhibits the sad fact that rational effort is always its own undoing. What at first looks like a way to explain something soon becomes a way of perplexing. Rational endeavor, in any area whatsoever, is "the high road to Pyrrhonism," to complete skepticism. In remark G of the article on Uriel Acosta (not included in these selections), Bayle summed up man's sad intellectual plight: ". . . it [reason] is a guide that leads one astray; and philosophy can be compared to some powders that are so corrosive that, after they have eaten away the infected flesh of a wound, they then devour the living flesh, rot the bones, and penetrate to the very marrow. Philosophy at first refutes errors. But if it is not stopped at this point, it goes on to attack truths. And when it is left on its own, it goes so far that it no longer knows where it is and can find no stopping place."

Having gone this far, Bayle announces over and over and over again that when man realizes the inadequacy and incompetency of reason to resolve any question, he should seek another guide—faith or revelation. The term "guide" suggests another of Bayle's favorites, Maimonides, the author of *The Guide for the Perplexed,* a work frequently referred to in the *Dictionary.* The French translation of "perplexed" in Maimonides' sense is usually *les égarés,* and over and over again Bayle speaks of the rational truth-seekers, the philosophers, the theologians, and the scientists, as ending up as *égarés,* or in *égarements* ("perplexities"), and needing a new "guide." (The nineteenth-century French translation of Maimonides' title is

Le guide pour les égarés. Bayle used a Latin edition.) In this
sense, one might say that the *Dictionary* was really intended as
a new *Guide for the Perplexed.* Maimonides had tried to show
how people became perplexed by failing to distinguish what can
properly be known by reason, what by faith, and what by both.
Their misuse, or use in the wrong areas on the wrong questions,
would lead to utter confusion, contradictions, and perplexities.
Maimonides left reason great areas to work in before it reached
its limits and intellectual chaos set in. Bayle reduced the size
of this area to just about zero, so that any and all rational inquiries led to perplexity, which could only be overcome by
finding a guide other than reason. Bayle's various discussions
are like the peeling of an onion and have the effect of removing layer after layer of conviction and assurance. Unlike
Bayle's friend Leibniz, the author of the *Dictionary* did not expect to find rational truth at the center from which he could
reconstruct the outer layers. Instead, this endless process leaves
the reader thoroughly perplexed about anything and everything. Then Bayle's "guide" for such unfortunates, the rational
animals of this world, points out the need for faith and the acceptance of revelation, *without reason,* lest one return to or
remain in the instability of the world of the perplexed.

No matter what the context of his remarks, whether sacred or
secular, Bayle makes it clear that reason fails to make the real
world intelligible. The revealed world, he insists, is in direct
opposition to the most evident maxims of reason and morality.
From Genesis onward, faith involves claims that reason cannot
understand, endorse, or live with. For example, Bayle contended
that rational man finds that the causal maxim, "Nothing comes
from nothing," is the clearest, most evident, most indubitable
principle of human reason, and it is completely shattered by
the unintelligible news that God created the world *out of nothing.* The most evident, rationally justified moral maxims are
undermined by the Biblical accounts of the heroes of the faith,
the Old Testament prophets, patriarchs, and others. Bayle always asserted, having posed this complete dichotomy, made as

bald and as blunt as possible in the "Clarification on the Pyrr-honists" (p. 421), that he was advocating revelation as the only secure and satisfactory haven for man.

Bayle's antirational and not very moral picture of the re-vealed world is not quite as strange as it looks at first sight. There are striking parallels between it and the versions of Christianity offered by later irrational fideists like Lamennais, Kierkegaard, and Chestov. In addition, the view expressed by Bayle in the *Dictionary*, and defended in the Clarifications and in his later writings, is very much like those parts of the extreme antirationalist theology advocated by Pierre Jurieu, in which the latter dealt with why there can be no rational evidence for the faith, and with the incomprehensible and amoral character of revealed truth. For example, Jurieu's view that grace alone can reveal the message and divine character of Scripture could easily lead to some shocking views about how the text would appear to nonbelievers. (And it is worth noting that Bayle speaks at length only about figures in the Old Testament and the post-Biblical Christian heroes and heroines, but not about anyone in the New Testament, except for a brief, insignificant article on St. John the Evangelist. There is a ribald article on St. Mary of Egypt [not in this group of selections], but not one on St. Mary Magdalene, who would seem to be an excellent subject for Bayle.)

But, in spite of all Bayle's protestations, Jurieu insisted that he and Bayle did not share either the same fideism or the same faith. And herein lies the heart of the matter. Was Bayle, in his forceful, skeptical way, trying to lead people to faith, or was he secretly trying to destroy it, as Voltaire and many others have since suspected, by making it so irrational, so lacking in moral-ity, and so ridiculous?[8] Jurieu knew Bayle and hated him for a host of personal reasons, so his suspicions may not be the best guide. Shaftesbury, who lived for a while under the same roof

---

[8] See, for instance, the quotation from the libertine St. Evremond, offered in the "Clarification on the Pyrrhonists," a statement on the nature of re-vealed truth (p. 431).

with Bayle, called him "one of the best of Christians." The text and texture of Bayle's writings certainly suggest an absence of a crucial religious element, found in Pascal, Kierkegaard, and others in this tradition, namely, that of ultimate concern. If one compares Bayle's calm and tepid statement on the debacle of reason and the need for divine guidance in remark C (p. 204) of article "Pyrrho" with Pascal's passionate and desperate *pensée* 434 (upon which Bayle's passage seems to be based)[9] or with Hume's anguished finale to the first book of *A Treatise of Human Nature,* where he could find no faith and no way of overcoming Bayle's ultimate doubts, then one definitely finds that some feature is absent. Bayle suffered, apparently, from no *Angst,* no fear and trembling. Unlike his nineteenth-century admirer, Herman Melville, Bayle was not desperately seeking God or trying to pierce the heart of Moby Dick. Unlike Kierkegaard, Bayle wrote no stirring positive religious works, though he certainly wrote negative and antirational ones similar to Kierkegaard's *Assault on Christendom* and *Training in Christianity.* The total absence of mystical or fervent religious expression in Bayle's writings makes one wonder what he *really* intended.

Bayle himself presented a picture of a religious attitude shorn of emotional content in remark M (p. 295) of article "Spinoza" that may well fit his own condition. He there describes two cases: People who have religion in their minds but not in their hearts, and those who have religion in their hearts but not in their minds. The first-named persons "are convinced of its [religion's] truth without their consciences being affected by the love of God," whereas the second "lose sight of it [religion] as soon as they seek it by the methods of human reasoning. They do not know where they are while they compare the pro and con. But as soon as they listen only to the proofs of feeling, the instincts of conscience, the weight of education, and the like, they are convinced of a religion; and they make their lives conform to it

---

9 *Pensée* 434 in the Brunschwicg edition (*pensée* 131 in the Lafuma classification).

as much as human weakness permits." Bayle's completely un-emotional statements about faith would indicate that he did not have "religion in the heart" in Pascal's sense, though he may well have had it in his own terms. When he tried to justify or understand it, all became doubtful and perplexing. When he could give up such rational endeavors, then a kind of tepid, un-emotional religion held sway.

In the interpretation I am offering (which is in disagreement with many others, ranging from those who see Bayle as a crypto-atheist or a deist, to those who see him as a fervent orthodox Calvinist), it is in the article "Bunel, Pierre" (p. 36), that Bayle's statement of faith appears. Pierre Bunel, the Renais-sance scholar from the area of Toulouse, who aided the develop-ment of modern skepticism by giving Montaigne's father a copy of Raimond Sebond's *Natural Theology,* is portrayed as the perfect Christian *because* he lived the lonely, quiet life of the scholar, caring not for worldly rewards. Bayle's dedication to the religious *cause* was the same as Bunel's. Bayle refused the pro-fessorship at Franeker. He spent his whole life revealing man's intellectual state through the most accurate scholarship and the most skeptical argumentation of his day. Bayle's version of the Christian life contains none of the fervor of the mystics, such as St. Francis of Assisi, San Juan de la Cruz, or Madame Guyon, and none of the anxiety of Pascal, Kierkegaard, or Dos-toevski. The quiet Erasmian scholar, living out his days in the city of Erasmus, examining man's intellectual heritage and intellectual world, could, by his patient erudition, undermine man's intellectual frame of reference, while remaining secure and tranquil in his unemotional religion of the heart.

This interpretation still leaves a major problem that may be fundamental in evaluating what Bayle was *really* asserting, namely, what extant religion best fits with Bayle's views, or what extant religion did Bayle actually accept or believe in? A note written to a friend the day he died, apparently his final statement on the subject, says "I feel that I have no more than a few moments to live. I am dying as a Christian philosopher, convinced of and pierced by the bounties and mercy of God, and I wish you a perfect happiness." Madame Labrousse, in her recent *Pierre Bayle*, Volume I, shows how minimal the Christian sentiments are in these final words. No mention is made of Jesus, of Calvinism, of Bayle's church, of the immortality of the soul, of sin, of repentance. Was Bayle possibly not a Christian except in some vague ethical sense? Was he, perhaps, actually an adherent of some other religion? I have speculated on some unusual possibilities that might account for some of his views and attitudes. Was he, perhaps, a Judaizing Christian, or a genuine Judeo-Christian, or even a secret Jew? These possibilities might explain his extraordinary knowledge of, and interest in, Judaism and his amazing tolerance on this score, which was far in advance of his time. Was he, perhaps, a genuine Manichean, a living survivor of the massacre of the Albigensians? (He came from their domain.) This might account for his extraordinary interest in their views and beliefs, his prolix examinations of why Christian theologians cannot answer the Manichean objections rationally, his attitude toward the Old Testament, and toward sexual aberrations. Bayle's critiques of various Socinian (Unitarian) views and deistical theories would seem to eliminate those possibilities. His persistence in remaining a member of the French Reformed Church of Rotterdam, despite all the troubles this caused him throughout the last twenty-five years of his life, suggests some genuine involvement and sincerity. Professor Sandberg's recent study, "Pierre Bayle's Sincerity in His Views on Faith and Reason," certainly shows that Bayle had no reason to fear persecution or censorship in Holland and could have lived and written as he pleased. His philosophical attack on Spinoza definitely suggests that his sympathies did not lie in that direction. Personally, I have found the attempt to define the actual beliefs and the actual religion of Bayle quite baffling. There are enough biographical and theoretical details to make it very difficult to assume that he was insincere in his almost lifelong adherence to Calvinism. But there are too many peculiarities in his views, his interests, his interpretations, to make it easy for me to accept the thesis that he really was a Calvinist in belief. Some of the other possibilities mentioned could account for some of these peculiarities but would then leave the biographical problem, why did he remain a member of the French Reformed Church of Rotterdam? Perhaps religion had no expressed or expressible content for him, but was only "in the heart" in some quite unemotional way, and when he tried to think and reason about it, he found too much plausibility in Manicheanism or Judaism. When he went back to pious study, he could preserve his composure as a "Christian philosopher" while destroying every form of intelligible Christian theology.

Until we can actually decide what Bayle did in fact believe and adhere to, we cannot ascertain the degree to which he was sincere, and the degree to which the next generation, the *philosophes* understood or misunderstood him. The avowed, the constant, and the continual statement of Bayle's message was that of the inadequacy and incoherence of man's intellectual endeavors, of the need for a different guide—faith and revelation—and of the picture of the Christian life in terms of the Erasmian goal of pious study. If this is, as I have assumed, at least part of what he believed, then he was certainly misunderstood by the thinkers of the Enlightenment. His destruction of certain views, however, was transformed by the Age of Reason into a positive affirmative of other views, into a new theology—scientism—that was to prove no more coherent or adequate than those Bayle had already denuded of all their pretensions and glory. Hume was to be one Baylean voice during this new enthusiasm, Hamann another, seeing that the newest philosophers, theologians, and scientists had really done no better than previous thinkers in making their formulations acceptable as man's understanding of man's world. The same kinds of skeptical problems that Bayle had raised against the theories of his day could be raised anew against the innovators of the eighteenth century. Both the critical and the positive views of the new spirits of the Age of Reason would turn out to be unable to withstand skeptical examination and probing. The ferocious efforts of Anthony Collins, Voltaire, Diderot, Tom Paine, *et al.*, to tear out the Judeo-Christian heart of our heritage, our understanding, and our hopes, were to turn out to be just as unsuccessful as all previous efforts to find the truth had been.

Perhaps only by rediscovering and fully appreciating Bayle's real legacy will we be able to realize the character of our present intellectual predicament—namely, that our philosophical and scientific guides are still inadequate to make our intellectual world coherent; that we seem to be unable to discover any other guides to replace or supplement our present ones; and that we no longer seem able to recapture a frame of reference within which the traditional guide of Judeo-Christianity can appear as a serious and complete alternative. Bayle, through his endless probing, undermined confidence in all the rational guides of his day. The problems he raised were not actually resolved by the new upsurge of confidence in man's reason during the Enlightenment, wherein the one guide Bayle left intact, that of faith and revelation, was undermined by this new confidence. Over two and a half centuries after Bayle, the destructive efforts initiated by Bayle have gradually undermined each new burst of enthusiasm and confidence in the ability of the latest achievements of man's rational endeavors to give us sure footing in the flux of the intellectual world we are trying to inhabit in our quest for understanding. The nonrational alternative Bayle offered us has been questioned and analyzed *ad nauseam* by techniques emerging from the folio columns of notes in Bayle, until the acceptance of faith and revelation that Bayle offered as a resolution to our perplexities looks like a preposterous and naïve suggestion that is unacceptable to modern enlightened man.

As a result of the two and a half centuries of erosion of all alternatives, growing out of Bayle's destructive efforts, we are in desperate need of someone wise enough and scholarly enough to write a new *Guide for the Perplexed*. We have many, maybe

far too many, subtle Arriagas, as Bayle's legacy, but no Maimonides, and perhaps no contemporary Bunel. This may be the
cause of the tragic emptiness in our world that so many of our
contemporary writers portray. In the age after the Age of Enlightenment we may have lost all possibility of finding or accepting any other kind of resolution. And this is, perhaps,
another and even the most harrowing of Bayle's contributions
to the "making of the modern mind." The realization and re-
assessment of what we have learned from Pierre Bayle and his
Dictionary, and what has happened to us as a result, may give
us some insight into the present crisis in the republic of letters and provide us with a basis for searching for new and more
hopeful means of resolving it.

Richard H. Popkin

La Jolla, California
December 1964

Selected Bibliography

BAYLE, PIERRE. *Dictionnaire historique et critique.* 5th edition, 4 folio vols., Amsterdam, Leiden, The Hague and Utrecht, 1740. A standard 18th-century edition, fairly readily available in major libraries.

————. *Dictionnaire historique et critique.* Edited by A.J.Q. BEUCHOT, 16 vols., Paris, 1820–1824. The last complete edition.

————. *Œuvres diverses.* 4 vols. The Hague, 1727. Collection of Bayle's writings other than the *Dictionary*, plus many of his letters. A photoreproduction of this edition was published by G. Olms, Hildesheim, 1964–1968. A fifth supplementary volume, 1982, contains a French version of some of Bayle's Latin works, plus some of the pamphlet literature about controversies Bayle was involved in.

————. *Dictionary, Historical and Critical.* 5 vols. London, 1734–1738. The first complete English translation.

————. *A General Dictionary, Historical and Critical.* 10 vols. London, 1734–1740. Contains all of Bayle's articles, plus many additional ones by the translators, especially on English subjects.

————. *Choix de textes.* With an Introduction by MARCEL RAYMOND. Paris: Egloff, 1948. Selections from a wide variety of Bayle's texts on many different subjects.

————. *Selections from Bayle's Dictionary.* Translated and edited by E.A. BELLER and M.DuP. LEE, Jr. Princeton: Princeton University Press, 1952. Contains fifteen of Bayle's articles. Somewhat difficult to use, since Bayle's notes are actually placed within the text of the articles.

————. *The Great Contest of Faith and Reason: Selections from the Writings of Pierre Bayle*. Translated and edited by KARL C. SANDBERG. New York: Frederick Ungar Publishing Co., 1963. Brief collection of items from Bayle's works up to and including the *Dictionary* (only parts of "Manicheans" and "Paulicians" used), on relation of faith and reason.

————. *Pensées diverses sur le Comète*. Edited by A. PRAQT and P. RÉTAT. Paris, Nizet, 1982.

————. *Ce que c'est La France toute Catholique*. Edited by E. LABROUSSE. Paris, J. Vrin, 1973.

————. "Unpublished Letters of Pierre Bayle." Edited by J.L. GERIG and G.L. VAN ROOSBROECK. *Romantic Review*, XXII (1931), 210–217; XXIII (1932), 20–23, 117–128, 206–224, 312–320; XXIV (1933), 17–20, 210–222, 303–314; XXV (1934), 15–24, 341–360. A series of letters in the collection of Columbia University.

————. *Choix de la correspondance inédite de Pierre Bayle*. Edited by ÉMILE GIGAS. Copenhagen and Paris, 1890. Contains some of the letters from the Royal Library of Copenhagen.

————. "An Unpublished Letter of Bayle." Edited by R.H. POPKIN. *Nouvelles de la République des Lettres* Vol. 2 (1981), 193–197.

A complete edition of all of Bayle's letters is being prepared by Elisabeth Labrousse and Ruth Whalen.

BARBER, W.H. "Bayle: Faith and Reason," in *The French Mind: Studies in Honour of Gustav Rudler*. Edited by W.G. MOORE, *et al.* Oxford: Oxford University Press, 1952, pp. 109–125. One of the first recent articles suggesting that Bayle was sincerely religious.

BRACKEN, HARRY M. "Bayle Not a Sceptic?" *Journal of the History of Ideas*, XXV (1964), pp. 169–180. An attempt to clarify the sense in which Bayle was a skeptic and a fideist, in answer to E.D. James.

————. "Toleration Theories: Bayle, Jurieu, Locke" in *Mind and Language: Essays on Descartes and Chomsky*, Dordrecht: Foris Publications, 1984, pp. 83–96. Shows importance of Bayle's contribution to modern views of toleration.

BRUSH, CRAIG B. *Montaigne and Bayle: Variations on the Theme of Skepticism*. The Hague: Nijhoff, 1966. Comparison of the two thinkers, showing some profound differences as well as general points of agreement.

COURTINES, LEO. *Bayle's Relations with England and the English*. New York: Columbia University Press, 1938. Discussion of Bayle's contacts with and influence on English philosophers, theologians, and writers, including Berkeley and Hume.

CROCKER, LESTER G. *An Age of Crisis: Man and the World in Eighteenth-Century French Thought*. Baltimore: The Johns Hopkins University Press, 1959. An important general study. Indicates Bayle's place in eighteenth-century thought.

DELVOLVÉ, JEAN. *Religion, critique et philosophie positive chez Pierre Bayle*. Paris, 1906. A major French study, began modern reconsideration and reevaluation of Bayle.

DESCHAMPS, ARSENE. *La Genèse du scepticisme érudit chez Bayle*. Liége, 1878. Until recent scholarship, the standard attempt to relate Bayle to previous skeptical thinkers.

DESMAIZEAUX, PIERRE. "La Vie de Monsieur Bayle" in the *Dictionnaire*, 5th edition. The first life of Bayle, written by the original editor of his works.

DIBON, PAUL (ed.) *Pierre Bayle, le Philosophe de Rotterdam*. Amsterdam: Elsevieer, 1959. An important collection of articles in French and English, written for the two hundred fiftieth anniversary of Bayle's death, reevaluating his views. Essays by P. Dibon, R.H. Popkin, H.C. Hazewinkel, A. Robinet, L. Kolakowski, P.J.S. Whitmore, E. Labrousse, R. Shackleton, C.L. Thijssen-Schoute, and E. Haase, plus some new documents about Bayle.

FEUERBACH, LUDWIG. *Pierre Bayle. Ein Beitrag zur Geschichte der Philosophie und Menschheit*. Leipzig, 1848. One of Feuerbach's major works, in which he sees Bayle caught between rationalism and the irrationality of Christianity.

HAASE, ERICH. *Einführung in die Literatur des Refuge.* Berlin: Duncker & Humblot, 1959. A monumental study of the French Protestant refugees. Places Bayle in the context of this group.

HAZARD, PAUL. *The European Mind, 1680–1713.* Translated by J. LEWIS MAY. London: Hollis & Carter, 1953. Reprinted in Pelican Books, 1964. A most important study of the intellectual climate of Bayle's time.

HEYD, MICHAEL. "A Disguised Atheist or a Sincere Christian? The Enigma of Pierre Bayle." *Bibliothèque d'Humanisme et Renaissance*, XXXIX (1977) 157–165. Examination of the problem of interpreting Bayle's real views.

JAMES, E.D. "Scepticism and Fideism in Bayle's *Dictionnaire.*" *French Studies*, XVI (1962), 307–324. Challenges the views of Popkin and others regarding Bayle's religious views.

JURIEU, PIERRE. *Le Philosophe de Rotterdam, accusé, atteint, et convaincu.* Amsterdam, 1706 [1707]. Criticism of Bayle by his leading enemy.

KEMP SMITH, Norman. *The Philosophy of David Hume.* London: Macmillan, 1941. Contains some analyses of sections in the *Dictionary* that influenced Hume, especially in *A Treatise of Human Nature.*

———. "Introduction" to David Hume, *Dialogues Concerning Natural Religion.* New York: Macmillan: 1947. Offers much material about what Hume drew from Bayle for the *Dialogues.*

KENSHUR, OSCAR. "Pierre Bayle and the Structures of Doubt." *Eighteenth-Century Studies* XXI (1988), 297–315. Most recent attempt to define and describe the nature of Bayle's skepticism, challenging Popkin's fideistic reading.

KNETSCH, F.R.J. *Pierre Jurieu: Theoloog en Politikus der Refuge.* Kampen: J.H. Kok, 1967. The definitive study of Bayle's chief enemey, Jurieu.

LABROUSSE, ELISABETH. *Bayle.* Translated by Denys Potts. Oxford: Oxford University Press, 1983. Overall view of Bayle's place in intellectual history by the leading present-day Bayle scholar.

————. *Inventaire critique de la correspondance de Pierre Bayle.* Paris: J. Vrin, 1961. An indispensable research tool covering almost all of the unpublished Bayle materials and identifying all of his correspondents.

————. *Notes sur Bayle.* Paris: J. Vrin, 1987. A collection of twelve important articles on Bayle and his work.

————. *Pierre Bayle.* Vol. I, *Du pays de Foix à la cité d'Érasme.* The Hague: Martinus Nijhoff, 1963. Second edition, 1985. The first modern biography of Bayle, based on monumental new researches.

————. *Pierre Bayle.* Vol. II, *Hétérdoxie et Rigorisme.* The Hague: Martinus Nijhoff, 1964. A very important study of Bayle's theology by the leading present-day Bayle authority.

————. *La Révocation de l'Édit de Nantes,* Geneva: Labor et Fides and Paris: Payot, 1985. A most important study of the developments over a century leading to the condemnation of Protestantism in France.

LEIBNIZ, GOTTFRIED W. VON. *Theodicy.* Translated by E.M. Huggard, edited with an introduction by Austin Farrer. London: Routledge & Kegan Paul, 1951. French original in *Die philosophischen Schriften von Gottfried Wilhelm von Leibniz.* Edited by C.J. Gerhardt. Berlin: Weidmann, 1875–1890. Vol. VI. (Photoreproduction edition issued by Georg Olms Verlag [Hildesheim, 1961].) Leibniz's attempt to deal with Bayle's views about the problem of evil, and the relation of faith and reason.

MASON, H.T. "Pierre Bayle's Religious Views," *French Studies,* XVII (1963), 205–217. An attempt to defend interpretation of Bayle as an irreligious thinker, against evaluations of Barber, Dibon, Popkin, etc.

————. *Pierre Bayle and Voltaire*. London: Oxford University Press, 1963. A comparison of the two, with an attempt to assess what Voltaire borrowed from Bayle.

NEDERGAARD, LEIF. "La Genèse du Dictionnaire historique et critique de Pierre Bayle." *Orbis Litterarum*, XIII (1958), 210–227. A study based on Bayle's notebooks preserved at the Royal Library of Copenhagen.

PAGANINI, GIANNI. *Analisis della fede e critica della ragione nella folosofia di Pierre Bayle*. Florence: La Nuova Italia Editrice, 1980. One of the most important recent studies of Bayle's thought.

PITTION, J.P. "Hume's Reading of Bayle: An Inquiry into the Sources and Role of the *Memorabilia*." *Journal of the History of Philosophy* XV (1977), pp. 373–386. Shows that Hume's debt to Bayle was greater than previously recognized.

POPKIN, RICHARD H. "Pierre Bayle," *Encyclopedia of Philosophy*, New York: Macmillan, 1967, Vol. I, 257–262. A new interpretation of Bayle.

————. *The High Road to Pyrrhonism*. San Diego: Austin Hill Press, 1980; Indianapolis: Hackett Publishing Co., 1989. Contains several articles dealing with Bayle's skepticism and his influence.

————. "Kierkegaard and Scepticism" in Josiah Thompson, editor, *Kierkegaard. A Collection of Critical Essays*. New York: Doubleday, 1972, 342–373.

————. "Manicheanism in the Enlightenment" in K.H. Wolff and B. Moore, Jr., editors, *The Critical Spirit. Essays in Honor of Herbert Marcuse*. Boston: Beacon Press, 1967, 31–54. Consideration of Bayle's revival of interest in Manicheanism and its effect on Voltaire, Hume and Gibbon.

————. "Scepticism in the Enlightenment" in Theodore Besterman, editor, *Studies on Voltaire and the Eighteenth Century*. Vol. XXVI, Geneva: Librairie Droz, 1963, 1321–1345. An examination of the skeptical legacy after Bayle during the eighteenth century.

————. "Theological and Religious Scepticism." *Christian Scholar*, XXXIX (1956), 150–158. An attempt to distinguish fideism and irreligious skepticism and to place various figures, including Bayle, in these categories.

RÉTAT, PIERRE. *Le Dictionnaire de Bayle et la lutte philosophique au xviii siècle*. Paris: Les Belles Lettres, 1971. Important study of the ways Bayle was interpreted and used during the Enlightenment.

REX, WALTER E. *Essays on Pierre Bayle and Religious Controversy*. The Hague: Martinus Nijhoff, 1966. Excellent study of Bayle's views in terms of the issues being debated in seventeenth-century French Protestant theology.

ROBINSON, HOWARD. *Bayle the Sceptic*. New York: Columbia University Press, 1931. Until fairly recently the only book-length study of Bayle in English. It presents the view that Bayle was an irreligious skeptic, a precursor of the Enlightenment.

SANDBERG, K.C. "Pierre Bayle's Sincerity in His Views on Faith and Reason." *Studies in Philology*, LXI (1964), 74–84. Interprets Bayle as a sincere Calvinist; shows Bayle had no need to fear censorship.

SERRURIER, CORNELIA. *Pierre Bayle en Hollande. Étude historique et critique*. Lausanne, 1912. An important study, first to see Bayle as religiously sincere. Interprets him as *un calviniste froid, mais sincère*.

Note on the Translation

It is hoped that the selections in this volume, even though they are small by comparison with the actual *Dictionary*, will convey some of the flavor, excitement, and importance of the original. Obviously, it is something of a contradiction in terms to condense Bayle's opus into one compact volume that can be carried in a coat pocket (though I do in fact own such an eighteenth-century volume, entitled *Bayle en petit*). No enthusiast of Bayle can actually conceive of the *real* Bayle without the folio columns. So, I can offer this edition only with genuine fears that the flavor of Bayle may in part vanish with the loss of bulk and the absence of the columns of tiny footnote print. The Talmudic look and flavor cannot be preserved without the entire forbidding apparatus of Bayle's notation system, his endless quotations, his marginalia. In reducing a work of seven to eight million words to less than 200,000 something is obviously lost. All one can hope is that not all has been.

Every student of Bayle will surely be sad to see that some of his favorite entries are missing. All sorts of fascinating articles, such as "Ovid," "Eve," "Ham," "Heloise," "Hobbes," "Pomponazzi," "Xenophanes," had to be omitted, as well as the fantastically lewd one, "Quellenec," and the delightful remark (ten pages long, in footnote print and folio size) from "Zueris," on whether one could really tell three days after the event if a preacher actually said before twelve hundred people that God commands us to hate our enemies. The puzzling remarks B and C of "Aristotle," on whether he was Jewish, or whether he filched his theories from a Jewish savant encountered during Alexander's campaigns, also had to be left out. Many articles containing some of Bayle's best bons mots were omitted. Obviously an editor must feel disheartened when he must leave out entries containing such observations as, "A girl who has been deflowered is like a wine that has lost its spirit," or "As the insensibility of a chaste wife is very disagreeable, so the ardor of a lewd mistress is a marvelous relish; this is an unfortunate cause of conjugal infidelity."

Bayle's *Dictionary* is a vast treasure house, loosely but definitely connected; unfortunately for modern readers, *nothing* can actually be omitted without losing a gem, a morsel of wisdom, a salacious story, a startling fact. My aim in selecting the material for this translation has been to preserve in miniature the overall character of the *Dictionary*—its variety of articles, differing so greatly in size and content—while emphasizing Bayle's central intellectual concern, that is, man's inability to construct a coherent and consistent picture of the world, and the struggle between the endeavor to accomplish this and the acceptance of the values of the Judeo-Christian tradition. Most of the articles that became the battleground for eighteenth-century intellectuals are included here, such as "David," "Manicheans," "Paulicians," "Pyrrho," "Rorarius," "Spinoza," and "Zeno of Elea."

Bayle intended that a reader, when consulting an article, also read the remarks (indicated by capital letters) associated with the article. The folio size and the small type of the original *Dictionary* permitted both an article and its remarks to appear on the same page. In a modern edition of smaller size and larger type this arrangement is virtually impossible. Because the remarks should not be separated from the article proper, the layout of each page in this edition is somewhat complex; the reader will note that when a remark is indicated in the article, the remark usually begins on that page. Since many of the remarks are quite long, three lines of the article and thirty lines of the remark will frequently occupy a page.

In order to save space, the less interesting or less important (at least in my judgment) remarks and footnotes in each selected article have been omitted. However, every article, itself, appears *in toto.* Only the article "Abimelech" (the first selection) has been presented with every remark and footnote that appears in the original. In order that the reader may conveniently consult the original text and locate the places from which these selections have been taken, the lettering and numbering of the remarks and footnotes of the fourth and fifth French editions have been preserved. In the main body of the article, only the capital letters indicating remarks actually appearing in these selections have been included; and in the remarks and articles, the only footnotes indicated are those that have been preserved. Thus, the reader will find, for instance, that in the article "Jonas" only remark C and footnotes 10 and 11 appear.

The omission of many remarks and footnotes will, it is hoped, make for easier and more continuous reading. For the same reason, digressive passages or long quotations have sometimes been eliminated from the text and are indicated by the use of ellipses. Most of the material in the footnotes refers to sources that are hardly known or available today. The page references have usually been dropped, since they would be of value only to specialists with access to the editions Bayle used. The references have been changed only in instances where an English edition of the work in question is readily available. In many cases, Bayle's references to chapter or book numbers have been altered to conform to current usage (as, for example, in the books of Aristotle's *Metaphysics* or Cicero's *De natura deorum*). For the reader's convenience, Biblical references have generally been removed from footnotes and placed in parentheses in the main body of the text; the King James version has been used throughout where Bayle quotes Biblical passages. In the very few places in this edition where Bayle quotes poetry, the English translations are sometimes taken from the English edition of 1734–38.

By and large, it has been felt that it would not be particularly helpful to identify the countless characters who appear as subjects, as figures in the careers of subjects, as sources, or as opponents. To do so would merely create an unholy clutter of additional notes and make the text less readable or comprehensible. Therefore, I have introduced my own notes (indicated by asterisks, daggers, etc., and enclosed in brackets) only when I really felt additional data would be of value to the reader. The major figures of Bayle's world, who make up the dramatis personae of the *Dictionary*, are discussed in the Introduction.

The reader may be interested in the accuracy of Bayle's references. In order to make some estimate of this, I checked his scholarship by using the resources of the Bibliothèque Nationale of Paris, the Universiteit Biblioteek of Amsterdam, and the British Museum of London. I found, in checking some of the more esoteric items, that Bayle was always accurate in the sense that his sources *always* say what he claims they say. Moreover, almost all the time he clearly differentiates between information he knows to be the case, information he has gathered from "reliable" sources, and information based on hearsay and rumor.

The text used for this translation is that of the fifth French edition, published in 1740, which has been checked against the first and second editions, the only two that appeared while Bayle was alive. All the selections have been completely translated anew, instead of making any attempt to revise the two archaic and sometimes inaccurate English translations of the early eighteenth century. I and Professor Brush, who has gone over every line of the translation, have tried to make the text as readable as possible without losing Bayle's original meaning and style. We sincerely hope that the reader will find Bayle as enjoyable and rewarding as we do, and that these selections, though representing merely a fraction of the original, will lead him to examine the full text.

R. H. P.

Historical and Critical Dictionary

SELECTIONS

Abimelech, King of Gerar, in the land of the Philistines, was a contemporary of Abraham. This patriarch retired with his family to Gerar. Although his wife Sarah was ninety years old,[a] she was not safe there. She was carried away by Abimelech, who found her so beautiful that he wanted her for his wife. Abraham could have prevented this unfortunate accident had he declared that he was Sarah's husband; but, since he was afraid of being killed, he said that she was his sister, and he begged her to say that he was her brother.[b] This was the second time that he employed this expedient,[c] which certainly does not merit the praise that St. Chrysostom bestows upon it (A). It is thought that the king of the

≪←

A. *(The praise that St. Chrysostom bestows upon it.)* We shall take notice in another place[1] of how much this dissimulation of Abraham deserves blame. Everyone may judge as he pleases about this relapse. The danger that Sarah's honor had endured before would seem at first to make Abraham's reiteration of the lie less excusable. But, on the other hand, does it not seem that a man can be more excused when he employs a remedy that has succeeded than when he tries a new one; and it is not beyond all doubt that Abraham's first attempt had had all the success he had hoped for? For not only was his life spared, but riches were heaped upon him, and his wife was returned without her being touched, which perhaps he had not expected. I use the word "perhaps"; for I would not dare to write what St. Chrysostom dared to preach. "You are aware," he said to his listeners,

---

a See the last remarks in the article "Sarah" [not included in these selections].

b Genesis 20.

c He had employed it before (see Genesis 12).

1 In the remarks of the article "Sarah" [not included in these selections].

3

Philistines was afflicted with a disease that rendered him impotent (B); and, however this may be, it is certain that Divine Providence prevented him from satisfying the passion he had

"that nothing exasperates a husband more than to see his wife suspected of having been in the power of another; and yet this just man does his utmost in order that the act of adultery can be accomplished."[2] One would expect the preacher to censure the patriarch after this; but, on the contrary, one finds that he bestows the highest praise on his courage and prudence: on his courage, for its having overcome all emotions of jealousy, so that he was able to give the advice he did; on his prudence, for its having pointed out to him this expedient which was so sure to extricate him from the troubles and perils that surrounded him. St. Chrysostom did not forget to portray in most lively fashion the fearful force of jealousy, so that one could comprehend the great courage that overcame this passion. But, on the other hand, he extolled Abraham's prudence by saying that, as he realized that Sarah was too beautiful to be able to escape the lasciviousness of the Egyptians whether she passed for his wife or for his sister, he resolved that she should be called his sister because he hoped in this way to save his own life. "See," St. Chrysostom cries out, "with what prudence this just man finds a good means to render vain all the ambushes of the Egyptians." Then he excuses him for having consented to his wife's adultery, on the ground that death, whose tryanny had not yet been overcome, filled him with a great deal of terror. Ὅτι οὔπω ἦν καταλυθεῖσα τοῦ θανάτου ἡ τυραννὶς· διὰ τοῦτο καὶ τῇ μοιχείᾳ τῆς γυναικὸς ἀρεῖται κοινωνῆσαι ὁ δίκαιος· καὶ μονονουχὶ ὑπηρετήσασθαι τῷ μοιχῷ εἰς τὴν τῆς γυναικὸς ὕβριν ἵνα τὸν θάνατον διαφύγῃ.[3] "Quia nondum mortis erat soluta tyrranis, propterea in adulterium uxoris consentit justus, et quasi servit adulterio in mulieris contumeliam ut mortem effugiat" ["Because the tyranny of death was not yet dissolved, therefore this just man consented to the adultery of his wife and was, as it were, subservient to the adulterer, to his wife's disgrace, in order to escape death"]. After having applauded the husband, he goes on to praise the wife and says that she accepted the proposal very cheerfully

---

[2] Ὁ μέν τοι δίκαιος καὶ σπουδάζει, καὶ πάντα ποιει ὥστε εἰς ἔργον τὴν μοιχείαν ἐκβῆναι (Chrysostom, *Homilies* XXXII, on Genesis).

[3] Chrysostom, *Homilies* XXXII, on Genesis.

conceived for Sarah. He was warned in a dream that she was
married to a prophet and that he would die if he did not give
her back to her husband. The king then returned her to him

and that she did all she could to play her part well in this comedy.[4]
After this, he exhorts women to imitate her and exclaims, "Who would
not admire this great facility to obey? Who could ever praise Sarah
enough, who, after such a chaste life, and at her age, was willing to
expose herself to adultery and to deliver her body up to barbarians,
in order to save her husband's life?"[5] I do not believe that a preacher
today would dare treat so delicate a subject as this in such a manner.
He would expose himself to the raillery of profane people. And I doubt
very much that the inhabitants of Antioch, who were naturally scan-
dalmongers, could have listened to such a sermon without indulging in
some malicious reflections. St. Ambrose gave Sarah's charity no less
praise,[6] and we shall see in the article "Acindynus, Septimius" [p. 16],
that St. Augustine had fallen into almost the same illusion. It is a very
strange thing that, with all their virtue and zeal, these great luminaries
of the Church did not know that it is unlawful to commit a crime in
order to save one's own life or that of another.

≪←

B. *(With a disease that rendered him impotent.)* To extinguish
the ardor of his lust, God afflicted him with a serious disease,
which frustrated all the skill of his doctors. God warned him in a
dream not to do anything to that foreigner's wife. Some time afterward, Abimelech, finding himself a little better, told his friends the
cause of his malady and gave Sarah back to Abraham. That is how
Josephus tells the story,[7] caring little, as usual, to make his version

---

[4] Πάντα ποιεῖ ὥστε τὸ δρᾶμα λαθεῖν. "Omnia facit ita ut fabula & fictio
illa lateant" (*ibid.*). ["She did everything she could so that the fiction might
be concealed."]

[5] Τὶς κατ᾽ ἀξίαν ταύτην ἐπαινέσειεν, ἥτις μετὰ τοσαύτην, καὶ ἐν ἑλικίᾳ
τοιαύτῃ ὑπὲρ τοῦ τὸν δίκαιον διασῶσαι, ὅσον εἰς τὴν οἰκείαν γνώμην καὶ εἰς
μοίχειαν ἑαυτὴν ἐξέδωκεν, καὶ συνουσίας ἡνέσχετο βαρβαρικῆς (*ibid.*).

[6] Ambrose, *De Abrah.* I. 2.

[7] Josephus, *Jewish Antiquities* I. 11.

and reproached him for their falsehoods. Abraham made his excuses and told him, among other reasons, that actually he was the brother of Sarah, born of the same father as she, though they did not have the same mother. This is what Scripture has him say. For the words of the sacred text Moreri substitutes im-

agree with the Mosaic account, or rather, being bold enough to contradict it. For does not Moses relate that after the dream, Abimelech, got up early and called all his servants in order to tell them what he had learned while sleeping?[8] Would he have been able to do this if he had been abandoned by the doctors? Josephus was aware of the difficulty, but in order to remove it he boldly supposes, contrary to the authority of Scripture, that this king told his friends about his dream only when his illness was subsiding, that is, some time after the dream. There are those who believe that Abimelech was not afflicted in person, but only through his wives;[9] and that when Scripture reports that God cured him, it only means that God removed the seals that had been placed on the wombs of the women in his palace.[10] I would not have to be pulled by the ear to accept this explanation; for I find no trace of Abimelech being diseased in the entire twentieth chapter of Genesis, except for the words of verse seventeen, "God healed Abimelech and his wife and his maidservants; and they bore children." But since the following verse only mentions the difficulties of these women, it is probable enough that this is the entire malady with which God afflicted Abimelech. Elsewhere I shall give the answer to the question that could be put to me:[11] "If he was well, why did this king not satisfy the passion that had led him to abduct Sarah?" I am not surprised at the reveries the Jews have set forth about this occurrence. I would be much more surprised at their conduct if they had not invented a hundred chimeras about our Abimelech. They relate that all the openings of the body were stopped up, throughout the palace, both in people and in beasts, both in males and in females, so that nothing could enter the body and nothing could leave it.[12] No

---

[8] Genesis 20:8.
[9] Saliani, *Annals*, I, 469.
[10] Genesis 20:18.
[11] In remark C, article "Sarah" [not included in these selections].
[12] According to Mercer. See Rivet, *Exercit. in Genes. Operum*, I, 395.

properly those of Josephus, who falsely supposes that Abraham said that Sarah was the daughter of his brother.[d] He has followed the same author regarding a fact about which Scripture does not say a word, namely, concerning an alleged alliance made between Abimelech and Abraham after Sarah was restored to her

one could eat or drink any longer, nor could anything go through their stomachs, and so on. Besides, the men were struck with such a great frigidity that Abimelech was in no condition to exercise any virile function, either with regard to Sarah, or with regard to anyone else. A famous Protestant theologian[13] accepts the last part of this tradition, but rejects all the rest as ridiculous or superfluous. He says that, since the devil sometimes prevents, by his ligatures,[14] married people from performing their conjugal duty, it is not altogether improbable that God sent a similar affliction to Abimelech's family for a good and holy end, which was to preserve the chastity of Sarah and to make it appear most clearly that she had not received any injury in the palace. He believes then that all the servants of Abimelech were struck with the malady of sterility: the males by an impotency like that which results from sorcery; the females by a complete closing of the gates of life, or by a contraction that made them incapable of conceiving. It will be said that *this amounts to doing twice as much as was needed; that the men were bewitched would have sufficed for God's plans.* But the reply must be made that, since Moses expressly mentions the closing of the feminine parts, there is then no way of looking upon it as superfluous. Here are two explanations of this fact which do not straighten out everything. The first claims that Moses meant that the wives and female servants of Abimelech could not deliver their babies when the time came. Indeed they had many pains, and it was as in the time of which the prophet Isaiah speaks, "Venerunt Filii usque ad os matricis, et vis non est ad partum" ["The children are come to birth, and there is not strength to bring them forth"].[15] The

---

[d] Josephus, *Jewish Antiquities* I. 12.

[13] Rivet, *ibid.;* Heidegger closely follows him in *De historia sacra patriarcharum exercitiones selectae,* II, 165.

[14] This is ordinarily called *nouer l'éguillette.* [This popular expression denoted a spell cast to make the male member impotent; literally, "to knot the lanyard."]

[15] Isaiah 37:3.

husband. Scripture is content to say that Abimelech gave great presents to this patriarch and gave him permission to reside wherever he wished in his dominions. It is true that there was a treaty between them, but it was made some years afterward.[e] This was the treaty of Beersheba. Josephus, as though he had

other explanation says that he meant that the women could no longer conceive. The first explanation cannot agree with Genesis unless it be supposed that all Abimelech's women were pregnant at the time of Sarah's abduction,[16] which is not at all probable. The second would require that Sarah had stayed much longer than she did in this king's palace, for it takes quite a bit of time to find out if a large number of women have lost the capability of conceiving. These difficulties have obliged a very learned interpreter to say that the punishment that God inflicted on Abimelech's family happened in such a manner as is unknown to us.[17] Besides, the rabbis do not note any great difference between the personal affliction of Abimelech and that of Sarah's first ravisher.[18] They say that the latter had the disease *ratan,* which is the most troublesome kind of ulcer and is especially the greatest enemy of amorous toils.[19] Solomon Jarchi claims that the plague of this king of Egypt was a headache, caused by a worm which had formed in his brain: "Morbus perturbati cerebri ob innatum ipsi vermiculum, quo qui laborant, iis concubitus gravis fit, & liberi gignuntur ulcerosi" ["He was stricken with a headache due to a worm formed in his brain; the social embrace is grievous to those afflicted with it, and they beget scabby children."].[20] Some will believe that these last words spoil everything; for they think it was necessary for Sarah's honor that Pharaoh's plague should have made him absolutely impotent. See our notes to the article on this holy woman.

---

e Genesis 21:31–32.

16 "For the Lord had fast closed up all the wombs of the house of Abimelech" (Genesis 20:18).

17 Mercer, according to Rivet, *Exercit. in Genes. Operum,* I, 395.

18 Pharaoh, king of Egypt.

19 According to Mercer, in Rivet, *Exercit. in Genes. Operum,* I, 395.

20 According to Heidegger, *Hist. Patriarch.,* Vol. II.

better sources than Moses (C), dares to place this treaty before the birth of Isaac, whereas Scripture places it after the rejection of Ishmael, which did not happen until after Isaac had been weaned. Moreri followed the same guide when he affirms that this same Abimelech "showed a great deal of good will" to

≪←

C. (*Better sources than Moses.*) For a long time I have been indignant at Josephus and at those who spare him on this account. A man who publicly professed Judaism, whose faith was based on the divinity of Scripture, dares to recount matters otherwise than they appear in Genesis. He changes, he adds, he suppresses items; in a word, he puts himself in opposition to Moses in such a way that one of the two must be a false historian. But is this to be tolerated? And must we not conclude that either he did not care how much he offended his people or he believed that the personal opinon he had with regard to the fallibility, and consequently the noninspiration, of Moses was commonly held among the Jews? He well deserved the blow that Theodore Beza gave him. "Hoc ego semel pronuncio, quod tu nunquam falsum esse ostendes, si verus est multis locis Josephus, mentitum esse multis locis Mosem et sacros omnes Scriptores. Sed nos potius istos pro veris ipsius Dei interpretibus, illum vero pro Sacerdote rerum sacrarum valde imperito, atque etiam negligente et prophano Scriptore, habebimus." ["I declare this once and for all, which you can never prove to be false, namely that if Josephus be true in a great many places, then Moses and all the sacred writers have told a considerable number of lies. But let us rather regard these writers as the true interpreters of God himself; and Josephus, not only as a priest who was very ignorant in religious matters, but even as a negligent and profane writer."][21] I believe that all the ancient historians have exercised the same license with regard to the old memoirs they consulted. They have tacked on supplements, and, not finding facts developed and embellished according to their fancy, they have enlarged and dressed them up as they pleased; and today we take this for history.

---

[21] Theodore Beza's answer to Baldwin; *Oper.*, II, 220.

Isaac, who had come into the land of Gerar. It is not impossible that this was the same Abimelech, but very likely it was the successor of the one who had carried off Sarah (D). What is quite

≪←

D. *(It was the successor of the one who had carried off Sarah.)*
I do not base my view on the great age that it would be necessary to attribute to Abimelech if he were still alive when Isaac went to Gerar. This journey occurs after Jacob's purchase of his brother's birthright. It can then be presumed that Isaac was eighty years old, since he was sixty when Esau and Jacob were born, and Esau was already a great hunter by the time he sold his birthright. On the other hand, Abimelech who abducted Sarah was both a king and a husband before Isaac came into the world. He would then have been a good hundred years old, at least, when Isaac journeyed to Gerar. But what is the problem here? In those days did people not live to be more than 150 years old?[22] It is hard to believe that there are learned people[23] who are capable of raising as an objection the words of Ecclesiasticus, "Omnis potentatus vita brevis,"[24] as though, in supposing the canonicity of this work, it would be contrary to revelation for a man to have reigned a hundred years. Who does not see that if this passage had the signification attributed to it, we would have to deny all the histories which tell us that there have been reigns that lasted more than fifty or sixty years? What is it, then, that leads me to believe that the Abimelech who abducted Sarah is not the same one as he who made an alliance with Isaac? It is this: This latter Abimelech credulously accepted, on Isaac's word, the notion that Rebecca was only his sister; and when he was disabused of this, not by Isaac's words, but by his deeds, Abimelech gently reprimanded him for his untruth without saying to him, "You are a chip off the old block. Abraham, your father, had already played the same trick on me." Now what chance is there that if he had already been tricked by Abraham, he would still have fallen into the same trap again? Or,

---

22 Abraham lived to be 175 years old, and Isaac, 180.
23 Pereira on Genesis 26, Preface. Saliani in *Annals*, I, 520.
24 The Geneva version renders it, "All tyranny is of short duration" (Ecclesiasticus 11:11).

certain is that when a famine was raging, Isaac withdrew into
Gerar, where *an* Abimelech then reigned. Rebecca's beauty was
the cause of her husband's making use of the same artifice that

if it did happen to him, that he would not have bitterly reproached
Isaac, for both his father's lies and his own? He would not have forgotten those of Abraham, which had caused him so much suffering.
St. Chrysostom found what I have just said so probable that he bravely
asserted from the pulpit that Abimelech reproached Isaac for his
father's deceit. "Rex adhuc habens recentem memoriam eorum, quae
tempore Patriarchae rapta Sara tulerat, increpabat eum reumque
arguens dicebat, cur hoc fecisti? . . . Hanc deceptionem & olim sustin-
uimus a patre tuo" ["The king, having fresh in his mind the suf-
ferings he had undergone in the time of the patriarch after he had
abducted his wife Sarah, finding Isaac guilty, reproved him, saying,
'Why did you do this? . . . In just this way did your father impose
upon me'."].[25] But all this has no other basis than the license of
rhetoric, which is sometimes extended almost as far as that of the poets
and painters.

> . . . *Pictoribus atque poetis*
> *Quidlibet audendi semper fuit aequa potestas.*
>
> [*Poets and painters may equally dare;*
> *In bold attempts they claim an equal share.*][26]

Two things seem to favor the view that Moreri has followed. First,
the king of Gerar in the time of Abraham had the same name as the
one in the time of Isaac; and there was a general called Phichol at
both times. Secondly, Rebecca, no matter how beautiful she may
have been, was not abducted as Sarah had been; and this is because
Abimelech had had time to grow old and remembered the unfortunate
consequences of Sarah's abduction. I reply, first, there have been
names borne by all the kings of a country, like that of Pharaoh by the
kings of Egypt. Why could not the name Abimelech have been the
common one for the kings of Gerar? Phichol was perhaps the name
of an office. Perhaps, also, the office had passed from father to son.
Secondly, I answer that Isaac's Abimelech could no longer have been

---

25 Chrysostom, *Homilies*, LI and LII, on Genesis.
26 Horace, *De arte poetica* 9–10.

Abraham had employed on account of Sarah's beauty. Isaac, being afraid that he would be killed if it became known that he was the husband of the beautiful Rebecca, passed her off as his sister. While looking through their window, Abimelech discovered, by a game (E) he saw going on between them, that

young, even if he were not the one who had abducted Sarah. I frankly believe that he was a good old man, since he formed no scheme to do anything to the beautiful Rebecca, who was unmarried, he thought; and since he did not tell Isaac that she had been in any danger from him, but only from his subjects. And because the latter lived in such a debauched way that any beautiful foreign woman, whom they believed to be unmarried, ran a great risk, I do not find any more reasonable explanation of Abimelech's continence than that of old age. "There comes a time when one is too well behaved," the young libertines say.

≪←

E. *(A certain game.)* Some think that Scripture wished to express discreetly, by use of the word "game," the conjugal duty that Isaac was rendering his wife when, chancing to look through the window, Abimelech saw such an activity. "Putant quidam honeste significari eo vocabulo copulam carnalem. Sed non fit verisimile Isaac prudentissimum et sanctissimum virum tam incaute rem habuisse cum uxore, ut id per fenestram prospicere, ut Scriptura inquit, Rex posset Abimelech. Credibilius igitur est eo vocabulo significatos esse tales jocos et blanditias in amplexando et osculando, quales inter conjuges agitari turpe non est: extra conjugium vero nefas est." ["Some think that by these words the conjugal embrace is modestly signified; but it is not probable that a person of Isaac's great wisdom and piety would have dallied so heedlessly with his wife that King Abimelech could see them through the window, as Scripture tells us. It is therefore more probable that by this word it is meant that they were kissing and toying in such a way as married persons are allowed to do without shame, though it is a crime for single persons."][27]

---

27 Pereira on Genesis 26.

such was not the case. He called Isaac to him and said, "Behold, of a surety she is thy wife: and how saidst thou, 'She is my sister?' What is this thou hast done unto us? One of the people might

Others will not listen to this kind of interpretation. They say that Isaac was too well behaved and orderly to have taken his precautions so badly, and that on these occasions he took care to be in a place where his neighbors could not see him through the window. "It is necessary then," they say, "to understand by the word 'game' certain pastimes, which, though not the last act of the play, are yet too strong to be allowed to be carried on between persons who are not married, no matter how they may otherwise be related." These pastimes must signify some other thing than familiar chattering, joking, and laughing together, for a brother and sister do all this very innocently without the conclusion being drawn that Abimelech drew from the game of Isaac and Rebecca. This interpretation seems to me to be incomparably more reasonable than the first. And yet it must be admitted that affection sometimes prevented Isaac from being as cautious as the rigid moralists would require a patriarch to be, for, finally, it cannot be denied that Abimelech, looking through the window, did catch him playing a certain game with Rebecca, from which he justly concluded that they were man and wife. Notice that they had been married for forty years. Isaac was then eighty years old. St. Augustine, in his books against Faustus the Manichean (a great critic of the patriarchs), makes a most solid apology for Isaac,[28] and in all honesty it is being too rigorous to wish that a patriarch or a married prelate not engage in some slight recreations with his wife without closing all the shutters of the windows. For we should have a high enough opinion of their character that, if nature prompts them to pass from little caresses to bigger ones, they will maintain their footing on this slippery road enough to arrange things so that nothing can be seen from the neighbor's windows. Cornelius à Lapide does not understand what he is refuting when he argues passionately against the authors of the first explanation. "Judaei impuri," he says,[29] "jocum hunc intelligunt copulam conjugalem. Sed apage hos cynicos. Quis credat Isaac

---

[28] Augustine, *Against Faustus* XXII. 46. Thiers quotes part of this passage in his *Traité des jeux et divertissmens*, p. 4.
[29] Cornelius à Lapide, on Genesis 26:8.

lightly have lain with thy wife (F), and thou shouldest have brought guiltiness upon us" [Genesis 26:9, 10]. At the same time he forbade all his subjects, under pain of death, to do the least injury to Isaac or Rebecca. Such a remonstrance and injunction

publice, et spectante Rege, tam inverecundum, lubricum, et cynicum fuisse?" ["The impure Jews by this game understand the conjugal embrace. But away with those cynics! For who can believe that Isaac would have been so shameless, dissolute, and cynical, publicly and in the king's sight?"] But this is not what is at issue. No one claims that Isaac was in the middle of the street at the time. He was in his room and had not carefully closed his windows. That is all; and if that is too much, you then have to condemn the patriarch yourself and play the Cato toward him. It is known that Cato threw one Manlius out of the senate for having given his wife a kiss during the daytime and in the presence of his daughter.[30] This Manlius would probably have been the consul at the next election. Some look for allegorical mysteries[31] in this game played by Isaac and Rebecca, which, no doubt, neither they nor the sacred historian ever dreamed of. I do not include these kinds of errors in the group of those I am compiling. This would be like trying to drink up the ocean. It is to be wished that most of these mystical speculations were unknown to the whole world.

≪

F. *(One of the people might lightly have lain with thy wife.)*
The Philistines must have been terrible people in matters of love since Abimelech, their king, is surprised that no one had lain with Rebecca, who passed only for Isaac's sister. From this we learn, at the same time, that they had respect for marriage. Concerning maidens, in those countries they rather believed that they belonged to the first man to possess them. Witness Dinah, the daughter of Jacob, when she wanted to take a walk. She was immediately grabbed. Someone enjoyed her and then spoke of marrying her.[32]

---

30 Plutarch, *Lives,* "Cato Major" XVII. 7.
31 See Pereira on Genesis 24.
32 Genesis 34.

could only proceed from a good heart, and this should make our modern authors watch their words more carefully when discussing Abimelech's character.[f] Isaac's prosperity lost him the king's friendship. When it had been observed that he had acquired great riches, he was told frankly that it would be best if he left. He obeyed, and he continued to prosper in spite of the obstacles that were raised against him at various places because of the wells he was having dug. Abimelech again desired to enter into an alliance with him, to which he consented.[g]

---

[f] Turselin, in his *Epit. Hist.* (Franeker, 1692), p. 10, is very much mistaken when he says, "Isaacus Gerarus annonae causa profectus, Dei numine conjugis pudicitiam ab Abimelechi Regis libidine intactam servat." ["Isaac, going to Gerar for corn, by the providence of God preserved his wife's chastity from the lust of Abimelech."]

[g] Drawn from Genesis 26.

Acindynus, SEPTIMIUS, was consul of Rome with Valerius Proculus, in the year that Constantine, son of Constantine the Great, was killed near Aquileia. He had been governor of Antioch, and something happened during his governorship that deserves to be reported. St. Augustine relates the matter. A certain man, neglecting to carry to the treasury the pound of gold he had been taxed, was put into prison by Acindynus, who swore to have him hanged if the sum were not paid by a certain day. The time limit was about to expire, without the poor man being able to satisfy the governor. Indeed he had a beautiful wife but one who did not have any money. Nevertheless, it was from that direction that he saw some hope of gaining his freedom. A very rich man, burning with love for this woman, offered her the pound of gold on which the life of her husband depended and asked as repayment only that he be allowed to spend a night with her. This woman, taught by Scripture that her body was not in her control but in her husband's, communicated the offers of this lover to the prisoner and told him that she was ready to accept them, provided he would give his consent, since he was the real master of his wife's body; and if he wanted to purchase his own life at the expense of her chastity, which belonged entirely to him, and which he could dispose of as he wished, it would be perfectly all right. He thanked her and ordered her to go to bed with the man. She did so, giving her body even on this occasion to her husband, not with respect to his usual desires, but with respect to his wish to go on living. The sum agreed upon was given to her but it was slyly taken away, and another purse was substituted in which there was only dirt. The good woman returned to her lodgings (for she had attended the lover at his country home), and no sooner had she discovered this fraud than she complained about it publicly. She demanded justice from the governor and very ingenuously told him the whole story. Acindynus began by admitting that it was his fault, since his severity and threats had made these good people seek such a remedy. He sentenced himself to pay the pound of gold to the treasury, and afterwards decreed that the woman should be awarded the piece of ground from which the dirt in her purse had been taken. St. Augustine does not dare decide whether this woman's conduct was good or bad, and he leans a good deal more toward approving it than toward condemning it, which is quite surprising (C). We have seen above[e] the same looseness of morality in St. Chrysostom concerning the conduct of Abraham and Sarah.

≪←

C. *(Which is quite surprising.)* Ought not so great a theologian know that our life, which is only a temporal and perishable good, should not seem so precious to us as to be thought worthy of being purchased at the price of disobeying God's law? For, since this disobedience is a sin that subjects us to an eternal punishment, and a moral evil that offends an infinite being, it is no less against prudence than against right reason to prefer to commit a sin rather than lose one's life. I shall say nothing about the abysses of corruption that would be opened up everywhere we tread if we were told that an act, which would be a crime if done without the intention of saving one's life, would become innocent if done to save one's life. Acindynus' prisoner would have been a disgraceful pimp and would have agreed to adultery, properly so called, had he permitted his wife to go to bed with the lover in order to obtain a pound of gold. But because he consents to it only to save his life, it is no longer an agreement to allow adultery to be committed; it is a permissible action. Who does not see that if such a morality were followed, there would not be a single precept of the Ten Commandments from which the fear of death would not give us a dispensation? Where are any exceptions found in favor of adultery? If a woman is not obliged to obey the commandment not to defile her body when she can save her husband from

---

e In article "Abimelech," remark A [p. 3].

execution, she would not be obliged to obey it when it is a question of saving her own life; for God has not required that we love anyone else more than ourselves. One could then transgress the law of chastity with impunity in order to avoid death. Why would a similar argument not make it permissible to commit murder, theft, perjury, abjuration of one's religion, and so on? The greatest men are apt to go wrong and lose their way, even on the best roads. Is is very difficult to realize that St. Paul did not at all claim that a husband can dispose of his wife's body in favor of any Tom, Dick, or Harry. I mean when St. Paul says that a woman does not have the power over her body and that this power is her husband's. Yet St. Augustine is perplexed by this passage of the apostle, and he makes a great deal of the qualifying circumstances, "not denying the authority of her husband when he orders her." We shall see elsewhere[7] that he made use of this doctrine of St. Paul to justify Abraham and Sarah with regard to Hagar's concubinage. Let us listen to a theologian who though he lived several centuries after this Church Father, was nevertheless a better moralist on this point. "It is surprising that so great a man should hestitate in this matter, since it is very evident from the Sacred Writings that the harm imposed by punishment must never be ransomed by a sinful act; but that we ought to lay down life rather than preserve it for ourselves or others when it cannot be preserved without offending God. In no manner are we to imagine, therefore, that it is lawful for a husband or wife to commit adultery to save the life of either; but rather that they should wait for death—nay, even voluntarily seek it— rather than betray each other's chastity; to preserve which, many of the most chaste women, not only among the heathens but even among the Christians, not only suffered others to kill them, but laid violent hands upon themselves, an action which, however, I do not approve."[8]. . .

---

7 In remark L of article "Sarah" [not included in these selections].
8 Rivet, *Opera*, Vol. I.

Andronicus, MARCUS POMPILIUS, a Syrian national, taught grammar at Rome. Applying himself too much to the study of philosophy (A), he could not carry on with enough diligence what was required of his profession as a grammarian; the result was that his school was unattended. When he saw that people not only preferred Antonius Gnipho to him, but also other grammarians who were inferior to Gnipho, Andronicus no longer desired to maintain his school or live in Rome. He retired to Cumae and devoted his leisure to writing books. This employment did not keep him out of poverty; he was so poor that he was obliged to sell the best of his works at a very low price. This work had been suppressed for a time, but Orbilius reclaimed it and published it under the author's name; at least he bragged that he had. Adronicus was an Epicurean, and he lived at the time of Cicero. Moreri has committed a great many errors here.

≪←

A. *(He applied himself too much to the study of philosophy.)* . . . This is a lesson to all those who want to attract a large number of disciples. It is necessary either that they apply themselves entirely to their profession, or that it not be known that they are applying themselves to other things. A humanist who wants to be a philosopher, who is curious about scientific experiments, who ardently examines whether Descartes has suceeded better than Gassendi, runs a great risk of seeing his class deserted. A doctor who is very interested in medals, mathematics, and genealogies, will watch the number of his patients diminish from day to day. This is the reason that Spon was very happy to tell the public that they would be very much mistaken if they thought that the study of antiquity was his chief interest.[1] He found by experience that this opinion did him great harm with regard to his medical practice. It is even indubitable that a professor, who is known to be engaged in writing several books, is not considered proper to train good students; it is thought that he does not have the time. That is why those who would seek to enrich themselves by instructing the young would be very wrong in involving themselves with being authors.

---

[1] See the letter that he wrote to the author of the *Nouvelles de la République des Letters*, January 1685, Article V. [The author at this time was Bayle himself. Spon was a famous authority on ancient coins, as well as a physician.]

Ariosta, *LIPPA,* concubine of Opizzon, Marquis of Este and Ferrara, by her faithfulness and political skill so reinforced the impressions that her beauty had made upon the heart of this marquis that at last he made her his lawful wife in 1352. He died the same year and left her the administration of his dominions, which she managed very well "during the minority of her eleven children. From her came all the house of Este, which still exists in the branch of the dukes of Modena, and of Rhegio." The author, from whom I borrow this, notes that Lippa Ariosta "gave more honor" to her family, which "is one of the noblest of Ferrara . . . than she took from it" (A). There are some reflections on this in the remark that I join to the article.

≪

A. *(She gave more honor to her family. . . than she took from it.)*
I have spoken elsewhere[1] of the singular efficacy of marriage. One cannot admire it enough, for, in short, it changes the nature of three kinds of time: the past is no less free from its influences than is the present or the future. "Do you not admire what force custom has, and what authority it exercises in the world? With three words, 'Ego conjungo vos' [I unite you in marriage], pronounced by a man, he makes a young fellow lie with a girl in the sight of, and with the consent of the whole world; and this is called 'a sacrament administered by a sacred person.' The same action, without these three words, is an enormous crime which dishonors a poor woman; and the man who arranged the affair is called, begging your pardon, a p——. The father and mother, in the first case, rejoice, dance, and themselves conduct their daughter to the bed. And in the second case, they are in despair. They have the daughter shaved, and they put her

---

[1] In remark D of the article "Ales" [not included in these selections].

in a convent. One must admit that the laws are very amusing."[2] This is not the most amazing part of the matter. The chief singularity consists in the retroactive effect. Our Ariosta had been a concubine. Her children were bastards. It was a blemish on her honor and on that of her household. But all this was erased, washed off, annihilated by the three words of the priest, "Ego conjungo vos." The marquis of Ferrara, marrying this mistress a little before he departed from this world, turned her into an honorable woman and made his children legitimate, though they properly deserved the contrary title. A like metamorphosis may be seen every day, and there are some who have claimed that the very children who were born at a time when their parents could not have been married, for want of a dispensation, *ought to be legitimatized by a subsequent marriage.* But the *parlement* of Paris decreed against this contention in 1664. It will be asked, perhaps, why this marquis waited until the year of his death. I could answer that a man who keeps a concubine, who feels himself close to his end, is much more disposed to conduct himself in this manner than if he still had hopes of living longer. The remorse of a conscience excited either by itself or by the arguments of a casuist is more lively when one is afraid of dying. Thus, one makes less difficulty about going through a disagreeable ceremony that sets this remorse to rest. In addition, a great noble, solicted for marriage by a mistress he is fond of, may imagine that she will be a thousand times more complaisant and faithful while she flatters herself with the hopes of becoming an honest woman, and that, when she reaches this state, she will reveal her haughtiness, her bad temper, and the like. It is therefore thought proper to keep her in suspense by the bare hope. But once a man sees himself beyond any hope of recovery, he renounces all these cautions. However this may be, there are some people who are so severe that neither the behavior of this marquis of Ferrara, nor that of his imitators, pleases them at all. They would prefer that a girl or a woman who has disgraced herself, and who has long been a scandal to a whole country, remain all her life in disgrace, and that the example of her rehabilitation not be able to serve as a lure to other girls and as a means of covering up, with such a hope, the infamy of their concubinage.

---

2 Bussy-Rabutin, Part IV, Letter 136, p. 192 (Dutch edn.).

Arodon, BENJAMIN D', a German Jew, author of a book* full of precepts for
women. It has been translated from German into Italian by
Rabbi Jacob Alpron. This version was reprinted at Venice in
5412, according to the Jewish calendar,[a] after having been carefully corrected by Rabbi Isaac Levita. This book is quite full
of observances, not only for the cleanliness of the body, but also
for the practice of prayers and good works. The observances of
the first kind often contain minutiae or superstitious regulations, and there is sometimes a great deal of *severity* in those
of the second kind (A). This will be seen more fully in the remark that accompanies this article.

≪←

A. *(There is a great deal of* severity *in the observances that his
work contains.)* For example, a husband and wife are ordered
not to say a word during the performance of their conjugal duty, and
to have only pious thoughts without any regard to pleasure; and it is
declared that if they should act in any other manner, their children
will be born deformed. . . . This ethic is excellent and very rigid at
the same time. See what is said in the *Nouvelles de la République des
Lettres*[3] about a book by Yvon, minister of the Labadists. Such a great
degree of purity is one of those blessings that is easier to wish than
to hope for. But, nevertheless, the casuists are to be commended when
they insist on it, and when they endeavor to introduce purity where
the furors of brutal lust have too much influence. Even if our rabbi
had believed, as the Church of Rome does, that marriage is a sacrament, he still would not have required that those who partake of it
should have more holy dispositions than he asked for. He imposes on

* [*Precetti da esser imparati dalle donne Ebree.*]
[a] I believe that this corresponds to our year 1652.
[3] For the month of November 1685, p. 1290.

them both at the same time the law of silence that the pagans recommended in their great mysteries, and that of lifting up one's heart
that the primitive Church never forgot to take notice of in her most
august ceremonies. In a word, it is certain that if this man had received
with an entire faith the doctrine of Jesus Christ, and if he had been
infused with the spirit of grace, he would not have given advice more
worthy of evangelical purity. This ought to shame those teachers of
looseness of morals who are so common among Christians.

Note that the doctrine of this rabbi hardly agrees with the advice
of medical doctors. These claim that a child conceived when the mind
is distracted—I mean, when one's thoughts are serious, grave, and
spiritual—is simple, silly, and imbecilic; and they give totally different
advice to those who want to have children. But, if we consider the
matter ever so little, we will agree that they are sending people to a
very bad school for chastity. Their precepts are designed only for
people who would like to limit all things to an animal, terrestrial,
sensual, Epicurean life. One has to go to this rabbi's school if one
wants to learn how to behave oneself with regard to these kinds
of duties, as a creature endowed with a spiritual soul, and as one
who does not wish to deserve this criticism:

> *O souls, in whom no heavenly fire is found*
> *Fat minds and ever groveling on the ground!*
> (Persius, *Satires* II. 61; Dryden tr.)

One will better comprehend how excellent and sublime is the morality
of this Jew if one recalls that it is directly opposed to the maxims
of those teachers of corruption who have filled their poems with so
many lascivious things. These dangerous poisoners take care not to
recommend silence. And this has led a modern writer to find some
proofs for an interpretation he has given to the words of a Greek
poet that contain a description of the cave of the nymphs. "Concerning the agreeable murmur of which Homer speaks," he says,[8]
"this is doubtless the endearing words of lovers . . . that accompany
the most favorable familiarities, and that caused the most knowing
of all of the poets in the art of love to say:

> *Her kind complaints, her melting accents hear,*
> *Whilst with fond sighs she wounds the listening ear.*
> (Ovid, *Art of Love* II. 723–724)

---

[8] La Mothe le Vayer, *Hexameron rustique*, Journée IV.

See how he speaks elsewhere:

> *The moving blandishments of sound she tried,*
> *And my dear life, my soul, my all she cried.*
>
> (Ovid, *Amores* III. 7. 11–12)

. . . The famous epithalamium of the Emperor Gallienus, which Trebellius Pollio thinks preferable to the writings of a hundred poets who made verses on the same subject, gives a most marvelous representation of that hollow and endearing murmur, and those caresses which are inseparable from it. . . ." To be diametrically opposed to these false teachers, to these plagues to youth, is very praiseworthy and a true sign that the ethic advanced is of an admirable purity. To all this must be added the judicious response that the famous Drelincourt gave to a bishop who made use of a remark that was totally unworthy, I will not say of a person of his character, but even of a layman who had any dislike of bantering style. "Instead of removing from his devotions," Drelincourt said, "these ways of speaking—that the Virgin Mary is the spirit and the life of Christians—he defends them by jests better left to actors on the stage." The bishop [Jean-Pierre Camus, Bishop of Bellay] answered, "As for you, pastors of the Protestant Church, who have dear better halves, not only as accidents inseparable from your substance, but as the bone of your bone and the flesh of your flesh, indeed, you who are but one flesh in two persons, you use many other more intimate terms, more endearing to those souls of your souls, to those lives of your lives, to those lives of your hearts and your souls, to those souls of your lives and your hearts—terms the world understands not. For you are those spiritual beings who judge everyone, even the angels, and more particularly the Roman Catholics, without being capable of being judged by anybody." Drelincourt replied, "I do not know who has taught him so much, and I cannot answer for what those who keep women secretly say; but a serious person who lives in a chaste marriage does not take pains to perfect such an extravagant rhetoric." The bishop answered him in the most ludicrous manner possible.

Arriaga, RODERIC DE, a Spanish Jesuit, was born in Lucrona on January 17, 1592. He entered the Society on September 17, 1606, and taught philosophy with great applause at Valladolid, and theology at Salamanca. Having learned from the letters of the general of the order that it would be for the greater glory of God if some Spanish Jesuits went to Bohemia to teach the most advanced subjects, he volunteered for this employment. He arrived in Prague in 1624. There he taught Scholastic theology for thirteen years, was the director general of studies for twenty years following, and was the chancellor of the University for twelve years. He solemnly received the degree of Doctor of Theology, and he gained a wide reputation. The province of Bohemia three times made him a deputy to Rome to attend the general congregations of the order there. He was requested several times to return to Spain, but in vain. He was highly esteemed by Urban VIII, Innocent X, and the Emperor Ferdinand III. He died in Prague on June 17, 1667. He published many books in which he exhibited much subtlety of mind. One finds that he was very much better in destroying what he denied than in establishing well what he affirmed; and for this it is claimed that he became an abettor of Pyrrhonism (B), though he made

«‹‹

B. *(It is claimed that he became an abettor of Pyrrhonism.)* This is the opinion of De Villemandy. "There are others," he says,[4] "who attack still more dangerously the sacred doctrines of the faith, as Arriaga in his *Theological Disputations upon Thomas Aquinas;* for they leave no stone unturned to pull down the opin-

---

4 Petrus de Villemandy, in *Scepticismo debellato.*

it known that he was no Pyrrhonist. Doubtless, there would be much injustice in suspecting him of the least prevarication and of having been a false friend of the dogmatists; for, if he em-

ions of others with their reflections and objections but build up nothing in place of them. . . . Roderic Arriaga is famous among the Schoolmen. . . . He dealt with philosophy and theology in many folio volumes but treats everything in such a manner as to endeavor to weaken the opinions of almost all others by various arguments, while supporting his own very feebly. If his temper may be determined by this, he may be counted as a true Pyrrhonist; but since he endeavors to strengthen his own opinions as much as possible and clings constantly to them, he cannot justly deserve that name." One can be sure that if reading the writings of this Jesuit inspires the Pyrrhonian attitude, it is by accident, and contrary to his intention. For he is as decisive as anyone else, and as ardent in confirming his views. But, either due to the weakness of the human mind, or to the difficulty of the subjects, he is in the same situation as a great many authors who admirably discover the weakness of a theory but who are never able to bring out its strength. They are like warriors who put the enemy's land to the fire and the sword, but who are not able to defend their own frontiers. Ancillon found this Jesuit was "quite peculiar in his way of writing," and freer "than the others, who, through an unworthy servitude, do not dare give up the views of the writers of the Society, and who follow them scrupulously as infallible. . . . Relating the view of Vasquez, he says plainly that 'upon the whole he does not put much stock in the solution of Father Vasquez.'[6] I have observed," adds Ancillon, "in reading Arriaga and Oviedo, that it is always the case that when one of these two Jesuits maintains the affirmative of a proposition, the other maintains the negative, which is rather rare, even among the theologians of the Roman Catholic religion in general, and I have hardly seen this except with Cornelius à Lapide and Estius." It is not a rare thing that on an infinite number of questions, as much in philosophy as in Scholastic theology, the Jesuits refute one another among themselves. It can even be said that this is very common. Suarez and Vasquez are an example of it.

---

[6] See the *Mélange critique de littérature,* Vol. I.

ploys all his strength to refute a great number of views, he
employs it also to maintain the views he embraced. It is easily
seen that he is acting in good faith in this, and that he does his
best; and if his proofs are inferior to his objections, this must
be attributed to the nature of things. The care with which he
has refuted all the subtleties invented by the Scholastics to
show that two contradictory propositions are sometimes true
and sometimes false (C) suffices to convince one that he had the
interest of the dogmatists at heart against the Pyrrhonists. On
several points in natural philosophy he gave up the most general
views of the Schoolmen, as, for instance, on the question of the
composition of the continuum, on rarefaction, and so on; and
that is why he took it upon himself to justify the innovators in
philosophical matters. It is too bad that such a clear and penetrating mind did not have more insight into the true principles,
for he might have been able to carry them much further. A
slight knowledge of hydrostatics would have led him to find

＜＜＜

   C. (*He has refuted carefully all the subtleties of the Scholastics to show that two contradictory propositions are sometimes
true and sometimes false.*) He has cleared up these sophisms very well.
See his second dispute on the *Summulae* of logic. I have seen some
professors at a great loss when these objections were made to them,
which really ought to be considered only as chicaneries invented at
the wrong time by men who had too much leisure, and who did not
claim, as Heraclitus did, that actually the same thing was and was
not. They intended only to give their minds some exercise. Note that
Aristotle does not believe that if Heraclitus said this, he also thought
so: "It is impossible that any man could think the same thing to be
and not to be, as some imagine Heraclitus did. For what a man says,
he does not necessarily believe."[8]

----

8 Aristotle, *Metaphysics* IV, 1005b, 23–26.

the explanation of a phenomenon (D), about which he tormented himself in vain. His efforts, his examples, and his dexterity in this matter make it regrettable that he traveled so rapidly on the wrong road.

≪←

D. *(He was not able to find the explanation of a phenomenon about whose explication he tormented himself in vain.)* This phenomenon is that wood lighter than water still does not float upon water with respect to its entire thickness. A beam floating in a river is part under water, and part above water. This cannot be explained according to the usual principles of heaviness and lightness. The vain efforts of Arriaga result from this.[9] The new philosophers* do not find any perplexity in this. See the theory of Gadrois.

---

[9] Arriaga, *Disputat. IV de generat.*, Sec. V, *De elementis.*, Subject VI.

* [The "new philosophers" is a name usually applied to the Cartesians and often to all those who believe that the natural world can be studied mathematically and mechanically. Hence, the term often applies to Galileo, Hobbes, Gassendi, Locke, etc., and their followers, as well as to Descartes, Malebranche, and the Cartesians. In Bayle's article "Pyrrho," remark B (p. 194), the "new philosophy" encompasses all theories that make the primary qualities–extension, motion, etc.—objective features of nature; and the secondary qualities—sound, color, taste, smell, etc.—subjective features that exist only in the mind of the observer. In this usage Bayle would include almost all the important seventeenth-century non-Scholastic thinkers as "new philosophers."

[Hume follows Bayle in this and in his *Treatise of Human Nature* (Bk. I, Pt. IV, sec. 4) makes the fundamental principle of modern philosophy the distinction between primary and secondary qualities, and the assigning of a different ontological status to each.]

Bonfadius, GIACOMO, one of the most elegant writers of the sixteenth century,
was born in Italy near Lake Garda. At Rome he was the secretary of the Cardinal de Bari for three years, after which, having
lost all of the fruits of his services through his master's death,
he went to Cardinal Ghinucci and served as his secretary until
a long illness made him give up this employment. When he was
cured, he found himself so disgusted by the court that he resolved to seek his fortune in another way. He could find nothing
in the kingdom of Naples, where he wandered for a long enough
time. Afterwards he went to Padua, and then to Genoa, where
he gave public lectures on Aristotle's *Politics.* He was charged
with lecturing on the *Rhetoric* too, and since he was quite
successful at it, he had a large number of students who came
to him to learn belles-lettres. His reputation grew daily, so that
the republic of Genoa made him its historiographer and gave
him a very good salary for this office. He applied all his talents
to the composition of the annals of that state and brought forth
the first five volumes of them. He spoke therein too freely and
satirically about some families, and in this way he made himself
many enemies who were sworn to destroy him. They accused
him of the unnatural sin [sodomy], and since witnesses were
found to convict him of it, he was condemned to be burned to
death. Some authors say that the sentence was carried out in
accordance with its form and tenor. But others affirm that the
solicitations of his friends changed the punishment, and he was
decapitated. This happened in 1560. Those who blame his
imprudence are not wrong but have themselves erred in imitating it (D). We have some *Harangues,* some *Letters,* and some
Latin and Italian Poems of his. He wrote a letter to Giovanni
Battista Grimaldi the day of his execution to give his thanks to

those who had tried to be of service to him. He promised to tell them how he was faring in the next world if he could do this

«««

D. *(Those who blame his imprudence are not wrong but have themselves erred in imitating it.)* I have in mind Boccalini who supposes that Bonfadius' complaints, coming out of the flames, were rejected by Apollo, and that this God of Parnassus declared to him, that even if he had been innocent of the crime imputed to him, he would have been justly punished for having been so mad as to tarnish the honor of some powerful families. It was told to him that a judicious historian imitates the grape-gatherers and gardeners. Before speaking of certain facts he waits for time to ripen them, that is to say, until the persons who have committed a bad action are dead, and until their children are unable to avenge themselves against him who publishes it. . . . Tacitus, who had exercised this precaution and preferred to offend the laws of history rather than to expose himself to danger, was cited as an example. . . . See how man knows the maxims of prudence better than how to practice them, for we have seen that Boccalini lost his life for having spoken too liberally against Spain.[15] The advice he puts in Apollo's mouth is no doubt judicious. Nothing is finer in theory than the ideas of the lawgiver of historians. He commands them not to dare to say anything that is false, and to dare to say everything that is true. But these are impractical laws, like those of the Decalogue, given the condition in which the human race finds itself. If it were permitted to compare human things with divine ones, one could say that the lawgiver of the historians has imitated the Lawgiver of the Jews. He has based his laws on the state of man in his innocence, and not on the state of man in sin. He has assumed that lost free will and the great powers man would have had if he had persevered in his original innocence. In addition, let us observe a great difference between such similar laws. Only a perfect wisdom can live according to the Decalogue; and it would be a complete folly to achieve the laws of history. Eternal life is the fruit of obedience to the Decalogue; but temporal death is the almost inevitable consequence of obedience to the lawgiver of historians.

---

[15] See article "Boccalini" [not included in these selections].

without terrifying them. He is not the only one who made such promises (E). He recommended to them his nephew Bonfadino, who perhaps is the Pierre Bonfadius whose verses are in the *Gareggiamento poetico del confuso accademico ordito.* This is a collection of verses, divided into eight parts and printed in Venice in 1611.

≪←

E. *(He promised to tell them how he was faring in the next world.... He is not the only one who made such promises.)* ... The Barnabite Baranzanus had made the same promise and did not fulfill it. I will speak about this in his article [not included in the present edition]. It is claimed that Marsiglio Ficino, having made the same promise, kept his word. . . .

The passage where Seneca relates the tranquility of mind with which Canius Julius went to his execution is admirable. This good man was condemned to death by Caligula and was executed ten days after his condemnation. He spent them without any uneasiness; and when he was informed that he had to go to the place of execution, he lost none of his gaiety. "Why are you grieving?"' he said to one of his friends. "You inquire whether the soul subsists after our death, I will soon know." The philosopher, who accompanied him, asked him, "What are you thinking of now?" "I propose," he answered, "to observe whether my soul will perceive its departure." He promised that if he discovered anything, he would come to see his friends and tell them of his condition. . . . Seneca does not tell us whether anyone had any news of this Julius as a result of the promise.

What is the nature of the proof drawn from the apparition of a soul? Perhaps some will be glad if I here examine two questions that naturally arise. The first is whether the friends of this Julius had a good basis for doubting the immortality of the soul by not receiving the news he had made them hope for. The second is whether they would have had a good basis for believing in the immortality of the soul if they had received some news from some phantom.

I. I reply with regard to the first point that such a basis for putting the immortality of the soul in doubt would be very bad. For though one could give a very good explanation for Julius' not keeping his promise by supposing that his soul no longer subsisted, it does not follow that one is right in employing this hypothesis to indicate the causes of his not keeping his word. When a phenomenon can be explained by three or four probable suppositions, there is not one of them that can lead to a just conviction. A demonstrative proof can be given only when hypotheses different from the one employed are either impossible or manifestly false. Since, then, by our supposing the immortality of the soul, good reasons can be given for why Julius did not come back to tell his friends about his condition, the hypothesis of the mortality of the soul can easily be rejected, even though it be very fitting to explain this matter. One can suppose with good reason either that a soul separated from its body does not remember the promise it made during this life, or that if the soul does remember the promise, it does not know the means for accomplishing it, or that it does not have the freedom to put it into operation, or that the soul does not dare or does not want to disobey some superior cause that forbids it to have anything to do with human beings. Let us say then that Bonfadius' friends would have been very bad reasoners if they had wished to infer the mortality of the soul from his not having kept the promise he made to them.

II. The second point is more delicate, and I will make a distinction at the outset. If any phantom calling itself the soul of Julius had shown itself to the friends of this Roman and had brought them news about the other world, they might have, as a result of this, been able to look upon the hypothesis of the immortality of the soul as extremely probable. But if they had taken this apparition as a demonstrative proof that Julius' soul still subsisted, they would not have judged well; for, as I have already said, a hypothesis does not furnish demonstrative proof when the fact that it explains can be explained by different hypotheses. A proof, to be demonstrative, must show that the contrary is impossible or manifestly false. Since, therefore, other possible causes can be given for the apparation of a phantom calling itself the soul of such and such a man, fulfilling certain promises that this man had made to his friends; since, I say, this can be explained by other possible hypotheses without supposing that the soul of man is immortal, it is clear that Julius' friends would not have philosophized with complete exactitude if they had taken such an apparition for a demonstrative proof that the soul of their friend was still living. "It is possible," someone could say to them, "that even though the soul of your friend be dead, you have seen a phantom that has said to you what he promised to come and tell you. There are several genii in the universe who know what we do, and who can act on our organs. Some one of them is having fun deceiving you. He has made you believe that he was the soul of Julius. By natural and convincing reasons we could not prove to you that this is true, nor could you prove to us that it is false. Hence, do not move so fast. Make no definite conclusion. Be content with taking it for a probable hypothesis." Julius' friends would reply that the very existence of these genii constitutes a proof of the immortality of the soul; for if these genii are immortal, why would our souls not be too? One could answer them and point out that these genii might have the power to do a hundred things, in the place of, and in the name of, the dead soul of Julius, even though they should be mortal. Are all men not mortal? Do they not all actually die, some sooner, some later? Would this prevent them from deceiving beasts in the supposition that I am going to set forth? Let us suppose that the soul of a dog should convince itself that it subsists after being separated from the body. Let us suppose that a particular dog had promised others to come and tell them how he was after death. Let us suppose in the last place that a man knew about this promise and the way in which the dog had agreed to keep it. Is it not true that this man could easily do what would be necessary to fool the other dogs? He would show them phantoms. He would make puppets and others bark. If the dogs would conclude from this, "Therefore our souls are immortal, for at least men are immortal," would they not be mistaken? It is easy to comprehend with a little reflection that the invisible spirits of the universe—what the Platonists call genii—might be able to do all that the art of necromancy attributes to them, even if they were mortal. It would be sufficient that their species should preserve itself in spite of the successive death of all the individuals, just as our species preserves itself even though all men die. To say that the generation of individuals among the genii is impossible is to decide rashly about what we do not and cannot know. The infinity of nature can contain a thousand ways of propagation not known to us. Note that there were pagans who believed in the mortality of genii.

Let us conclude from all this that what is called the return or apparition of spirits is not, strictly speaking, a necessary proof[23] either

---

[23] It is necessary to note carefully these two phrases, "strictly speaking" and "necessary proof."

of the immortality of the soul or of the immortality of demons. I do not at all deny that it would be a proof to which one could acquiesce prudently and reasonably. But I am speaking here about demonstrative proofs which can only be eluded by chicaneries, the defenders of which can be quickly reduced to absurdity.

Bunel, PIERRE, a native of Toulouse, was one of the most polished writers in the Latin tongue to appear in the sixteenth century. He studied in Paris at the Collège de Coqueret, and he distinguished himself in a brilliant way by the perfection of his genius. Having returned to Toulouse and not finding any means of subsisting within his family, he sought his fortune elsewhere. He went to Padua and was supported there by Emilius Perrot. Then an advantageous post was obtained for him with Lazare de Baïf, François I's ambassador in Venice. He spent three agreeable and profitable years there and was even aided in the study of Greek by his master the ambassador. After having become well versed in the knowledge of that language, he studied Hebrew. Georges de Selve, Bishop of Lavaur, who succeeded Lazare de Baïf as François I's ambassador to Venice, took Bunel into his service. They were so happy with each other that when the bishop went back over the Alps and confined himself to his diocese, as a good prelate should, he found that Bunel was completely disposed to spend his days in this retreat of Lavaur. This learned man found there what was most suitable to his temperament, a great deal of tranquility, much time to devote to study, and the pleasure of not having to look at the mighty examples of the corruption of that age. After the death of his bishop,[a] he returned to Toulouse. There he would have suffered the persecutions of poverty, had not the Messires du Faur, protectors of virtue and learning, extended their liberality toward him generously and unasked. One of them gave his son to Bunel to instruct and to take to Italy. Bunel did not complete this trip, for he died of a high fever at Turin. He had lived only forty-seven years. He was a

---

[a] He died in 1541.

man even more notable for his fine conduct than for the delicacy
of his style. He was not seen running after riches or seeking
lucrative employments. Content with the bare necessities of life,
he devoted himself only to improving the faculties of his soul
(C). Such conduct is almost as rare in the republic of letters as
anywhere else. He did some *Latin Epistles,* which are written
with the utmost purity, and which contain some curious facts
(E).* Some persons believe that he was the son of the Guillaume
Bunel of whom I spoke in the preceding article [not included
in these selections]; but this is not probable at all since one
cannot find any trace of the matter either in his letters or in
writers who discuss him. Would Sainte Marthe, who notes that
Pierre Bunel's father was a Norman, have forgotten so honorable
a matter as that he was Doctor Regent in a famous university?
The Capitouls of Toulouse have erected a marble statue in
honor of Pierre Bunel and have placed it in the city hall.†

≪←

   C. *(Content with the bare necessities of life, he devoted himself only to improving the faculties of his soul.)* Here is what he
wrote to Du Ferrier: "Though the smallness of my fortune seemed to
require that I should make a provision for myself in the time to come,
yet I will confess the truth: I cannot be unlike myself. After God, my
whole delight is in my studies, which I will endeavor to order so that
they may all turn to His service. You will say that a man who is oppressed with poverty cannot do anything excellent. I grant it; but
then as I have always been content with little, I believed I should

---

   * [Remark E appears on p. 41.]
   † [At the beginning of the essay "Apology for Raimond Sebond," Montaigne mentions that Pierre Bunel, "a man with a great reputation for
learning in his day," stayed with Montaigne's father for a few days at the
family château and left him as a parting gift a copy of Raimond Sebond's
Theologia naturalis. It is this copy of Sebond's work that Montaigne claims
his father rediscovered shortly before his death and asked his son to translate into French; and, of course, it is the translation and the "Apology"
occasioned by it that made Montaigne the central intellectual figure in the
revival of skepticism in the Renaissance.]

never want much; and this hope has never yet deceived me." What he wrote to Reynold Chandon deserves to be considered. This was a man who was very fond of him, and who had gotten him a post with the French ambassador, an honorable and useful employment. . . . A few years later Chandon tried to help him and to set him on the road to making his fortune. But Bunel answered him that he had no ambition and cared little to rise to high office, even were it the case that public affairs were well managed; that he had better cause to renounce such posts inasmuch as they are the rewards of vice; and that he did not have the bad qualities necessary to be appointed to them. "If I saw public affairs ordered with justice, and that the way to the highest honors lay open to me, yet I would not strive to rise further. Now, since I see that these signs of desert are awarded, not to virtue and industry, but to wickedness and sluggishness, I ought not (if I would act consistently with my principles) to wish for such rewards; nor, as I am unfurnished with those arts by which they are procured, ought I to hope for them." He adds that if one wished to assist him in terms of his own tastes, it should be known that he endeavored only to live quietly, and that he had chosen the retreat of the study as a haven where he could be safe from the storms of ambition and envy; that men have need of things only in proportion to their desires; that as for himself, he had set strict limits to his desires, which meant that he did not consider himself poor in not having what he did not wish for; that those who would despise his resolution can run as much as they please in the direction that their blind cupidity pushes them; that he himself is not concerned about it [i.e., their attitude toward him], provided that they will leave him in peace in the bosom of his Christian philosophy. . . . There is no doubt at all that here he gives a faithful description of what is in his heart. He was therefore an honest man; he was the one Diogenes was looking for. This is the way in which all men ought to direct their minds, and it is chiefly what Christians ought to do. But this is not what they actually do. There is hardly one in six thousand who does so. The Protestants have a small catechism, the first question of which is, "Why has God placed us in the world?" The catechumen answers, "In order to know and serve Him." This is generally the principle of all Christians, but it is only a theoretical and purely speculative principle. If one's answer were proportional to one's moral practices, then all Christians, with a few exceptions, would answer that God has placed them in the world so that they may enrich themselves and obtain positions; for in actuality this is the goal of all their concerns. Many, indeed, at first think only of making their lives modestly comfortable; but when they achieve enough of this, they immediately aspire to greater things, and by degrees they propose to rise to the most exalted positions. This attitude directs a father, as much for himself as for his children, and he communicates it to them as soon as they are old enough to understand. No one is satisfied with the station to which he is born. Everyone tries to cut a finer figure than his father. The son of a lowly artisan employs all his strength in order to raise himself to the condition of a wealthy citizen. If his covetous and insatiable activity enables him to obtain great riches, he squanders his money in order to obtain posts and to play a part in the government. No amount of expense will seem excessive to him, provided that it helps him obtain the influence of the mediate or immediate distributors of magistracies. The persons who are most involved in terms of their function of putting into practice the precepts of Jesus Christ concerning the contempt of worldly things forget this obligation a little too often. They take a little too much advantage of the opportunities for amassing wealth, advancing their family, and raising their dependents. This puts me in mind of what a worthy man told me one day. He was at Mr. ———'s house, with nine or ten people who were discussing various things. Finally the conversation turned to the qualities of a certain minister. One of these gentlemen criticized him quite freely on some accounts; another spoke, and without justifying him very much on these matters, he set forth other very favorable aspects of his character. He insisted chiefly on the matter of friendship. "One has never seen a better friend than this minister," he said, "nor anyone more zealous to help those who had supported his interests. He has procured pensions for so and so; another has obtained, on the basis of his recommendation, a post worth two thousand pounds a year and as a result is on the way to making a great fortune. Others have made their coaches roll on the basis of the secret advice he gave them to buy certain goods that would become expensive in a short time. Others, who had a passionate desire to become magistrates, have, by his help, removed the obstacles that stood in their way." Having run through his catalogue, he let the others speak, and Mr. ——— said right away, "I am very much shocked at the way in which you praise a successor of the apostles. I would not find it odd if you had praised a pagan in this fashion or even some laymen of our religion. But I cannot bear to hear you present those actions as highly worthy of a minister of Jesus Christ. Is it the business of such as him to know if goods are going to be more expensive at such and such a time?[17] Does it suit him well to alert his friends to this and to smooth the way for them that leads to riches and dignities? Is this not pouring oil on the fire of avarice and ambition, a fire that is his duty to extinguish in the souls of all his flock in so far as he can? Does he not know that the riches and honors of this world are the food of vanity, and manifold obstacles and stumbling blocks in the way of salvation? It would be as praiseworthy if he were to obligate his friends to give to the poor what they spend in self-aggrandizement, as it is blameworthy that he encourages their ambitions. If he had gotten some friend to give up his coach, to walk on foot, and to sell his equipage for the benefit of hospitals, I would consider this the action of a genuine friend. Such is the duty of your hero."*

Doubtless these thoughts are truly Christian; but in the state of corruption in which we live these are Platonic ideas. One scarcely finds any longer either in the world or in the Church that contempt of wealth and dignities that characterized our Bunel. To complete the corruption, there is practically no one who does not despise those who preserve this indifference. So true is it that the truths of the Gospel, which are read and heard read every day of the week, make so little impression on our hearts! Praised and admired is a learned man who enriches himself, who climbs from one post to another, and who, in order to make his fortune, divides his leisure time in half, one part for his books, the other for courting the favor of the great and thrusting himself into the social whirl everywhere. Such a man, though basically very despicable, is not at all despised. Bunel and those who are like him, though basically very worthy of esteem, are regarded with contempt. What a way to portion out approval! Bunel follows a right course, the others the wrong one; Bunel, I say, who prefers the tranquility of his studies to all the pomp of worldly honors. . . . Had Bunel been in line for preferments or academic honors, and if he

---

17 It is about such things that one can say of an ecclesiastic that not to know this information is as glorious as understanding an obscure passage of St. Paul.

* [In portraying the immoral and unchristian minister, it seems highly probable that Bayle had in mind here his enemy Pierre Jurieu.]

had not been promoted to them when his turn came because such was not in the interests of a more powerful faction, do you think that he would have been chagrined about it, and that in order to wipe away this alleged dishonor, he would have joined the stronger party? I do not believe so. He would have been more philosophical than thousands of others are. Being deprived of these rewards afflicts them, they yield sooner or later, by which I mean that they follow the road to favor. Their inconstancy would be excusable if exclusion were a sign of lack of merit; but when it only proves that their party is weaker in influence, it does not in the least tarnish the glory of a person. It can even contribute to make it more brilliant both for the present and for the future. What is said of martyrs—that it is their cause and not the torments they suffer that make them such—is true both in this sense and in the contrary sense. For it is not the deprivation of dignities that dishonors, but it is the cause of the privation. Therefore those who do not rise to preferments because they adhere steadfastly to the cause of justice, though of less immediate success, ought to consider this not as a dishonor but as a mark of glory. This is what our Bunel would have done.*

«‹-

E. *(And which contain some curious facts.)* I will give an example of them. In his letters, we are told that a professor at Padua criticized in his lectures those who, because they were more devoted to philosophical studies than is necessary for a Christian, neglected the study of sacred writings all their lives or did not examine them until very late. The arguments of this professor were so strong that they affected some of those who deserved his criticism. But a letter of Sadoletto relaxed their resolution. They had begun to renounce their concubine, that is, philosophy, in order to devote themselves to theology, a chaste wife, when the letter from Sadoletto plunged them anew

---

* [This description and evaluation of Bunel is obviously semiautobiographical. Bayle's fairly minimal academic career and worldly success were partly a function of his refusal to engage in false flattery and favor-seeking, and of his dedication to fighting for the myriad number of unpopular causes he supported. Throughout the *Dictionary*, the note appears and reappears suggesting the value of quiet study and serious scholarly achievement over all the usual signs of worldly success.]

into concubinage. "Hearing that some are so moved by Sadoletto's authority and eloquence that they do not persevere in their resolution but rather have divorced Theology (whom they a little before had married as a most chaste wife) and are returned to their old harlot (whom they had intended to cast aside) and her wanton allurements. . . ." This is the occasion of this letter. Reginald Pole, writing to Sadoletto,* requested him to arrange it so that Lazarus Bonamicus would devote himself to sacred writings, or at least give up rhetoric in order to apply himself to the study of philosophy. Pole had hopes that this study would not hold up Bonamicus very long, and that it would lead him much further. He believed that Bonamicus would see that the lights of philosophy can only guide a man to the point where he will admit that he knows only that he knows nothing; that this is the *non plus ultra* of philosophy, from which it ought necessarily to be concluded that the mind of man requires another light to dissipate its ignorance. Now, where can this other light be found except in revelation? . . . Sadoletto answered that he found it odd that philosophy was thus condemned since theology could not subsist without it . . . and thereupon he amply exhibited the advantages of philosophy. Bunel clarifies this and shows that the actual opinions of Sadoletto are not those which appear at first reading of this letter. But, be this as it may, I find that Pole's judgment is the most sensible one that can be made about philosophy; and I am extremely pleased that such an author gives me an opportunity of confirming what I have set down in various places, namely, that our reason is only suitable for making everything perplexing and for raising doubts about everything. No sooner has it built something than it provides the means for destroying it. Reason is a veritable Penelope, unraveling during the night what she had been weaving during the day. Thus, the best use that can be made of the study of philosophy is to realize that it is a misleading way, and that we ought to look for another guide, which is the light of revelation.

---

* [Jacopo Sadoletto, Cardinal and Bishop of Carpentras, was an important figure in the humanist revival in the Renaissance and wrote in favor of philosophy against some of the skeptical attacks on the merits of human reasoning. Reginald Pole, Cardinal and Archbishop of Canterbury (1556–1558), was an important figure in the theological discussions of the sixteenth century and had strong fideistic leanings. He played a major role in the Church's struggles against Henry VIII.]

Caniceus, JAMES,* author of some love letters. I relate this fact only on the testimony of Agrippa,[a] and to excite the curious to discover who this writer was, whose name I have not found in any bibliography; no more than of James Calandrus, an author of the same type, according to the same Agrippa.[b]

---

* [This is the entire article, including all the notes.]
[a] Agrippa von Nettesheim, *The Vanity of the Sciences,* chap. 64.
[b] *Ibid.*

Chrysis, a priestess of Juno at Argus, was by her negligence the cause of the goddess' temple being burned to the ground. She had placed a lamp too near the sacred ornaments. They caught fire; and as she was so deeply asleep that she did not wake up soon enough to prevent the consequences of this accident, the fire burned down the entire temple. Some say that she herself perished in the midst of the flames (A); but others assert that she escaped that same night to Phlius. She had reason to fear the resentment of the Argives, for instead of recalling her they selected another priestess. This post was quite important for them since it was the priestess who regulated their dates and their chronology. This conflagration occurred in the ninth year of the Peloponnesian War.

St. Jerome in his first book against Jovinian has observed that our Chrysis, the priestess of Juno, was a virgin. Marianus Victorius errs in asserting, in his notes on this passage, that this Church Father was speaking of Chrysëis whom Agememnon abducted.

≪←

A.′ (*Some say that she . . . perished in the midst of the flames.*) Not only does Arnobius assert this, but he uses this to construct an argument against the pagans. "Where was Queen Juno when the same flames destroyed her celebrated temple and burned her priestess, Chrysis, at Argos?" Clement of Alexandria had provided him with all this, both the fact and the conclusion. It was poor judgment to make use of such a proof against the pagan gods; for, besides the fact that Lucretius makes use of the very same argument to destroy the worship of the gods in general, could not the question be thrown back on Arnobius himself? Could not one ask him where the God of Israel was when the king of Babylon pillaged and burned down the temple of Solomon? I do not know what the Church Fathers were thinking about in some of their arguments against the gentiles.

David, King of the Jews, was one of the greatest
men in the world and a man after God's own
heart, even if he is not considered a royal prophet. The first
time Scripture has him appear on the stage, it is in order to tell
us that Samuel appointed him king and performed the ceremony of anointing him. David was then only a simple shepherd.
He was the youngest of the eight sons of Jesse the Bethlehemite
(A). After this, Scripture tells us that he was sent to King Saul to

««-

A. *(He was the youngest of the sons of Jesse.)* Jesse was descended in direct line from Judah, one of the twelve children
of Jacob, and dwelt in Bethlehem, a small city of the tribe of Judah.
Some modern rabbis say that when David was conceived, Jesse believed that he enjoyed not his wife but his maidservant, and it is in

* [After the first appearance of Bayle's *Dictionary* there was so much
opposition to the "scandalous" character of the article "David" that Bayle
agreed, in discussions with the Consistory of the French Reformed Church
of Rotterdam, to which he belonged, to amend the article and remove the
objectionable parts. As a result, a much emasculated article "David" appeared in the second edition. Both the body of the article was cut, as well
as several of the major notes. The text presented here is that of the original
1697 version, except for the additional portion of remark A. In the revised
article, besides deletions and changes in the body of the article and notes,
remarks D, E, H, and I were suppressed.

[This is the only article so affected by criticism. With many articles Bayle
merely expanded the text in the second edition; and in the cases of the
others definitely singled out as objectionable by the Consistory, namely,
articles "Manicheans," "Paulicians," and "Pyrrho," he added appendices to
clarify his claims.

[A most illuminating and interesting discussion of the background of
this article appears in the recent two-part article by Walter Rex, "Pierre
Bayle: The Theology and Politics of the Article on David," *Bibliothèque
d'Humanisme et Renaissance,* XXIV (1962), 168–189; XXV (1963), 366–
403.]

cure the latter of his fits of frenzy by the sound of musical instruments. A service of such importance made him so beloved by
Saul that that prince kept him in his house and made him his

this way that they explain the fifth verse of Psalm 51, where David
declares, "Behold, I was shapen in iniquity; and in sin did my mother
conceive me." This, they say, signifies that Jesse, "his father, committed an adultery when he was begotten, because, although he begot
him on his wife, he thought he begot him on a maidservant, whose
chastity he had tried to corrupt."[1] This explanation does not conform
much to the doctrine of original sin, and it is for this reason that
Father Bartolocci,[2] having reported this view of the modern rabbis,
felt that the occasion obliged him to examine whether the ancient
Jews acknowledged the truth of this doctrine. If the supposition of
these rabbis were true, they would be quite right in saying that Jesse
had committed adultery; but, on the other hand, it would have to be
said that he would not have committed a sin if he had gotten his maid
with child when he sincerely believed he was enjoying his wife. This
rabbinical supposition is very far from the tradition that St. Jerome
mentions. He says that it was believed that Jesse, David's father, never
committed any actual sin, and that there was no spot in him but the
one he brought from his mother's womb. "It is a wonderful thing
that St. Jerome relates of the life of Jesse, David's father, that he
was never guilty of any other sin than what he had originally contracted. For the passage wherein we read that 'Amasa went in to Abigail, the daughter of Nahash, sister to Zeruiah,' is thus expounded by
St. Jerome: 'Nahash signifies a serpent; for they say he was guilty of
no deadly sin but the one he originally contracted from 'the ancient
serpent. Now Nahash is the same with Jesse, the father of David.'
Abulensis mentions the same tradition and observes that Nahash is
the same with Jesse or Isai, the father of David, which de Lyra had
likewise taught before."[3] Those who would like to adopt the impertinence of these rabbis concerning the conception of David might

---

[1] See the *Journal des Savans* for July 14, 1692.

[2] In *Bibliotheca magna rabbinica,* Part II, cited in the same *Journal des
Savans.*

[3] These words and the citations that accompany them are from Father
Camart, *De rebus gestis Eliae,* pp. 126–127.

armor-bearer. Scripture then says that he returned from time
to time to his father's house to take care of the flocks, and that
one day his father sent him to Saul's camp with some provisions,
which he intended for his three sons who bore arms. David, in
executing the order, heard that a Philistine named Goliath,

easily proceed to another impertinence, which would be placing
David among the illustrious bastards. The physical reason that is
given why bastards are so frequently born with so many natural
talents should apply here with respect to the father's part.

[In the revised article "David," Bayle added the following to remark A.]

I have just read an Italian book[4] in which this story of the rabbis
is reported in this way. David's father was in love with his maidservant,
and after having cajoled her many times, he told her finally that she
should prepare herself to go to bed with him that night. She, being no
less virtuous than beautiful, complained to her mistress that Jesse
would give her no rest from his solicitations. . . . "Promise to please
him tonight," her mistress told her, "and I will go and put myself in
your place." The project was put into execution two or three nights
in a row. When Jesse found that his wife, with whom he had not been
to bed for a long time, was nevertheless pregnant, he accused her of
adultery and would not believe her tale of the bargain she had made
with the servant. Neither he nor his sons cared to lay eyes on the child
that she brought into the world. They considered him a bastard. He
treated her with the utmost contempt and arranged to have the child
brought up in the country among the shepherds. He did not tell his
neighbors his secret. He hid this domestic shame for love of his children. Things remained in this state until the prophet Samuel came
to seek a king in Jesse's family. Since his choice did not fix on any of
the sons he was shown, it was necessary to fetch David. They sent for
him with repugnance because they were afraid that the shameful
secret would be discovered. But when they saw that this supposed

---

4 This book is entitled *Precetti da esser imparati dalle donne Ebree* [Pre-
cepts to Be Learned by Hebrew Women]. See article "Arodon," remark A
[p. 23].

proud of his strength and his gigantic stature, came every day
to offer a challenge to the Israelites, without any of them daring
to accept it. David had an earnest desire to go and fight the
giant, whereupon he was brought to the king and assured him
that he would triumph over the Philistine. Saul gave him his
armor; but, since David found himself encumbered by it, he
put it aside and resolved to use only his sling. He was so successful with it that he knocked down the bully with one shot of a
stone, and then he killed him with Goliath's own sword and cut
off his head, which he presented to Saul. This prince had asked
his general, when he saw David march against Goliath, "Whose

bastard was the person whom the prophet sought, they soon changed
their minds. Nothing was heard but fine hymns. David began with a
Te Deum; he praised God who had heard his prayers and had delivered him from the mark of bastardy. Jesse continued and said, "The
stone that the builders refused has become the headstone of the corner
that shall support the whole house." His other sons, Samuel, and
everyone also spoke sentences of praise. The rabbi adds that Jesse's
intention was good. His wife was old, his maid was young, and he
wished to beget more children. . . . Oh, what a fine apology! If such
excuses sufficed, what a multitude of lewd people might be protected
from criticism. Have there ever been doctrines concerning the direction of intention more convenient than this?*

---

* [Bayle could assume that the literate reading public of his day was
familiar with the "direction of intention" as taught by the Jesuit casuists,
because Pascal had ridiculed their doctrine in his widely-read *Provincial
Letters*. Generally speaking, directing the intention amounted to living according to the principle that the end (in Jesse's case, having an heir) justifies
the means (adultery). In his seventh letter Pascal applied the doctrine as he
found it in several Jesuit works and came to the conclusion that Jesuits could
kill Jansenists who successfully criticized the Society.]

son is this youth?" (C) The general answered that he did not
know and received orders from Saul to find out. But Saul learned
the answer himself from the mouth of the young man, for when

≪←

C. *(Saul had asked his general . . . "Whose son is this youth?")*
It is a little strange that Saul did not know David that day since
the young man had played on musical instruments several times in
his presence to calm the dark vapors that disturbed him. If a narration like this were found in Thucydides or Titus Livy, all the critics
would unanimously conclude that the copyists had transposed the
pages, forgotten something in one place, repeated something in
another, or inserted additional passages into the author's work. But
it is necessary to be careful not to have such suspicions when it is a
question of the Bible. Nevertheless, there have been some people bold
enough to claim that all the chapters or all the verses of the first book
of Samuel are not placed in their original order. The Abbé de Choisi,
it seems to me, nicely eliminates the difficulty. "David was brought to
Saul," he says, "at first he did not recognize him, although he had
seen him several times during the period when he had had him
brought in to play the harp. But, since it had been several years back
—for David was quite young when he was brought to court as a
musician, and he was then seen dressed as a shepherd—one should not
be amazed that a king, overwhelmed by his affairs, and whose mind
was not well, had forgotten the facial characteristics of a young man
who was not important." I would only wish that he had not said: (1)
that "it had been several years back" since Saul had seen David, and
(2) that "David was quite young" when he came to Saul's court as a
musician. There is no indication that he was much older when he
killed Goliath than when he came for the first time to Saul's Court;
for at the time of this first arrival he was "a mighty valiant man, and
a man of war, and prudent in matters" (I Samuel 16:18). He was only
thirty years old when he was elected king after Saul's death; and it
must necessarily be the case that many years passed from the death of
Goliath until that of Saul. . . .

he was brought to him after the victory, he asked him, "Whose son art thou?" and David answered that he was the son of Jesse. Saul then retained him in his service without allowing him to return to his father's home any more. But since the songs that were sung throughout all the cities about the defeat of the Philistines gave ten times more honor to David than to Saul, the king developed a violent jealousy, which increased more and more, because the posts that he gave David to keep him away from the court served only to make him more illustrious and to gain for him the affection and admiration of the Jews. As a political maneuver Saul desired to have him for his son-in-law. He hoped that the condition on which he would give him his second daughter would get rid of this object of aversion, but he was thwarted by his own ruse. He demanded for his daughter's dowry one hundred foreskins of the Philistines. David brought him two hundred all told, so that, instead of perishing in this enterprise, as Saul had hoped, David returned with a new burst of glory. He married Saul's daughter and thereby became all the more formidable to the king. All his expeditions against the Philistines were very successful. His name grew famous and he was held in very high esteem; so much so that Saul, who knew much less of his son-in-law's virtue than of the attitude of his people, thought that the death of David was the only way that could prevent his being dethroned. He therefore resolved to get rid of him once and for all. He confided his plan to his eldest son, who, very far from being as jealous as his father, warned David of this dark plot. David took flight and was pursued from place to place, until he had given incontestable proofs of his probity and his loyalty to his father-in-law, to whom he did not do the least harm on two favorable occasions when he could have killed him if he so wished. This made Saul resolve to leave him in peace. But because David feared that this prince might resume his wicked plans, he took care not to relax his precautions. On the contrary, he provided himself a safer refuge than before, in the land of the Philistines. He asked the king of Gath for a city to dwell in, from which he made frequent incursions into the neighboring countries (D); and it was not his fault that he did not fight against the Israelites (E),* under the banner of that Philistine prince, in the unhappy war in which Saul perished.

≪≪

D. *(He asked the king of Gath for a city . . . , from which he made frequent incursions into the neighboring countries.)* David, having stayed some time in the capital of King Achish, with his little band of six hundred bold adventurers, was afraid of being burdensome to that prince and begged that he would assign him another dwelling place. Achish assigned him the city of Ziklag. David moved there with his followers and did not allow their swords to rust in their scabbards. He often led them out on sorties and killed man and woman without mercy; he left only the cattle alive, which was all the booty he returned with. He was afraid that the prisoners would reveal this secret to King Achish, for which reason he took none along with him but put both sexes to the sword. The secret that he did not want to have discovered was that these ravages were committed not on the lands of the Israelites, as he made the king of Gath believe, but on the lands of the ancient inhabitants of Palestine. To tell the truth, this conduct was very bad. To hide one fault he committed a greater one. He deceived a king to whom he had obligations; and to conceal this deceit he exercised extreme cruelty. If David had been asked, "By what authority do you do those things?" what could he have answered? Has a private person such as he was, a fugitive, who finds shelter in the territories of a neighboring prince, a right to engage in hostilities on his own account and without a commission from the ruler of the country? Had David any such commission? On the contrary, did he not act in opposition to the intentions and interests of the king of Gath? It is certain that if a private person, no matter how great his birth may be, should behave nowadays the way David did on this occasion, he could not avoid having very dishonorable epithets applied to him. I know very well that the most famous heroes and the most famous prophets of the Old Testament have sometimes approved of putting everything alive to the sword, and thus I should

---

* [Remark E appears on p. 53.]

He returned to Judea after the death of Saul and was there declared king by the tribe of Judah. However, the other tribes submitted to Ish-bosheth, the son of Saul; the fidelity of Abner

be very far from calling what David did cruelty if he had been authorized to do it by the orders of any prophet, or if God himself had commanded him to do so by inspiration. But it clearly appears from the silence of the Scripture that he did this all of his own accord.

A Reflection on David's conduct toward Nabal. I shall add a word about what he had decided to do with Nabal. While that man, who was very rich, was shearing his sheep, David asked him very civilly for some gratuity. His messengers did not fail to say that Nabal's shepherds had never been harmed by David's people. Since Nabal was very surly, he rudely asked who David was and reproached him for having thrown off his master's yoke. In a word, he declared that he was not such a fool as to give to strangers and vagabonds what he had provided for his own servants. David, enraged at this answer, armed four hundred of his soldiers, put himself at their head, and firmly resolved not to allow a single soul to escape being slain by the sword. He even bound himself to this by an oath; and if he did not execute this bloody plan, it was because Abigail came and appeased him with fair words and presents. Beautiful and intelligent, Abigail was Nabal's wife and a woman of great merit; she pleased David so much that he married her as soon as she became a widow. Let us speak frankly. Is it not indisputable that David was going to commit an extremely criminal action? He had no right to Nabal's goods, nor any authority to punish him for his surliness. He ranged up and down the land with a band of trusty friends. Indeed he might have been allowed to ask for some payment from people who could afford it; but if they refused, he ought to have accepted this patiently; he could not compel them to it by military action without plunging the world again into the terrible confusion called the "state of nature," in which no other law is recognized except that of the strongest. What would we say today about a prince of the blood royal of France, who, being out of favor at court, should take refuge where he could with such friends as should be willing to follow his fortune? What judgment, I say, should we make of him, if he got the idea of raising contributions in the lands where he should station himself, and he put to the sword all those in the villages who should

was the reason for this. This man, who had been general of the
army under King Saul, placed Ish-bosheth on the throne and
kept him there against all of David's efforts; but, unable to bear

refuse to pay him taxes? What should we say if this Prince should fit
out vessels and cruise at sea to take all the merchant ships he could
light upon? Frankly, did David have a better authority to exact contributions from Nabal, and to massacre all the men and women in the
country of the Amalekites, and others, and to take all the cattle he
found there? I agree that I may be answered that we are nowadays
better acquainted with the Law of Nations, the *Jus belli et pacis,* about
which such fine systems have been written; and therefore such behavior was more excusable in those times than it would be now.
But the profound respect we ought to have for this great king, this
great prophet, ought not to prevent us from disapproving the blemishes that are to be found in his life; otherwise we should give the profane occasion to reproach us and to say that to make an action just
it suffices that it be committed by certain persons whom we revere.
Nothing could be more fatal to Christian morality. It is of great
concern to true religion that the lives of the orthodox be judged by
the general concepts of right and order.

≪≪

E. (*It was not his fault that he did not fight against the Israelites.*) While David with his small roving band was exterminat-
ing all the infidel countries wherever he could penetrate, the Philistines in their dominions were making preparations for war against
the Israelites. They assembled all their forces; and David and his
bold adventurers joined the army of Achish and would have fought
like lions against their brethren had the suspicious Philistines not
led Achish to dismiss them. It was feared that in the heat of battle
they would fall on the Philistines in order to make their peace with
Saul. When David was informed that because of these suspicions he
was obliged to quit the army, he became angry. He resolved therefore
to contribute with all his might to the victory of the uncircumcised
Philistines over his own brethren, the people of God, and the professors of the true religion. I leave it to nice casuists to judge whether
these views were worthy of a true Israelite.

Ish-bosheth's criticisms of his having taken one of Saul's concubines, he negotiated with David to put him in possession of Ish-
bosheth's kingdom. The discussion would soon have been concluded to David's satisfaction if Joab, to avenge himself for a
private quarrel, had not killed Abner. The death of that man
only hastened the ruin of the unfortunate Ish-bosheth. Two
of his chief captains killed him and brought his head to David,
who, far from rewarding them as they had expected, gave orders
that they be put to death. Ish-bosheth's subjects hardly waited at
all to submit voluntarily to David's rule. That prince had reigned
for seven and a half years over the tribe of Judah; after that
he reigned about thirty-three years over all Israel. This long
reign was notable for great successes and glorious conquests.
It was hardly troubled except by the criminal conspiracies of
the prince's own children (F). These are usually the enemies

«««

    F. *(His reign was only troubled by the criminal conspiracies of
his own children.)* The greatest of their conspiracies was the
revolt of Absalom, who forced this great prince to flee from Jerusalem,
in mournful garb with his head covered and his feet bare, melting
into tears, and having his ears greeted by nothing but the groans of
his faithful subjects. Absalom entered Jerusalem as if in triumph;
and, in order that the zeal of his partisans should not grow cold because of the feeling that this quarrel between father and son would
come to an end, he did something that was most likely to convince
them that he would never be reconciled with David: he went to bed
with the ten concubines of that prince, in full view of everybody. It
is very probable that he would have been forgiven for this crime;
the extreme grief in which David was plunged by his death is a
proof of this. He was the best father that was ever seen. His indulgence toward his children went beyond reasonable limits, and he
was the first who suffered from this leniency. For if he had punished
the infamous action of his son Ammon[16] as it deserved to be, he

---

    [16] He violated Tamar and was killed for this crime by order of Absalom,
Tamar's brother by both father and mother.

from whom a sovereign has the most to fear. David was very near being forced to return to the low condition in which Samuel had found him. Humanly speaking, this reversal of fortune would have been inevitable (G) had he not found some people to play the role of traitors to his son Absalom. David's

would not have had the shame and the displeasure of seeing another avenge the insult done to Tamar; and if he had chastised—as he should have—the one who avenged this injury, he would not have run the risk of being completely dethroned. David's destiny was that of most great princes. He was unfortunate with his family. His eldest son violated his own sister and was killed by one of his brothers because of that incest. The author of this fratricide slept with David's concubines. What a scandal it must be for pious souls to see so many infamous actions committeed in the family of this king!*

≪≪

G. (David was very near being forced to return to the . . . condition in which Samuel had found him. . . . This reversal of fortune would have been inevitable.) It can be seen from this example that there is no basis for depending on the fidelity of the people; for, in short, David was both a good and a great king. He made himself beloved and esteemed, and he had all the imaginable zeal for the religion of the country. His subjects, then, had reason to be content; and if they had to choose a prince, could they have wished for one with any other qualities? Yet they were so unsteady in their duty to David that his son Absalom, in order to have himself declared king, had only to make himself popular for a while and to keep some emissaries in contact with each tribe. The maxim, "She is chaste who has never been asked the question," can be applied to the people. If we do not see more kings dethroned, it is because the people have not been solicited to revolt by properly conducted intrigues. That is all that is necessary. If the prince is not a bad one, he can easily be made to appear so, or as the slave to wicked counsel.

---

* [This last sentence, giving the moral of the remark, was omitted in the revised version of the article.]

piety is so conspicuous in his Psalms and in many of his actions that it cannot be sufficiently admired. There is one thing no less admirable in his conduct, namely, that he happily reconciled so much piety with the loose maxims of the art of reigning. It is commonly believed that his adultery with Bathsheba, the murder of Uriah, and the proscription of the people are the only faults with which he can be charged. But this is a great mistake; for there are many other things in his life that deserve criticism (H). He is a sun of holiness in the Church; there by

≪≪

H. *(It is commonly believed that his adultery, etc., are the only faults with which he can be charged. . . . There are many other things in his life that deserve criticism.)* We have already taken notice of some that relate to the time when he was a private person. Here are others that refer to the period when he was on the throne.

I. His polygamy cannot be quite excused, for although God tolerated the practice in those days, we must not think that it could be carried very far without leading too much to sensuality. Michal, Saul's second daughter, was David's first wife. She was taken from him during his disgrace. He successively married several others and yet asked for her return. To restore her to him, they were obliged to take her away forceably from her husband who loved her greatly, and who followed her as far as he could, weeping like a child. David made no scruple to ally himself with the daughter of an uncircumcised person; and though he had children by several wives, he took concubines at Jerusalem. He chose, without doubt, the prettiest he could find, so that it cannot be said that he took much pains to mortify nature with regard to the pleasures of love.

II. As soon as he heard of Saul's death, he set himself to secure his succession, without any loss of time. He went to Hebron, "and immediately on his arrival there, the whole tribe of Judah, whose chief men he had won over by presents, acknowledged him to be king."[21] If Abner had not preserved the rest of the succession for the son of Saul, there is no doubt that by the same method—I mean, "by win-

---

[21] Abbé de Choisi, *Histoire de la vie de David.*

his works he spreads a marvelous light of consolation and piety, which we cannot admire enough. But he had his faults; and even in his last words we find the indirect dealings of policy (I).* Holy Scripture relates them only historically, for which reason everyone is at liberty to make a judgment of them. Let us conclude by saying that the history of King David may reassure several crowned heads against the fear that strict casuists might give them in maintaining that it is hardly possible for a king to be saved. The life of this great prince, published by the Abbe de Choisi, is a very good book and would have been much better if he had taken the trouble to set down in the margin the years of each action and the passages from the Bible or Josephus that furnished him his data. A reader is not pleased to be left ignorant about whether what he reads comes from a sacred source or a profane one. I shall not take notice of many of Moreri's faults. The article on David, which I have just read in the *Dictionary of the Bible,* will furnish me with matter for a remark. I have forgotten to observe that it would be unreasonable to blame David for excluding his eldest son from the succession.

ning over the chief men by presents"—David would have become king of all Israel. But what happened after Abner's fidelity had preserved eleven entire tribes for Ish-bosheth? The same thing that would have happened between two infidel and most ambitious princes. David and Ish-bosheth made incessant war on one another to see which of the two could get the other's share in order to enjoy the entire kingdom without division. What I am going to say is a great deal worse. Abner, discontent with his master the king, resolves to dispossess him of his dominions and to deliver them up to David. He lets David know of his intentions and goes to him himself to agree on means for putting them into execution. David listens to the traitor and is willing to gain a kingdom by intrigues of this nature. Can it be said that these are the actions of a saint? I admit that there is nothing in all this that is not in keeping with the maxims of politics and the ways of human prudence. But I shall never be convinced that

---

* [Remark I appears on p. 60.]

the strict laws of equity and the severe morals of a good servant of God can approve such conduct. . . .

III. I make the same judgment about the stratagem David employed during Absalom's revolt. He would not allow Hushai, one of his best friends, to accompany him but ordered him to go over to Absalom's side, so that he might give bad advice to that rebellious son and be able to inform David of all the plans of the new king. This stratagem is, without doubt, very commendable if we judge things according to human prudence and the policy of sovereigns. It saved David, and from that time to our own it has produced an infinite number of results, beneficial to some, harmful to others. But a rigid casuist will never take this stratagem for an action worthy of a prophet, a saint, or an honest man. An honest man, as such, would rather lose a crown than be the cause of his friend's damnation. And it is to damn our friend, as much as lies within our power, to urge him to commit a crime. And it is a crime to pretend to espouse zealously a man's cause, to pretend, I say, in order to ruin that man by giving him bad advice and giving away all the secrets of his cabinet. Can there be a more treacherous piece of villainy than this action of Hushai? As soon as he sees Absalom, he cries out, "God save the King, God save the King." And when he is asked why he is so ungrateful that he does not accompany his intimate friend, he gives himself devout airs and offers reasons of conscience, "I will be his whom the Lord hath chosen."

IV. When David, because of his old age, could not get warm under all the clothes they covered him with, it was thought proper to look for a young girl to nurse him and lie with him. For that purpose he allowed them to bring him the most beautiful maiden who could be found. Can this be said to be the action of a very chaste man? Will a man who is filled with the ideas of purity and completely resolved to do what decency and strict morality require of him ever consent to these remedies? Can a man consent to them unless he prefers the instincts of nature and the concerns of the flesh before those of the Spirit of God.

V. David has long been blamed for having committed a crying injustice against Mephibosheth, the son of his intimate friend Jonathan. . . . Note well the view of Pope Gregory. He admits that Mephibosheth was slandered, and yet he insists that the sentence which stripped him of his entire estate was just. He insists on this for two reasons: (1) because David pronounced the sentence, and (2) because a secret judgment of God intervened. . . . The author whom I cite [Théophile Raynaud] reasons another way. Since the holiness of David, he says, is well known to us and since he never ordered any reparation of the wrong that he had done to Mephibosheth, we have to conclude that the sentence was just. This is to establish a very dangerous principle. We must no longer examine the actions of the old prophets in terms of the ideas of morality, in order to condemn those who might not conform to them. As a consequence, libertines might accuse our casuists of approving certain actions that are obviously unjust, of approving them, I say, in favor of certain people and by making exceptions. Instead, let us say and apply to the saints what is remarked about great wits, . . . "The greatest saints have need of pardon in some respects."

.   .   .   .

VII. The conquests of David shall be the subject of my last observation. There are some rigid casuists who do not think that a Christian prince can lawfully engage in a war merely from a desire to aggrandize himself. These casuists only approve of defensive wars, or, in general, those that tend only to restore to every man the possessions belonging to him. On the basis of this view, David had frequently undertaken unjust wars; for, besides the fact that Scripture often presents him as the aggressor, we find that he "extended the limits of his empire from Egypt to the Euphrates."[37] In order that we may not therefore condemn David, we had better say that conquests may sometimes be allowed; and that, consequently, care should be taken lest, in declaiming against modern princes, our criticisms fall inadvertently on that great prophet.

But if, generally speaking, the conquests of that holy monarch have increased his glory without prejudice to his justice, it will be difficult to admit this proposition when we enter into particulars. Let us not, by our conjectures, pry into secrets history has not revealed to us. Let us not conclude that since David was willing to take advantage of the treason of Abner and of Hushai, he therefore had no qualms about employing all sorts of stratagems against the infidel kings whom he subdued. Let us confine ourselves to what the Sacred History has told us of the way in which he treated the vanquished. "And he

---

[37] Choisi, *Histoire de la vie de David.*

brought forth the people that were therein and put them under saws, and under harrows of iron, and under axes of iron, and made them pass through the brickkiln: and thus did he unto all the cities of the children of Ammon" (II Samuel 12:31). The Geneva Bible observes in the margin of this verse that "these were different ways of putting people to death that were used in ancient times." Let us see how he treated the Moabites: "And he smote Moab and measured them with a line, casting them down to the ground; even with two lines measured he to put to death, and with one full line to keep alive" (II Samuel 8:2). That is to say, he decided to put precisely two-thirds of them to death, neither more nor less. Edom received yet a harsher treatment. He slew all the males there. "For six months did Joab remain there with all Israel, until he had cut off every male in Edom" (I Kings 11:16). Can it be said that this way of waging war is not to be condemned? Have not the Turks and the Tartars a little more humanity? And if a vast number of pamphlets complain every day about the military executions of our time, which are really cruel and much to be blamed, although mild in comparison to David's, what would the authors of those pamphlets not say if they had the saws, the harrows, and brickkilns of David, and the general slaughter of all of the males, young and old, to condemn?

≪←

I. *(Even in his last words we find the indirect dealings of policy.)*
Understand me correctly. I do not mean that David, when in those circumstances, did not state his real thoughts; but that the frank and plain way in which he opened his heart is a demonstration that he had previously, in two noteworthy instances, sacrificed justice to utility. He knew well that Joab deserved death, and that allowing the assassinations with which that man's hands were polluted to go unpunished was a flagrant affront to law and reason. Joab nevertheless had kept his posts, his interest, and his authority. He was brave. He served his master the king faithfully and to good purpose; and dangerous mutinies were to be feared if there were attempts to punish him. These were the political reasons that made the law give way to utility. But when David had no further use for that general, he gave orders that he should be put to death. This was one of the

clauses in his will. Solomon, his successor, was charged with a similar order against Shimei. This man, having heard that David was fleeing from Jerusalem in great disorder due to Absalom's revolt, came to insult him on his way and employed reproaches still harder than the stones he threw at him. David bore this injury very patiently. With marks of singular piety he acknowledged and adored the hand of God in it; and when his affairs were settled, he pardoned Shimei, who was one of the first to submit and to beg his mercy. David swore that he would not put him to death, and he was as good as his word until he was dying; but finding himself at his last moments, he ordered his son to put that man to death, an evident proof that he had only let him live first to gain the glory of being a merciful prince and later to avoid being reproached to his face with having broken his word. I should like to know whether, strictly speaking, a man who promises his enemy his life keeps his promise when he orders him to be put to death in his will?

From all that has been said in the preceding remarks and in this one, it may be easily inferred that if the Syrians had been as great writers of libels as Europeans are nowadays, they would have strangely disfigured David's glory. What infamous names and titles would they not have used for that band of adventurers who joined him after he had left Saul's court? The Scripture informs us that all those who were persecuted by their creditors, all the discontented, and all those who were in bad circumstances went to him, and he became their captain. Nothing is capable of being more maliciously misrepresented than a matter of this kind. Those who have written the history of Cataline and of Caesar would furnish a satirical painter with a great many colors. History has preserved a small specimen of the abuses that were heaped upon David by the friends of Saul. This specimen shows that they accused him of being a man of blood and looked upon Absalom's rebellion as a just punishment for the damage they said David had done to Saul and to his entire family. I put the words of Scripture in a note,[48] and here are those of Josephus: "But when

---

[48] According to Scripture, the words of Shimei are, "Come out, come out, thou bloody man, and thou man of Belial. The Lord hath returned upon thee all the blood of the house of Saul, in whose stead thou hast reigned; and the Lord hath delivered the kingdom into the hand of Absalom thy son; and, behold, thou are taken in thy mischief because thou art a bloody man" (II Samuel 16:7–8).

David came near a place called Bachora, there came a kinsman of
Saul, named Semei . . . who threw stones at him and reviled him;
and when his friends protected him, he abused him still worse, calling him a bloody man who had done much damage, and he bade him
leave the land as an impure and execrable person. And he gave
God thanks that He had deprived him of the kingdom and punished
him by means of his own son for what he had committed against his
master."[49] They carried things too far. It is true that by the testimony of God himself, David was a man of blood; for which reason
God would not permit him to build the Temple. It is also true that
to appease the Gibeonites he delivered up to them two sons of
Saul and five grandsons, all of whom were hung. But it is false that he
ever made any attempts either on the life or crown of Saul.

An important notice with relation to what has been said above.
Those who may think it strange that I should state my opinion of
certain actions of David, comparing them with natural morality, ought
to consider three things: (1) They themselves have to admit that this
prince's behavior toward Uriah is one of the greatest crimes that can
be committed. Therefore, the only difference between us is with
regard to the number of his faults; for I recognize as well as they
do that the failings of this prophet are no argument against his having been a man full of piety and extraordinary zeal for the glory of
the Lord. He was alternately subject to passions and grace, a misfortune adhering to our nature ever since the sin of Adam. The grace
of God guided him often; but on several occasions his passions got
the upper hand, and policy silenced religion. (2) It is perfectly permissible for private persons like myself to judge facts contained in
Scripture when they are not expressly qualified by the Holy Ghost.
If Scripture in reporting an action blames or commends it, one
is no longer allowed to appeal from that judgment. Everyone
ought to regulate his approval or disapproval on the model of
Scripture. I have not acted contrary to this rule. The facts on which
I have given my humble opinion are related in the Sacred History
without any indication of approval.[52] (3) Great harm would be

---

49 Josephus, *Jewish Antiquities* VII. 207–208.

52 I have observed that Scripture acquaints us that David consulted and
followed the orders of God when aggressors were to be repulsed (II Samuel
23, 30); but that he did not consult God when he was going to destroy Nabal,

done to the eternal laws and consequently to true religion if libertines were given a chance to object to us that, as soon as a man has a share in the inspirations of God, we look upon his conduct as the rule of manners, so that we do not dare to condemn those actions that are diametrically opposed to the conceptions of equity when it is he who has committed them. There is no middle ground. Either these are unworthy actions, or actions like these are not wicked. Now, since we must necessarily choose one or the other of these two propositions, is it not better to consider the interests of morality rather than the glory of a particular person? Otherwise, will we not have to say that we would rather expose the honor of God to criticism than that of a mortal man?

---

or when he went to exterminate the neighbors of Achish and made the latter believe that he ravaged Saul's dominions. It is a sign that God did not approve of such actions.

Dicaearchus, a disciple of Aristotle, wrote a
great many books that were greatly
admired. Cicero and his friend Pomponius Atticus valued them
highly, and I think that their esteem extended even to the work
in which he attacked the immortality of the soul (C). Moreri

≪←

C. *(. . . I think that their esteem extended even to the work in
which he attacked the immortality of the soul.)* He had composed two treatises on this subject, each divided into three books.
"Dicaearchus, in that discourse that was held by some learned men
disputing at Corinth and that he has given us in three books, introduces several interlocutors in the first book, and in the other two,
one Pherecrates, an old man of Phthia, whom he makes a descendant
of Deucalion, and who argues that the soul is nothing more than an
empty name, that the term 'animal' has no signification since there
is no soul either in man or beast, and that the whole power whereby
we either do or feel anything is equally diffused through all living
bodies and is not separable from body, the soul being nothing in
itself nor anything else other than simple body, so modified that it
lives and feels by the disposition of nature. . . . Dicaearchus, who is
my delight, has argued strenuously against this immortality: for he
wrote three books, which are called Lesbian because the discourse is
supposed to have taken place at Mitylene, wherein he endeavors to
prove that our souls are mortal."[21] In some of his letters Cicero says
that he had need of these two works and begged Pomponius Atticus to
get them for him.

*An invincible objection against Dicaearchus on the immortality of
the soul.* I shall say in passing that this view of Dicaearchus is not
worthy of a philosopher. To reason in this manner is to have no

---

21 Cicero, *Tusculan Disputations,* I. 10 and 31.

attributes this work to another Dicaearchus who was from Lacedaemon and was a student of Aristarchus. But he is wrong in
making him the author of several books, since Suidas, who is
perhaps the only one who has spoken of that Dicaearchus, does
not ascribe any kind of book at all to him. This provides me
with a remark against Meursius. There is a passage in Pliny
that shows that Dicaearchus was commissioned by some princes
to measure the height of the mountains. Geography was one
of his principal studies, and we still possess a treatise he wrote

principles. It is to overturn the harmony of a system. If you once
suppose, with this author, that the soul is not distinct from the body,
that it is only a power equally distributed through all living things,
and that it makes but one simple being with the bodies that are
called living, then either you do not know what you are saying, or
you have to maintain that this power always accompanies the body.
For what is not distinct from the body is essentially the body; and
according to the first principles of reason, it is a contradiction to say
that a being ever exists without its essence. From this it obviously
follows that the power of feeling does not cease in dead bodies, and
that when they decay the parts of living bodies carry away with
themselves their life and soul. There is then no basis for telling oneself that sensation will cease after death, and that one will be subject
to no pain. If a body is capable of feeling pain when it is placed in
connection with nerves, it is also so capable in other situations in
which it may be located, either in stones, in metals, in the air, or in
the sea. And if an atom of air was once destitute of all thought, it
seems completely impossible that its conversion into that substance
called "animal spirit" would ever make it capable of thinking. This
seems as impossible as to give a definite location to a being that had
been for some time without such a location. Thus, to reason logically,
it has to be established either that the substance that thinks is distinct
from the body, or that all bodies are substances that think, inasmuch
as it cannot be denied that men have thoughts. From this it follows,
according to the principles of Dicaearchus, that there are a certain
number of bodies that think. Cicero, however, argues very poorly
against Dicaearchus. He claims that according to this philosopher, a
man should not feel pain, since he would not be aware that he had

on this. The work that he composed about the republic of
Lacedaemon was very much honored. He held to the maxim
that one ought to make oneself beloved by everybody, but that

a soul. Dicaearchus could easily have answered, "I do not deny that
he feels, and that he is aware that he feels. But I do deny that he
knows that what feels in him is a soul distinct from the body." It is
very true that he does not feel this, he knows it only by reasoning.
Lactantius makes use of this paralogism of Cicero.

I have just noticed that one could develop an illusory argument
against the one I have opposed to the system of Dicaearchus. This
obliges me to forestall an objection. Someone will tell me that feeling
could be a modification of body. From which it would follow that
matter, without losing anything essential to it, could cease to feel
as soon as it was no longer enclosed in the organs of a living machine.
I answer that this theory is absurd, for all the modalities of which we
have any knowledge are of such a nature that they cease only to give
way to another of the same kind. There is no figure destroyed but
by another figure, nor is any color driven out but by another color.[25]
I admit that, according to the old philosophy, cold and heat, which
expel one another out of the same subject, are not accidents of the
same species. But at least one will grant me that they belong to
same genus of qualities that are called "tangible." Thus, to reason
carefully, one should say that no sensation is driven from its substance except by the introduction of some other sensation. Nothing
precludes the possibility that the sensation may be a genus that has
other genera under it, before we reach what is called *species infima*.
According to this, my objection is not weakened by the answer I
am refuting; and I still have a basis for saying that if animal spirits
do not have outside the nerves the same sensation that they have in
them, they have only lost this sensation by acquiring one of another
kind. I will doubtless be told that there are modalities that cease,
without being succeeded by another positive one. The example of
motion will be offered, for one would not dare offer that of figures:
it is too obviously against the defenders of Dicaearchus. But I answer
that motion and rest are not different, as one supposes, in the same
way as positive modalities and privations are. Rest and motion are

---

25 Only bodies visible to man are intended here.

one ought to develop intimate friendships only with reputable persons. What he criticizes in Plato deserves criticism. Vossius should not have attributed a treatise on dreams to him. Lactan-

both very real and positive local presences. They differ only in external and entirely accidental relations. Rest is the duration of the same local presence. Movement is the acquisition of a new local presence. And consequently, what ceases to move does not lose its modality without acquiring another of the same nature. It always has a position equal to its extension among the other parts of the universe. When somebody gives us an example of some body that loses a place without acquiring another, we will agree that certain bodies may lose one sensation without acquiring another. But, since it is impossible that such an example be given, we are justified in maintaining that every body that feels once will always feel. Is not the conversion of being into nothing impossible in the natural order? Would not the conversion of figure into the absence of all figure, or the conversion of location into the absence of all location, be a conversion of something real and positive into nothing? This would then be impossible in the order of nature. Therefore, the conversion of sensation into the absence of all sensation is impossible, for it would constitute a conversion of something real and positive into nothing. Finally, I say that all the modes of bodies are based on the essential attributes of bodies, which are the three dimensions. This is why the loss of a figure or a definite location is always accompanied by the acquisition of another figure or another definite location. Extension never ceases. It never loses anything. This is why the decay of one of its modes is necessarily the generation of another. For the same reason, a sensation can only cease by the existence of another. For in the system I am refuting, the sensation would be a mode of body, just as figure and place are. But if you wish to base sensation on some attribute of matter other than the three dimensions, and unknown to our minds, I would answer you that the changes of this attribute ought to resemble the changes of extension. These latter can never make all figure and all location cease; and so the changes of this unknown attribute would not cause all sensation to cease. They would only bring about the passage from one sensation to another, as the motion of extension is only the passage from one place to another.

tius did not know where to place him. I was never more surprised than to see the sterility of the Jesuit Jerome Ragusa on so illustrious a subject as Dicaearchus, who has done so much honor to his native Sicily.

A person, who does not wish to make himself known, has sent me some objections that I am going to examine. They deal with the argument I offered against Dicaearchus on the subject of his view about the nature of the soul (L). This will afford me the opportunity to say a word about a dispute that has caused much excitement in England (M).*

≪←

L. *(A person . . . has sent me some objections that I am going to examine . . . on the subject of his view about the nature of the soul.)* The author of these objections begins by unfolding the system of our philosopher. He claims that Dicaearchus meant that living bodies differ from nonliving ones only in the shape and arrangement of their parts. He compares this theory with that of Descartes in the following manner. If a dog differs from a stone, it is not because the dog is composed of a body and a soul, and the stone of a body only. It is solely because the dog is composed of parts so put together that they make a machine, which the arrangement of the parts of a stone do not. This is Descartes' view. This presentation is very helpful for understanding the theory of Dicaearchus. We only have to suppose that he extended to all living things what the Cartesians said only with regard to beasts. We need only suppose that he reduced man to the condition of a machine. From this will follow that the human soul is not distinct from the body, but that it is only a construction, a mechanical disposition of several parts of matter. Assuming this is supposed, the author of the objections claims that I do not really undermine the system of Dicaearchus because I have not shown that the difficulty I advanced cannot be overcome. I maintained that Dicaearchus either did not know what he was saying, or he was obliged to hold that the power he said the soul consisted in

---

* [Remark M appears on p. 72.]

always accompanied the body. The answer is made that he only had to maintain that it [this power] always accompanied the living body. It is added that had I always joined together the two terms, "body" and "living," my conclusion could have been completely accepted by Dicaearchus and would have done no damage to his system. It is claimed, therefore, that he can deny that, if the soul is a power of living bodies, then it follows that it exists in cadavers. For if the soul consists only of the mechanical arrangement of certain bodies, as he supposes, it obviously follows that it ought to cease as soon as the arrangement ceases, as soon as the machine no longer exists. Thus, the answer goes on, a Cartesian would reply to those who might assert that, according to this hypothesis, the souls of beasts exist even after the beasts have been killed. "You are wrong," he would answer, "for since I suppose that it consists only in a certain disposition of organs, I ought to suppose necessarily that it perishes as soon as that disposition is destroyed." The author of the objections supposes "that it has never been proven against the Cartesians that the power of feeling does not cease in dead bodies, and that the parts of living bodies each carry away with them their life and soul when they decay." It is certain that this conclusion has not been raised as an objection against the Cartesians. But this is due to the fact that they do not attribute any sensation to the souls of beasts; for if they did, then the same difficulties I raised against Dicaearchus would apply to them, and they would also be obliged to find an answer. Lastly, the objection is raised against me concerning the remarks I made to the effect that all modalities known to us only cease being such by being replaced by other modalities of the same kind. From this it follows that a body that had sensation on some occasions would never cease having it. The objection that is raised against me is that it has little to do with Dicaearchus, for "he attributed life to matter *only* after it possessed the modification necessary to make it a living body, that is, the various arrangements of its parts. I had therefore no right to make him hold that there was life in any of the parts of matter after its dissolution, although before and after it really was a body but not a living body." This is the conclusion of the author of the objections. Note that he is not trying to defend Dicaearchus' doctrine itself. He recognized both its falsity and its impiety. He only wanted to show that I was wrong in accusing Dicaearchus of inconsistency, and that the system does not fall apart just because this philosopher

has not admitted sensation and imperishable life to be in bodies that
have once been alive.

You clearly see here the entire state of the question. It is solely
to determine whether a philosopher who believes that there are
bodies that think, and bodies that do not, reasons logically. I maintain that he does not; and that whoever once admits, for example,
that a collection of bones and nerves feels and reasons ought to maintain, on pain of being declared guilty of not knowing what he is
talking about, that every other assemblage of matter thinks, and that
the thought which existed in such a collection exists in other modifications of the disunited parts after the collection has been dissipated.
I shall not repeat the proofs I have already given of this, nor is it
necessary that I add any new strength to them; for the author of the
objections has not attacked them. He has only observed that Dicaearchus does not have to be troubled about the matter, since he
has asserted that matter only begins to live after a certain arrangement of its parts. But, it is here, principally, that I would want to
accuse him of not knowing what he is saying. He did not understand
by life, simply breathing, eating, walking; he understood it to involve
all the operations of man, the actions of the five senses, imagination,
reflection, reasoning, and the like. I maintain that something is being
supposed that has hitherto been inconceivable to all mankind, if
one supposes that the arrangement of the organs of the human body
alone make a substance that had never thought to become a thinking
one. All that the arrangement of the organs can accomplish is reduc-
ible, as in the case of a clock, to various different kinds of local
motion. The difference can only consist in the greater or lesser degree
of motion. But just as the arrangement of the several wheels that
make up a clock would be of no use in producing the effects of this
machine if each wheel, before being placed in a certain way, did not
actually possess an impenetrable extension, a necessary cause of
motion as soon as it is pushed with a certain degree of force; so
I also say that the arrangement of the organs of the human body
would be of no use to produce thought, if each organ before being
put in its place was not actually endowed with the ability to think.
Now this capacity is quite different from impenetrable extension, for
all that you can do with this extension, by pulling it, hitting it,
pushing it, in every way imaginable, is a change of situation whose
whole nature and essence you fully conceive without having need

to suppose any sensation in it, and even if you deny that there is any sensation in it. There have been some great geniuses who have been a little too *halfhearted in believing* the distinction between the soul of man and the body. But up to now no one I know of has ever dared to say that he conceived clearly that, in order to make a substance pass from the absence of all thought to actual thought, it sufficed to move it[51] so that this change of situation would be, for example, a feeling of joy, an affirmation, an idea of moral virtue, and so forth. And even if some people should boast that they clearly conceived this, they do not deserve to be believed. They ought to be shown the passage of Aristotle that I cited in another place.[52] Would it not be an absurdity to maintain that there are two kinds of color, one which is the object of sight and nothing more, the other the object of sight and of smell also? It is still more absurd to maintain that there are two kinds of roundness, one kind consisting merely in the parts of a body's circumference being equidistant from the center; and the other kind being, besides this, also an act whereby the round body perceives that it exists and sees several other bodies around it. The same absurdity occurs in maintaining that there are two kinds of circular motion, one that is only the change of situation on a line whose parts are equidistant from the center, the other that, besides this, is an act of love of God, a fear, a hope, and so forth. What I have said of roundness with regard to vision may be applied to all sorts of figures with regard to all sorts of thoughts; and what I have said about circular motion is not less forceful with regard to all the other lines along which a body can move either slowly or quickly. And thus we ought to conclude that thought is distinct from all modifications of body of which we have knowledge since it is distinct from all figure and all change of situation. But as this is not the question here, let us content ourselves with concluding that Dicaearchus, in order to reason consistently, ought to have admitted that thought is in every kind of matter; for otherwise it would be absurd to claim that if several veins, several arteries, and the like, were placed to-

---

51 Note that the Peripatetics, in attributing thought to beasts, do not give matter this property but ascribe it to a substantial form, which according to them is neither matter nor body, and which is produced anew in matter without being composed of matter. Thus, they agree that matter never acquires either sensation or knowledge.

52 See above, article "Arriaga," remark C and footnote 8 [p. 28].

gether like the parts of a machine, this would produce the sensation
of color, taste, sound, smell, cold, heat, love, hate, affirmation, negation, and so forth.

≪←

M. *(This will afford me the opportunity to say a word about a
dispute that has caused much excitement in England.)* It
seems to me that if I had simply and absolutely asserted that no one
up to now had boasted of having a clear idea of a modification of
matter that is an act of sensation, I should not have been too rash;
for I have just read in the *Nouvelles de la République des Lettres*
that Locke, one of the most profound metaphysicians in the world,
frankly acknowledges that a body endowed with thought is an incomprehensible thing. And note that he makes this admission in
replying to an objection based on this incomprehensibility. It was
therefore greatly to his interest to deny the basis of this objection. One
must conclude then that his admission is most sincere, and an effect
of the force of truth, and a proof that the greatest efforts he made to
understand the union of the materiality of a substance with thought
were of no avail. Now, if a man of such superior intellect admits this,
is it not probable that no one has dared to claim that he understood
such a union? This would be too vague if I did not add something.
Let me say then that the question whether the soul of man is distinct from matter came up in the famous dispute between Dr. Stillingfleet[54] and Locke. The first maintained that matter is incapable
of thought, and thereby became the defender of a fundamental article
of philosophical orthodoxy. He made use of this argument, among
others, "that we cannot conceive how matter can think."[55] Locke
himself admits the truth of this principle and contents himself with
denying the consequence; for he claims that God can do things incomprehensible to human understanding, and thus, just because
man cannot comprehend how a portion of matter could acquire
thought, it does not follow that God, who is all-powerful, "cannot,
if he wishes, give some degree of sensation, perception, and thought,
to certain collections of created matter, combined together as he

---

[54] One of the most learned men in Europe. He died as Bishop of Worcester in 1699.
[55] *Nouvelles de la République des Lettres,* November 1699, p. 500.

thinks proper. . . ."[56] "All the difficulties that are constructed," he says, "against the possibility that there is matter that thinks, drawn from our ignorance or the narrow limits of our conception, do not affect in any way the power of God if he wishes to give matter the power of thinking and if it cannot be proven that he has not actually given it to certain parts of matter, disposed as he thinks proper, until it can be shown that it is contradictory to suppose such a thing."[57] Here is a formal admission of the incomprehensibility of the thing, and a recourse to the extent of God's power on effects that are beyond the limits of our understanding. It is in much the same manner that the Schoolmen suppose that there is in creatures an *obediential* power, by which God might raise them, if he wished, to any state whatsoever. A stone might become capable of the beatific vision, a drop of water might become capable of washing away all the pollution of original sin. Note that to refute this *obediential* power of matter with regard to knowledge, a proof could be employed that Dr. Stillingfleet does not appear to have used.[58] It has always seemed to me very proper to show the impossibility of joining together the three dimensions and thought in the same subject. You will find a summary of this proof in the book that I cite.[59] A theologian who was very passionate against the Abbé de Dangeau, who made use of this argument, criticized him as well as he could and only produced poor arguments.[60]

Take notice of the expression "philosophical orthodoxy," which I have used, for I am not claiming that Dr. Stillingfleet is superior to Locke with respect to theological, evangelical, or Christian orthodoxy. To insist that, because the soul of man thinks, it is immaterial is good reasoning to my mind and is, besides, a way of establishing a very solid foundation for the immortality of the soul, a doctrine that ought to be considered as one of the most important articles of good philosophy. But this truth, in so far as it is grounded upon such a principle, does not belong to the faithful nor to Christian theology.

---

[56] *Ibid.,* p. 497.

[57] *Ibid.,* p. 506.

[58] In the extracts of the *Nouvelles de la République des Lettres,* November 1699, Article I.

[59] *Nouvelles de la République des Lettres,* August 1684, Article VI.

[60] See the same *Nouvelles,* January 1685, p. 12. [Among the references in this article to the *Nouvelles de la République des Lettres* only those references in footnotes 59 and 60 are of the period when Bayle was the editor of this journal.]

A Christian theologian—and every Christian in general, as a Christian—believes in the immortality of the soul, the existence of heaven and hell, and so on, because these are truths that God has revealed to us. It is in this respect only that his faith is a truly religious act, a meritorious one,[61] acceptable to God, a condition for being a child of God and a disciple of Jesus Christ. And those who may believe in the immortality of the soul solely on account of the philosophical ideas that reason furnishes to them would be no further advanced in the kingdom of God than those who believe that the whole is greater than the part. Since Locke bases his conviction of the immortality of the soul on Scripture, he has as much theological, evangelical, and Christian orthodoxy as anyone can have. What he says on this subject is admirable.[62] I will probably cite it in some other place.[63]

---

[61] Here the hypothesis of the merit of works is assumed to be true.

[62] See the *Nouvelles de la République des Lettres,* November 1699, p. 510; and the book entitled *Parrhasiana,* pp. 388ff [by Locke's friend, and Bayle's opponent, Jean le Clerc].

[63] In remark L of the article "Perrot, Nicholas" [not included in these selections].

Eppendorf, HENRY OF, a German gentleman, would be very little known today in the republic of letters, had he not been engaged in a great controversy with Erasmus. He carried on this quarrel vigorously, and the great Erasmus perhaps never met with an adversary who reduced him to such disagreeable terms of agreement. Because the articles of this pacification were not being observed, Eppendorf raised a great clamor and published a work that contains an account of this controversy. We learn therein that he had left his country in order to improve himself in the sciences; that he had been a student of the famous Zasius, professor of law; that he spent a long time at Strasbourg; and that he remained neutral among the violent factions that Luther's Reformation produced in Germany (C). It must be said that, in order to obtain justice for an abusive pamphlet that had been written against him, he made use of a method very proper to restrain the most slanderous authors (D).*

⫷

C. *(He remained neutral among the . . . factions that the Reformation produced in Germany.)* Without doubt he was one of those who believed that the Roman Church had need of reforming, and that the Protestants did not reform it very well. Thus he offended both sides. People went so far as to accuse him of being in the pay of the papists and the Lutherans at the same time. He portrays himself as a man who sought to live under shelter during this storm and who, not knowing yet which side was right, was waiting for the weather to clear so that he could better see the affair. Here are his words: "I have lately seen some letters, written to a very important

---

* [Remark D appears on p. 77.]

person, in which the writer, a most wicked wretch, asserts that I received five hundred ducats from the Lutherans and as many from the papists, and that I cheat them out of their money and laugh at both parties, because I care neither for the new nor the old religion. What should I do? I laugh at the wretch's impudence. Being recently invited to participate in a conversation with a man who is very zealous for the Roman Church, I was asked by him what I thought of the present state of affairs. I told him my views very freely. On the other hand, I told the Protestants just as freely that (according to my opinion, I who am but a very young man) there were insufficient reasons for either the explosion or the innovations. And thus I have made myself but little acceptable to both sides. I have continued, determined to this very day, not to meddle with that evangelical business, as they call it; and I pray that in this fatal and memorable innovation nothing but what is happy and good may befall us miserable men. Nor shall I follow any sect unless some new Solon lead me to it; but in that case, I will have you know that I will adhere to the soundest doctrine, though it should cost me my life." If we judge of things only by the principles of the natural light, Eppendorf's choice seems most reasonable. He wished to wait for the outcome of this affair before ranging himself on either the side of those who maintained the abuses or those who fought against them. Both sides seemed too violent to him, and the tempest from both sides too strong. He said with Cicero, "I know whom to avoid but not whom to follow." He was too great a lover of peace to engage in that religious war. But it was in vain that he hoped to remain on the shore, a quiet spectator of that boisterous sea. He found himself more exposed to the storm than if he had been in either one of the fleets. This is the inevitable fate of those who wish to remain neutral in the political or religious civil wars. They are exposed to attack from both sides at the same time. They make themselves enemies without making any friends. Whereas, if they had wed themselves with ardor to one of the causes they would have had friends as well as enemies. O deplorable condition of man, O obvious vanity of philosophical reasoning! It makes us regard the tranquility of the soul and the calmness of our passions as the end of all our labors and the most precious fruit of our most difficult meditations. However, experience shows that, according to the ways of the world, there is no condition less appreciated than that of souls who do not wish to abandon themselves to the surges of factions, nor is there a condition less troublesome than that of men who howl with the wolves and who follow the violent current of the most impetuous passions. People in this latter condition have, among other advantages, that of not knowing they are wrong. For there are no persons more incapable of knowing the defects of their own side and the good qualities that can be found on the other side, than those who are carried away by an ardent zeal and a violent anger, and who are bound by a strong prejudice. "Blessed are the peacemakers," says the Bible. This is very true in terms of the other world; but in terms of this one they are very miserable. They do not want to be the hammer, and because of this they are continually the anvil, beaten from all sides.

«««

D. (He made use of a method very proper to restrain the most slanderous authors.) He brought his case before the judges, and he demanded, among other satisfactions for the injuries committed against him, that the aggressor be condemned to pay a fine to the poor. Here is a most efficacious remedy for the bile of a great many writers. They are both more quarrelsome and more difficult to reconcile than warriors. The reason for this, some say, is that warriors eliminate their dispute with sword in hand and risk their lives thereby. But authors who quarrel do not expose themselves to spilling their blood. It only costs them paper and ink. If they had to expose their skin to the point of a sword as they do to the point of a pen, they would be more peaceful. Let us also say that if their purse were exposed to some danger for every injurious expression, their style would be more moderate and civil. Thus our Eppendorf hit on a good method. Authors ought to be permitted to criticize each other with regard to their learning or their false reasoning. Civil judges have no concern with this; but one might wish that they would exert their legal power by at least fining authors who attack their neighbors and cover them with injuries in other respects. This would banish an infinite number of abusive phrases from books and would introduce moderation into the controversies of Parnassus, a quality that is not common.

Guarini, BATTISTA, was born in Ferrara in the year 1538. He is better known for his tragicomedy *Il Pastor Fido* than for any of his other works or for any of his achievements in the service of his master the duke. This play was his favorite work, as he clearly showed by his anger with a critic who had attacked it only indirectly. He has therein painted the mysteries of love so vividly that it is claimed that the work has led to fatal consequences to the chastity of several members of the fair sex. This seems to be in strong opposition to a maxim of La Fontaine (C). I do not know if Guarini

«←

C. (*This seems to be in . . . opposition to a maxim of La Fontaine.*) Nicius Erythraeus, having said that *Il Pastor Fido* is reprinted almost every year, and that all nations, no matter how barbarous, have translated it into their own languages, adds that it is perhaps not a book that contributes to the purity of manners. And here are the reasons he offers. "For it is related that many virgins and married women have had their chastity shipwrecked by its sweets and allurements, in the same way that Ulysses was led astray in a sea infested with Sirens." Let us examine the maxim of La Fontaine: "After all, is there any reason why one should be alarmed by a little pleasantry? I should much rather fear that the cajolery of a lover would set fire to the house. But ye lovely fair ones, banish your suitors, and peruse my book. I myself will answer for you, body for body."

Here is how this author extricates himself from a very great difficulty. People had complained that his Tales were only fit to excite a thousand unchaste desires in the minds of his readers. La Fontaine replies that, if women who read his book do not allow any gallant to approach them, they will not lose their honor. This answer smells like a sophism, for it requires a condition, the practice of which is made very difficult by the very book in question. You want us to read

would have wished to use such a maxim in his own defense, and if he would not have found it easier to have recourse to a more common view (D). I do not imagine there is anything stronger

your book and to banish our suitors. You are not fair to demand this because your poems deprive us of the power of banishing our suitors. They fill us with love, they heat us up, they set us on fire, they make us wish ardently for the presence of those gentlemen. With what good grace, then, can you say after this that nothing bad will befall us provided we banish them? Another objection can be raised against La Fontaine, namely, that even if they banish their suitors, the ladies would find themselves exposed to many impure passions excited by the reading of his Tales. And is this not a great enough fault? In order to give a just apology for this author, one would have to suppose that his book is not capable of prejudicing chastity, and that nothing can damage that virtue but the sight of lovable objects and actual courtship. But this cannot be supposed if it is really the case, as has been claimed, that the reading of *Il Pastor Fido* has undone many ladies and virgins. Thus I have given sufficient commentary on my text.

Even if what is said about the pernicious effects of that poem should be false, it would nevertheless be true that the reading of certain books is very pernicious for young people of both sexes. There are doctors who have prescribed the reading of the *Priapeia* for those who are having difficulty exciting themselves for love-making; and I have observed that the Emperor Aelius Verus, a prince who had abandoned himself to lewd sensual pleasures, always had the love poems of Ovid in his bed, and that he was partial to the verses of Martial. . . . I remember having read in Tassoni that study excites lewd desires because, among other reasons, it acquaints readers with a thousand lascivious things that are found in books. In this way he explains why several learned women, whom the ancient writers mention, were very lustful. . . .

≪≪

D. *(He would* perhaps *have found it easier to have recourse to a more common view.)* He could perhaps have said that his pastoral tale did not teach his readers anything they did not already

in his work than the scene that has been so well translated into French by the Countess de la Suze. There he deals with one of the most incomprehensible mysteries of nature (E).* The number of editions and translations of *Il Pastor Fido* is incredible. Guarini died in Venice at an inn in 1613. His funeral, solemnized by the Academy of Humorists, indicates that he was held in high esteem.

He was the great-grandson of Guarini of Verona, and he taught moral philosophy in the Academy of Ferrara. Notwithstanding the exalted reputation he had gained by the above-mentioned poem, he could not endure being called a poet because he thought that such a title does not do the least honor to those who bear it, while it exposes them to contempt. One imagines on reading his verses that he composed them without any difficulty at all. But this is not true. The verses cost him great sweat and tears, requiring many changes and erasures. He was not stricken with a fever for amassing riches but he did like pomp and show. Because of this he did not have, when fortune turned her back on him, the resources that a more careful economy would have provided had he carefully managed the generous sums his master, Alfonso II, had bestowed upon him. This prince ceased to favor him, and then Guarini attached himself successively to Vincenzio de Gonzaga, to Ferdinand de' Medici, Grand Duke of Florence, and to Francesco Maria da Montefeltro, Duke of Urbino. All these changes only brought him great esteem for his wit and for his compositions. He retired finally to his native land, where, like an oracle, he was consulted on the means for bringing peace to Italy.

know, or that, if young people did come across something they had not known before, they would have learned about it somewhere else. Therefore, there would have been no point in not having published *Il Pastor Fido* on this account. A friend of La Fontaine's has delicately

---

* [Remark E appears on p. 82.]

touched upon this kind of defense. "It is prudent for persons entrusted with the education of the young," he says, "not only to forbid them from reading works like La Fontaine's but still more to prevent them from learning much more by frequenting bad company. It is not always books that teach people what they should not know." This is to insinuate very clearly that, the way things go on in this world, those who do not learn from La Fontaine's book what they should not know will learn by a hundred other ways. Someone [Bayle] offered a similar view to refute the unjust complaints of those who did not want to censor the dirty passages in Juvenal and Martial. This kind of defense is better than that of La Fontaine's maxim, but it is, nevertheless, not a good one. For in the end, no matter how inevitable lewd disorders may be, each person should prefer that, even if he does not contribute to them, they arise from some other source than his own actions. And note that this applies to those who invent obscene stories or who translate them with new embellishments, and not to those who cite a passage of Martial and others as a proof of some incident which they are obliged to mention either because of the nature of their work or because they are historians, commentators, and the like. On the whole we have to admit that all the salacious things that one might learn about in books are communicated by conversations and without the aid of literature. It is incredible how many things of this kind are known by those who are still very young, and who have not yet learned to read. The progress that is made in this science is surprising and does not require a great number of years. Let us listen to Montaigne: "Let women dispense a little with ceremony and express themselves with freedom in discourse, we are but babes compared to them in the knowledge of this science. Listen to them talk of our addresses and conversations, they will plainly show that we teach them nothing that they had not learned and digested without us. Shall we say with Plato that they were formerly rakish boys? My ears happened one day to be in a place where they could overhear, unsuspected, some discourse among women. Would that I were allowed to relate all I heard! By Our Lady, said I, let us go now and learn phrases from Amadis and study Boccacio and Aretino to appear clever. We will be using our time well indeed; there is not a word, an example, or a single step but it is better known to them than to the authors who have written on that subject. This is a science that is born in their veins, 'and Venus herself inspires them' (Virgil), so that those good schoolmasters—nature, youth, and health—are perpetually infusing it into their souls. They have no need to learn it, for it is engendered in them. . . ."[14]

They learn these things from one another. The old ones teach the young ones; and if the ignorant ones passionately desire this knowledge, the learned ones are no less avid in their desire to communicate their wisdom. It could be said that they regard it as an accepted axiom that knowledge is useless unless it can be communicated to others. Thus, an Italian upbringing—the great care that is taken in keeping girls away from the company of boys—does not remove the danger. Besides, women, in those countries where they are restrained, are allowed to be mixed helter-skelter with men at marriage ceremonies. Now, can one find a more scandalous school for impurity than the assemblies, diversions, and feastings at weddings? How many ridiculous and obscene things are said there? St. Cyprian was right in not wanting to allow virgins to attend them. He told them that their virginity would be tainted by the time they returned. "Some women do not blush to be present at weddings, to intermix immodest words with the loose conversations usual at such times, to hear what I dare not repeat, to observe and be present at the obscene discourses and drunken revelings, by which the fire of lust is raised, and which animate the bride to submit to the losing of her virginity and invigorate the husband to attack it. What is learned, as well as seen there? How greatly does a virgin fail in her purpose, when she returns immodest from thence, though she was modest when she went? For although she is still a virgin with respect to her body and mind, nevertheless, by her eyes, ears, and tongue, she has been partly despoiled of what she brought with her to those entertainments. . . ."[17]

≪←

E. (*He . . . deals with one of the most incomprehensible mysteries of nature.*) He introduces a maiden who, being a prey to the arbitrary will of two tyrants—love and honor—who are enemies, is envious of the happiness of beasts, who are guided by no other

---

[14] Montaigne, *Essays*, Bk. III, chap. 5 [the line from Virgil is *Georgics* III. 267]

[17] Cyprian, *De disciplina et habitu virginum* XIV.

regulations in their love-making than love itself. She cannot understand the opposition she finds between nature and law. The first attaches an extreme pleasure to certain things, and the second a severe punishment to them. This is her conclusion:

> *Doubtless either Nature is imperfect in itself*
> *In that it gives us a disposition that the law condemns,*
> *Or the law should be considered too severe*
> *That condemns a disposition that Nature gives.*

Without the revelation we have received from Moses it would not be possible to make any sense of this, and I am very surprised that the ancient philosophers paid so little attention to this matter. I am talking only about the philosophers who knew of the unity of God; for, according to the established religion of their country, those who admitted a plurality of gods would not have found any difficulty here. They only had to suppose that one god was the cause of the natural impulse and that other deities impressed the instincts of conscience and the ideas of honor on us. The difficulty only concerned those who were convinced that the universe is the work of an infinitely holy God. How can it come to pass, in that case, that the human race should be attracted toward evil by an almost irresistible allurement—I mean, by the sensation of pleasure—and should be steered away from it by the fear of remorse, or by that of infamy and several other punishments; and that mankind should spend their whole lives in this conflict of passions, pulled sometimes one way, sometimes the other, sometimes conquered by pleasure, sometimes by the fear of the consequences. Manicheanism is apparently the result of a deep meditation on this deplorable state of man.

Guillemete of Bohemia, head of an infamous sect
that began in Italy in the thirteenth
century, had deceived the world so well by exhibiting the appearance of an extraordinary devotion and had played the
comedy so well during her lifetime that she not only died in the
odor of sanctity but was also venerated as a saint for rather a
long time after her death. Finally her imposture was discovered,
as well as the charms she had employed. Her body was disinterred and burned in 1300. She had died in 1281 and had been
buried in Milan in the cemetery of San Pietro del Horto. Six
months later she was moved to the convent of Caravalla, where
a monument to her was erected, whose ruins can still be seen
in the cemetery of the monks. Two learned men, Puricellus
and Bossius, have written on this sect and are not in agreement
about everything. Bossius was the first who defamed this sect
because of its contaminating the flesh (A); but Puricellus has

≪←

A. *(Bossius was the first who defamed this sect because of its
contaminating the flesh.)* A practice was imputed to this sect,
of which several other assemblies have been accused at various times
and places. It was said that the followers of Guillemete would assem-
ble at night in a cave, and that after having recited certain prayers,
they would extinguish the candles, and the men would couple with
the women as chance arranged it. . . . It is added that a rich merchant,
whose wife used to steal away frequently to this cave, once followed
her secretly, enjoyed her, and convinced her of this by a ring he took
off her finger. He became an informer against this sect. We have seen
above that the same story is told about the Fratricelli. I believe that
sometimes there is slander in this kind of accusation. But no doubt
many lewd acts are very often committed at such assemblies; and I
am not surprised that so many husbands disapprove of their wives'

maintained that the disorder did not pass from the spirit to the
flesh, and that Guillemete and her followers were only guilty

zeal for attending certain devotional meetings; for sooner or later love
gets involved and we cannot admire enough the docility of the fair
sex with regard to the doctrines that are most opposite to that of chastity. I am not so much amazed that in ancient paganism one could
persuade women to prostitute themselves; it was said that this was a
type of divine worship. That is how the goddess Venus was honored.
But it is astonishing that in the midst of Christendom, after all the
efforts that are used to restrain the impulses of nature, and in spite
of all the wise counsel of mothers and the strong exhortation of preachers, the first hypocrite they come across can persuade them to commit
thousands and thousands of abominations. Let him say to one of his
female devotees what St. Aldhelm did, "Come lie next to me in bed
and I will see if you will be a sufficiently powerful instrument in the
hands of Satan to make me succumb to temptation," and she does so.
Let him say, as certain heretics who were punished by the Inquisition
of Toulouse did: "Let us lie down completely nude next to each other,
on one another. Let us kiss each other, let us tickle each other. In this
way we will give proofs of our spiritual strength."[6] And he is obeyed.
Can a greater docility be found? Would she not do more if he wished?
Has she not acquiesced on several occasions to the order to defile herself with the first person she met after the candles have been extinguished during the assemblies of the group?

Let us speak about another docility, less criminal, but quite strange,
however. Wherever there are infirm men who have need of some res-
toration of natural warmth, there will also be girls or women who
will go to bed with them to render them this service. A panegyrist of
the fair sex will furnish me with a rather remarkable passage on this.
"Doctors cannot conceal the fact," he says,[7] "that the delicate warmth
of a young woman's breast applied to the stomach of an old man may
revive, preserve, and augment in him the natural heat of life. This
was also not unknown to the royal prophet David, who chose the
beautiful Shunamite damsel to warm up in him in this manner the

---

[6] From the trials of the Inquisition of Toulouse, published in Amsterdam in 1692.

[7] Billon, *Fort inexpugnable de l'honneur du sexe feminin.*

of abominable fanaticism, which he proves by the investigations
of the Inquisition (B). Guillemete's festival was celebrated three
times a year at her grave; on St. Bartholomew's Day, which was

frigidity of his old age. And, on the basis of this example, it is probable that the grandfather of the last deceased king of Navarre, called
Monsieur d'Albret, at the age of one hundred and twenty kept two
lovely young ladies for this purpose. He lived for a long time on their
milk without any other nutriment whatsoever, as he lay between them.
For this they were also honored as princesses of his palace. To be sure, it
is not suitable for all men to do likewise because the same thing might
often take place as happened once with a notary of the Châtelet in Paris
who was called Master Martin Maupin. He, taking good advantage of
such stories, made his jealous wife believe that, because he was often afflicted with David's malady, she should allow him to make use of his
servant-maid to warm his stomach a little; and the poor woman was
sometimes deceived in this way." I shall observe in passing that St.
Jerome does not approve of taking the story of the Shunamite lady
literally. He has recourse to allegory and claims that what should be
understood by it is that David in his old age was more intimately
united to wisdom. No one could reject the literal sense with more
indignation than this Father of the Church did. "Are you not of the
opinion that by following the letter, which kills, you make a mere
farcical fiction of it? . . . What, therefore, is that Shunamite woman,
both wife and virgin, so hot as to repel the cold, so holy as not to pro-
voke him when heated to lust? Let the most wise Solomon describe
his father's delights, and let the pacific man relate the embraces of the
warlike one: May you possess wisdom, receive understanding, and the
like."[8]

≪–

B. *(By the investigations of the Inquisition.)* These inquiries,
drawn up in 1300, report that André Saramita and Mayfreda
Pirovana, the chief followers of Guillemete, maintained that she was
the Holy Ghost incarnate in the female sex and was born of Con-
stantia, wife of the king of Bohemia; that she was dead only according

---

[8] Jerome, *Epist. ad Nepotianum.*

the day of her death; on the day when her body was removed to Caravalla; and on the day of Pentecost. Her visions were never completely eradicated (C).

to the flesh; that she would rise before the general resurrection and would ascend to heaven in the sight of her disciples; that she had left as her vicar on earth Mayfreda Pirovana, a nun of the order of the *Humilitae;* that this nun would say mass at the tomb of Guillemete; and that finally she would occupy the Holy Apostolic See at Rome; that she would drive away the cardinals; and that she would have four learned men who would compose four new Gospels. Puricellus deals amply with all these frightful impieties. His book has not yet been printed, and it is not even known whether it ever will be published. It does not seem that Guillemete herself boasted of this alleged incarnation. It even seems that because of false modesty she affected not to be in agreement about it.

«‹‹

C. *(Her visions were never completely eradicated.)* The author of the continuation of the chronicle of Nangis reports, for the year 1306, that a certain Dulcinius of Vercel put forth similar doctrines concerning the Holy Ghost. Postel and his mother, Jeanne, did not have lesser fantasies; and it would be easy to show that this kind of fanaticism sprouts up again from time to time. It seems that there may be a conspiracy among the demons to make religion fall under feminine control, and in spite of the poor results of a great number of attempts they are not disheartened, and they try again from time to time in different places.

Hall, JOSEPH, one of the most illustrious prelates in England in the seventeenth century, was first professor of rhetoric at Cambridge University and then successively, Rector at Halsted, Dean of Worcester, Bishop of Exeter, and finally Bishop of Norwich. He was a deputy at the synod of Dordrecht and attended it for a while, but having become ill he was forced to withdraw from that famous assembly. He published many books, several of which have been translated from English into French by Théodore Jaquemot. These books contain beautiful thoughts, a very sound morality, and even a great aura of devotion. He died in 1656 at the age of eighty-two. He liked to study so much that he passionately wished that his health would have allowed him to do this to excess. His writings, when the occasion presented itself, show that he was very strong against popery. He disapproved hardly less of those who separated themselves from the Established Church without extreme necessity. What he said about Arminius shows this. He deplored the divisions among the Protestants, and he wrote something to put an end to this state of affairs. The great pacifier Duraeus was very much pleased as a result. Among other controversial subjects, he dealt with the vow of celibacy (F); and when he learned that Marc Antoine de

≪←

F. *(Among other controversial subjects, he dealt with the vow of celibacy.)* The third letter of his second Decad is entitled "An Apologetical Discourse Concerning the Marriage of Ecclesiastical Persons." It took the author only three hours and three pages to deal with this and takes up twenty-three duodecimo pages in Jaquemot's French translation. Twelve years after it had appeared, an English Roman

Dominis planned to return from England to Italy, he wrote him a letter to show him the necessity of continuing his separation from the Church of Rome. This letter has been inserted in its entirety in the answer of Marc Antoine de Dominis. His *Epistles* are good; they are undated; but since they are dedicated to Prince Henry, the eldest son of James I, one must conclude that they were written before 1613. He remarks in his dedicatory epistle that it was not yet an English custom to publish discourses in the form of letters, as was done in other countries. In the catalogue of the Oxford library a work in Latin is attributed to him entitled *Mundus alter et idem, sive terra australis antehac semper incognita longis itineribus peregrini academici nuperrime lustrata, autore Mercurio Britannico* [*Another World, or the Southern Lands Formerly Unknown, Lately Traveled over by a Foreign Scholar, by Mercurius Britannicus*]. He did not approve at all of English noblemen traveling in foreign countries, and he wrote a book on this, which he dedicated to the nobility.* His Christian Seneca has been translated into several languages. It is a very solid treatise.

Catholic priest refuted it in a writing of 380 pages. Joseph Hall answered him extremely promptly in a book entitled *An Apology for the Honor of the Marriage of Ecclesiastical Persons, against the Wicked Calumnies of C.E., a Pseudo-Catholic Priest.*† He published it in English in 1620. Jaquemot's French translation was published in Geneva in 1665 and contains 362 duodecimo pages. The author wished to prove his diligence, "so that my self-conceited adversary and his seduced abettors may see how little a well-ordered marriage is guilty of deadening our spirits, or slacking our hands." Although he was married, he finished his answer and wrote it ("twice written it over

---

* [*Quo Vadis? Or a Just Censure of Travell as It Is Commonly Undertaken by the Gentlemen of Our Nation* (1617).]

† [This is only the second half of Hall's title. The full title reads *The Honour of the Married Clergy, Maintained Against the Malicious Challenges of C.E., Mass-Priest; or, The Apology Written Some Years Since for the Marriage of Persons Ecclesiastical, Made Good Against the Cavils of C.E., Pseudo-Catholic Priest.*]

with mine own hand") in very little time, even though he worked at it as "but the recreation of the weightier business of my calling which now did more than ordinarily urge me." This gives us grounds for conjecturing that the English Roman Catholic priest had made use of the commonplace that marriage turns a man too much from his studies. Inadvertently Hall used some expressions which seemed to indicate that continency was impossible, and he was embarrassed a little by the conequences that were drawn from this thesis. Here is one of the English priest's objections. "Master Hall was absent in France. Flesh is frail, temptations frequent. Yet both then and before his marriage he would take it in great scorn to be suspected for dishonest. If Master Hall could, for so long together, live a chaste life, why not more?" He answers that this conclusion is worthless and compares it to the following: "A good swimmer may hold his breath under the water for some portion of a minute: why not for an hour? why not for more? A devout papist may fast after his breakfast till his dinner in the afternoon: therefore, why not a week? why not a month? why not as long as Eve, the maid of Meurs?" After this, among other things he says that St. Paul, having permitted married persons to part "with consent for a time, that ye may give yourselves to fasting and prayer," commands them to "come together again that Satan tempt you not for your incontinency" (I Corinthians 7:5). This supposes that though one can be continent for several days, it does not follow that one could do it all one's life. "Where there is impossibility," it has been objected to Hall, "or necessity, there is no sin, no counsel; as no man sins in not making new stars, in not doing miracles." He answers that this is "a stale shift, that oft sounded in the ears of Augustine and Prosper from their Pelagians." Another objection made to Hall is this: "The father cannot blame his child for incontinence. To contain implies impossibility; . . . to provide a husband or a wife is not a work of an hour's warning; in the meantime what shall they do?" Hall answers: "Sure, the man thinks of those hot regions of his religion where they are so sharp set that they must have stews [brothels], allowed of one sex at least. Else, what strange violence is this that he conceives? As our Junius answered his Bellarmine in the like, 'This man appears to be speaking of stallions rushing on mares, or of the hippomanes, and not of rational men.' He speaks as if he had to do with stallions, not with men, not with Christians, amongst whom is to be supposed a decent order and due regard of seasonableness and expediency." Lastly, the case of divorce is raised as an objection to Hall. " 'The husband and wife are separated upon some discord or disease. What shall they do? To live continent with this man is impossible.' I [Hall] answer: If only their will sunders them, that must yield to necessity; dissension may not abridge them of the necessary remedy of sin. If necessity, that finds relief in their prayers, if they call on Him who calls them to continency by this hand of His, He will hear them and enable them to persist. 'And why not then in the necessity of our vows?' This is a necessity of our own making: that is of His. He hath bound Himself to keep His own promises, not ours."

Whoever examines impartially these answers of Hall will find them a bit weak. It is actually a campaign like that of a general, who, having advanced too far into enemy territory, can only retreat by losing his rear guard. Any minister who admits that continency is beyond human capacity and who gives this as the reason why he is married will raise strong suspicions about the period that preceded his marriage when he was even younger than when he took a wife. For, if, in order to vindicate his character with regard to that period, he asserted that he had lived without love, but that at last a certain woman, having affected him by means of certain sympathies that exist in nature and by means of certain mechanical proportions that exist between objects and our faculties, he found himself deprived of the power to contain himself as he had previously; if, I say, he had employed such an apology, he would expose himself to very difficult and embarrassing questions. "What did you do," he would be asked, "after that fatal meeting when you fell in love? You spent five or six months, or perhaps a year, courting the object of your love, and in settling the marriage contract with her relatives. Your love deprived you of your continency. You must have fallen into a dissolute way of life. But what would you have done if it was a married woman who had happened to strike you by those sympathies or by those proportions of which you speak? Could you have then been continent? If so, love and continency are not incompatible, and you contradict yourself. If it had not been in your power to be continent, you would have committed adultery, either actually or in intention. But, if after your marriage your maid, who will perhaps be prettier and younger than your wife, should be situated in those mechanical proportions with regard to you, then you will find yourself in love with her and incapable of containing yourself. The same thing will happen if a married woman is encountered in the same proportions, and thus your virtue cannot be depended upon. All the time there will be fear of what scandal your conduct will lead to, or at the very least you will be considered as a person whose virtue is based upon a very weak foundation." It is certain that a man whose profession requires not only that he should live morally but also that he should be considered chaste cannot well and honestly acknowledge that he married only because it was impossible for him to contain himself. He ought to say that he could have done so, and that he married only in order to have children, to have domestic companionship, a person he could trust, and so on. Let us conclude that the controversy over celibacy cannot be well handled unless one is careful not to expose oneself too much to the enemy's cannons. Hall is on much stronger ground when he insists on the bad effects of monastic vows. He has no lack of quotations. Here is one of them: "Do not our histories tell us that during the reign of Henry Third, Robert Grosthead, the famous bishop of Lincoln, during a visitation 'was fain to explore the virginity of their nuns, by nipping of their dugs.' *Indignum scribi* [it is shameful to mention it], as Matthew Paris [writes]?"

To conclude, it is not only in Protestant communions that it has been believed impossible to be continent. There have been Roman Catholics who have had the same view. For they made fun of those prelates who abstained from adultery and fornication, and regarded them as either eunuchs or sodomites, and there were parishes where the curate was required to keep a concubine. Without this, people would not have believed that the honor of their wives was safe, and even this precaution did not put all danger out of the way. . . .

Hegesilochus was one of those who committed a thousand atrocities on the island of Rhodes when the democratic government was changed into an aristocracy through the influence of Mausolus, King of Caria. Athenaeus has preserved for us some instances of the debauchery of these new masters. They committed adultery with the wives of the most eminent citizens and ravished several boys. Finally they carried their licentiousness to the extent of staking the honor of their women on the throw of three dice (A). They established the rule that the loser would be obliged to bring the woman gambled for to the winner, and that he would have to employ all possible means and artifices to place her in the winner's arms. They allowed no foul play. Persuasion and violence were to succeed each other, the one preceding or following the other as the case required, until the gambling debt was paid. The one who most often and most shamelessly engaged in this new game of chance was Hegesilochus. His drunkenness and other disorders rendered him so incapable of managing his affairs that he lost his dignity, and even his friends considered him infamous. He must not be confused with that Hegesilochus who was the Rhodian ambassador to Rome, after being among the principal dignitaries of the state. This latter lived at the time of Perseus, King of Macedon; and the former, at the time of Philip, the father of Alexander the Great.

⋘

A. *(He was one of those Rhodians . . . who carried licentiousness to the extent of staking the honor of their women on the throw of three dice.)* The Abbé Lancelot of Perugia had a good opportunity here for fortifying the admirers of the present age. For I do not believe that any country in Europe in our own century has had such debauchery as the Rhodians did. I have heard that the servants of a great minister of state, who has not been dead very long, used to play at dice or cards for captains' commissions. But, in addition to the fact that this story is very uncertain, it does not amount to very much. Each of these servants would receive for his Christmas present the promise that a certain number of companies would be given to those whom he recommended. They played with these promises as stakes; and when someone lost a company, it was not he, but the winner who would confer it on somebody. In spite of all this disorder, it was easy to prevent commissions from being given to improper people. Thus, this is in no way comparable to the debauchery of those petty tyrants of Rhodes. They gambled with the virginity and the cuckolding of the elite of the society, and they gave the loser no peace until he had delivered the prey. It was not enough that they risked the honor of the most beautiful women, inseparable from that of their husbands, as it is commonly held to be, but they also risked their own reputations, for the loser had to play the role of a pimp. This was enough to make a man cry out, "O tempora! O mores!"

Hipparchia, the wife of the philosopher Crates, had been so charmed by the discourses of that Cynic that she wanted to marry him at no matter what cost. She was sought after by a great number of lovers who were distinguished by their nobility, their wealth, and their good looks. Her family pressed her to choose a husband from among these rivals, but nothing could tear her away from her desire for Crates. She declared that Crates was more important to her than anything else, and that if they would not marry her to him, she would stab herself. The family, on hearing this declaration, went to Crates and implored him to use his eloquence and all his authority with the young woman to cure her of her passion. To achieve this he employed all his ability, without getting anywhere with the obstinate girl. Finally, when he saw that his arguments and advice had no effect on her, he displayed his poverty before her; he showed her the hump on his back; he placed his stick, his wallet, and his cloak on the ground, and said to her: "This is the man you will have and the furniture you will find in his home. Consider the matter carefully. You cannot become my wife without leading the kind of life that our sect prescribes for us." Hardly had he finished speaking, but she announced that the proposal pleased her infinitely. She put on the habit of the order, I mean the Cynic's dress; and grew so attached to Crates that she roamed everywhere with him, went to banquets with him, and did not even scruple to perform her marital duty with him in the middle of the street (C). It was one of the tenets of this sect that one should not be ashamed to exercise any bodily function that nature requires of us (D).*
One day when Hipparchia was dining with the atheist Theo-

---

* [Remark C appears on p. 96, D on p. 97.]

dorus at Lysimachus' house, she made a subtle objection to him
to which he made no verbal reply (E).* He had recourse only to
his hands; and whatever he was able to say or do afterwards, he
found her so bold and resolute that nothing could daunt her.
She wrote some books, which have not survived. Moreri has
committed some errors in this article. Lorenzo Crasso has also
done so. I forgot to mention that Hipparchia and her brother
Metrocles, who was a disciple of Crates, were born in Maronea.
They flourished in the time of Alexander. From the marriage of
Hipparchia and Crates a son was born, named Pasicles.

«‹‹‹‹-

C. (*She did not even scruple to perform her marital duty with
him in the middle of the street.*) It is not at all astonishing that
the philosopher Hipparchia set herself above custom with regard to
the first two items I have just mentioned since she was capable of
trampling decorum underfoot with regard to the third matter. Contempt for custom cannot be carried any further. This was a great triumph of love. The most natural virtue of the fair sex was sacrificed
to it; I refer to that shame, that decency, which is a thousand times
more deeply rooted in the female heart than even chastity. And what
is yet more surprising, Hipparchia was ready from the beginning to
commit this type of impudence. It was not necessary to lead her to it
little by little, and by degrees. Juvenal observes that nothing seems
difficult to women when it is a question of gratifying their love. If they
have to go on a sea voyage with husbands of whom they are weary, they
cannot resolve themselves to make the trip, the inconveniences of the
sea are too great. If they are to travel with lovers, they have the best
stomachs in the world, and there is nothing more pleasant than the
life of a sailor. Hipparchia proves the truth of this observation. She
was mad about Crates. He wanted all shame put aside. . . . "These
mysteries cannot otherwise be celebrated," he probably said. She wanted
to do so in order to please him. Several authors relate this fact; Sextus
Empiricus and Theodoret assert it, and I have already cited others
about it. But St. Augustine had a unique opinion on this matter. He
believed that the Cynics only postured and made useless efforts. Latin

---

* [Remark E appears on p. 102.]

is more proper than French to set forth his view.* "It would seem to me that Diogenes and the others who are said to have done this only actually exhibited some motions to others' sight, who were ignorant of what was going on under the cloak. This is easier for me to believe than that such a pleasure can be tasted when other persons are looking on. For these philosophers did not blush to appear to do what lust itself blushed to perform."[10] A modern writer has set himself up as Cato against this Church Father and has reprimanded him rather sharply on this subject. "When he adds," he says, "that he cannot believe that Diogenes and his followers, who were reputed to have done everything in public, took any real and true pleasure in it, however, imagining that they only imitated under the Cynic cloak the movements of those who are entwined in an embrace, thus deceiving the spectators, though actually they could not even erect their muscles before witnesses; this is what I am ashamed to relate, and what I beg you to consider in his own words.[11] . . . Is it possible that so great a man has allowed his imagination to penetrate into the inner recesses of these Cynic mysteries and that St. Augustine's hand had no scruples about lifting up Diogenes' cloak to show us the motions going on under it, which shame, though this philosopher claimed to have none, made even him hide under Diogenes' cloak?"[12]

≪←

   D. *(One should not be ashamed to exercise any bodily function that nature requires of us.)* . . . Some people believe that the Cynics were so named because, in imitation of dogs, they lay with

---

* [Occasionally Bayle makes a point of not presenting certain material in French, either because of its obscenity or irreligious content. However, he rarely gave French translations for his Latin quotations anyway. He usually paraphrased the content in French and then gave his source in Latin. He also assumed that a large number of his readers could easily read Latin. In the case above, he is obviously not trying to keep anything secret from non-Latin readers since he first paraphrased St. Augustine's view and then presented La Mothe le Vayer's criticism of it in French. He discusses the problem of whether he should have kept all the obscene material in Latin in the Fourth Clarification (p. 436).]

[10] Augustine, *The City of God* XIV. 20.

[11] He here transcribes the above passage from St. Augustine.

[12] La Mothe le Vayer, *Hexameron rustique.*

their wives in the streets. . . . The Cynics claimed that their behavior was based on reason; for, they said, if it is lawful to know one's wife, it is lawful to know one's wife in public. Now, it is lawful to know one's wife; therefore, it is lawful to know her in public. . . . This is a miserable sophism, that of drawing a general and absolute inference from what is said with regard to some particular case or circumstance. It is as though one should argue, "It is good to drink wine, therefore it is good to drink wine when one has fever." These philosophers were not aware that there are several actions which are only good in certain circumstances, so that the absence of these circumstances could make an action bad that otherwise would have been good. To lend a friend money so that he can pay his creditors is a very commendable action; to lend him money so that he can get drunk, or that he can gamble, is a bad action. There are actions that are by nature bad. They can never be good, no matter what collection of circumstances be present. But there are other actions that are sometimes good and sometimes bad, depending upon the times, places, and other circumstances under which they occur. I admit that this does not suffice to refute the Cynics, for they could present their argument in this way: When an action is good and lawful in itself, there should not be any shame in committing it. Now, the marital duty is an action that is good and lawful in itself; therefore, there should be no shame in performing it. Therefore, it can be lawfully performed in public; for if anything could spoil this public action, it would only be that one lacked shame in a situation in which one should be obliged to have it. The problem then is reduced to this single question: Is it necessary to be ashamed of performing the marital act in public view? A nice question, I will be told, and who doubts that the answer is yes? "I," Diogenes would answer, "and prove to me that I am wrong." He would be answered that shame with regard to those actions is a natural sentiment, and that, thus, it is to act unnaturally to have no shame in such situations. "But," he will reply, "if it were a natural sentiment, then animals, who so faithfully follow natural instincts, would seek shadows and dungeons when they wanted to procreate. Now, nothing is more false than this. It would at least have to be the case that all men would, in such situations, seek the darkest and most hidden recesses, which again is false; for several groups in the Orient perform the act of generation in the sight of all who go by." This is what the famous Pyrrhonist, Empiricus, observes in order to show that the usual practice is not based upon an immutable and eternal law of nature, but simply upon customary regulations and the effect of education. . . . A modern writer has pointed out that certain peoples have made love "in the temples themselves," and that they have said, "that if this action displeased the gods, they would not have allowed it among the rest of the animals."[17] He adds that a "Mohammedan sect still practices this nowadays," and that "the new world appeared to us in this state of innocence." Diogenes could be answered that it suffices that civilized peoples are subject to shame, and one ought not to be disturbed by what barbarous people do. But, he will reply in turn that the people called barbarians have much less deviated from the laws of nature than those peoples who have so multiplied the laws of decency and civility in accordance with the subtleties of their minds; and that, after all, since natural law never loses its authority, everyone is allowed to return to it at any time and place whatsoever, without regard to the arbitrary yoke of customs and the opinions of his countrymen.

A reflection on the weakness of reason. This may be said to show how much human reason is capable of misleading us. It has been given to us to direct us to the right road but is an uncertain, changeable, and flexible instrument, which may be turned in all directions like a weather vane. See how the Cynics used it to justify their abominable impudence. I may add, for the honor and the glory of the true religion, that it alone furnishes us with excellent arms against the sophisms of those people; for even though one could not show an explicit precept in Scripture concerning the darkness in which the private actions of a marriage ought to take place, it suffices to say in the first place, that the spirit of Scripture obliges us to avoid all that could weaken the impressions of decency. In the second place, there are precise texts forbidding us to do anything that offends decorum or that scandalizes our neighbors. I do not know whether any of the casuists, who have made such poor use of their leisure by examining somewhat farfetched cases of conscience, ever thought of looking into the question of what kind of a crime the impudence of a Crates or a Diogenes ought to be classified as. These philosophers did not believe that there was any divine law on this matter, or that men were obliged to conform to local customs on this. They believed that in

---

[17] La Mothe le Vayer, *Dialogues d'Orasius Tubero*. He cites Herodotus, II.

not conforming to them the only blame they might receive would be that of being country bumpkins or of failing to comply with accepted customs. To be impolite, boorish, and a poor observer of customs is not a criminal action or an evil one, morally speaking. What could one then say against the Cynics if they are not condemned by revealed truths? I have never read anything whatever on this subject; and I do not know whether anyone has ever asserted that at the present time a Cynic action would be criminal solely, (1) because of the offense that it would give to neighbors, (2) because of its contempt for local customs, and (3) because of its neglect in preserving the limits of chastity. I am supposing here a man convinced that the action in itself has not been explicitly forbidden in Scripture, and that it is not contrary to natural law. If it were contrary to this, the sentences by which judges order a congress* would be just as criminal, for which the judges would be accountable.

No doubt there are some casuists who would consider masturbation or the sin of onanism, which Diogenes committed in the market-place, greater crimes than the congress of Crates and Hipparchia. It is a strange and entirely scandalous thing to see Chrysippus, that famous and severe Stoic, praise Diogenes' action.[19] This Cynic could not have justified himself by his sophism, "It is lawful to perform the marital duty; therefore, it is lawful to perform it in the street," for his action is bad both in private and in public. Sextus Empiricus agrees that it was looked upon as detestable, even though Zeno, the founder of Stoicism, had approved of it, and many others engaged in it as if it were a good thing. . . . Diogenes made use of another sophism; he claimed that what some fishes do is a lesson of nature to us; but this sophism is no better than the one based on the practice of the Lydians. To conclude, although the Cynics sought in vain for arguments to cover up their dreadful impudence, they did not dare to keep up their practice. It is probable that public indignation served as a more severe brake upon them than the notions of decency.

---

* [Bayle discusses the nature of a congress at great and bawdy length in the article "Quellenec," one of the leading martyrs of the St. Bartholomew's Day Massacre. A congress was the legal means of testing a wife's charge that her husband was impotent. The couple were examined, prepared, and placed together to ascertain whether or not coition could occur.]

19 Plutarch, *Moralia*, "De Stoicorum repugnantiis."

St. Augustine notes that natural modesty gained the ascendency even over these people.[22] . . .

An observation for those who might be shocked by what I have just related. Those who will find it strange that I relate obscenities as horrible as those above have need of being told that they have not considered carefully enough either the rights or the duties of a historian. Any man nowadays who writes the history of either an ancient philosopher or some other person who gained a reputation during preceding centuries has the right to relate all the items that books tell us about him, whether they deserve to be praised or whether they deserve the horror and execration of the reader. And if he collected only what is praiseworthy, he would fulfill very poorly the duties that the nature of his work imposes upon him. When one is writing the life of a modern person, one has more liberty; for if that person has committed some very obscene actions unknown to the public, one can pass them by silently in accordance with the judgment that one must prevent certain problems that might arise from the publication of such things. But, when it is a question of a fact related by hundreds of authors, one is not free to exercise such discretion; and if one chooses to suppress something, one gives in to a very useless scruple; for the readers will easily find by other means what one wished to hide from them. The impudence of Diogenes the Cynic is so well known by everybody that there are even some sayings current about him that are not based on the testimony of any ancient writer. "Du Moustier reminded me of the book by the same Orléans, entitled *The Human Plant to the Queen.* This is a ridiculous title, which made me recall Diogenes' saying, 'I plant a man.' " These words are from the Cardinal du Perron. Numberless persons relate the same story in their private conversations. It is found in several books in which it is asserted that Diogenes, embracing a woman in the middle of the street, was asked, "What are you doing?" and that he answered, "I am planting a man." None of the ancient writers that I know of has told this story. And Du Rondel, whom I consulted about it, told me that he had found this tale only in the works of modern authors. Now since such a poorly grounded story about the effrontery of this ancient philosopher is spread about, what the authors whose words I have cited about him say should not be unknown. What would be

---

[22] Augustine, *The City of God* XIV. 20

accomplished then if I suppressed those facts? I should at least, you will tell me, have chosen phrases and expressions that would have placed a thick veil over these infamies. I reply that this would have been the way to diminish the horror of them; for those delicate and oblique means that are employed nowadays when one speaks of impurities do not disgust the reader as much as a blunter, stronger wording would do, and which would fill the reader with much more indignation inasmuch as the author does not amuse himself in inventing circumlocutions, which, strictly speaking, are only ways of disguising matters. I add that it is more useful and more important than one imagines to set forth clearly the horrors and abominations that pagan philosophers have approved of. This can humiliate and mortify our reason, and convince us of the infinite corruption of the human heart, and teach us a truth that we ought never to lose sight of—that man has had need of a revealed light, which might make up for the defects of the philosophical light; for you see that the Stoics, who devoted themselves to moral philosophy more than other philosophers did and who had quite sublime ideas about it, still approved of Diogenes' shameless obscenities. So, we can apply to them in particular the general claim of St. Paul against the pagans: "Professing themselves to be wise, they became fools" (Romans 1:22).

《《←

E. (*Hipparchia . . . made an objection . . . to which the atheist Theodorus made no verbal reply.*) It was a sophism which was easy to solve and to turn against her. "If I were to perform," she said to him, "the same action that you may lawfully do, I could not be accused of having done something unlawful. Now, you act lawfully when you beat yourself. Therefore, if I were to beat you, I could not be accused of having done something unlawful." Theodorus did not waste any time answering her as a logician. He threw himself upon her and untied her gown. Considering the manner of attire, and speaking in present-day terms, we would say that he "raised her petticoat." This is the explication that Ménage gives of the words of Diogenes Laertius. . . . This is a very gay and cavalier way of replying to a woman's sophisms. Hipparchia was not disconcerted at all; and when

Theodorus cited her the verse from a tragedy which told of a woman who had left her female duties and her spinning wheel, she replied to him, "I recognize myself in this. I am that woman. But do you think that I made the wrong choice by preferring to use my time to philosophize rather than to spin?" Let us see now what Theodorus might have been able to answer had he wished to take the trouble. Answering directly, he could have said that the action of Theodorus beating himself and the action of Hipparchia beating Theodorus are two different actions and not actions of the same species. There were then four terms in Hipparchia's syllogism. In order that two actions be similar, it must be the case that relation in one between the agent and the receiver, exist also in the other. Now this is not the case in Hipparchia's hypothesis. If Theodorus had wanted to turn the argument against Hipparchia and to perplex Crates' wife, he could have said to her, "If I were to perform the same action that your husband may lawfully do, I could not be accused of having done something unlawful. Now your husband acts lawfully when he kisses you, etc. Therefore, if I were to kiss you, etc., I could not be accused of having done something unlawful." One would have seen whether Hipparchia, who was very dissolute, would have dared to answer before witnesses with: "I grant you everything."

Jonas, *ARNGRIMUS,* an Icelander by nationality, gained a reputation in the sixteenth and seventeenth centuries for the works he had published. He was still alive in 1644 and was then more than ninety years old. Just four years earlier he had gotten remarried to a young girl. He was learned and reputable and much respected by all scholars. He had been coadjutor to Gundebrand of Torlac, Bishop of Hola in Iceland. This Gundebrand was an Icelander and a man of great learning and probity. He had been a disciple of Tycho Brahe and understood astrology well. After Gundebrand's death, Arngrimus refused the bishopric of Hola, to which the king of Denmark wanted to promote him. He begged that ruler to excuse him, both so that others would not envy him and so that he could apply himself more peacefully to his studies. The books that he published are mostly either histories and descriptions of Iceland or apologies for his country. Blefkenius had reported some detrimental items about Iceland, both with regard to witchcraft and with regard to dissoluteness (C). Arngrimus refuted him.

He died in 1649. He had been pastor of the church of Melstad and superintendant of the churches in the neighborhood of the diocese of Hola.

≪←

C. (. . . *with regard to dissoluteness.*) "Blefkenius says that the Germans who trade in Iceland set up tents near the ports in which they land and that they there display their wares, which are coats, shoes, mirrors, knives, and a great many trifles, which they trade for what the Icelanders bring them. Some girls, who are very pretty on that island but very poorly dressed, go to see these Germans and offer, in exchange for some bread, some biscuits, or some other small reward, to go to bed with those who have no wives. Even fathers present their daughters to the foreigners; and if the daughters become pregnant, they consider it an honor. These girls are considered more desirable by the Icelanders on that account and are more sought after by suitors, who press hard for their hands. When the Icelanders have bought (that is to say, exchanged for) wine or beer from the foreign merchants, they invite their relations, their friends, and their neighbors to come and drink with them. And they do not stop so long as there is a drop left. While they are drinking, they sing of the heroic deeds of their captains. . . . It is considered rude among them to leave the table to urinate while they are all drinking. The girls, who are not ugly in that country, as I have noted, glide under the tables and present the drinkers with chamber pots. Arngrimus Jonas insists that this raillery is false. He got very angry at Blefkenius for the outrageous things that that author had said about the honor of the girls of Iceland. This good man [Arngrimus Jonas] could not bear to hear his countrymen treated with contempt and pictured as barbarians."[10] If ever it was right for an apologist to become angry, Arngrimus could not be blamed. For it is not at all probable that the Gospel, which has been known in Iceland for so many centuries, would have left the people there in such a state of criminal brutality. Nor is it likely that if the Christian religion had been so ineffectual in changing the behavior of these islanders, that the king of Denmark would allow them to have so little regard for public decency and welfare. The customs that prevail at their festivities are not, I think, faithfully reported. The matter has been exaggerated to amuse readers. Has one ever heard of such an occupation as that of the girls mentioned here, or of such ridiculous laziness? Here are men who

---

[10] Isaac la Peyrère, *Relation d'Islande*. [La Peyrère (1594–1676) was the author of the preadamite theory that there were people before Adam, and was an early anthropologist. He was a friend of Gassendi and La Mothe le Vayer and, after being persecuted for his novel ideas, retired to the Oratory. Bayle, in his article "Peyrère, Isaac la," remark G, quotes a letter from a person who dined with La Peyrère at this religious institution. One of the leaders of the order got La Peyrère to confess that he was always writing books, which, the religious leader whispered to Bayle's informant, would be burned as soon as the author died. The letter concludes, "La Peyrère was the best man in the world, the sweetest, who tranquilly believed very few things."]

not only do not want to take the trouble to get up from the table to urinate, but who do not even want to make the smallest motions with their hands. This is the picture the story gives us; otherwise, why would we be told that the girls present the chamber pots under the table? The pots could be easily given to the guests in other ways if the only point was to spare them the trouble of getting up. If all that Blefkenius has just told us were true, we would have to admit that jealousy is not useless in this world.[11]

An objection drawn from the shamelessness of some peoples. If it were permitted to lie for the sake of the truth, one should deny all that is told about the shamelessness of certain peoples; for the libertines gain great advantage from the claim that there are, it is said, certain nations which do not consider the practice of female prostitution infamous. The Icelanders would be a case in point, if we accepted Blefkenius' account. In fact, they would go even further since they regarded it as an honor for a girl to be with child by a stranger to whom she had prostituted herself, and the fathers would consider themselves very happy that their offer of the virginity of their daughters had been accepted by people from another land. Then, one might ask, where is that natural impression that makes all men distinguish between good and evil? Here are Christian nations that not only have no regard for chastity in their practices but also take no account of it in theory. From which it follows that in this respect their consciences are devoid of any perception of natural law. Is this not an indication that the ideas of virtue depend on education and custom, and not on a natural impression? How can these people be cured since their consciences are entirely dead or inert? For if it is possible that a conscience endowed with the notions of good and evil enjoy only a precarious security, would not such a condition be inevitable where these notions have been extinguished? It is not necessary to answer this objection since Arngrimus Jonas denies the fact on which it is based. To him we must refer all those who claim to show something from his adversary's account. And if they would advance some indisputable facts, then we should not lack a reply.

---

[11] See *Nouvelles lettres contre le calvinisme de Maimbourg*, pp. 542ff [by Bayle].

Jupiter, the greatest of all the gods of paganism, was the son of Saturn and Cybele. There is no crime he did not commit; for, besides dethroning his own father, castrating him, and weighing him down with chains in the lowest depths of hell, he committed incest with his sisters, with his daughters, and with his aunts, and he even tried to violate his own mother. He debauched an infinite number of virgins and wives, and, in order to accomplish this, he took on the form of all kinds of animals. He was guilty of the unnatural sin [sodomy], for he abducted the beautiful Ganymede and gave him the office of cupbearer to the gods so that he might be available whenever Jupiter desired him. Frauds and perjuries, and, in general, all actions punishable by the laws were very familiar events to him. One has even gone as far as to assert that he ate up one of his wives. Hence, there can be nothing more monstrous than paganism, which regarded such a god as the supreme master of all things, and which adapted to that idea the religious worship it paid to him. The Church Fathers have greatly stressed this proof of the falsity of pagan religion; and it can be said that this system was very apt to corrupt human behavior (D). I shall say nothing about the fables concerning either the

«←

D. (*The system of pagan religion was very apt to corrupt human behavior.*)[31] "From these infamous actions of Jupiter, Christian writers have developed potent arguments to convince pagans of the falsity of their gods, as can be seen in several places in Lactantius, Tertullian, Clement of Alexandria, Arnobius, and many others.

---

[31] See Arnauld in his *Ve Dénonciation du peché philosophique.*

birth or the education of Jupiter. Moreri has touched on some
of these matters, and they can be found in a great number of
books that students have their hands on every day. I will only
speak about the eagle that brought him nectar.* This fact is not
so well known. Charpentier does not faithfully report an item
that he cites from Homer.

For, besides the fact that such horrible crimes cannot be compatible
with the divine nature, gentiles could have found a just pretext in
this for abandoning themselves to all sorts of wickedness . . . not
believing that they might err in imitating their gods. This is also
what Euripides' Ion intends, in the tragedy bearing his name:

> We must not censure wicked wretches
> Who imitate the deities, but those,
> For setting such examples."
> (Euripides, *Ion* 449–451)

Meziriac makes this observation on a passage of Ovid, where Phaedra
remarks that it was all right to have qualms about incest in the crude
times of Saturn, but that under his successor it ought to be allowed
that a woman may lie with her son-in-law. This is authorized, she says,
by the fact that Jupiter married his sister.

> Let not mere names—step-mother, son-in-law—
> Affright; these scruples under rustic Saturn
> Were good, but banished in politer times.
> Jove bids enjoy whatever we approve;
> And all permits, since he his sister married.
> (Ovid, *Heroides* IV. 129–134)

Ovid falls into a grievous error here since it is certain that Saturn
was married to his sister, just as Jupiter was with his. One could add
to the passage from Euripides that Meziriac cited a hundred others
of equal strength. Nothing is more common in the ancient poets than
to find people excusing their crimes by maintaining either that they
are only imitating the gods or that the gods led them to commit evil.
But, in order not to hide anything, it must be said to the glory of
the pagans that they did not live in accordance with their principles.
It is true indeed that corruption and depravity were great in the

---

* [In remark E, which is not included in these selections.]

For quite a long time, what the pagans said about the origin of Jupiter seemed so strange to me that the more I thought about it, the more monstrous it appeared to me, so that, in a word, it seemed impossible to me that philosophers could have accepted it. But finally I realized that they might have fallen into this error by I know not what arguments (G) whose weak-

pagan world, but there were many people in it who did not follow the example of their false gods and preferred the ideas of virtue to so great an authority. What is strange is that Christians, whose system of religion is so pure, yield almost nothing to the gentiles in respect to engaging in vices. It is a mistake to believe that the moral practice of a religion corresponds to the doctrines of its confession of faith.

≪≪≪

G. *(They might have fallen into this error by I know not what arguments.)* Let us first see what Hesiod said about the genealogy of the gods. He begins with Chaos. This is the first being he presents. Then he brings in Earth and Love, and adds that Erebus and Night were engendered by Chaos and that Aether and Day sprung from the marriage of Erebus and Night, and that Earth, without contracting any marriage, begot Heaven and Sea, and then, having married Heaven, she brought forth Ocean, Rhea, Themis, Tethys, Saturn, and others. This extraordinarily prolific marriage gave hardly any pleasure to Earth, since her husband Heaven imprisoned all their children as soon as they were born. She provoked them to vengeance and was so successful that with a single stroke of a scythe Saturn lopped off his father's unmentionable parts and tossed them into the sea. These produced a foam from which the goddess Venus was born. The children of Saturn and Rhea were Vesta, Ceres, Juno, Pluto, Neptune, and Jupiter. This is what I have gathered from Hesiod's poem. There were some other genealogists who said that Aether and Day, the children of Erebus and Night, were the father and mother of Heaven and that their brothers and sisters were Love, Fraud, Fear, Work, Jealousy, Fate, Old Age, Death, Gloom, Misery,

ness was not easy for them to discover. They did not believe that the creation of anything was possible, and they did not admit that there were any substances completely distinct from extension. Now when these two hypotheses have once been established, it is almost as easy to imagine that refined matter could become a god, as to believe that the soul of man is material, as most philosophers believed. See remark G. In Arcadia there was a temple dedicated to the "good god." Pausanias

Dreams, and so on. We have seen above[44] how Carneades made use of this genealogy for refuting the theology of the Stoics. Let us be satisfied here with saying that according to this genealogical tree, there necessarily had to be some god whose father was not a god; for if on the one hand it had been admitted to Carneades that Heaven, Aether, Day, Erebus, and Night were deities, it would have been denied to him on the other hand, that Chaos, who was anterior to all of these divine beings, was a god. And consequently, one was forced to say that the gods had been formed from a matter that was not god, and without an efficient cause that possessed the nature of a god. This is certainly an idea that contradicts the most solid and evident notions of natural reason. But, nevertheless, there have been great philosophers who have supposed the generation of the gods and have attributed a cause of them that was not a god. "Anaximenes ascribed the causes of all things to the boundless air, nor did he deny that there were gods, nor was he silent with regard to them; yet he did not believe that the air was created by them, but that *they sprung from that element.*"[45] The theory of Anaximenes can be better understood by these words of St. Augustine than by the following ones of Cicero, "Anaximenes thought that the air was god, that it was procreated, was immense and infinite and always in motion."[46] It is not probable that Cicero has properly related the view of this philosopher; for since he ascribed to air the characteristics of the principle of all things, namely immensity and infinity, it must be believed that he supposed it to be both eternal and unproduced and that, if he called it god in terms of this conception, he did not believe in the

---

[44] Footnote 87, article "Carneades" [not included in these selections].
[45] Augustine, *The City of God* VIII. 2.
[46] Cicero, *De natura deorum* I. 10.

conjectures that this temple was consecrated to Jupiter. His reason for this is that this adjective ought to apply most properly to the greatest of the gods. It is certain that Jupiter's goodness was indicated by several of the surnames under which he was worshipped. But he was also worshipped under several names that showed what a terrible deity he was. His role as thunderer was designated solely in terms of his descent to earth. There are some places where it is claimed that he demanded

generation of god in this respect. Therefore, when he said that infinite air had been the cause of all beings and that even the gods had been produced by it, he did not ascribe the name and nature of god to it in the same sense that he attributed it to the gods who owed their origin and existence to air. This is, perhaps, his view. He was willing, in order to avoid disputes about words, to apply the term "god" to the immense and infinite air that he considered to be the principle of all things; but that he did not claim that Saturn, Rhea, Jupiter, Juno, Neptune, Minerva, and the other gods whom the pagans worshipped were this air or had produced it. On the contrary, he claimed that this air was their principle, or source, no less than that of all the other beings who make up the universe. He ascribed perpetual motion to this principle, and from this we can conclude that he considered it as an immanent cause that produced in itself an infinity of effects without end and continuously; and that he counted among these effects not only the stars, meteors, plants, stones, and metals, but also gods and men. Such a view is at bottom Spinozism; for according to what has been said, the god, or eternal and necessary being of Anaximenes, was the sole substance of which heaven and earth, animals, and the like, were only modifications. Thales, perhaps, had had a similar view since he had taught that water was the principle of all things. He perhaps had called it god on that account. This was the god he claimed to be speaking about when he said that god, not having been produced from anything, was the oldest of all beings. He added that since the world was the work of god, it was the most beautiful of all beings. Spinoza would have admitted as much. He does not deny that god is the cause of all things, that is, the immanent cause that modifies itself in an infinite number of ways, from which all that is called the world and

that men be sacrificed to him. I will mention elsewhere[d] that the book entitled *Cymbalum mundi* contains many jokes about Jupiter's actions; but I do not know whether it is possible to go further than Arnobius did on such a subject. His imagination rushes on like a torrent, and since he had just before been a rhetorician by profession, there were no colors or figures with which he did not animate his language. I have cited some of his thoughts at various points in this dictionary, and the reader

the universe in general results. If Thales also said that the world is alive and full of spirits, this perhaps signified that water, the principle of all things, the uncreated god, had so modified itself that it had formed a soul diffused through all bodies and particular spirits like the gods who were worshipped by the pagans. This would help us to understand what we have seen elsewhere[51] and what is doubtless surprising, namely, that Thales and other natural philosophers who came before Anaxagoras explained the generation of the world without supposing it to have been directed by a divine intelligence. Thales and Anaximenes could not admit such an intelligence, if the one supposed that water, the other that air, was the eternal and uncreated principle of all things; for, although to avoid a battle about words they called this universal and uncreated principle "god," they could not consider it an intelligent cause antecedent to the particular beings that it formed since it produced them in itself and from itself as an immanent cause, and not as an external cause distinct from its matter. But because Anaxagoras was the first who acknowledged a spirit distinct from the matter of the world, a pure spirit unmixed with bodies, he must have reasoned differently than preceding natural philosophers had done. He could have said, reasoning logically, that the world had been formed according to the direction of a spirit that disentangled and arranged the parts of matter. His hypothesis allowed for an intelligence antecedent to the formation of the world. The other hypotheses only allowed the world to be preceded by Chaos, or by water, or by air, or the like, and thus they had to attribute a beginning to intelligent beings and not only to the crudest of beings. All things issued from the first principle by way of generation or production. Jupiter, the greatest of the gods, his father,

---

d In article "Periers" [not included in these selections].

51 In remark D of article "Anaxagoras" [not included in these selections].

may have seen elsewhere the joke he made about the fact that
the great Jupiter used up nine nights to conceive a child, when
he had had need of only one night to make fifty virgins pregnant.
It is probable that his memory failed him here, and that he confused some things. He had read that Jupiter devoted nine nights
to the production of the muses, and he applied this to a completely different subject, I mean the adventures of Alcmena.
Lively authors are rather subject to such mistakes. Jupiter

Saturn, his grandfather, Heaven, his great-grandfather, Aether, and
anyone you want to mention further back, were particular beings,
who owed their origin, their birth, their existence, to eternal and
uncreated matter, the principle of all things, Chaos according to
Hesiod, water according to Thales, air according to Anaximenes. But,
it will be said, did not Thales assert that the gods know the very
thoughts of men? What does this prove, I will reply? All that can be
concluded is that he attributed a very extensive knowledge to some
of the beings whom water had engendered, and who were called
Jupiter, Juno, Venus, Neptune, and so on. Observe that Homer, who
so eloquently describes the power of the gods, supposes that they were
all born of the Ocean. . . . The great and prodigious absurdity of these
hypotheses is to say that the gods, endowed with great knowledge,
were formed from a principle that knows nothing; for neither chaos,
nor air, nor sea are thinking beings. Then, how could they have
been able to constitute the complete cause of those divine beings, who,
in the system of the poets and the most ancient natural philosophers,
knew so many things? But, no matter how false and ridiculous these
hypotheses may be, I am no longer surprised, as I used to be, that
they have been able to be accepted by philosophers. Most of them
supposed that the soul of man was corporeal. They therefore believed
that it was made of the most subtle parts of blood or of seed. Once one
has taken this step, things move along very quickly in short order. Set
aside experience. Consult only the ideas of theory, and it will not
appear easier for the matter received in the womb to transform itself
into a child, who, by eating and drinking, becomes a man of great
genius, than for a child to be born of a tree. On this basis, a pagan
finds it possible that in the beginning men were born either from
the slime of the earth or from some liquid that fell from the sky. As
soon as this seems possible, one easily moves on to believing what the

made love both in heaven and on earth. He gathered in partners on all sides. Goddesses and women were equally to his liking. Arnobius did not forget this item and made most of the point that the bodies of mortals, completely transparent though they were for Jupiter, nevertheless possessed enough charms to inspire him with a lewd passion. It is proper to observe that the ridiculous stories that the poets had told about this god served

poets say about the birth of Venus. It is no longer found strange that, by the fermentation that disentangled the chaos or formed various degrees of rarefaction and condensation in infinite extension, the stars might have begun to exist in the firmament, and the gods in heaven, just as plants and animals might have begun on the surface of the earth. The usual view of the pagans about divine nature only allowed for a difference of degree between men and gods. Now, as a result of this, nothing prevented them from imagining that the most refined and subtle parts of matter had formed the gods since such parts as were big and solid, and which, as the dregs and sediment of everything, had formed the earth, had not failed to transform themselves into men. Observe that it was imagined that to animate the big and solid parts it sufficed that some spiritual particles fell from heaven, and it is in this fashion that Lucretius acknowledges that living bodies have a celestial origin.[58] . . .

Let us conclude from all this that nothing is more dangerous or more contagious than starting from some false principle. It is a bad leaven that, even when small, can spoil all the dough. An absurdity once set forth leads to many others. Err only about the nature of the human soul; imagine falsely that it is not a substance distinct from extension; this error is capable of making you believe that there are gods who first sprung from fermentation and who afterwards multiplied through marriage. I cannot end this remark without observing something that completely amazes me. Nothing seems to me to be based on clearer and more distinct ideas than the immateriality of that which thinks; and nevertheless, there are some philosophers in Christendom who maintain that matter is capable of thinking,[59] and these are philosophers of great ability and acumen. Can one rely on

---

[58] Lucretius, II. 991.
[59] See above, article "Dicaearchus," remark L [p. 68].

as a foundation for pagan religion and that there have been
serious persons who have tried to explain them, either allegorically or in terms of scientific theories; but this was as ridiculous
an endeavor as that of the poets (N), and one which quite often
terminated in serious impieties. See remark N, where I shall
discuss those who say that Juno was the air, and Jupiter was
the aether.

the clarity of ideas after that? Besides, do these philosophers not see
that on such a basis the ancient philosophers could have gone so far
astray as to claim that all intelligent substances had a beginning and
that only matter was eternal? This was the view of the philosopher
Anaximenes, as we have seen above. It was the theory of his master
Anaximander. This difficulty is not overcome by contending that
matter only becomes something that thinks through a special gift of
God. This would not prevent it from being true that its nature was
susceptible of thought; and that to make it actually something that
thinks, it would suffice to agitate it, or to arrange it in a certain way;
from which it would follow that an eternal matter without any intelligence but not without movement would have been capable of producing gods and men, as the poets and some pagan philosophers
have foolishly maintained.

≪

N. (*Serious persons . . . have tried to explain the stories of the
poets, either allegorically or in terms of scientific theories; but
this was as ridiculous an endeavor as that of the poets.*) We have seen
above[79] how Cicero made fun of the philosopher Chrysippus, who had
gone to so much trouble to reconcile the fables of the ancient poets
with the theology of the Stoics. Here is a passage which will give us
a specimen of that attempt. "This subject was treated by Zeno, afterwards by Cleanthes, and amply explained by Chrysippus; for all
Greece was formerly of the opinion that Caelus [Heaven] was emasculated by his son Saturn, who in turn was bound in chains by his son
Jupiter. The profane fables include an elegant physical meaning; it

---

[79] In footnote 49 of the article "Chrysippus the Philosopher" [not included in these selections].

was intimated thereby that the highest, celestial, and ethereal nature, namely fire which produces all things by itself, is void of that
corporeal part that requires the conjunction of another in order
to procreate. Saturn they affirmed to be that being that contains the
course and change or revolution of spaces and times. The name Saturn
is given him because he is filled with years; he is also said to devour
the children he begets because age or time consumes its various
periods and is filled with such years as are past without being satiated.
He is bound in chains by Jupiter to prevent his going to immoderate
lengths and to check him by the bands of the stars."[80] It is not necessary to go further to show the ridiculousness of these explanations.
They cannot be read without feeling pity for those philosophers who
used their time so badly. And, if we deplore, on the one hand, the
bad consequences of the fictions of poets and the unrestrained licence
with which they have toyed with a subject that deserved so much
respect, we are diverted, on the other hand, by the artistry of their
inventions, while we consider them as clever witticisms. But, when we
see philosophers who in all seriousness are searching for mysteries in
these follies, we can no longer bear their aberrations, and we toss the
following saying at them:

> 'Tis shameful to employ our time in trifles,
> Which, the more difficult, are the more ridiculous.
>   (Martial, *Epigrams* II. 86)

The greatest evil is that while desiring to protect themselves from
one impiety they fell into another; for, in rejecting the gods of the
poets, animated and living ones, they substituted others who had
neither life nor knowledge. Let us see how Cicero rebukes them.
"The same Zeno says elsewhere that the aether is god, if we can form
in our imagination a god wholly insensible, who never attends upon
our prayers, our wishes, or our vows. However, in other books, he
imagines that a certain divine nature is diffused over the whole nature of things. The philosopher in question ascribes the same thing
to the stars, to years, months, and the changes of years. But when he
would interpret the *Theogony* of Hesiod, he takes away all the common and accepted notions relating to the gods; he does not permit
Jupiter, or Juno, or Vesta, or any one so called, to be ranked in the
number of the gods but teaches that these names are ascribed, in a

---

[80] Cicero, *De natura deorum* II. 24–25

certain signification, to inanimate and mute things."[82] By these false interpretations they got people used to supposing that the blue sky overhead was Jupiter. . . . As for Juno, they reduced her to being the air, as Cicero teaches us. "But the air, as the Stoics assert, lying between the sea and the sky or heaven, is consecrated by the name of Juno, who is Jupiter's wife and sister, because it resembles the aether and is intimately united to it. But they made it feminine (if I may employ that expression) and attributed it to Juno, because nothing can be softer than the elements of the air."[84] From whatever side one looks at this hypothesis, one cannot avoid either absurdities or impieties. Here is the proof of this. Let us ask these philosophers a few questions: You therefore believe that the Jupiter of the poets and the one who is worshipped in the capitol and everywhere else is that vast space where we see so many stars, and that this Juno, the sister and wife of Jupiter, so jealous, so haughty, so powerful, to whom the Argives and other peoples paid so many honors, is the air that surrounds the earth and that enters into the lungs of animals, and in which clouds, rain, and the like, are formed. But is it not obvious that this celestial space and this air are part of the matter of the world, and that matter, considered as such, does not think? Do we not know clearly that air has no more life or knowledge than does snow or hail? Thus, if Juno is nothing but the air, it is ridiculous to direct prayers to her and to offer her sacrifices. For she hears nothing and knows nothing. Therefore, your theory overthrows religion directly. It is a materialistic atheism. You divest Juno of all her divinity, and you leave her only the vain and empty name of goddess. And you are more absurd than Epicurus since you worship what is only an illusory and imaginary name. Juno is here only one example; but Jupiter and Neptune and all the other deities fall in the same way by the force of the same argument. If you say that you do not consider air as a simple body when you maintain that Juno is the air, then explain to me, I beg of you, what other idea you have of it. Do you claim that air is united to the Goddess Juno, that she is the soul of it, and that air is the body of that goddess? But is this not supposing a kind of animal of which we have no idea? Is not the notion of an animal that of an assemblage of parts that form one entire continuum? Does it not exclude what is called "discrete quantity"? And is it not certain that

---

82 *Ibid.*, I. 14
84 *Ibid.*, II. 26.

the parts of air are continually separating one from another, and that the smallest stone that is thrown breaks the continuum and ought to constitute a grievous wound if the air were an animal? What sort of problems do you expose the divinity of Juno to by making her the soul of the air? Is she not constantly receiving an infinity of wounds? If you reply to me that deity is united to the air, not in the capacity of soul, but only to make it act, then you fall into another absurdity that is no less ridiculous than if you were to say that a pilot is a ship, and a rider is a horse. Will you reply to me that there is a great deal of difference between these cases since a pilot is not united to a ship the way that Juno is united to the air? Then explain to me what kind of union this is, and pay careful attention to the difficulties Aristotle raises for you when he says that it is contrary to reason to assert that air and fire are animals; but in case they have souls, it is absurd to say that they are not animals. Consider seriously his words. "For which reason, if a soul be in air, or fire, why does it not form an animal as it does in mixtures of elements, particularly since it seems to be more excellent in them? Anyone may also ask the reason why that soul that is in the air is of a more noble and durable nature than that with which animals are informed.* Something absurd and irrational results in either of these cases; for to advance that fire or air is an animal is in no way rational; and, again, to assert that they are not animals, if they are endowed with a soul, is certainly extremely absurd."[85] You are here between two precipices. If Juno is the soul of the air, without its being the case that she and air make up an animal, this is an untenable absurdity. And, if they constitute an animal, this is an absurdity as well as a horrible impiety. Carneades, with the great power that he possessed, completely destroyed the contention that such a type of animal exists.[86]

I will conclude with an observation furnished me by Pausanias. He relates that one day he disputed with a Sidonian in a temple of Aesculapius. This man claimed that the Phoenicians were much more skillful than the Greeks in matters concerning the deity, and in others also. They say, he added, that Aesculapius is the son of Apollo, and they do not contend that a woman was his mother, for he is the air,

---

* ["Informed" is the Scholastic term for the act or action of giving a form to something.]

[85] Aristotle, *De anima* I. 5. 411a.

[86] See his argument in Cicero, *De natura deorum* III. 17.

the source of health as much for mankind as for animals. Apollo, who is the sun, is rightly considered to be the father of Aesculapius since, by the vicissitudes of the seasons that his motion bring about, he makes the air wholesome. Pausanius agreed to all these claims, but he insisted that they did not belong to the Phoenicians more than to the Greeks and that it is obvious even to children that man's health is an effect of the sun's motion. Judge from this the orthodoxy of the gentiles. Those who claimed to be best acquainted with the doctrines of theology showed, when they expressed themselves clearly, that they did not acknowledge any other gods than air, the stars, and the like. This was at bottom a true atheism. It amounted to converting the necessity of nature into god. I have noticed a passage in Euripides in which Jupiter is invoked without actually knowing what he is. It is admitted that he governs all things justly by occult methods, but he is found extremely difficult to know, and one cannot tell if he is the necessity of nature or human intelligence. What a faith! A Spinozist would just about agree to this.

> *O vehicle of earth, residing on it,*
> *Whoe'er thou be, inscrutable to us,*
> *Necessity of nature, or men's minds,*
> *O Jupiter, I invoke thee; thou who guid'st*
> *Men's actions right, thro' fate's still hidden paths.*
> (Hecuba, in Euripides, *Trojan Women* 884–888)

Lacydes, a Greek philosopher from Cyrene, was a disciple of Arcesilaus, and his successor in the Academy. Some claim that he did not follow his master's doctrine, but I think that they are mistaken. He was poor in his youth but managed to achieve a great reputation by his diligent, hard work. Besides this, he spoke most gracefully. He taught in a garden that Attalus, king of Pergamus, had had constructed. He told this ruler, who had requested him to come to the court, that the pictures of kings should be viewed from afar. He taught philosophy for twenty-six years and gave up his post to two of his students. He imitated his master in one praiseworthy matter: he liked to do good without caring that it was known. The affection that a goose had for him was very remarkable. He died of paralysis from having drunk too much (E). What Numenius tells about him has all the air of a humorous

≪←

E. *(He died of paralysis from having drunk too much.)* Athenaeus relates that Lacydes and another philosopher named Timon were invited for two days together to a feast and that, in compliance with the mood of the gathering, they drank copiously. Lacydes left the party the first day and retired when he felt that he had had enough. Timon, seeing him leave, claimed the victory; but the next day he succumbed first: he could not empty the goblet that was brought to him. Lacydes was even with him. This is most unseemly. Philosophers should never dispute for such a victory. They should be blamed not only for winning but also for trying to; and although the ignominy of the victor is greater than that of the vanquished, the latter too deserves severe criticism. How many Christian philosophers, how many theologians even, have imitated Timon and Lacydes!

fiction (F). Moreri has committed some very egregious errors. The difference that Father Rapin found between Arcesilaus and Lacydes is just an illusion. Philosophy, he says, became restless in the former's view and vexatious in the latter's. It is certain that it was never more vexatious than in the hands of Arcesilaus.

≪≪

F. *(What Numenius tells has all the air of a humorous fiction.)* Here is a summary of his story. Lacydes was very stingy in the management of his household. He never trusted his servants with anything. The place where provisions were kept was not accessible to them. He himself put in and took out whatever was needed, and he never left the place open. So that he would not have to be troubled with the key, he put it into a hole, which he sealed, and then let his seal fall into the pantry through the lock. His servants, having discovered this, deceived him whenever they wished. It was easy for them to obtain the key, to put it back where he had placed it, and to seal up the hole. They drank, they ate, they plundered whatever they liked, while making fun of him at the same time. Lacydes, on his side, quite readily perceived the diminution of his wine and provisions; and not knowing who was taking them, he remembered having heard that Arcesilaus taught that neither our senses nor our reason understand anything. He attributed the emptiness of his bottles and baskets to that incomprehensibility. Such are the auspices under which he began philosophizing according to the manner of the school of Arcesilaus, that is, against the certainty of human knowledge. He even used his household experience to prove that he was right in suspending his judgment about all things. "I am not offering you hearsay," he insisted gravely to one of his friends. "I myself am acquainted with what I am going to tell you. I can speak of it without any doubt whatsoever." He then proceeded to relate to the friend the adventure of his pantry. "What could Zeno," he added, "have said against an argument of this strength, which has demonstrated to me so clearly the *acatalepsia* [the incomprehensibility of things]? Am I not right in mistrusting all things, since, though I myself shut, sealed, unsealed, and opened my pantry with my own hands, I do not find in my pantry the provisions I left in it? I find nothing but my seal, and this fact does not allow me to believe that I am being robbed." It was at this point that his friend could no longer contain himself. He burst into such fits of laughter that the philosopher realized his mistake and resolved to take better care of his seal. His servants were not troubled by this; and, whether they had learned from the Stoics or elsewhere how to dispute with him, they unsealed his key without bothering to put his seal on it again. They would use another seal, and sometimes even none at all. Lacydes would get angry when he discovered their knavery. But they insisted that they had not unsealed anything and that he had forgotten to use his seal. He would then hold forth in a long discourse to show them that he remembered perfectly having applied his seal, and he would even swear to this. "You want to play jokes," they would answer, "and make fun of our simplicity. A philosopher like you has no opinions and no memories. Why, the other day you maintained in our presence that memory is just opinion." He refuted them with arguments different from those of the Academic skeptics. But they had recourse to a Stoic philosopher who taught them how to answer their master and to get around all his proofs by means of the doctrine of the incomprehensibility of all things, which they did with many pleasantries. The worst of it was that they continued to plunder the provisions, and Lacydes saw his belongings disappear day by day. He found himself very puzzled. His principles, instead of being helpful to him, were the very opposite; and he was obliged to behave like ordinary men. The whole neighborhood was filled with his cries and complaints. He swore by all the gods and goddesses that he was being robbed. Finally he decided not to go out at all but to keep watch on the door of his pantry. What did he gain by disputing with his servants? He used the method of the Stoics against them, and they replied by the method of the Academic skeptics. They beat him with his own weapons. Here is how the affair ended. Wanting to free himself once and for all from the intolerable perplexities he was in, Lacydes spoke from his heart and simply told his servants, "My children, we dispute in one way in the schools, and we live in another way at home." . . .

This is a pretty story; and if it were put into the hands of La Fontaine, he could make it most diverting. But who does not see that it was fabricated by a pious fraud of the Stoics? This method is used at all times and in all countries. Men have always tried, and still try, to ridicule the doctrine and the person of their adversaries. To achieve

this they invent thousands of stories, the smallest pretext being employed to strain maliciously the consequences of the adversaries' views.
This passion has been followed so blindly against the Pyrrhonian skeptics that not only good faith but probability as well have been set aside.
For these skeptics have never denied that in the ordinary course of life
men have to conduct themselves by the testimony of the senses. The
skeptics have only denied that it was certain that the absolute nature
of objects is entirely such as it appears. . . .

Leucippus, a Greek philosopher. There is no agreement about the place of his birth but almost all authors agree that he invented the theory of atoms, and that the testimony of Posidonius should not be taken seriously. It cannot be denied that in some respects the Cartesian theory is like that of Leucippus (B) and that Epicurus ought to be blamed for the fact that he did not admit that he had profited from the inventions of this philosopher (C). Those who have ridiculed the invention of atoms so much did not make the necessary distinctions (D).

I have often been astonished that Leucippus and those who followed in his footsteps did not assert that every atom was animated. Such a supposition would have enabled them to solve some of the objections that were made against their theory (E), nor would this supposition have been more unreasonable than the eternity and self-movement that they attribute to their indivisible particles. Let us observe that there was a sect of Oriental philosophers who admitted the hypothesis of atoms and the vacuum (F), but they had improved it, for they attributed the creation of atoms to God. Let us also say that the vacuum, which Gassendi revived and which Descartes refuted, gains ground all the time and has become the favorite idol (G)* of the most famous mathematicians.

《《←

B. *(It cannot be denied that in some respects the Cartesian theory is like that of Leucippus.)* The malady I have just mentioned has appeared in our age in reference to Descartes. People try to rob him of all the glory of invention by dividing it among several

* [Remarks C, D, E, F, and G appear on pp. 125, 126, 129, 134, and 135, respectively.]

other philosophers, both ancient and modern. I shall not enter into
this examination. I will content myself with saying that about certain
things one is right to say that he has only renewed some old ideas.
For instance, is not his hypothesis of vortices the same as that of Leucippus? The learned Huet proves this very clearly. "Leucippus, Democritus, and Epicurus have supposed that the first matter or elements
of things were divided into several vortices. From this we may judge
how much the Cartesians are well grounded in boasting of the invention of these vortices. What I have asserted of those ancient philosophers is plain from Diogenes Laertius and from Hesychius; for they
observe that an infinite number of corpuscles gathered together made
up a vortex; and the particles that were in the middle resisting those
next to them made the whole turn round and whirl about. From this
whirling both the separation and the conjunction of the parts arose,
and from the conjunction came a globular heap."[5] Further, one finds
in Leucippus' theory the germs of that great principle of mechanics
that Descartes employed so efficaceously, namely, *that bodies that are
whirled about recede from the center as much as they can*. The ancient philosopher teaches that the most subtle atoms tend toward
empty space, as if darting forth. Descartes would also have supposed
such a motion in his subtle matter had he followed his own principle.
But by a consequence that cannot be sufficiently admired he drives
all that subtle matter to the center of the vortices and the most solid
globules to the circumference. I have mentioned elsewhere[8] those who
assert that with regard to vortices and to the causes of gravity Descartes only copied from Kepler. They ought to have added that Kepler
copied from Leucippus.

≪←

    C. (*Epicurus ought to be blamed for the fact that he did not
    admit that he had profited from the inventions of Leucippus.*)
This is a malady of great minds. It is hard for them to acknowledge
that they are indebted to their neighbors for their knowledge. They
would have the world think that they had gotten it all from their
own brains and that they had no other teacher but their own genius.
This is what Epicurus has been charged with, for it is claimed that he

---

[5] Pierre-Daniel Huet, *Censura Philosophica Cartesianae*, chap. 8.
[8] In remark D of the article "Kepler" [not included in these selections].

only improved certain aspects of the theory of Democritus, of which Leucippus was the original author. Cicero will be our witness for all this. "For you people used to repeat these things as so many lessons which Epicurus carelessly uttered to you, who, as we see in his writings, boasted that he never had a master; which, had he not even so asserted, I could as easily imagine, just as I would the maker of an indifferent building who should boast that he had no architect to direct him. . . . Epicurus might have heard Xenocrates. What a man! Good gods! Some assert that he did really hear him, but he denies it; I believe him rather than any man in the world. He tells us that he heard at Samos one Pamphilus, a disciple of Plato. . . . But Epicurus heartily despises this Platonic philosopher; so much does he fear lest he should seem to have learned anything. If we bring up to him Nausiphanes, the follower of Democritus, he has nothing to answer, for he admits that he heard Nausiphanes, and yet he heaps all manners of reproach upon him. But if the theory of Democritus was not taught to him, then what did he study? What is there in the natural philosophy of Epicurus that is not borrowed from Democritus? For though he altered some things, such as the one I mentioned before concerning the inclination of atoms, yet his theory is for the most part the same, involving atoms, vacuum, images, infinity of space, and innumerable worlds, their formation and dissolution, and almost everything in the economy of nature."[9] Father Lescalopier observes that Heraclitus also boasted that he was indebted to no man for what he knew and showed thereby that he was not ashamed to suffer from the sacred malady, that is, arrogance. That is a strange name to give to pride. This could be pardoned in those who had known the haughtiness of the clergy under the popes of Rome. If any sort of vanity deserved this name, it would be on some occasions that of persons who glory in not owing their knowledge either to reading or to the lessons of professors. You claim then, they might be told, to have been inspired.

≪←

   D. (*Those who have ridiculed the invention of atoms so much did not make the necessary distinctions.*) Lactantius employs all his strength to refute the hypothesis of Leucippus, as much on the

---

   [9] Cicero, *De natura deorum* I. 26. Others have made the same charge against Epicurus. See Gassendi, *De vita et moribus Epicuri libri octo*, Bk. I, chap. 4, and Bk. V, chaps. 1 and 2.

origin and direction of atoms as on their qualities. He succeeded very well on the first point, but he is pitiable on the second. The terms "madman," "dreamer," "visionary" are appropriate to anybody who claims that the fortuitous meetings of an infinity of corpuscles has produced the world and is the continual cause of generations. But if one applies the same names to those who assert that the diverse combinations of atoms form all the bodies we see, one shows clearly that one has no taste and no idea of true physics. Let us admit that there are good and bad objections in the words of Lactantius, which you are going to read. This is due to the fact that he mixes up things that he ought to have distinguished. "There is no need for Providence, says he, for there are seeds which swim through void space, which uniting together by chance produce everything. But why then do we not feel or see them? Because, says he, they have neither color, nor heat, nor smell, and also they lack taste and moisture; they are also so small that they cannot be cut asunder or divided. Thus, since he set out upon false principles he has been led to absurdities by an unavoidable consequence. For where are, or from whence come these corpuscles? Why did no man dream of them except Leucippus himself? By whom Democritus was taught and left that foolish theory as an inheritance to Epicurus. For if these atoms be really corpuscles, and even solid ones, they must certainly be visible."[11]

Lactantius expands on these objections in another book. "In the first place, I ask, where are, and whence come these minute seeds by the fortuitous concourse of which they assert that this whole world was made to hang together? Who ever saw those seeds? Who felt them? Who heard them? Was Leucippus the only man who had eyes and understanding? Leucippus, I say, who alone was blind and silly since he asserted such nonsense as no man lightheaded by a fever could fancy, nor a person dream in his sleep. The ancient philosophers maintained that all things were made up of four elements. He denied it lest he should seem to follow in the steps of others. But he claimed that the very elements were composed of other *principles,* which can neither be seen nor touched nor felt by any part of our body. They are so small, he says, that there is no edge of a knife sharp enough to cut or separate them; for which reason he called them *atoms.* But he observed that, if all the atoms were of one and the same nature, they could not produce so many different things with such a variety as we see there

---

[11] Lactantius, *Divinae institutiones* III. 17.

exists in the world. He supposed therefore that there were some smooth, some rough, some round, some angular, and some crooked or hooked. How much better would it have been to be silent than to make use of one's voice for such a wretched and silly purpose! I am afraid that whoever tries to refute him will not appear less ridiculous. However, let us answer him as if he had talked sense. If the atoms be smooth and round, they cannot stick together so as to make up a body, as though one would attempt to make one mass out of a number of grains of millet; the very smoothness of the grains would prevent their sticking together. If the atoms be rough, angular, and crooked so as to be able to stick together, then they are divisible and may be cut asunder. For the angles and hooks must of necessity jut out so that one may cut them off. And what can be thus cut and separated must be visible and capable of being taken hold of."[12]

Nowadays one would make fun of a man who would offer such objections. For since the chimerical qualities that the Schoolmen invented have been banished, the only course left to take was that of admitting insensible particles in matter, whose shape, angles, hooks, motion, and place constitute the particular essence of the bodies that strike our senses. Cicero introduced a person who showed Lactantius the false method of not making distinctions; for he brings the same qualifications to bear on the subject of the shape of atoms and on their fortuitous meetings.[13] The modern thinkers have known better how to make distinctions. They reject the eternity of atoms and their fortuitous motion; but by otherwise sticking to the hypothesis of Leucippus, they have built a very beautiful theory. That is what Gassendi has done, who differs from Descartes on the first principles of bodies in that he believes in retaining the vacuum. Lactantius' objections against the indivisibility of atoms are the weakest that can be made against the atomists. The Aristotelians and the Cartesians offer much stronger objections. But after all, they can only assert a possible divisibility of all kind of extension; but as for the actual division, all sects are obliged to fix a limit to it at some point. It is too obvious that there must be an infinity of corpuscles that are never divided, which suffices to invalidate the objections of Lactantius by turning them back against him. . . .

---

12 Lactantius, *De ira Dei* X.
13 Cicero, *De natura deorum* I. 24.

≪≪

E. *(Such a supposition would have enabled them to solve some
of the objections that were made against their theory.) From the
supposition that each atom is not animated, it follows that a collection
of atoms feels nothing.* They might have answered an objection
they were never able to resolve. It is the one that Plutarch proposed
to the Epicurean Colotes, and that Galen has set forth forcefully, as
has been seen above.[16] It consists in this: that, since each atom is destitute of a soul and a sensitive faculty, it is obvious that no collection
of atoms can become an animated and sensible being. But if each atom
had a soul and feeling, we could understand how collections of atoms
might constitute a composite being capable of certain particular modifications, both with regard to sensations and knowledge and with regard to motion. The difference noticed between the passions of rational and irrational animals could be explained in general by the
different combinations of atoms. It is therefore very surprising that
if Leucippus did not recognize the interests of his theory in this respect, those who came after him were not any more aware and did not
add this supposition to it. For the shock of disputes and the ability to
correct what is lacking in the inventions of others might have led
them to carry their view further than our Leucippus had done. There
are reasons to believe that Democritus had in some fashion remedied
this great defect in the theory. The passages I have cited in another
place[17] seem to tell us that he attributed a soul to all atoms, and this
can be confirmed by the testimony of Plutarch. "Democritus supposes that all things are endowed with a kind of soul, including even
dead bodies, in so far as they obviously still have some warmth and
some feeling, even though most of it has passed away."[18]. . . But since
we no longer possess the writings of Democritus, it is not easy to give a
just and exact statement of his thoughts on this matter. Be that as it
may, we know that this opinion has not been followed by the sect of
atomists. Neither Epicurus nor his successors have said that atoms
were endowed either with life or with feeling; and they have considered the soul as a composite of several parts. They maintain that all

---

16 Footnote 68 of article "Epicurus" [not included in these selections].
17 In remark P of article "Democritus" [not included in these selections].
18 Plutarch, *Moralia*, "De placitis philosophorum" IV. 4.

feeling terminates with the separation or the breaking apart of the parts of this composite. See below[19] the examination of a critical observation by Plutarch against Epicurus. The hypothesis of animated atoms would have had another great advantage, for their indivisibility could have furnished some reply to the unanswerable objection to which the view of those who maintain that matter can think (that is to say, have feelings and knowledge) is subject. This objection is based on the unity, properly speaking, that ought to belong to thinking beings. For if a thinking substance was unified only in the way a sphere is, it would never see a whole tree at once; it would never feel the pain produced by the blow of a stick. Here is a way of convincing everybody of this. Consider the shape of the four parts of the world on a globe. You will never be able to see anything on this globe that contains all of Asia or even an entire river. The part that represents Persia is not the same as the one that represents the kingdom of Siam. And we distinguish a right and left side in the part that represents the Euphrates. It follows from this that if this globe were capable of knowing the shapes with which it has been decorated, it would contain nothing that could say, "I know all Europe, all France, the whole city of Amsterdam, the whole Vistula"; each part of the globe could only know the portion of the shape that fell to it; and since that part would be so small as not to represent any place entirely, the globe's capability of knowing would be absolutely useless; no act of knowledge would result from this capability; and at least it would be the case that these acts of knowing would be very different from those that we experience; for they make us know an entire object, an entire tree, an entire horse, and so on, which is complete proof that the subject that is affected by the entire image of these objects is not at all divisible into several parts, and consequently that man in so far as he is a thinking entity is not corporeal or material or a composite of several beings. If he were such, he would not feel any blows from a stick since the pain would divide itself into as many particles as there are in the organs that are struck. Now these organs contain an infinite number of particles; and thus the portion of pain that would belong to each part would be so small that it would not be felt. If you should answer me that each part of the soul communicates its passions to the others,

---

[19] In remark Q of the article on the poet Lucretius [not included in these selections].

I would make two or three replies that would again throw you into the mire.

I would tell in the first place that it does not seem to be more possible for the parts of a globe to communicate pain to each other than it is possible for them to communicate their motion to each other. Now it is certain that each of them keeps the portion of motion that falls to it, and that it communicates none of it to the others. Push a globe; the motion that you communicate to it is distributed equally to all its parts, to each according to its mass, and from that time on until the globe stops moving there is no division again of the motion among its parts. Why would you suppose there are other conditions with regard to thought, for example, with regard to the pain you might cause in that globe by kicking it? Ought you not say that this pain is distributed throughout the globe and that each part of the globe takes some of it in proportion to its mass and retains what falls to it? In the second place I pose this small question to you. How does part A of the soul communicate its pain to parts B and C, and so on? Does it give it to them by divesting itself of it so that the same numerical pain that was in part A is afterwards in part B? If this be so, then here is the destruction of a most certain and most true maxim, that accidents do not pass from one subject to another. Still further, this is the destruction of your own claims. You want to make us understand how the pain of a kick must be very sharp though it be divided into an infinite number of parts; and you suppose that the part that falls to one section of the soul leaves this section and passes to another. But this way of communicating will not augment the feeling; for if one section of the soul loses its pain at the same time as it communicates it to another section, this is a sure means of preventing the augmentation that is called "intensive,"[21] and thus the difficulty remains in its entirety. One cannot see how it can occur that a pain divided into an infinite number of parts can be an unbearable sensation. You will say that a part of the soul communicates its pain to others and nevertheless retains it, that is to say that it produces in the neighboring parts a sensation like its own. But my objection still remains. Is not this similar sensation that is produced anew received in a subject that is infinitely divisible? It will consequently be divided

---

[21] The Schoolmen call "extensive" the propagation of a quality in different parts of the subject, and "intensive" the acquisition of new degrees in the same part of the subject.

into an infinite number of parts just as the first one was; and as a result of this division, each subject or each piece of the substance will have only so small, so slight a degree of pain, that it will not be felt at all. Now experience teaches us the contrary only too well. My third reply will be that you introduce an infinite number of superfluous things into the world. You can maintain your view only by making an inconceivable assumption, namely, that the image of a horse and the idea of a square, being received into a soul composed of an infinity of parts, are preserved in their entirety in each part. This is the absurdity of intentional species that the Schoolmen hardly dare put forth any longer. It is a much greater absurdity than that of the professors who claim that the soul is entirely in the whole body, and entirely in every part of it. But I will not insist upon this. I will rest content with asking you if your supposition does not manifestly include this monstrous consequence, namely, that in a hungry dog there are an infinite number of substances that feel hungry, and in a man who reads there are an infinite number of things that read and each one knows that it reads? However, each one of us knows by experience that there is only one thing in himself that knows that it reads, that it is hungry, that it feels pain or pleasure, and the like. What purpose then does this infinity of substances serve that read within every reader, that are hungry or thirsty within every animal, and so on? You cannot deny this consequence since, in order to get rid of the difficulties to which you expose yourself by supposing that every thought is divided into as many parts as there are parts in the substance of a material soul, you are forced to answer that the sensation is preserved entirely in every part of the soul by those parts communicating to each other their respective modifications. This reminds me of a very good argument that a sect of philosophers, whom I will speak about in the following remark [p. 134], used to maintain concerning the spirituality of God. If God is a body, they say, his divine perfections are either in all the individual substances of his body, or in one only; if they are found in all, then there are several Gods; if they are in only one, the others are superfluous.[23] . . .

Whether the perception of a body is formed successively in the soul. You will perhaps tell me that the soul does not see all the parts of a horse at once but one after another, that this succession is so quick that it is imperceptible, and that the impression received at the first

---

[23] Moses Maimonides, *Guide for the Perplexed*, Pt. I, chap. 77.

instant can last long enough to be united with the impression of the following instants, from which it happens that the soul thinks it sees the parts of the object that no longer act upon it. It is thus that it believes it sees a circle of fire when a lighted piece of wood is whirled around. The soul sees each part of this circle successively, and nevertheless it seems to it that it sees them simultaneously. This is due to the fact that the impression that the soul receives lasts a longer time than does the action of the object in making an impression. I reply to you that this subterfuge will not get you out of the difficulties. It is of no use against my last objection, nor against several of the others. It can only throw dust in the eyes with regard to the disproportion between the bigness of the object and the smallness of the thinking substance. But after all, what answer could you give me if I say to you that when a man looks very fixedly at an immobile object, a wall for example, the same part of the object that strikes him in the first of these imperceptible instants that you spoke of ought to strike him in all the following instants? For no reason can be imagined why it would cease acting on the soul. It strikes it therefore at the same time as all the other parts. But tell me, if you can, how the image of a wall can place itself entirely at the same instant in a subject divisible to infinity. This and several other reasons that can be found in the writings of some modern thinkers invincibly prove the incompatibility of thought with a composite being.[24]

I have dwelt upon this matter to confirm what I have already put down as a fact: that Leucippus, Epicurus, and the other atomists could have protected themselves from various unanswerable objections if they had been advised to attribute a soul to each atom. By this means they could have joined thought to an indivisible subject; and they had no less right to suppose that atoms were animated than they had to suppose that they were uncreated, possessing the attribute of the power of self-motion. It is as difficult to conceive of this power in an atom as to conceive of its having sensation. Extension and solidity make up the whole nature of an atom according to our ideas of it. The power of self-motion is not contained in that idea. It is something that our ideas find alien and "extrinsic" to bodies and extension in

---

24 See above, article "Dicaearchus," footnote 58 [p. 73]. I note that no one, it seems to me, has treated this important question more nobly and forcefully—on the immateriality and indivisibility of all that thinks—than Dom François Lami, a Benedictine monk of the Congregation of St. Maur, in his excellent work *De la connoissance de soi-même*.

the same way that knowledge does not seem to belong to them. Therefore, since the atomists suppose the power of self-motion to be in their
corpuscles, why do they take thought away from them? I am well aware
that by attributing thought to them they would not have avoided all
the difficulties. They could still be overwhelmed by most unanswerable objections.[25] But it is no small thing to be able to parry some
of the blows. Let us observe that some very great philosophers have
made the principle properties of the soul consist in the power of self-
movement.[26] They have characterized and defined it by this attribute.
Would it have been found strange then that those who attributed the
principle of motion to atoms might also have given them a soul?

《←

 F. (*There was a sect of Oriental philosophers who admitted the
  hypothesis of atoms and the vacuum.*) The famous Rabbi Maimonides amply discusses this sect of philosophers. They are called "The
Speakers."[27] They dealt chiefly with these four points:[28] (1) that the
world is not eternal, (2) that it has been created, (3) that its Creator
is one single being, (4) that he is incorporeal. This rabbi tells us of
the twelve principles they used as the foundation of their view. The
second was that there is a vacuum, and the third, that time is composed of indivisible moments. It does not seem that their atoms were
like those of Leucippus, for they did not attribute any size to them,
and they made them all alike. Maimonides attacks them greatly for
their being obliged to deny that one moving body goes faster than
another and that the diagonal of a square is longer than a side. These
difficulties led them to say that the senses deceive us and that only the
understanding is to be trusted. Some of them were even led to deny
the existence of the square shape. Let us say in passing that they could
have thrown these difficulties back upon their adversaries; and let
us defy all the partisans of infinite divisibility to give satisfactory
answers to the arguments that prove that the diagonal of a square is

---

 [25] See those that St. Augustine proposed to them in his fifty-sixth epistle.
 [26] See Aristotle, *De anima* I. 2; and Plutarch, *Moralia,* "De placitis
philosophorum" IV. 2.
 [27] See the marginal note of Buxtorf at the beginning of chap. 69 of the
first part of his translation of the *Guide for the Perplexed* by Maimonides.
 [28] Maimonides, *ibid.,* chap. 73.

not longer than one of the sides. For the rest, these Arabic philosophers supposed in part what I have said that Leucippus should have supposed. They taught that each atom of a living body was alive, and that each atom of a sensing body was sensitive, and that understanding resided in an atom. There was no controversy among them on this theory. But with regard to the soul they were divided into two camps. One said that it consisted of atoms of which man, for example, is composed. The other camp said it was composed of several very subtle substances. The same division existed among them regarding knowledge. Some supposed that it was lodged in a single atom, and others that it was in each of the atoms that made up the knower. . . .

«««

G. (*The vacuum . . . has become the favorite idol of the most famous mathematicians.*) Plutarch asserts: (1) that from Thales to Plato, everyone denied the vacuum; (2) that Leucippus, Democritus, Demetrius, Metrodorus, and Epicurus admitted an infinite vacuum; (3) that the Stoics taught that there is a plenum in the world and that beyond the world there is an infinite, empty space; (4) that Aristotle admitted only as much empty space beyond the world as heaven needed to breathe, for, he added, heaven is made of fire. I do not know where Aristotle set forth such a doctrine, but I do know where he denied that there were bodies beyond heaven, which presupposes that he admitted an empty infinity beyond the world; for nothing would be more absurd than to admit an empty and limited space above the last heaven. Take notice that he teaches at this point that there is neither place, nor emptiness, nor time beyond the last heaven. But this is only a difference about words. For he rejects the vacuum only because he defined it as a space that does not contain any bodies and can contain them. He maintained that there could not be any bodies beyond the world. He therefore could not admit the vacuum, in terms of this definition. But he would have been absurd if, taking the term "vacuum" simply and generally to mean that which does not enclose or contain any bodies, he had said that there was no vacuum beyond the last celestial sphere. The Christian philosophers who profess his doctrines have taught what Plutarch attributes to the Stoics, that all is full in the world and that outside the world there is an infinite vacuum. They call it "the imaginary spaces," and they do not believe that it is, properly speaking, a vacuum even though it does not enclose any bodies; for they call a vacuum a space that does not contain any bodies and is surrounded on all sides by bodies. It is evident that this definition does not fit in with the imaginary spaces. As to the fullness of the world, they have admitted it as a fundamental point, dear and precious to nature, since they have asserted that she has such an abhorrence of a vacuum, that she would rather violate her own laws than permit it to turn up anywhere. Nature makes light bodies descend and heavy bodies rise any time that a vacuum threatens, they say. These movements are contrary to her own laws, and they do violence to the elements. But what is to be done about this? Of two evils, is it not lawful and just to avoid the worse? The modern philosophers have made fun of these fancies. Galileo and his successor Torricelli revived the doctrine of the vacuum. Gassendi, the great restorer of Leucippus' theory, brought it into fashion and claimed to have proven it demonstratively. Descartes has declared himself for the plenum and carried it much further than the Aristotelians had done. For not only did he maintain that there was no vacuum, but also that it was absolutely impossible that there should be one. He based this on the contention that if the vacuum had all the properties and the entire essence of bodies, that is to say, the three dimensions, it would be a contradiction in terms to claim that the vacuum was a space where there were no bodies. A great paradox was discovered in the *identity* that he established between space and body; and men cried out that he diminished the divine omnipotence since he taught that God, even acting by a miracle, could not make a barrel that remained a barrel and was not filled with some matter. This is doubtless a consequence of his doctrine, but one that does not at all concern the omnipotence of God. It is not at all a question of this omnipotence; it is a question only of knowing if everything that has three dimensions is a body. Descartes' arguments have appeared very strong to many people. They have believed that by means of his subtle matter, one might easily reconcile together motion and plenitude, and they have found a paralogism in the alleged demonstrations of Gassendi.[37] The reign of the plenum seemed then to be more firmly established than ever, when to everybody's surprise some great mathematicians appeared holding another view. Huygens declared himself in favor of the

---

[37] See [Nicole and Arnauld,] *L'Art de penser (Port-Royal Logic)*, Pt. III, chap. 18, no. 4; and note that Aristotle, in *Physics* IV. 7, gives the outline of the answers the gentlemen of Port Royal make to Gassendi.

vacuum;[38] Newton took the same side and fought strongly on this point against Descartes' hypothesis, contending that it is incompatible with motion, gravity, and other phenomena.[39] Fatio is of Newton's opinion, and I have heard him say that the existence of the vacuum is not problematical but is a fact that is certain and has been mathematically demonstrated. He added that the empty space is much larger than the full space. This new sect of protectors of the vacuum paint the universe as an infinite space in which some bodies have been scattered hither and yon, which in comparison to this space are only like a few vessels dispersed on the ocean, so that those who possess good enough vision to discern what is full and what is empty would cry out, "Few here and there in the abyss are seen."[40] What is distressing for the new adherents of the vacuum is that they cannot deny that the arguments of the Cartesians against space's being nothing are very strong. I mean that they dare not maintain as the Scholastics did that space is nothing and that it is a pure privation. Then when they are asked what are these spaces that really have three dimensions, and that are distinct from bodies, and that allow themselves to be penetrated by bodies without making any resistance, they do not know what to say and are almost ready to adopt the chimera of some of the Peripatetics who have dared to say that space is no more than the immensity of God.[41] This would be a very absurd doctrine, as Arnauld has shown in the writing[42] in which he claims that Father Malebranche seems to attribute to God a formal extension. Note that Hartsoeker, a good physicist and mathematician, has adopted a middle position between Descartes and the new adherents of the vacuum; for if on the one hand he claims that motion would be impossible in the Cartesian theory, he asserts on the other hand that the fluid extension in which bodies swim and flutter about very easily is not a pure space nor a penetrable extension.[43]

Let us gather two conclusions from this. One conclusion is that these great mathematicians who demonstrate that there is a vacuum give more pleasure than they think to the Pyrrhonian skeptics. Here

---

[38] See his *Discours de la cause de la pesanteur.*
[39] Newton, *Philosophiae naturalis principia mathematica.*
[40] Virgil, *Aeneid* I. 118.
[41] See Derodon, *Physique abregée,* Pt. I, chap. 6.
[42] See, among other items, his *Défense,* printed in 1684.
[43] Hartsoeker, *Principes de physique,* Chap. I.

is how. The mind of man has no ideas more clear and distinct than those of the nature and attributes of extension. These are the basis of mathematics. Now these ideas show us manifestly that extension is an entity that has parts distinct from each other and is, consequently, divisible and impenetrable. By experience we know of the impenetrability of bodies; and if we look for the source and a priori reason for this, we find it with the utmost clarity in the idea of extension and in the distinction of the parts of an extended being. And we can imagine no other foundation for it. We conceive extension, not as a genus which contains two species under it but as a species that contains only individuals under it.[44] From which we conclude that the attributes that are found in one extension are found also in all others. However, here are mathmaticians who demonstrate that there is a vacuum, that is to say an indivisible and penetrable extension, so that a sphere of four feet [in volume] and the four feet of space that fill it up make only four feet of extension. There is then no longer any clear and distinct idea on which our mind may depend since the idea of extension has been found to have misled us miserably. It had convinced us that everything that is extended has parts that cannot be penetrated; and here is the existence of space demonstrated mathematically, of a space, I say, that has three dimensions, that is immobile, and that allows other dimensions to pass and repass through it without stirring, without giving way in the least. The second conclusion I have to mention is that the theory of Spinoza agrees very poorly with this twofold extension of the universe, the one penetrable, continuous, and immobile; the other impenetrable and separated into pieces that are sometimes one hundred leagues from one another. I believe that the Spinozists will be very perplexed if they are forced to accept the demonstrations of Newton.

I have mentioned above[45] a remark of the philosophers of the sect of Speakers. Rabbi Maimonides refutes it in this way;[46] "If you examine that assertion of theirs, you will find that it is based on their first and fifth propositions, and therefore is of no weight at all. For one might tell them that the body of God is not, as you say, composed or made up of the union of such individual particles as he created himself but is one continuous body or being that does not admit of

---

44 See *La Défense* of Arnauld, Pt. V.

45 Footnote 23 [p. 132].

46 Moses Maimonides, *Guide for the Perplexed.*

any actual division except in thought." The response that this rabbi supposes could be made is not far from the claim of those who admit a positive space which is the divinity itself.

Mammillarians, a sect among the Anabaptists. I am not sure of the date when this new schism developed, but it is said that Haarlem is the birthplace of this subdivision. It owes its origins to the liberty a young man took by putting his hand on the breast of a girl whom he loved and wanted to marry. This touch became known to the Church, which deliberated on the punishments the delinquent ought to suffer. Some claimed that he ought to be excommunicated; others said that his fault was pardonable and therefore they would never agree to his excommunication. The dispute grew so hot that it led to a total rupture between the contending parties. Those who had favored being indulgent toward the young man were called Mammillarians (A). In one sense, this affair does honor to the Anabaptists; for it proves that they carried moral severity much further than those who are called Rigorists in the Spanish Netherlands (B). I shall relate a story on this topic that is told about Labadie (C). I have heard that some able people maintained in a conversation one day that there will never be "Baisarians" or "Oscularians" among the Anabaptists (D).*

≪←

A. *(Mammillarians.)* There is no need to play the etymologist here. All those who understand French know that the word *mammelle,* which is no longer good usage, means the same as *téton* [breast, teat].

---

* [Remarks B, C, and D appear on pp. 141–143.]

《《←

B. (*The Anabaptists . . . carried moral severity much further than . . . the Rigorists in the Spanish Netherlands.*) The least strict casuists, the Sanchezes and Escobars, condemn the touching of the breasts. They agree that it is an impurity, and a type of lewdness, one of the seven mortal sins. But, if I am not mistaken, they do not impose a very severe penance on the guilty party. And there are several countries in Europe where they are almost compelled to treat this like the minor faults that are called *quotidianae incursionis* [daily occurrences]. This wicked practice is so usual in those countries, and it is so common a spectacle, even in the middle of streets, especially among the ordinary people, that the casuists mitigate their severity and are convinced that this commonness eliminates half the crime. They believe that it is not considered in the category of a very indecent freedom and that the scandal it gives the spectator is very small. This is why they treat this article of confession lightly. I do not believe that any Rigorist has ever deferred the absolution of his penitent on this account even in those climates where this kind of toying is least in use and is considered as one of those liberties which persons of the fair sex ought to resent a great deal. Thus the Anabaptists are the most rigid of all of the Christian moralists since they condemn with excommunication anyone who touches the breast of a woman he wishes to marry and they break off communion with those who do not want to excommunicate such a lover.

《《←

C. (*I shall relate a story on this topic that is told about Labadie.*) All those who have heard of this person know that he recommended some spiritual exercises to devout people of both sexes and that he trained them in interior recollection and mental prayer. It is said that he once signaled out a point of meditation to one of his female students and, having strongly recommended that she apply herself for a few hours to such an important object, he approached her when he believed that she was at the height of her interior recollection, and he put his hand to her breast. She repulsed him brusquely and indicated great surprise at this event; she was about to rebuke him when he forestalled her by saying, without being disconcerted in the least and with a devout air: "I see clearly, my child, that you are still very far from perfection. Humbly acknowledge your failings. Ask God for forgiveness for your having paid so little attention to the mysteries on which you ought to have been meditating. If you had bestowed all the necessary attention to these matters, you would not have been aware of what was happening around your bosom. But you were so little detached from the senses, so little preoccupied with the divine, that it did not take you a moment to realize that I touched you. I wanted to test whether your fervency in prayer had raised you above the material world and had united you to the Supreme Being, the living source of immortality and spirituality. And I see with much sadness that you are making very little progress, that you are only creeping on the ground. May this make you ashamed, my child, and bring you, in the future, to perform better the holy duties of mental prayer." It is said that the girl, who had as much good sense as virtue, was not less indignant at Labadie's words than at his action and that she never wanted to hear him spoken of again. I do not guarantee the certainty of all these facts. I am content to assert that it seems highly probable that some of these very spiritual believers who make people hope that strong meditation will ravish the soul and render it insensible of the actions of the body do so in order to play with their lovely disciples, and to do even worse. This is what the Molinosists are accused of. In general, there is nothing more dangerous for the soul than devotions that are too mystical and too intense. The body, no doubt, runs some risk in doing them; and many people wish for the kind of deceptions that may ensue.

«‹

D. *(There will never be "Baisarians" or "Oscularians" among the Anabaptists.)* These would be people who would be thrown out of their communion because they did not want to sanction the excommunication of those who kiss their girl friends. Here is the basis of the view of those who deny that such a schism could arise. It is impossible, they said, unless there are some casuists who are so unyielding as to hold that a kiss deserves to be punished with excommunication, just as certain rigid people have wished to apply this punishment for touching a girl friend's breasts. But these two cases are not similar. The laws of love-making of certain peoples, they continue, have established from generation to generation, especially among persons of the third estate, that a kiss is almost the first favor, and a touch of the breast practically the last, or the penultimate. When one is raised on such principles, one believes people suffer little by kisses, but much by the handling of the breasts. Thus, although the administrators of canon law have raised a great outcry against the young man whom the Mammillarians protected, it does not follow that they would make the same outcry against the other kind of love-making. They would defer to custom; they would pardon those liberties that are considered only as the first elements, or the beginning of the alphabet of amorous civilities. I only report these things to show that there is no subject to which the conversation of reputable people does not sometimes descend. It is not useless to make known this weakness of able people. Now seriously, does this sort of speculation deserve to be examined [namely, whether or not there will ever be "Baisarians" or "Oscularians" among the Anabaptists]? And, after all, would it not be more prudent not to give positive answers about what may or may not happen in the future? . . .

.   .   .   .

Manicheans, heretics whose infamous sect, founded by a certain Manes, sprang up in the third century, and took root in several provinces, and lasted a long time. Nevertheless, they taught what should have struck everyone with the greatest horror. The weak side of their view did not consist, as it appeared at first, in the doctrine of the two principles, one good and the other wicked; but in the particular explanations they gave of this and in the practical consequences they drew from it. It must be admitted that this false doctrine, much older than Manes, and incapable of being maintained as soon as one accepts Scripture, in whole or part, would be rather difficult to refute if maintained by pagan philosophers skilled in disputing (D). It was fortunate that St. Augustine, who was so well versed in all the arts of controversy, abandoned Manicheanism; for he had the capability of removing all the grossest errors from it and making of the rest of it a system, which in his hands would have perplexed the orthodox. Pope Leo I exhibited a great deal of vigor against the Manicheans; and as his zeal was supported by the laws of the empire, the sect was dealt a very severe blow. It became formidable in Armenia in the ninth century, as I shall discuss elsewhere,[a] and it appeared in France during the Al-

⟪⟪⟪

D. (. . . *would be rather difficult to refute if maintained by pagan philosophers skilled in disputing.*) They would soon have been defeated by a priori arguments; their strength lay in a posteriori arguments. With these they could have fought a long time, and it would have been difficult to defeat them. My point will be better

---

[a] In the article "Paulicians," remarks B and D [not included in these selections].

bigensian century.* This cannot be denied; but it is not true
that the Albigensians were Manicheans. The latter, among other
errors, taught that the souls of plants were reasonable, and they
condemned farming as a murderous activity, but they allowed
their auditors to practice it for the benefit of their elect (F).†

In this article, in "Marcionites" and "Paulicians," and in
some others, there are some things that have shocked many
people and seemed capable of making them believe that I had
wished to support Manicheanism and inspire doubts in the
minds of Christian readers. I here give notice that a Clarification
will be found at the end of this work, that this can cause no
injury to the foundations of the Christian faith [p. 409].

understood from the exposition that follows. The most certain and
the clearest ideas of order teach us that a Being who exists by himself, who is necessary, who is eternal, must be one, infinite, all-powerful, and endowed with every kind of perfection. Thus, by consulting
these ideas, one finds that there is nothing more absurd than the
hypothesis of two principles, eternal and independent of each other,
one of which has no goodness and can stop the plans of the other.
These are what I call the a priori arguments. They lead us necessarily
to reject this hypothesis and to admit only one principle in all things.
If this were all that was necessary to determine the goodness of a
theory, the trial would be over, to the confusion of Zoroaster and all
his followers. But every theory has need of two things in order to
be considered a good one: first, its ideas must be distinct; and second, it must account for experience. It is necessary then to see if the
phenomena of nature can be easily explained by the hypothesis of a
single principle. When the Manicheans tell us that, since many things
are observed in the world that are contrary to one another—cold and
heat, white and black, light and darkness—therefore there necessarily
are two principles, they argue pitifully. The opposition that exists
among these entities, fortified as much as one likes by what are called
variations, disorders, irregularities of nature, cannot make half an
objection against the unity, simplicity, and immutability of God. All

---

* [The Albigensians flourished in France from the eleventh until the
thirteenth century.]

† [Remark F appears on p. 153.]

these matters are explained either by the various faculties that God has given to bodies, or by the laws of motion he has established, or by the concourse of intelligent occasional causes by which he has been pleased to regulate himself. This does not require the quintessences that the rabbis have imagined and that have furnished an Italian bishop with an *ad hominem* argument in favor of the Incarnation. "The author speaks amply of this union, bringing instances with which the rabbis abound, some of which are the same that our theologians make use of to explain the Incarnation, that it is nothing but an "insefiration," that is, two natures sefirated, and the Divinity at the same time as the substratum."[46] They say that God has united himself with ten very pure intelligences called "Sefira," and that he operates with these in such a way that all the variations and the imperfections of effects have to be attributed to them. "By ascribing to God in the Scriptures acts inconsistent with each other and imperfect in order to secure his immutability and perfection, they have supposed ten most pure intelligences by means of which, as instruments of his power, he performs everything, but in such a manner that all variety, imperfection, and change are ascribed to them only."[47] The simplicity and immutability of the ways of God can be saved without going to this expense. The establishing only of occasional causes suffices for it, provided only bodily phenomena have to be explained and not things concerning man. The heavens and the whole universe declare the glory, the power, and the unity of God. Man alone— this masterpiece of his Creation among the visible things—man alone, I say, furnishes some very great objections against the unity of God. Here is how:

Man is wicked and miserable. Everybody is aware of this from what goes on within himself, and from the commerce he is obliged to carry on with his neighbor. It suffices to have been alive for five or six[48] years to be completely convinced of these two truths. Those who live long and who are much involved in worldly affairs know this still more clearly. Travel gives continual lessons of this. Monuments to human misery and wickedness are found everywhere—pris-

---

[46] Joseph Ciantes, Bishop of Marsica, in the *Journal d'Italie,* August 27, 1668.

[47] *Ibid.*

[48] By this age one has done and suffered malicious acts, one has felt chagrin and pain, one has sulked many times, etc.

ons, hospitals, gallows, and beggars. Here you see the ruins of a flourishing city; in other places you cannot even find the ruins.

> *Now corn grows where Troy stood; the Phrygian soil*
> *Fattens with human blood.*
>   (Ovid, *Heroides* I. 53–54)

Read the following fine words taken from a letter written to Cicero. "Returning from Asia, as we sailed from Aegina towards Megara, I began to survey the surrounding shores. Behind me lay Aegina, before me Megara, Piraeus on the right hand, and Corinth on the left—once flourishing cities all, but now they lie prostrate in ruins."[51] Scholars who never leave their study acquire the most knowledge about these two matters because in reading history they make all the centuries and all the countries of the world pass in review before their eyes. Properly speaking, history is nothing but the crimes and misfortunes of the human race. But let us observe that these two evils, the one moral and the other physical, do not encompass all history or all private experience. Both moral good and physical good are found everywhere, some examples of virtue, some examples of happiness; and this is what causes the difficulty. For if all mankind were wicked and miserable, there would be no need to have recourse to the hypothesis of two principles. It is the mixture of happiness and virtue with misery and vice that requires this hypothesis. It is in this that the strength of the sect of Zoroaster lies. . . .

To make people see how difficult it would be to refute this false system, and to make them conclude that it is necessary to have recourse to the light of revelation in order to destroy it, let us suppose here a dispute between Melissus and Zoroaster. They were both pagans and great philosophers. Melissus, who acknowledged only one principle, would say at the outset that his theory agrees admirably with the ideas of order. The necessary Being has no limits. He is therefore infinite and all-powerful, and thus he is one. And it would be both monstrous and inconsistent if he did not have goodness and did have the greatest of all vices—an essential malice. "I confess to you," Zoroaster would answer, "that your ideas are well connected; and I shall willingly acknowledge that in this respect your hypothesis surpasses mine. I will renounce an objection that I could employ, which is that infinity ought to comprehend all that is real, and malice

---

[51] Sulpicius to Cicero, in Cicero, *Epistulae ad familiares* IV. 5. 4.

is not less real than goodness.[53] Therefore the universe should require that there be wicked beings and good beings. And since supreme goodness and supreme malice cannot subsist in one subject, it is the case that in the nature of things there must be an essentially good being, and another essentially bad being. I renounce, I say, this objection.[54] I allow you the advantage of being more conformable to the notion of order than I am. But by your hypothesis explain a little to me how it happens that man is wicked and so subject to pain and grief. I defy you to find in your principles the explanation of this phenomenon, as I can find it in mine. I then regain the advantage. You surpass me in the beauty of ideas and in a priori reasons, and I surpass you in the explanation of phenomena and in a posteriori reasons. And since the chief characteristic of a good system is its being capable of accounting for experience, and since the mere incapacity of accounting for it is a proof that a hypotheisis is not good, however fine it appears to be in other respects, you must grant that I hit the nail on the head by admitting two principles and that you miss it by admitting only one."

Doubtless we are now at the main point of the whole affair. Here is the great chance for Melissus. . . . Let us continue to listen to Zoroaster.

"If man is the work of a single supremely good, supremely holy, supremely powerful principle, is it possible that he can be exposed to illnesses, to cold, to heat, to hunger, to thirst, to pain, to vexation? Is it possible he should have so many bad inclinations and commit so many crimes? Is it possible that the supreme holiness would produce so criminal a creature? Is it possible that the supreme goodness would produce so unhappy a creature? Would not the supreme power joined to an infinite goodness pour down blessings upon its work and defend it from everything that might annoy or trouble it?" If Melissus consults the ideas of order, he will answer that man was not wicked when God created him. He will say that man received a happy state from God, but not having followed the lights of his conscience, which according to the intention of his author would have

---

[53] That is to say, malicious action. I add this note so that one cannot tell me that evil is only a privation.

[54] I have read in the *Journal d'Italie*, August 31, 1674, that Piccinardi refutes the thesis, "Another God is possible," maintained by Father Conti against Columera.

conducted him along the virtuous path, he became wicked, and he deserved that the supremely just and supremely good God made him feel the effects of His wrath. Then it is not God who is the cause of moral evil; but he is the cause of physical evil, that is to say, the punishment of moral evil—punishment which, far from being incompatible with the supremely good principle, necessarily flows from one of God's attributes, I mean that of justice, which is no less essential to man than God's goodness. This answer, the most reasonable that Melissus could make, is basically fine and sound. But it can be combatted by arguments which have something in them more specious and dazzling. For Zoroaster would not fail to set forth that, if man were the work of an infinitely good and holy principle, he would have been created not only with no actual evil but also without any inclination to evil, since that inclination is a defect that cannot have such a principle for a cause. It remains then to be said that, when man came from the hands of his creator, he had only the power of self-determination to evil, and that since he determined himself in that way, he is the sole cause of the crime that he committed and the moral evil that was introduced into the universe. But, (1) we have no distinct idea that could make us comprehend how a being not self-existent should, however, be the master of its own actions. Then Zoroaster will say that the free will given to man is not capable of giving him an actual determination since its being is continuously and totally supported by the action of God. (2) He will pose this question, "Did God foresee that man would make bad use of his free will?" If the answer is affirmative he will reply that it appears impossible to foresee what depends entirely on an undetermined cause. "But I will readily agree with you," he will say, "that God foresaw the sin of his creature; and I conclude from this that he would have prevented it; for the ideas of order will not allow that an infinitely good and holy cause that can prevent the introduction of moral evil does not stop it, especially when by permitting it he will find himself obliged to pour down pains and torments upon his own work. If God did not foresee the fall of man, he must at least have judged that it was possible; therefore, since he saw he would be obliged to abandon his paternal goodness if the fall ever did occur, only to make his children miserable by exercising upon them the role of a severe judge, he would have determined man to moral good as he has determined him to physical good. He would not have left in man's soul any power for carrying himself toward sin, just as he did not leave any power for carrying himself toward misery in so far as it was misery. This is where we are led by the clear and distinct ideas of order when we follow, step by step, what an infinitely good principle ought to do. For, if a goodness as limited as that of a human father necessarily requires that he prevent as much as possible the bad use which his children might make of the goods he gives them, much more will an infinite and all-powerful goodness prevent the bad effects of its gifts. Instead of giving them free will, it will determine its creatures to good; or if it gives them free will, it will always efficiently watch over them to prevent their falling into sin." I very well believe that Melissus would not be silenced at this point, but whatever he might answer would be immediately combatted by reasons as plausible as his, and thus the dispute would never terminate.[55]

If he had recourse to the method of retortion, he would perplex Zoroaster greatly; but in granting him for once his two principles, he would leave him a broad highway for reaching the discovery of the origin of evil. Zoroaster would go back to the time of chaos: this is a state with regard to his two principles much like what Thomas Hobbes calls the state of nature, which he supposes to have preceded the establishments of societies. In this state of nature man was a wolf to man; everything belonged to the first who had it; no one was the master of anything except by force. In order to get out of this abyss each agreed to give up his rights to the whole so that he would be given the ownership of some part. They entered into agreements; war ceased. The two principles, weary of the chaos in which each confounded and overthrew what the other wanted to do, mutually consented to agree. Each gave up something. Each had a share in the production of man and in forming the laws of the union of the soul. The good principle obtained those that give man thousands of pleasures, and consented to those which expose man to thousands of pains; and if the good principle consented that moral good in mankind should be infinitely small in proportion to moral evil, that principle made up for that loss in some other species of creatures in which the proportion of vice would be correspondingly smaller than that of virtue. If many men in this life have more misery than hap-

---

[55] All this is more fully discussed in the remarks of the article "Paulicians" [p. 166].

piness, this is recompensed in another state; what they do not have under the human form, they will find under another form.[57] By this accord chaos was unraveled; chaos, I say, a passive principle that was the battlefield of the two active ones. The poets have represented this unraveling with the image of a quarrel being terminated. There is what Zoroaster could have claimed, priding himself that he did not make the good principle responsible for the intentional production of a work that would be so wicked and miserable except after it had found that it could not possibly do better nor more effectively oppose the horrible plans of the bad principle. To render his hypothesis less shocking he could deny that there had been a long war between these two principles, and he could toss out all those combats and prisoners that the Manicheans have spoken of. The whole business could be reduced to the certain knowledge that the two principles could have had, that the one could only obtain from the other such and such conditions. The accord could have been made on this basis for eternity.

A thousand great difficulties could be proposed to this philosopher; but as he would still find answers and after that demand that he be given a better hypothesis and claim that he had thoroughly refuted that of Melissus, he would never be led back to the truth. Human reason is too feeble for this. It is a principle of destruction and not of edification. It is only proper for raising doubts, and for turning things on all sides in order to make disputes endless; and I do not think I am mistaken if I say of natural revelation, that is to say, the light of reason, what the theologians say of the Mosaic Dispensation.* They say that it was only fit for making man realize his own weakness and the necessity of a redeemer and a law of grace. It was a teacher —these are their terms—to lead us to Jesus Christ. Let us say almost the same thing about reason. It is only fit to make man aware of his own blindness and weakness, and the necessity for another revelation. That is the one of Scripture. It is there that we find the means to refute invincibly the hypothesis of the two principles and all the objections of Zoroaster. There we find the unity of God and his

---

57 Note that all those, or most of those who have admitted two principles, have held the doctrine of metempsychosis.

* [*Dispensatio* was, in theology, the word chosen to translate the Greek οἰκονομία, "economy," i.e., divine or religious systems, as in the Jewish, Mosaic, Christian Dispensations.]

infinite perfections, the fall of the first man, and what follows from it. Let someone tell us with a great apparatus of arguments that it is not possible that moral evil should introduce itself into the world by the work of an infinitely good and holy principle, we will answer that this however is in fact the case, and therefore this is very possible. There is nothing more foolish than to argue against the facts. The axiom, "From the act to the potency is a valid inference," is as clear as that two plus two equal four.[59] The Manicheans were aware of what I have just pointed out. That is why they rejected the Old Testament. But what they retained of Scripture furnished enough strong arms to the orthodox. Thus it was no difficult task to confound those heretics, who, in addition, childishly embarrassed themselves when they entered into details. Now since Scripture furnishes us with the best solutions, I was not wrong in saying that a pagan philosopher would be very difficult to defeat on this matter. That is the subject of this remark.

Long as it is, I shall not finish without informing my reader that I still have three observations to make that I will come back to in another article.[61] First, I will discuss whether the Church Fathers have always argued well against the Manicheans and whether they have been able to push them to the end; secondly, I will show that according to the doctrines of paganism the objections of Zoroaster did not have much strength; and thirdly, I will discuss in what sense it can be said that the Christians did not reject the theory of the two principles. It is harder for them than for the pagans to clear up these difficulties by rational means because they have disputes to settle among themselves concerning liberty, in which the aggressor always seems to have the better of the argument;[62] and also because the small number of the elect and the eternity of the torments of hell furnish objections that Melissus would have had no reason to be afraid of.

---

[59] See below, article "Paulicians," remark F [p. 179].

[61] In that of "Paulicians," remarks E [p. 166], G [not in these selections], and H [p. 186].

[62] See remark F in the article "Marcionites" [not included in these selections].

«‹-

F. *(They allowed their auditors to farm for the benefit of their
elect.)* The Manicheans were divided into two orders, the elect
and the auditors. The former were not allowed to engage in farming
or even gathering fruit. The others were allowed to do so, and they
were assured that the murders they were committing by doing this
would be pardoned through the intercession of the divine particles
which were liberated from their prison. The elect ate them. Thus the
remission for these murders was based upon the fact that these events
provided nutrition for the elect and obtained freedom for the particles of the divine substance that were locked up in the plants. St.
Augustine related these fantasies very well and makes fun of them, as
he should. . . .[70]

---

[70] Augustine, *De Haeres*. XLVI.

Naples, JOANNA II, QUEEN OF, descended from Charles of Anjou, brother of St. Louis, was the daughter of that Carlo di Durazzo who had put Queen Joanna I to death. She was born in 1371 and married William of Austria around 1403. She was left a widow in 1406. After her brother Ladislaus, King of Naples, died in 1414 without lawful issue, she succeeded to the kingdom and married Jacques de Bourbon the following year. This prince, not able to tolerate her leading such a scandalous life, deprived her of both her lover and all authority. But he was not cunning enough to defend himself against the ruses of this princess. She gained the upper hand and carried matters so far that he was forced to return to France, where he became a monk. The queen, freed from such a husband, soon found herself in new difficulties. She so annoyed the brave Sforza di Cotignola that he tried to persuade Louis of Anjou to conquer the kingdom of Naples, and he put himself at the head of the malcontents. Pope Martin V took the side of Louis of Anjou, who besieged Naples by sea and by land and would have captured it had not Alfonso of Aragon sent the queen powerful help. He did it because she had promised to adopt him. She kept her word but was so mistreated by that ingrate that she revoked the adoption and transferred it to Louis of Anjou. This prince recovered the cities that had gone over to the Aragonese, and he treated her so well that when he died in November 1434, the grief she felt was the cause of her own death soon after. She made René of Anjou her heir, but he did not have the strength to establish himself in the kingdom of Naples and thus left his heirs only an empty title and vain pretensions to the crown. He was better qualified to make a tranquil state happy than to subjugate rebellious subjects, and he used to spend more time painting than in preparing warlike expeditions. The real successor of this princess was Alfonso of Aragon, whom I will speak of in the following article ["Naples, Alfonso I, King of," not included in these selections]. No one denies that she disgraced herself by her dissoluteness. Brantôme gives very poor excuses for her (G). It was perhaps to expiate her sins that she endowed the Church and permitted Capistrano to persecute the Jews (H). I have spoken elsewhere[h] of Caraccioli, one of her lovers. What Brantôme says of him is taken from Collenuccio. I must say a few words here about Bartolomeo Coglione (I).*

«‹‹

G. (*Brantôme gives very poor excuses for her.*) Here are his words, "The history of Naples tells us that this queen . . . was always in love with someone, having given pleasures to her body in many ways and with many men. However, this is the least blameworthy vice in a queen, great and beautiful princess that she was; and if this be the least vice that she might have, a very great one would be if she were bad, malicious, vindictive, and tyrranical, as some have been. It is this latter that causes the poor people to suffer much, but they suffer little from her love affairs, as I have heard a great man maintain." It is almost in this manner that Paulus Jovius tries to excuse the voluptuous life of Leo X, as we have seen above.[38] We have also given our reflections on this kind of apology. But I add that there is a great difference between the public lewdness of a king and the scandalous loves of a queen. It is no doubt better for the subjects that their sovereign scandalize them by the multitude of his bastards than that he load them with taxes and oppress them. And it is very possible that a ruler who is extremely dissolute with women may preserve good order in his dominions, make justice and trade flourish there, and not oppress his subjects in the least. I also admit that people are happier under a lewd queen if she otherwise treats them gently and wisely than under a chaste queen who is avaricious, cruel, and ambitious. This is not open to dispute. But it seems to me

---

[h] Above, in the article "Caraccioli" [not included in these selections].

* [Remark H appears on p. 157, I on p. 158.]

[38] Remark O of article "Leo X" [not included in these selections].

that it is morally impossible that, in a country where the laws of religion and human honor are as severe against female lewdness as they are in the West, a kingdom could be happy under a queen who tramples under foot chastity and the most special virtue of her sex. The indulgence of human honor towards the unlawful amours that occur in the life of a king prevents us from concluding that, since he lets this passion go unbridled, he is not capable of moderating himself in other matters. But the severity of this same code of honor against the public impurities of a woman, no matter who she be, leads us to believe that a queen who passes by this barrier is capable of all sorts of excesses. She must have lost all shame and modesty; she must have no regard for her reputation; she must have a base soul since she is able to resolve to sacrifice her honor, her conscience, and her public reputation to gratify a criminal passion that she has conceived either for one of her servants or one of her subjects. Can the populace have any esteem for a princess whom by very plausible reasoning they have come to think of in this way? Can they prevent themselves from despising her? And is not this contempt the seed of sedition? Further, it is almost inevitable that the lewd conduct of a queen will lead the ladies of her court into similar disorders and thereby disperse throughout the whole kingdom a pernicious relaxation of the laws of propriety and decency, which contribute so greatly to preserving on this earth what still remains of chastity. What was only despised then becomes odious and detestable to all those who are concerned about the public good. What can be expected from this but factions and rebellions? A male sovereign keeping a concubine does not expose himself to the same consequences. Ambition, a desire to get ahead, a false idea of grandeur almost always play more of a part in the fall of his mistresses than does love. On the other hand, only by the brutal passion of carnal lust is an amorous queen thrown into disorders that overwhelm her. Let us add another consideration. A queen who prostitutes herself to her lovers becomes their slave. She cannot refuse them anything. It is they who really rule. Their vanity, their other passions, a fruitful source of disorders by themselves, become still more disastrous as the result of the jealousy they excite in the minds of important people. The latter try to oust the lovers, they intrigue, they divide into factions, and they stir up the people. Can the subjects be happy under such a government? Experience confirms all I have just said, for history provides us with prac-

tically no examples of amorous queens whose lewdness was carried
to excess, and whose reigns were not also unhappy. How many troubles were to be seen in the kingdom of Naples under our two Joannas?
How many wars of every kind? How many sackings? Thus we can
conclude, contrary to Brantôme, that it is a capital defect and a most
blameworthy vice in a queen to abandon herself to impure conduct.
It is a defect whose consequences are most dreadful for the populace.

.   .   .   .

≪-

H. *(It was perhaps to expiate* her dissoluteness *that she endowed
the Church and permitted . . . to persecute the Jews.)* De Sponde
says this expressly about her desire to be buried with a minimum of
pomp. "She was buried in the Church of the Annunciation of the
Blessed Virgin in a very private manner, as she had ordered herself
to do penance for her dissolute life which had disgraced her very
much." Here follows what is added regarding the care she took to
promote the interests of the faith. "Notwithstanding the vices in
which she indulged herself, she has done many pious actions, both
for the good of the churches and in behalf of the state, which
Giovanni Summonte enumerates. Among these was her giving power
to Friar Juan Capistrano, an eminent Franciscan, not to permit the
Jews to practice usury or to do other things prohibited by the
Church and to force them to wear the sign of the letter *thau* so that
they might be distinguished from the Christians." A man as ardent
as this Franciscan, who was set up as inspector of the conduct of the
Jews, and who required them to wear the letter *thau* so they could
be recognized, definitely has the earmarks of having made them suffer
many afflictions.*

* [In the article "Capistran, Jean" (San Juan Capistrano), remark E,
Bayle describes some of this saint's policies toward the Jews: "The power
of his eloquence was not limited to handsome achievements about inanimate things. He made the Jews feel it in a terrible way. For he was the
cause of many of them being burned to death throughout Silesia, on the
pretext that they had behaved irreverently toward the consecrated wafer."
[By the letter *thau* the Greek letter *tau* or the ancient Hebrew letter *tav*
(Thamudenic, Safahitic, etc.; not the modern printed *tav*) is probably
meant. This letter was chosen as a reminder of the cross on which Christ
died.]

≪←

I. *(I must say a few words here about Bartolomeo Coglione.)* He was one of the most famous captains of his century.
"He was born in the neighborhood of Bergamo, and his whole household had been put to the sword during the quarrels between the
Guelphs and the Ghibellines. He had been a beggar until he was
eighteen, when he found himself in Naples. After no one dared to
dispute with him for either the prize in wrestling or running because
of his prodigious strength and incomparable agility, Joanna II, Queen
of Naples, who valued men only on the basis of the vigor of their
bodies, made him her minion. But he soon grew tired of that infamous
employment and stole away from the court in order to apprentice
himself to learn about arms under the celebrated Braccio."[47] It will
not be superfluous to let the reader know that these facts appear in
the eulogies of Paulus Jovius; for the authority of the French historian
alone would not eliminate all doubt about them. . . . From this
passage, you may know the nature of this queen. During the solemn
performance of the public games, she saw a good-looking adventurer,
of so good a constitution that he won the wrestling, the running, and
the jumping prizes from all those who dared to contend with him.
He threw the javelin farther than any of them. She was not interested
in anything else about him and chose him for her favorite. Apply to
her then the fable of the mare that appears in the *Mercure Galant*
for 1673. If I remember it well, it ends with this moral: "I know many
women whose modest countenances deceive us. They are of a mare's
taste; it does not matter who comes to them, or how, if he has but a
good strong back and broad shoulders."

---

[47] Varillas, *Anecdotes de Florence.*

Nihusius, BARTHOLDUS, made himself very well known by his writings in the seventeenth century, and perhaps we should call him "a famous proselyte and converter." He was born at Wolpe in the dominions of the duke of Brunswick in 1589, and after having studied for a while at the College of Verden and the one at Goslar, he went to the University of Helmstedt around 1607. Because he did not have much money, in order to subsist it was necessary for him to seek employment with a master. He put himself in the service of Cornelius Martinus, who taught logic. He lived with him for four years and made progress in the sciences, for his master did not keep him so busy that he did not have time for studying. The master himself took pains to instruct him. He became esteemed for his good qualities and for his genius and was recommended to the bishop of Osnabrück and obtained a pension from him. He wanted to show his gratitude by writing some verses for the birthday of that prelate, but not being a poet he made use of a borrowed poem and published it under his own name. The liberality of this patron did not prevent Nihusius from being reduced to skimpy circumstances despite the fact that he gave lessons to the richest students after receiving his degree of Master of Philosophy in 1612. Fearing a very powerful faction that was opposed to those who had been disciples of Martinus and of Caselius, he was torn between the study of medicine and theology. He experienced the ill will of that faction when he wanted to maintain some metaphysical theses in 1614. He received a serious affront that led him to become disgusted with the Lutheran Church. Two years later he was appointed preceptor to two gentlemen whom he accompanied to the University of Jena. Afterwards he obtained a similar post at the court of Weimar. He received a good salary there and was considered a most honorable person. Nevertheless, he left without saying a word to anyone and went to Cologne, where he became a Catholic around 1622. The first post bestowed on him was that of director of the College of Proselytes. He wrote some controversial letters to Horneius and to Calixtus,* in which he used all his endeavors to prove that Christians need a judge whose word could settle their disputes infallibly; for since Scripture is a law that can only speak through the sense that is given to it, and since controversies are based on the diverse interpretations given to Scripture, it is a necessity, he said, either that Christian controversies cannot be ended or that there be in the Church a speaking authority to whom all members are obliged to submit. He placed this authority in the person of the pope; and when the bad lives of various popes were raised as an objection to him, he had the audacity to say that this objection also applied to the authors of Scripture (E). His letter to Calixtus was printed more than once. This renowned professor, not wishing to answer him in writing, decided to refute him in class and announced this to his students by means of a written notice. This notice was printed in 1625, unbeknownst to its author; and as it was rather satirical, it annoyed Nihusius tremendously, who returned some time after to the territory of Brunswick to be the director of a convent of nuns. He was appointed abbot of Ilfield in 1629 when that monastery was taken away from the house of Brunswick—where Michael Neander and his successors had trained some very good disciples. The following year he published a German

≪←

E. *(He had the audacity to say that this objection also applied to the authors of Scripture.)* Cursed effect of obstinacy! A man who has once adopted a hypothesis and regards it as his very own will spare nothing, either sacred or profane, to maintain it and to escape from an objection. He would prefer that it cost Scripture some-

---

* [Georg Horn (1620–1670), historian and theologian; Georg Callisen (1586–1656), Lutheran theologian.]

work in which he inveighed greatly against Calixtus. And
finally in 1633 his favorite work appeared. It was a new method
for confounding heretics, which was refuted in a very learned
fashion by Calixtus. Nihusius managed things so well that he
was appointed titular bishop of Mysia and was made suffragan
to the archbishop of Mainz. He was carrying on these functions
when he died at the beginning of 1657. He made friends at
Rome and arranged to publish in Germany some works written
in Italy. I ought to note that when the Swedes chased him from
his abbey, he took refuge in Holland, where he remained for
several years. He frequently saw Vossius there and used to tell
him among other things that the principal reason that he remained in the Church of Rome was simply that the sects which
separated from it could not prove any of their claims demon-

thing rather than let people see him without an answer. And as long
as he can keep his opinions from being insulted, it does not matter
to him that the reputation of sacred writers suffer. He tries to save
himself at their expense. He exposes them to attack so that the enemy
may not overthrow him except by trampling on them, or so that
the respect given them stops his being attacked. He makes use of
the stratagem that was so advantageous to the Spaniards when they
retook Maastricht in 1576. They placed the women of Wich[8] in front
of their soldiers so that the inhabitants of Maastricht did not dare fire
their cannon on the Spaniards, for they feared killing their relatives,
or at least their fellow female citizens. Be that as it may, when Nihusius had to answer Calixtus, who had said to him that it did not become the wisdom of God to establish religion on the authority of certain people as wretched as the popes have been during whole centuries, he asserted that those who wrote the Bible were very wicked
men, either openly, as David, or perhaps in a secretive way. . . . It was
not very difficult for the professor from Helmstedt to confound him
for employing so false and so detestable a reply. There is a great difference between a holy man who commits great sins of which he immediately repents and those who spend their entire lives in sin.

---

[8] It is the part of the town on the other side of the bridge.

stratively (H). Nicolaus Rittershusius, when accused of plagiariz-
ing from Nihusius, gave an answer that deserves consideration.
The author of the *Memorabilia ecclesiastica saeculi decimi
septimi* has not carefully indicated the time when Nihusius set
forth a new view about the invocation of saints.

≪←

H. *(Could not prove any of their claims demonstratively.)* It has
already been seen that Vossius considered him a learned and
subtle man. Let us add that he found him also full of civility and
charm. Nihusius, strongly biased in favor of his new method and
imagining that no one would be able to withstand it, wished to have
a conference with Vossius. He told him that if the Lutherans or Calvinists could offer him some proofs that would eliminate all doubts,
he would return to Protestantism. "Let them choose," he said, "whatever subject they please, for instance, the one in which they think they
have the greatest strength. All I ask of them is one good argument.
But if they have only probabilities to offer, they will allow what I
maintain to them—that they should return to the Church from which
our ancestors separated." . . . His strongest argument was the following: "Tell me, Vossius, why your father left the Church of Rome?
Give me a good reason for this." Vossius told him of the difference
which exists between this Church and the primitive Church. But, after
several discourses he fixed upon this: the theologians of the Church
of Rome interpret Scripture in such a way that they give it a sense
that is manifestly forced, and sometimes contradictory, and, in general, far removed from the doctrine of the ancient Church Fathers.
And not content with this, they put to death those who would not
adopt such interpretations. It was therefore just to break away from
such interpreters of the Word of God and to form new assemblies in
order to worship according to one's conscience as well as to preserve
a life that can be of value to one's country, one's Church, and one's
family. . . . No matter how reasonable this answer was, Vossius did
not have complete confidence in it. He begged his good friend Grotius
to examine the matter and to give him his views. . . . The only answer
he received was that he had justified very well the separation of the
Protestants from the Church of Rome.

Paraphrase of Nihusius' views. It is clear that Nihusius had reasoned in this way: When a person finds himself in a certain communion by education and by birth, the inconveniences that he suffers
in it do not constitute a legitimate reason for his leaving it unless he
can gain by the change, that is to say, by moving into a position where
he can be completely comfortable. For what good would it do us to
abandon the communion in which we were born and raised if in
leaving it we only changed ailments? Let us put this matter to a trial.
Let us imitate those poor invalids who, being tired of lying in bed,
think they would feel much more comfortable if they could sit in an
easy chair. Let us leave the Church of Rome and let us join the Protestant one. But, like these same invalids who no sooner have found that
the easy chair does not give them any comfort than they have put
themselves back in bed, let us go back to popery as soon as we feel that
the Protestant divines do not remove our difficulties. They offer us
only disputable reasons, nothing convincing, no demonstrations. They
prove, and they object. But their proofs and objections are answered.
They reply, and they are answered. This never ends. Is this worth a
schism? What greater inconveniences did we have in the Church in
which we were born? We lacked demonstrations there. Nothing was
offered to us that could serve our minds as a certain foundation. Objections were found against all the doctrines and against all the replies
ad infinitum. That was our greatest problem. We find it again in the
Protestant Church, and therefore we ought not to live in it. Let us
return to the communion which has the advantage of possession on
its side. And if it is necessary to be badly housed, is it not better to be
so in one's own country and in one's father's house than in the inns
of foreign countries? Besides, it is more disadvantageous to dispute
from the Protestant point of view than from the Catholic one. The
latter has all its enemies in front of it. The same arms that serve to
attack and repel one group serve to attack and repel the others. But
the Protestants have their enemies both in front and in the rear. They
are like a ship fighting between two fires. Popery attacks them from
one side, and Socinianism from the other. The arms they use against
popery hinder rather than help when they have to refute a Socinian;
for this heretic employs against them the arguments they have used
against the Church of Rome, so that a Protestant who has just fought
with a papist and is preparing to fight against a Socinian is obliged
to change his armor, at least part of it. These are without doubt the

chimeras that Nihusius fed upon and which persuaded him that, in order to convince the Protestants that they were wrong in quitting the Church of Rome, it sufficed to ask them for a demonstrative proof of their belief; I say, a proof to which there would be nothing to reply, no more than against the demonstrations of mathematics. He knew well that they would never take him at his word. Most theologians agree that the controversial points of religion cannot be carried to so high a degree of evidence. A famous minister has just taught us that not only is it a very dangerous error to assert that the Holy Ghost makes us know the truths of religion with complete evidence, but also that this is a doctrine the Protestants have rejected up to now.[35] He maintains that the faithful soul embraces these truths without their being evident to his reason, and even without knowing that it is evident that God has revealed them; and he says that those who insist that the Holy Ghost at least makes us see evidently the testimony that God has given to these truths are pernicious innovators. I am very sure that Nihusius did not expect anyone to give him the demonstrative argument he asked for. What was he then thinking of when he promised to go back to Lutheranism upon such a condition? Was he acting like a serious man? Had he been very reasonable, he would have accepted fully the answer that was given him by Vossius. It was very judicious and solid. But let us admit that Nihusius did not always base his views on illusions. He applied a good principle badly, namely that *a person should not leave his situation if the change is not an improvement.* The minister I just spoke of made use of this axiom. He is a rigid predestinarian and a strong particularist, and he groans under the weight of the objections to which his system is exposed.

---

35 "The question is to know if Saurin is right in saying that 'faith obtains its certitude by means of evidence, particularly in the problem of the divinity of Scripture.' There is a factual question, namely whether the opinion of Saurin is that of the entire Reformed Church, and whether the one of Jurieu is new and peculiar to Jurieu and Beaulieu, his master and professor. On the first question, it is not very surprising that Saurin should have been so mistaken. There are grosser errors than these, though there are hardly any more dangerous. But, on the second question—the factual one—it is extremely surprising that a man who appears as an author should commit such an error as to give the name of 'new opinion, rising error' to an opinion as old as the world, and extended as far as the Christian religion, and which until our time has been combatted only by heretics" (Pierre Jurieu, *Défense de la doctrine universelle de l'Eglise contre les imputations de M. Saurin*).

But he does not change hypotheses, because he does not find any that can ease him of the burden. He would not find anything to satisfy his reason in the hypothesis of the Molinists or in the other relaxed methods of explaining grace. He prefers therefore to stay where he is rather than to take up another position that would not cure his problems.[36] This makes very good sense.

---

[36] See the book entitled, *Jugement sur les méthodes des rigides et relâchées d'expliquer la providence et la grace*, p. 23. [This work by Jurieu (Rotterdam, 1686) attacks many Protestant liberals and rationalists for their "relaxed methods," which the author contends lead to Pelagianism, Socinianism, and Spinozism. It also sets forth the claim Bayle mentions here, that the "orthodox" predestination theory is beset with insoluble difficulties, but so is every other theory. This work is one of Jurieu's best, containing a forceful statement of his views, an interesting critique of Malebranche's theology, as well as one of a "pre-established harmony" theory. Bayle, in spite of all his criticisms of Jurieu, claimed to have found his own entire theological view in this work. Perhaps out of perversity, Bayle often attempted to show that his most astounding contentions were direct consequences of what Jurieu had presented as orthodox Calvinism in the *Jugement sur les méthodes*. The latter went to great lengths, after Bayle's death, to show that Bayle had misunderstood and misrepresented his position in that work. See Jurieu's *Le philosophe de Rotterdam, accusé, atteint, et convaincu* (Amsterdam, 1706 [1707]), pp. 110–131.]

Paulicians. It is thus that the Manicheans in Armenia were called when a certain Paul became their leader in the seventh century. "They became so powerful, because of either the weakness of the government, or the protection of the Saracens, or even perhaps the favor of the Emperor Nicephorus, who was very friendly to this sect, that, when they were finally persecuted by the Empress Theodora, the wife of Basil, they were in a position to build towns and to take up arms against their rulers. These wars were long and bloody during the reign of Basil the Macedonian, that is, at the end of the ninth century."[a] Moreover, so great was the slaughter of these heretics by the Empress Theodora that it seemed that they would never again be able to recover. It is thought that the preachers whom they sent to Bulgaria established the Manichean heresy there, and "that it is from there that it soon spread to the rest of Europe."[b] They condemned the worship of saints, and the images of the Cross, but this was not their principal view. Their fundamental doctrine was that of two coeternal principles, independent of one another. One is horrified as soon as he hears this doctrine, and therefore it is strange that the Manichean sect was able to seduce so much of the world. But, on the other hand, it has been so difficult to answer their objections about the origin of evil (E) that we

≪←

E. *(It has been so difficult to answer the Manichean objections about the origin of evil.)* I have prepared my readers[13] to find three observations here that I would have placed in the article on

---

a Bossuet, *Histoire des variations des églises protestantes,* Bk. XI.
b *Ibid.*
13 In article "Manicheans," footnote 61 [p. 152].

should not be surprised at the fact that the hypothesis of two principles, one good and the other evil, had dazzled several ancient philosophers and has found so many adherents in Christendom, where the doctrine that teaches of the basic hostility of the devils for the true God is always accompanied by the doctrine that teaches of the rebellion and fall of a group of the good angels. This hypothesis of the two principles would probably have made even more progress if the details of the view had been presented less crudely, and if it had not been accompanied by several odious practices,ᶜ or if there had been as many disputes then about predestination as there are today (F),* in which Christians accuse one another of making God the author of sin or of depriving him of the government of the world. The pagans could better answer the Manichean objections than the Christians could; but some of their philosophers found it difficult to do. It will be necessary to indicate in what sense the orthodox seem to admit two first principles (H),† and in what sense it cannot be said that, according to the Manicheans, God is the author of sin. We shall also criticize a modern author who has denied that the doctrine that makes God the author

the Manicheans had I not wanted to avoid being too prolix there. Let us now keep our promise and not frustrate the expectations of those who wish to follow up our cross reference. My second and third observations will appear separately afterwards.14 Here is the first one.

The Church Fathers, who so well refuted the Marcionites, the Manicheans, and, in general, all those who admitted two principles, hardly gave a good answer to the objections that deal with the origin of evil. They should have given up all a priori reasons as the outposts of a place that can be attacked but not defended. They should have contented themselves with a posteriori reasons and put all their strength behind these battlements. The Old and New Testaments are two parts of the revelation that mutually confirm one another. Then, since these heretics acknowledged the divinity of the New, it would not

---

ᶜ See article "Manicheans," remark D [not included in these selections].

* [Remark F appears on p. 179.]

† [Remark H appears on p. 186.]

14 In remarks G and H [only H is included in these selections (p. 186)].

of sin leads to irreligion. He has even said that this doctrine raises God to the highest conceivable degree of glory. The ancient Fathers were not unaware that the question of the origin of evil was a most perplexing one. They were not able to resolve it by employing the Platonic hypothesis, which is basically a type of Manicheanism, since it admits of two principles; they were obliged to have recourse to the privileges of man's free will. However, the more one reflects on that way of untangling the difficulty, the more one finds that the natural light of philosophy supplies arguments that tighten and entangle this Gordian knot still more (M).* A learned man claims that the Pythagoreans gave rise to this thorny question. They searched for the super-latives in all things; that is to say, their investigations aimed at a knowledge of that which is the highest degree of each species. They asked, for example, what is the strongest, the oldest, the most common, and the truest thing? To the last item the answer was given that men are wicked and that God is good. This gave rise to another question, how does it happen that if God is good, men are wicked? The solution of this problem seemed to be of great importance to Simplicius.

have been difficult to prove the divinity of the Old to them, after which it would have been easy to destroy their objections by showing that they are contrary to experience. According to Scripture there is only one′ principle, a good one, and yet moral and physical evil have been introduced into the human race. Therefore it is not contrary to the nature of the good principle to permit the introduction of moral evil and to punish crimes; for it is no more evident that four and four make eight than it is evident that if a thing has happened, it is pos-sible. "From the act to the potency is a valid inference" is one of the clearest and most incontestable axioms of all metaphysics.[15] This is an impregnable rampart, and it should render the cause of the orthodox victorious even though their a priori reasons can be re-futed. But some may say to me, "Can they actually be?" Yes, I will answer: the way in which evil was introduced under the government

---

* [Remark M appears on p. 187.]

[15] See article "Manicheans," remark D, footnote 59 [p. 152].

of a supreme, infinitely good, infinitely holy, and infinitely powerful being is not only inexplicable, but also incomprehensible. And all that can be opposed to the reasons why this being has allowed evil agrees more with the natural light and the ideas of order than do the reasons themselves. Consider carefully this passage from Lactantius, which contains an answer to an objection of Epicurus. Epicurus says, "God is either willing to remove evil and cannot; or he can and is unwilling; or he is neither willing nor able to do so; or else he is both willing and able. If he is willing and not able, he must then be weak, which cannot be affirmed of God. If he is able and not willing, he must be envious, which is also contrary to the nature of God. If he is neither willing nor able, he must be both envious and weak, and consequently not be God. If he is both willing and able—the only possibility that agrees with the nature of God—then where does evil come from? Or why does he not eliminate it? I know that most philosophers who assert there is a Providence are perturbed by this argument and are forced, almost against their will, to acknowledge that God does not concern himself with the government of the world, which is the very view that Epicurus is trying to establish. But this formidable argument is easily overthrown by clear reason. For God can do whatever he pleases, and there is no weakness or enviousness in him. Consequently, he is able to remove evil but is not willing to do so, and, nonetheless, he is not envious. He does not remove evil for this reason: because he also (as I have shown) bestows wisdom, and there is more good and satisfaction in wisdom than there is painfulness in evil. It is by wisdom that we come to know God, and by that knowledge attain immortality, which is the chief good. And therefore unless we first know evil, we shall not be able to know good. But neither Epicurus nor anyone else has noticed this point: If evil were to be removed, wisdom would also have to be removed. No trace of virtue would remain, since virtue consists in bearing with and overcoming the pains of evil. And so, the price of the small advantage of removing evil would be the deprivation of the greatest, the most real and proper good. It is evident therefore that all things, evil as well as good, were intended for the benefit of mankind."[16]

The full force of the objection could not be more accurately stated. Epicurus himself could not have set it forth more precisely and force-

---

[16] Lactantius, *De ira dei* XIII.

fully. See footnote 17. But the answer of Lactantius is pitiful. It is not only weak, but it is full of errors, and perhaps even heresies. It supposes that God had to produce evil because otherwise he would not have been able to communicate either wisdom, virtue, or the knowledge of goodness to us. Is it possible to find anything more monstrous than this doctrine? Does it not overthrow all that the theologians tell us about the joys of paradise and the state of innocence? They tell us that in that happy state Adam and Eve felt, without any admixture of discomfort, all the pleasures available to them in the garden of Eden, that delightful and charming place in which God had put them. The theologians add that if they had never sinned, they and all of their descendants would have enjoyed this happiness without ever being subject to diseases or sorrows, and without either the elements or the animal kingdom ever being unkind to them. It was their sin that exposed them to cold and heat, to hunger and thirst, to pain and sorrow, and to the misfortunes that certain beasts cause us. It is so far from being the case that virtue and wisdom cannot subsist in man without there being physical evil as well, as Lactantius claims, that it is necessary to maintain, on the contrary, that man has only been subject to this evil because he gave up virtue and wisdom. If the doctrine of Lactantius were sound, we would necessarily have to suppose that the good angels are subject to thousands of discomforts, and that the souls of the blessed change alternately from joy to sorrow; so that in the mansions of glory, and in the very bosom of the beatific vision, none is safe from adversity. Nothing is more contrary to the unanimous opinion both of theologians and of right reason than this. *One can experience one of two contraries without having ever experienced the other.* It is even the case that according to sound philosophy it is in no way necessary that our soul should have to experience evil in order that it might enjoy good, or that it should have to change successively from pleasure to pain and from pain to pleasure in order that it be able to tell that pain is an evil and pleasure a good. And thus Lactantius' view is no less shocking to the natural light than to the theological light. We know from experience that our soul cannot feel pleasure and pain at the same time. It must then necessarily have first felt either pain before pleasure or pleasure before pain. If its first

---

17 Note that this objection of Epicurus does not concern moral evil. If it did it would be even more difficult to answer.

feeling had been that of pleasure, it found that state to be agreeable even though it was unaware of pain; and if its first feeling had been that of pain, it found that state to be disagreeable even though it was unaware of pleasure. Suppose that its first feeling had lasted for several consecutive years without any interruption. You recognize that during all that time it was either in an agreeable or in a disagreeable state. *Why custom dulls feeling.* And do not appeal to experience against me. Do not tell me that a pleasure which lasts a long time becomes insipid, and that pain in time becomes bearable; for I will reply that this happens as a result of a change in the organ, so that, although the feeling continues to be the same with regard to its species, it is not so with regard to its degree. If at first you had a feeling of six degrees, it will have, at the end of two hours or at the end of a year, not six degrees but only one degree, or a quarter of a degree. It is in this way that custom dulls the edge of our feelings. Their degrees correspond to the agitation of parts of the brain. This agitation diminishes with frequent repetition, and as a result the degrees of feeling also diminish. But if pain or joy were communicated to us at the same degree for a hundred consecutive years, we would be as unhappy or as happy in the hundredth year as on the first day. This plainly shows that a creature can be happy with a continuous good, or unhappy with a continuous evil, and that the alternative that Lactantius speaks of is a bad solution. It is not based either upon the nature of good and evil, or upon that of the subject who receives them, or upon that of the cause which produces them. Pleasure and pain are no less proper to be communicated the second moment as the first, the third moment as the second, and so forth. Our soul is as susceptible of them after it has experienced them one moment, as it was before having experienced them; and God who gives them is not less capable of producing them the second time than the first one. This is what we learn from the natural ideas we have of these objects. Christian theology invincibly confirms this, in that it tells us that the torments of the damned will be eternal and continuous, and as strong at the end of one hundred thousand years as they were the first day, and that on the contrary the joys of paradise will last forever and continuously without their strength ever diminishing. I would very much like to know whether, supposing something very simple, namely, that there were two suns in the world, one of which rose when the other set, we would not have to conclude that darkness would be unknown to mankind. According to the lovely philosophy of Lactantius, we would also have to conclude that man would not know light, would not know that it was day, that he saw objects, and so on. . . .

What I have just said invincibly proves, it seems to me, that nothing would be gained against our Paulicians if they were told that God has mixed good and evil together only because he foresaw that pure good would seem insipid to us in a short time. They could answer that this property is not contained in the idea that we have of good, and that it is in direct opposition to the usual doctrine about the happiness of paradise. And with regard to what experience teaches us only too well: (1) that the joys of this life are only felt to the degree that they deliver us from an annoying state; (2) that they entail that after them we feel a disgust no matter how short a time they have lasted; the Paulicians maintain that these phenomena are explicable only if we have recourse to their hypothesis of two principles. For if we depend, they will say, on only one cause, all powerful, infinitely good, infinitely free, and which universally disposes of all beings according to the good pleasure of its own will, then we ought not to feel any evil, all our goods ought to be pure, and we ought never to experience the least disgust in them. The author of our being, if he is infinitely beneficent, ought to take continual pleasure in making us happy and in preventing everything that might trouble or diminish our pleasure. That is an essential characteristic contained in the idea of supreme goodness. The fibers of our brains cannot be the cause of God's diminishing our pleasures; for according to you he is the sole author of matter, he is all powerful, and nothing prevents him from acting in accord with the full extent of his infinite goodness. He need only will that our pleasures not depend on the fibers of our brains; and if he wishes that they so depend, he can preserve these fibers forever in the same state. He need only will either that they not wear out, or that the damage they suffer be quickly repaired. Therefore you can only explain our experiences by the hypothesis of two principles. If we feel pleasure, it is the good principle that gives it to us. But if we do not feel it in completely pure fashion, and if we are soon disgusted with it, it is because the bad principle thwarts the good one. The latter acts in the same way. It makes it such that pain is less aggravating when we are used to it, and it always gives us some resource even when we are afflicted with the greatest evils. This, and the good use that is often made of adversity, and the bad use that is often made of good fortune are phenomena that are admirably explained by the Manichean hypothesis. These are the things that lead us to suppose that the two principles have made an agreement that reciprocally limits their operations. The good one cannot do us all the good that it wishes to. It was necessary that in order to do us much good, it consented that its adversary do us as much harm; for without this agreement chaos would always have remained chaos, and no creature would ever have experienced what is good. Thus the supreme goodness, finding a better means of satisfying itself in seeing the world sometimes happy and sometimes unhappy than in never seeing it happy, made an agreement that produced the mixture of good and evil that we find in the human world. By ascribing to your principle an almighty power and the glory of alone enjoying eternity, you have deprived it of an attribute that precedes all others, for *optimus,* the best, always precedes *maximus,* the greatest, in the manner of the most learned nations when they speak of God. You suppose that with nothing to prevent him from bestowing good things on his creatures, he oppresses them with evils; and if he raises any of them above this state of affairs, it is in order that they may fall further. We clear him of any guilt on this score. We explain it without impeaching his goodness and saying of it what can be said of the inconstancy of Fortune, the jealousy of Nemesis, and of the continual game that Aesop makes the occupation of God. He elevates, Aesop says, the things that are low and abases those that are high. We say, however, that he could not obtain a better agreement from his adversary. His goodness went as far as it could. If he does not give us more good, it is because he cannot. Thus we have nothing to complain about.

Who will not admire and deplore the fate of our reason? Behold that here the Manicheans, with a completely absurd and contradictory hypothesis, explain experiences a hundred times better than do the orthodox, with their supposition so just, so necessary, and so very true of an infinitely good and all-powerful first principle.

Let us show by means of another example the lack of success the Fathers have had in their dispute with the heretics regarding the origin of evil. Here is a passage from St. Basil: "But to say that evil did not proceed from God is a pious assertion; for no contrary can arise from its contrary. . . . But if evil is not innate, you will say, and does not come from God, then where does it come from? For nobody alive will deny that evil does exist. What then must be said? My answer is that evil is not a living essence, endowed with a soul, but that it is a quality of the soul, contrary to virtue, planted in the slothful and lazy because they have departed from good. Do not therefore look around and seek for evil elsewhere, nor imagine that there is a first principle of malignity, but let everyone acknowledge himself as the author of his own wickedness. For those things that happen to us are partly the result of nature—for example, old age and illness—and they are partly the result of their own natures—for example, sudden accidents from external causes . . .—but, also, they are partly the result of activities within our own powers—such as our ability to mortify our desires, to moderate our pleasures, to govern our passions, to lay our hands on someone who has injured us, to speak the truth or to lie, to be meek and even-tempered, or to be filled with pride or arrogance. Therefore do not look anywhere else for the source of those things of which you yourself are the master, but know that what is properly evil results from free will and choice."[22] The German theologian[23] who cites this passage is right in saying that this Father grants the Marcionites more than he ought to; for St. Basil does not even want to admit that God is the author of physical evil, such as illness and old age, or of the hundreds of things that result from external causes and that happen unxpectedly. Thus, in order to extricate himself from difficulties, he adopts errors, and maybe even heresies. But there is another fault in his answer. He imagines that he will get himself out of difficulties by exonerating Providence, provided that he claims that vices have their origin in the human soul. How is it that he did not see that he is either evading the difficulty or offering as his solution the very point in which the chief difficulty lies? The claim of Zoroaster, Plato, Plutarch, the Marcionites, the Manicheans, and in general of all of those who admit a naturally good principle and a naturally bad one, both eternal and independent, is that without this supposition one cannot give an account of how evil came into the world. You answer that it came by way of man. But how can this be, since according to you man is the product of an infinitely holy and infinitely powerful being? Would the product of such a cause not be good? Could it be other than good? Is it not more impossible that darkness should result from light, than that it be possible that the

---

22 Basil, *Hexaëmeron*. Homil. II, according to Tobias Pfanner, *System. Theologiae Gentilis,* Chap. IX.

23 Tobias Pfanner, *ibid*.

product of such a principle be bad? That is where the difficulty lies.
St. Basil could not be unaware of it. Why, then, does he say so coldly
that we only have to search for evil inside man? But who put it there?
Man himself in misusing the grace of his creator, who, being supreme
goodness, had produced him in a state of innocence. If you give this
answer you are begging the question. You are disputing with a Manichean who maintains that two contrary creators were involved in the
production of man and that man has received what is good from the
good principle, and what is bad from the bad principle; and you
reply to his objections by supposing that man's creator is one being,
supremely good. Does this not amount to giving your own thesis for
an answer? It is obvious that St. Basil argues badly. But since this is a
problem that reduces all philosophy to helplessness, he should retire
into his fortress; that is to say, he should have proven by the Word
of God that the author of all things is one, and infinite in goodness
and in all kinds of perfections; that man, having come from his hands
both innocent and good, lost his innocence and his goodness by his
own doing. This is the origin of moral and physical evil. Let Marcion
and let all the Manicheans reason as much as they please in order
to show that under an infinitely good and holy Providence this fall
of innocent man could not happen. They will be arguing against a
matter of fact, and consequently they will make themselves ridiculous.
I am always supposing that they are such people who may be reduced
by *ad hominem* arguments to acknowledge the divinity of the Old
Testament. For if one had to deal with Zoroaster or Plutarch, it would
be another matter.

In order that one may see that it is not without reason that I am
urging that these sectarians should be opposed only with the maxim,
"From the act to the potency is a valid inference," and this short en-
thymeme, "This has happened, therefore this is not contrary to the
holiness and goodness of God," I will show that one cannot enter into
this dispute on any other grounds without some disadvantage. The
reasons for the permission of sin which are not drawn from the mysteries revealed in Scripture have this defect: that no matter how good
they are, they can be opposed by other reasons both more convincing
and more in conformity with the ideas we have of order. For example,
if you say that God has permitted sin in order to manifest his wisdom,
which shines forth more in the midst of the disorders that man's
wickedness produces every day than it would in a state of innocence,

you will be answered that this is to compare God either to a father who allows his children to break their legs so that he can show everyone his great skill in mending their broken bones, or to a king who allows seditions and disorders to develop through his kingdom so that he can gain glory by overcoming them. The conduct of this father and this monarch is so contrary to the clear and distinct ideas by which we judge goodness and wisdom and in general all the duties of a father and a king, that our reason cannot conceive how God could act in this way. But, you will say, the ways of God are not our ways. Stop at this point, it is a text of Scripture,[27] and do not reason any further.[28] Do not tell us any more that without the Fall of the first man the justice and mercy of God would have remained unknown, for you will be answered that nothing could have been easier than to have made man know these two attributes. The idea alone of a supremely perfect being clearly teaches sinful man that God possesses all of the virtues that are worthy of an entity that is infinite in all respects. How much more would it have taught an innocent man that God is infinitely just? But had he never punished anyone, this very state of affairs would have made his justice known. This would have been a continuous act, a perpetual exercise of that virtue. No one would have deserved to be punished; and consequently, the prevention of all punishment would have been an exercise of justice. Please tell me your answer to this: There are two princes, one of whom lets his subjects fall into a miserable state, so that he can rescue them from it when they have languished there long enough; and the other keeps them in a prosperous state. Is not the latter better and even more merciful than the former? Those who teach the doctrine of the Immaculate Conception of the Virgin demonstratively prove that God poured out his mercy and the benefits of redemption upon her more than upon any other members of the human race. One does not have to be a metaphysician to know this; a peasant clearly knows that it is a greater act of goodness to prevent a man from falling into a ditch than to let him fall into it and then rescue him an hour later, and that it is much better to prevent a murderer from killing anyone than to break him on the wheel after he has been allowed to do his killing. All of this warns us that we should not dispute with the

---

27 Isaiah 55:8. ["For my thoughts are not your thoughts, neither are your ways my ways, saith the Lord."]
28 See remark M of this article, toward the end [pp. 191ff].

Manicheans until we have established the doctrine of *the elevation of faith and the abasement of reason*.[31]

Those who say that God permitted sin because he could not have prevented it without destroying the free will that he had given to man, and which was the best present he made to him, expose themselves greatly. The reason they give is lovely. It has a *je ne sais quoi*, an undefinable something, that is dazzling. It has a grandeur. But in the end it can be opposed by arguments more easily understood by all men, and based more on common sense and the ideas of order. Without having read the fine treatise of Seneca on benefits, everyone knows by the natural light that it is essential to a benefactor not to bestow gifts that he knows will be abused in such a manner that they will only serve to bring about the ruin of the person to whom they are given. There is no enemy so impassioned, if this were the case, who would not load his opponent with gifts. It is the essence of a benefactor to spare nothing to see that his bounty makes the person he bestows it upon happy. If he were able to bestow upon him the knowledge of how to make good use of it, and he refused to do so, he would be a poor benefactor indeed. He would not be any better if, being able to keep the person he was helping from making bad use of his gifts, he did not do so by ridding him of his bad inclinations. These are notions as well known to ordinary people as to philosophers. I admit that if one could only prevent the bad use of a gift by breaking the arms and legs of the recipients or by putting them in leg irons in a dungeon, one would not be obliged to prevent it. It would be better to refuse to give them the gift. But if one can prevent it by changing the heart and giving man a taste for good things, one ought to do so. Now this is what God could easily do if he so wished. . . . There is no good mother who, having given her daughters permission to go to a dance, would not revoke that permission if she were assured that they would succumb to temptations and lose their virginity there. And any mother who, knowing for sure that this would come to pass, allowed them to go to the dance and was satisfied with exhorting them to be virtuous and with threatening to disown them if they were no longer virgins when they returned home, would, at the very least, bring upon herself the just charge that she loved neither her daugh-

---

31 Amyraut has produced a book that has this title. [Moïse Amyraut was a leading French Protestant theologian who taught at the Academy of Saumur.]

ters nor chastity. It would be in vain for her to try to justify herself by saying that she had not wished to restrain the freedom of her daughters or to indicate that she distrusted them. She would be told this type of behavior was preposterous and was more indicative of a provoked, cruel stepmother than of a mother, and that it would have been better to keep her daughters in her sight than to give them the privilege of freedom and the signs of her confidence for such a bad end. This shows the temerity of those who offer us as an explanation the consideration that God had for the first man's free will. They would be better off believing and keeping quiet than offering reasons that can be refuted by the examples I have just made use of. Cotta, in a book of Cicero's, offers so many arguments against those who say that the faculty of reason is a gift the gods bestowed upon man, that Cicero did not find himself capable of resolving these difficulties. For if he had found that he was capable of so doing, he would have refuted them, since his Academic skeptical spirit was in its element when he was able to show that the pro and the con could be maintained ad infinitum. In view of this, since he let the arguments of Cotta go without any answer, we have to assume that he did not know what to say against them. Cicero, however, was one of the greatest geniuses there ever was. Cotta, having shown that reason is an accomplice in all crimes, and that thus the gods should have given it to us if they wanted us to commit evil, then offered the usual solution, which is that men make bad use of the heavenly gifts. . . . Then he replies that this misuse should have been prevented, and that men should have had a reason that would drive away evil, and that those who give what they know will be pernicious cannot be excused. He proves this by several examples. "Men should have been given such a type of reason as might have excluded vice and guilt. Where then was there room for the mistake of the gods? We leave estates to children in hopes that those children may do well, and we may be deceived. But could a god be deceived? Either as Phoebus was when he took his son Phaëton on up into his chariot, or as Neptune was, when Theseus destroyed Hippolytus after the former had been granted three free wishes by his father Neptune? These are the fictions of poets, but we wish to be philosophers, dealing with realities not fables. And yet these poetical gods would be thought culpable for bestowing these favors, had they known they would prove pernicious to their children. And if it be true. as Aristo the Chian used to say, that philosophers did harm to those who misinterpreted their good sayings (for dissolute persons might emerge from the school of Aristippus, and cruel persons from that of Zeno), undoubtedly if auditors departed corrupt because they misconstrued the philosophers' views, it would be better for the philosophers to be silent than to harm those who hear them. So, if men turn the reason, given to them with good intention by the immortal gods, into fraud and wickedness, it would be better not to give it at all than to give it to mankind. Just as a physician would be much to blame if he prescribed wine for a patient, and if he knew that the patient would drink it undiluted and would die immediately, so also would that Providence of yours be to blame if it should give reason to those who it knows would misuse it wickedly and perversely; unless perhaps you will say that it does not foresee this. I wish it were indeed so! But you will not dare to say it, for I know what a value you put upon that name [Providence]."[36] By means of these reasons it is easy to show that the first man's free will, which was preserved full and complete in him in circumstances in which he was to make use of it to bring about his own downfall, the ruin of the human race, the eternal damnation of most of his descendants, and the introduction of a terrible flood of evils, of guilt, and punishment, was not a good present at all. We will never understand that this privilege [of free will] was preserved in him as the effect of goodness and for love of holiness. Those who say that it was necessary that there be free beings so that God might be loved by a love of choice[37] are aware that this hypothesis is not satisfactory to reason. For when it is foreseen that those free beings will choose not the love of God, but sin, it is clearly seen that the desired end has disappeared, and that thus it is in no way necessary that free will be preserved. I will examine this again in remark M [p. 187]. . . .

≪-

F. *(If there had been as many disputes then about predestination as there are today.)* If the Manicheans had remained at this point, they would have given up their principal advantages. For the more terrible objections are the following ones: (1) It is incon-

---

36 Cicero, *De natura deorum* III. 31.
37 See the *Traité de morale* by Father Malebranche.

ceivable that the first man could have received the faculty for doing wrong from a good principle. This faculty is vicious; and everything that can produce bad is bad, since evil can only arise from a bad cause; and thus the free will of Adam is the result of the action of two contrary principles; insofar as it was able to move in the right way, it depended upon the good principle; but insofar as it was able to embrace evil, it depended upon the bad principle. (2) It is impossible to understand that God only permitted sin; for a simple permission to sin adds nothing to free will and would not have enabled anyone to foresee whether Adam was going to persevere in his innocence or whether he was going to fall from it. Besides, according to the ideas we have of a created being, we cannot comprehend at all that it can be an originating source of action; that it can move itself; and that, while receiving its existence and that of its faculties every moment of its duration, while receiving it, I say, entirely from another cause, it should create in itself any modalities by virtue of something that belongs exclusively to itself. These modalities must be either indistinct from the substance of the soul, as the new philosophers claim, or distinct from the soul's substance, as the Peripatetics assert. If they are indistinct, then they can only be produced by the cause that is able to produce the substance of the soul itself. Now it is obvious that man is not this cause and that he cannot be it. If they are distinct, they are created beings, beings produced from nothing, since they are not composed of the soul, or of any other pre-existent nature. They can then only be produced by a cause that can create. Now all the sects of philosophy agree that man is not such a cause and that he cannot be one. Some contend that the motion which pushes him comes from causes other than himself, but that, nonetheless, he can stop it and fix it upon a particular object.[39] This is contradictory, since it does not require any less force to stop something moving than to move something at rest. Seeing therefore that a creature cannot be moved by a simple permission to act, and that it does not have the principle of motion in itself, it must necessarily be the case that God moves it. Therefore, he does something more than just permitting it to sin. (3) This may be shown by a new reason, namely, that one cannot comprehend that a simple permission would bring contingent events out of the class of things that are just possible, or that this

---

[39] Father Malebranche in *Traité de la nature et de la grace*.

would put the divinity in a position of being completely sure that the creature will sin. A simple permission cannot be the basis for divine foreknowledge. It is this fact that has led most theologians to suppose that God has made a decree that declares that the creature will sin. This, according to them, is the foundation of foreknowledge. Others claim that the decree declares that the creature will be placed in the circumstances in which God has foreseen that it would sin. Thus some contend that God foresaw the sin by reason of his decree, and others contend that he made the decree because he had foreseen the sin. No matter how it is explained, it obviously follows that God wished that man sin, and that he preferred this to the perpetual duration of innocence, which was so easy for him to bring about and ordain. Reconcile this, if you can, with the goodness that he ought to have for his creatures, and with the infinite love that he ought to have for holiness. (4) If you join with those who come closest to exonerating providence, by saying that God did not at all foresee the Fall of Adam, you will gain very little; for at the very least he certainly knew that the first man ran the risk of losing his innocence and introducing into the world all the evils of punishment and guilt that followed his revolt. Neither his goodness, nor his holiness, nor his wisdom could allow that he risked these events; for our reason convinces us in a most evident manner that a mother, who would allow her daughters to go to a ball when she knew with certainty that they ran a great risk of losing their honor there, would show that she loved neither her daughters nor chastity. And if one supposes that she possesses an infallible preservative against all temptations and that she does not give it to her daughters when she sends them to the dance, one then knows with complete assurance that she is guilty and that she hardly cares whether her daughters keep their virginity. Let us push this comparison a little further. If this mother went to the ball, and if she should see and hear through a window that one of her girls was defending herself only weakly in the corner of a study against the demands of a young lover; if she should see that her daughter was but a step away from giving in to the desires of her tempter, and if she would not go to her aid and rescue her from that trap, would we not rightly say that she would be acting like a cruel stepmother and that she would be quite capable of selling her own daughter's honor?[40]

---

40 See below, footnote 50 [p. 184].

Now this is the picture of God's conduct that the Socinians paint. They cannot say that he only knew of the sin of the first man as a possible event. He knew all the stages of the temptation, and he must have known a moment before Eve succumbed that she was going to ruin herself. He must have known it with such certitude, I say, that it makes it inexcusable that the evil was not prevented, and he cannot make the claim that, "I had reason to believe that this would not happen; I still had great hopes." There are no people so little experienced who, without seeing what goes on in the heart, cannot tell by signs when a woman is ready to yield, if they should happen to see through a window how she defends herself when her fall is imminent. The moment of consent is preceded by certain signs that cannot be deceptive. With much stronger reason, God, who knew all Eve's thoughts as they were formed (the Socinians do not take this knowledge away from him), could not doubt that she was about to succumb. He therefore wished to let her sin. He wished this, I say, at the very time that he foresaw that she would certainly sin. Adam's sin was still more certainly foreseen, for Eve's example gave some light for better foreseeing the Fall of her husband. If it had been God's purpose to preserve man and his innocence and to keep out all the misfortunes that would be the infallible result of sin, would he not have at least fortified the husband after his wife had fallen? Would he not have given him another wife who was sound and perfect instead of the one who allowed herself to be seduced? Let us say then that the Socinian system, in depriving God of foreknowledge, reduces him to slavery and to a pitiful form of government, and does not remove the great difficulty which it ought to and which forces these heretics to deny the foreknowledge of contingent events.[42]

I refer you to a professor of theology, who is still alive,[43] who has shown as clearly as day that neither the method of the Scotists, nor that of the Molinists, nor that of the Remonstrants, nor that of the Universalists, nor that of the Pajonists, nor that of Father Malebranche, nor that of the Lutherans, nor that of the Socinians can resolve the objections of those who impute the introduction of sin to

---

[42] See Arnauld, *Réflexions sur le système du P. Malebranche,* Bk. I, chap. 13, where he shows that, unless God combines by particular wills the wills of men and the movements of matter, the events that are called contingent would be so even with respect to God.

[43] I am writing this at the beginning of April 1696.

God, or of those who claim that its introduction is not compatible with his goodness, or his holiness, or his justice.[44] Inasmuch as this professor finds nothing better elsewhere, he keeps to the hypothesis of St. Augustine, which is the same as that of Luther and Calvin, and as that of the Thomists and the Jansenists. He keeps to it, I say, "discomforted with the amazing difficulties" he has set forth in it, and "overwhelmed by the weight of them." Since Luther and Calvin appeared on the scene, I do not believe a year has gone by without someone accusing them of making God the author of sin. The professor of whom I am speaking admits that the accusation is just with regard to Luther. The Lutherans nowadays make the same claim about Calvin. The Roman Catholics make the claim about both of them. The Jesuits say it is the case with Jansenius. Those who are somewhat fair and moderate do not take as insincere the protestation that the adversary makes that he does not impute man's sin to God, that he does not make God the author of it. They are quite willing to agree that he does not teach this formally and that he does not see everything that his doctrine involves; but they add that a "protestation contrary to fact proves nothing," and that if he will take the trouble to set down exactly what God would have had to do in order to be the author of Adam's sin, he will find that, according to his own view, God has done everything necessary to accomplish that. "You therefore act," they add, "just the opposite of Epicurus. The latter basically denied that there were any gods, and yet he said that there were some. You, on the contrary, deny verbally that God is the author of sin, but, at bottom, you teach it."

Let us come at last to the text of this remark. The disputes that have arisen in the West among Christians since the Reformation have so clearly shown that a man does not know what course to take if he wants to resolve the difficulties about the origin of evil, that a Manichean would be much more formidable than previously; for he would refute each side by the others. "You have used up," he would tell us, "all your mental ability. You have invented something called

---

44 Jurieu, *Jugement sur les méthodes rigides et relâchées d'expliquer la providence et la grace.* See above, article "Nihusius," footnote 36. [Bayle is again trying to needle his enemy Jurieu. The translator's comments following footnote 36 (p. 165) describe this work of Jurieu and the role the work played in the Bayle-Jurieu controversy.]

*scientia media** as a *deus ex machina* to get you out of your chaos.
This invention is chimerical. It cannot be understood how God could
see the future other than in his decrees or in the necessity of causes. It
is no less incomprehensible in metaphysics than in ethics that he who
is goodness and holiness itself should be the author of sin. I refer you
back to the Jansenists. See how they attack your 'middle science' both
by direct proofs and by throwing your arguments back at you; for it
does not prevent all the sins and miseries of man from proceeding
from the free choice of God; nor does it prevent one from comparing
God—Absit verbo blasphemia [I mean this without blasphemy], see
footnote 50—to a mother, who, knowing with certainty that her
daughter would give up her virginity if, at such a time and in such
a place, she were asked by a certain person, should then arrange that
interview, lead her daughter there, and leave her to conduct herself
as she sees fit. The Socinians, overwhelmed by this objection, try to
get out from under it by denying foreknowledge. But they have the
disgrace of seeing that their hypothesis vilifies the government of
God without exonerating him of the guilt, and that it does not at all
avoid the comparison of this mother. . . . I refer them to the Protestants
who have knocked them down and demolished them. As to absolute
decrees, the certain source of foreknowledge, take a look, I beg of
you, at the way the Molinists and the Remonstrants attack them.
There is a theologian as resolute as Bartolus, who admits, almost with
tears in his eyes, 'that there is no one more perplexed than he by the
difficulties' of these decrees, and that he remains in this condition only
because he found that, when he wished to adopt more mitigated methods, 'he found himself even more overwhelmed by these same pres-
sures.'[51] He explained himself even more forcefully elsewhere on
this, and you cannot deny that he has completely and thoroughly
refuted all these methods. And, consequently, you have no other
recourse unless you adopt my system of the two principles. In that
way you will get yourself out of the problem. All the difficulties will
vanish. You will fully exonerate the good principle, and you will

---

* [This refers to the Molinist doctrine.]

[50] This comparison has shocked several Protestants. But I beg them to
consider that it is only to give the Jesuits and the Arminians some of their
own medicine. They make the most horrible comparisons in the world
between the God of the Calvinists, as they say, and Tiberius, Caligula, etc.
It is good to show them that they can be fought with the very same weapons.

[51] Jurieu, *Jugement sur les méthodes.*

realize that you are only passing from a less reasonable Manicheanism to a more reasonable one; for if you examine your own system
carefully, you will see that you, just as I, admit that there are two
principles, one of goodness, and one of badness; but instead of locat-
ing them, as I do, in two subjects, you combine them together in one
and the same substance, which is monstrous and impossible. According to you, the sole principle, which you admit, desired from all eternity that man should sin, and that the first sin should be contagious,[53]
that it should ceaselessly and endlessly produce all imaginable crimes
over the entire face of the earth. In consequence of which he prepared
all the misfortunes that can be conceived for the human race in this
lifetime—plague, war, famine, pain, trouble—and after this life a
hell in which almost all men will be eternally tormented in such a
way that makes our hair stand on end when we read descriptions of
it. If such a principle is also perfectly good and loves holiness infinitely, do we not have to recognize that one and the same God is
simultaneously perfectly good and perfectly bad, and that he loves
vice no less than he loves virtue? Now is it not more reasonable to
divide these opposing qualities and to attribute all the good to one
principle and all the bad to another principle? Human history will
prove nothing to the disadvantage of the good principle. I do not
say, as you do, that of his own accord, of his pure and free will, and
solely because it had been his pleasure, he submitted the human race
to sin and misery when it was within his power to make mankind
happy and holy. I suppose that he only consented to this in order to
avoid a greater evil, and that he did it as if he were defending himself. This exonerates him. He saw that the evil principle wanted to
destroy everything. He opposed it as much as he could and managed
to achieve the state of affairs to which things are now reduced. He
acted as a monarch who, in order to avoid the destruction of all his
dominions, is obliged to sacrifice a part of them for the good of the
rest. It is a great inconvenience, which at first frightens human reason, to speak of a first principle and of a necessary being as an entity
that does not do all that it wishes to, and that is constrained to submit to combined actions by virtue of its own impotency. But it is still

---

[53] According to the Molinists, God decreed that men be placed in the
circumstances in which he knew with complete certainty that they would
sin, and that he could have either placed them in more favorable circumstances, or not placed them in those particular ones.

a greater imperfection to be able from wantonness to resolve to commit evil when one was capable of doing good." That is what that heretic could say. Let us conclude by showing the good purpose for which I made these remarks.

What use can be made of the dispute reported above. It is more useful than one would think to humiliate man's reason by showing him with what force the most foolish heresies, like those of the Manicheans, may play games with it in order to confuse the most fundamental truths. This ought to teach the Socinians, who want reason to be the rule of faith, that they are throwing themselves onto a road to perplexity that is only fit to lead them step by step to denying everything, or doubting everything, and that they are laying themselves open to being beaten by the most abominable people. What must be done then? Man's understanding must be made a captive of faith and must submit to it. He must never dispute about certain things. In particular, he must only fight against the Manicheans by appealing to Scripture, and by the principle of submission, as St. Augustine did. . . .

≪←

H. *(The orthodox seem to admit two first principles.)* It is a view continually spread throughout Christendom that the devil is the author of all the false religions; that he is the one who leads the heretics to dogmatize; that he is the one who inspires errors, superstitions, schisms, lewdness, avarice, intemperance, in a word, all the crimes committed among men; that he is the one who made Eve and her husband fall from the state of innocence; from which it follows that he is the source of moral evil and the cause of all of the misfortunes of man. He is then the first principle of evil; but, nonetheless, since he is neither eternal nor uncreated, he is not the basic wicked principle in the Manichean sense. This has furnished these heretics with I know not what sort of material for boasting and for insulting the orthodox. You do much more harm to the good God than we do, they could tell them, for you make him the cause of the bad principle. You claim that he is the one who has produced it, and that, having been able to stop it from taking its first step, he allowed it to usurp so great an empire on this earth with the result that the human race was divided into two cities, that of God, and that of the

devil,[75] of which the first has always been very small and was so small
for several centuries that it did not have two inhabitants while the
other had two million. We are not obliged to look for a cause that
accounts for the wickedness of our bad principle; for when an uncreated thing is such and such, it cannot be asked why it is that way.
That is its nature. One must necessarily stop there. But with regard
to the qualities of a created being, one ought to look for the reason
for them, and one can only find this in its cause. You would then
have to say that God is the author of the devil's malice, that he himself produced it such as it is, or that he sowed the seeds of it in the
soil he created. This is to do a thousand times more harm to God than
to say that he is not the only necessary and independent being. This
leads back to the objections set forth above concerning the fall of
the first man. It is not necessary to insist on this further. It is necessary to acknowledge humbly that all philosophy comes to a halt here,
and that its weakness ought to lead us to the lights of Revelation,
where we will find a sure and firm anchor. Observe that the heretics
made bad use of the passages in Holy Scripture in which the devil
is called "the prince of this world" (John 14:30) and "the god of
this world" (II Corinthians 4:4).

≪←

   M. *(However, the more one reflects . . . the more one finds that
   the natural light . . . supplies arguments that . . . entangle this
Gordian knot still more.)* I found this out by experience in rereading
this article when I had to get it ready for the second edition. Some new
thoughts occured to me[120] that convince me all over again, and more
strongly than ever, that the best answer that can be naturally[121] made
to the question, "Why did God permit man to sin," is to say, "I do
not know; I only believe that he had some reasons for it that are
really worthy of his infinite wisdom, but which are incomprehensible
to me." By offering this answer you will stop the most obstinate dis-
puters short, since if they want to continue arguing, you will leave

---

[75] See Augustine, *City of God.*

[120] See also the new remarks in the article "Origen" [not included in
these selections].

[121] That is to say, without consulting Revelation, but only philosophical
ideas.

them to talk to themselves, and they will soon be quiet. If you should enter into a dispute with them, and if you should take on the task of maintaining before them the contention that the inviolable privileges of free will constitute the real reason that led God to allow men to sin, you will have to satisfy them about the objections they will make to you on this score, and I do not know how you might be able to do this, since they would be able to offer you two objections that seem most evident to our reason:

I. The first is that since God gave being to his creatures as an effect of his goodness, he also gave them, in his role as a beneficent cause, all the perfections proper to each species. We therefore have to say that he has shown more love to those that received very excellent qualities than to those that received less excellent ones. It is then as a result of a particular goodness that he bestowed free will on men, since that quality raises them above all other beings on earth. Now it is inconceivable that a beneficent being would give such an important gift unless it would contribute greatly to the happiness of the recipient; and consequently it would have to be the case that he arranged that they gain such an advantage from it, and that he prevent them, if possible, from being desolated and completely ruined by it. If there be no other way of avoiding this result than by revoking his donation, he would have to do this. This would better preserve his character as patron and benefactor than anything else he might do. This would not involve any change with regard to the recipient and would preserve without the slightest variation the good will with which the present had been given. The same goodness that leads to giving something that one judges is capable of making the recipients happy leads to withdrawing it as soon as it is seen that it will make them unhappy; and if the benefactor has time and sufficient strength, he will not delay taking back this present until after it already has become the cause of misery. He will take it away before it does any harm. This is where the ideas of order and the notions by which we are able to judge of the essence and characteristics of goodness lead us, whether it be with regard to a creator or a creature, father, master, or king, and so on. And this is what gives rise to this dilemma; either God has given men free will as an effect of his goodness, or without any goodness. You cannot say that it was done without any goodness. Therefore you say that it was done with a great deal of goodness. But it follows necessarily then that he should have deprived them of it at any cost rather than wait until it should result in their eternal damnation through the production of sin, a monstrosity that he abhors essentially. And if he was so patient as to leave so dismal a present in their hands until the evil occurred, it is a sign either that his goodness had changed even before they left the right road, which is something that you would not dare say; or that free will was not given to them as the effect of goodness, which is contrary to the supposition granted in the dilemma stated above.

There are conditions involving strict obligation. They ought not to be dispensed with except in cases of necessity. But when these cases occur, the conditions ought to be set aside. A son who sees his father about to jump out a window, either in a fit of frenzy, or because he is temporarily insane, would do well to bind him with chains if there be no other way to restrain him. If a queen fell into the water, the first servant who could get her out, either by embracing her or by pulling her by the hair, even though he might pull off more than half of it, would do very well in so acting. She would certainly not complain that he failed to show respect for her. And what excuse could be more frivolous for allowing a finely dressed lady to fall down a precipice than to say that she could only be stopped by putting her ribbons and her coiffure in disarray? In such situations the force and violence used on people is an effect of goodness; and even if people were snatched from the jaws of death against their own wills, it would be an act of charity to do so, even if one ran the risk of dislocating their limbs if they could not be saved in any other way. Those who are saved will be the first to give thanks when their frenzy is over. The maxim that to save a man against his will is the same as killing him does not apply here; and the strongest advocates of tolerance will tell you that the alleged commandment, "Compel them to come in," ought to be obeyed in the literal sense if the sole, sure, and certain way of saving heretics were to make them go either to Protestant services or to Mass by using a pitchfork. I offer the testimony of the philosophical commentator. "If I saw," says he,[124] "a man in front

---

[124] *Commentaire philosophique sur ces paroles de Jesus Christ, Constrains les d'entrer,* Pt. III. [The philosophical commentator is, of course, Pierre Bayle himself. The passage in question is from section 8 of the *Commentaire philosophique,* Pt. III, in *Œuvres diverses* (The Hague, 1727), II, 452–453. The passage is then followed by Bayle's analysis showing why this scheme of saving souls by force would not work (though it was being tried

of the door of a house who was very wet during a heavy rain, and if, out of pity for him, I wished to rescue him from the sorry situation in which I found him, I could make use of these two means: either I could ask him to come into the house, or I could take him by the arm, if I was stronger than he, and push him inside. These two methods are equally good for achieving the desired goal, that of preventing the man from being drenched; and in terms of that goal, it is of little importance whether he enters the house willingly, or whether he is forced to; for whether he enters by his own action, or whether he waits until he is asked, or whether he is pushed, he is equally protected from the rain. If hell could be avoided in the same way, I grant that those who are trying to convert people would be on firm ground; for if it sufficed to accomplish that end that a person be under the vaults of a church, then it would matter little whether he came into it voluntarily or were dragged in with hands and feet bound; and thus the strongest laborers or porters in the world should be used to grab heretics as soon as they turn up on the streets and to transport them on their shoulders to the nearest church; and still further, if necessary, they should blast open the heretics' doors, pull them from bed, in order to carry them quickly to some church." What we have said about the right that man has, by virtue of the laws of charity, to annoy and attack people in order to prevent their deaths by these means, is even truer with respect to fathers. They would neglect all their duties if they did not take a knife or a sword away from a son when they saw he was about to make bad use of it to wound himself. They would be obliged, in spite of his tears, to snatch away those presents; and if they saw him on the verge of ruining his life by some disastrous course of action, they ought to restrain him from it by force, even by appealing to secular authority. If they neglect the welfare of their sons, and if they claim that they do not want to use force since they would thereby be treating their sons as if they were slaves, they show either that they have no love or that they are not aware of its proper function.

---

by Catholic dragoons in France at the time). Bayle argues that those who are engaged in conversion by force also admit that a necessary condition for anyone to be converted is that the person consent to being converted. Hence, dragging people into churches and giving them the sacraments will not help to save them unless they want to be saved in this manner.]

All these things show us clearly that those who would like to submit the conduct of God's providence to the judgment of reason with respect to the allowance of the first sin would infallibly lose their cause if they had nothing to say but that the privileges of free will ought not to be violated. They would be answered: How can you conceive that God is the father of men, and yet say that he prefers to spare them the slight disturbance by making them give up a pleasant conversation in which they were about to make bad use of their freedom, than to spare them the eternal damnation they would incur by misusing their free will? Where do you find such ideas of parental goodness? To have regard for man's free will, to abstain carefully from interfering with the inclination of a man who is going to lose his innocence forever and is going to condemn himself eternally, do you call that a legitimate observation of the privileges of freedom? You would be less unreasonable if you should say to a man who had fallen down near you and had broken his leg, "What kept us from preventing your fall is that we were afraid of undoing some of the folds of your gown; we have too much respect for symmetry to do anything to disturb it, and it seemed to us that it was better to let you run the risk of breaking your bones."

I do not deny that the permission to make use of something and to abuse it has sometimes had the character of a very special favor, but then this permission carries with it the impunity for the abuse. This then has nothing to do with the present case.[126]

II. But the second item that is left for me to set forth will be more troublesome still for the defenders than was the other. I have argued up to now on this principle: When those whom one loves cannot be protected either from death, or infamy, or some other major evil unless they are made to experience a lesser pain, then one is obligated to make them experience it. To be complacent about, or tolerant of, their capricious acts or their bad inclinations would be less an act of kindness than one of cruelty; and as they would be first to get angry when they could see what the consequences would be, they would also be the first to thank those who hurt them for their own good. The self-evidence of these propositions leaps to everybody's eyes, and it can-

---

126 The right way of conferring a benefit is not to allow that it may be misused, but to add to it the art for using it correctly. Without that a present is a body without a soul, as Horace says to Tibullus (Epistles I, 4. 6). . . .

not be doubted that Adam and Eve would have looked upon God's restraining them from falling as as great a favor as the preceding ones.

That is what my first observation is based on and leads to. But now I will make use of another approach. I will grant my opponents all that they wish. I will agree that they have established that, in view of the fact that man had received the privilege of free will, he was to have complete possession and use of it, and not the slightest constraint was to be placed upon him. I will agree if they say that it was not the right time for saving someone by pulling him by the arm or by the hair, by throwing him to the ground, and by telling him, "It is hard for thee to kick against the pricks" (Acts 9:5). Let them say that free will was an absolutely inviolable barrier and a privilege that was not allowed to be challenged. I will agree. Were there not enough other means to prevent the Fall of man, even taking all this into account? It was not a question of opposing a bodily motion. Such an opposition causes pain. It was only a question of an act of the will. Now all philosophers cry out that the will cannot be constrained, . . . and there is a contradiction in saying that a volition is forced, since every act of the will is essentially voluntary. Now it is infinitely easier for God to imprint on man's soul whatever act of the will he may wish, than it is for us to fold a napkin. Therefore, etc. Here is another observation that is even stronger. All theologians agree that God can infallibly produce a good act of the will in the human soul without depriving it of its free functions. A pleasing delectation, the suggestion of an idea that weakens the impression of a tempting object, and a thousand other preliminary ways of acting on the mind and on the sensitive soul will surely make it the case that the rational soul makes good use of its freedom and directs itself toward the right road without being invincibly pushed to it. Calvin would not deny this with regard to Adam's soul during the period of his innocence; and all the theologians of the Roman Catholic Church, not even excepting the Jansenists,[129] agree to this with respect to man the sinner. They acknowledge that his actions can be meritorious although he

---

129 That is to say, by taking them at their word when they maintain that they condemn the propositions of Jansenius in the sense in which the pope has condemned them. [This was a crucial point in the dispute between the Jansenists and Rome. Rome had condemned five propositions of Jansenius, which were taken as the core of the Jansenist doctrine. Leading Jansenist theologians—e.g., Arnauld and Quesnel—refused to accept the papal con-

acts only by means of a grace, whether it be efficacious in itself, or whether it be sufficient to such a degree that it be infallibly followed by its effect. Then they have to acknowledge that a proper assistance furnished by God to Adam, or some help that was so arranged that it would have infallibly prevented his Fall, would have been in complete accord with the use of his free will, and would not have led him to feel under any constraint or difficulties, and would have left him sufficient room to act meritoriously.

Thus the opponents are driven from their defenses. Will they say, as their last resort, that God owes nothing to his creatures and that he is not obliged to supply them with a necessitating or infallible grace? But then why did they say earlier that he was obliged to have regard for human freedom? If he was obliged to preserve this prerogative for man and to abstain from interfering with it, then he has some obligations to his own creations. But, leaving this *ad hominem* argument aside, can they not be answered that, if he is in no way obligated to his creatures, he is completely obligated to himself and cannot act contrary to his essence? Now it is of the essence of a holiness[131] and of an infinite and omnipotent goodness not to permit the introduction of moral and physical evil.

Yes, they will finally say, but "Shall the thing formed say to him that formed it, 'Why hast thou made me thus?' " (Romans 9:20). This is well put, and there is where the matter should rest. We are back at the beginning of the discussion. It would have been better to have remained there; for it is useless to enter into a dispute, if, after it has gone on for some time, one is forced finally to shut oneself up in one's own thesis. The doctrine that the Manicheans oppose ought to be considered by the orthodox as a truth of fact, clearly revealed; and since it must finally be admitted that the causes and the reasons for it cannot be understood, it would be better to say this from the outset, and stop there, and allow the objections of the philosophers to be considered as vain quibblings, and to oppose nothing to them but silence along with the shield of faith.

---

demnation as a condemnation of Jansenism and insisted that they agreed that the five propositions in question were heretical in the sense condemned by the pope, but not in the sense in which they interpreted them, and as also claimed, not in the sense in which Jansenius, the late Bishop of Ypres, intended them.]

131 That is to say, it seems so to the light of our feeble reason.

Pyrrho, a Greek philosopher from Elis in the Peloponnesus, was the disciple of Anaxarchus and accompanied him as far as India. They were no doubt in the entourage of Alexander the Great, which tells us when Pyrrho flourished. He had been a painter by profession before he devoted himself to the study of philosophy. His views were hardly different from those of Arcesilaus, for he was very close to teaching, as the latter did, the theory of the incomprehensibility of all things. Everywhere he found reasons for affirming and for denying; and this is why he suspended judgment after having carefully examined all the arguments pro and con, and always concluded that the matter should be looked into further. All his life he was searching for the truth, but he always managed things so as not to grant that he had found it. Although he was not the inventor of this method of philosophizing, it nevertheless goes by his name; the art of disputing about all things and always suspending one's judgment is most commonly called "Pyrrhonism." It is rightly detested in the schools of theology (B), where it tries to gain new strength, which turns out to be only illusory. But it may have its value in making men conscious of the darkness they are in, so that they will implore help from on high and submit to the authority of the faith

≪≪

B. *(It is rightly detested in the schools of theology.)* Pyrrhonism is dangerous in relation to this divine science, but it hardly seems so with regard to the natural sciences or to the state. It does not matter much if one says that the mind of man is too limited to discover anything concerning natural truths, concerning the causes producing heat, cold, the tides, and the like. It is enough for us that we employ ourselves in looking for probable hypotheses and collecting

(C).* Since what I relate^c about a conference where two *abbés*
disputed about Pyrrhonism may perplex many of my readers, I
intend to clarify this matter in a supplement at the end of this
work [p. 421]. We must consider as bad jokes or impostures the
stories of Antigonus Carystius to the effect that Pyrrho did not
prefer one thing to another and that neither a chariot nor a
precipice could ever make him take a step forward or backward
and that his friends who followed him around often saved his
life. There is no indication that he was this mad, but it cannot
be doubted that he taught that the honor and infamy of actions
and their justice or injustice depend solely on human laws and
customs. No matter how abominable this doctrine may be, it
flows naturally from the Pyrrhonian principle that the absolute
and internal nature of objects is hidden from us and that we
can only be sure of how they appear to us in various respects.
Pyrrho's indifference was astonishing. He did not like anything,

data. I am quite sure that there are very few good scientists of this
century who are not convinced that nature is an impenetrable abyss
and that its springs are known only to Him who made and directs
them. Thus, all these philosophers are Academics and Pyrrhonists in
this regard. Society has no reason to be afraid of skepticism; for
skeptics do not deny that one should conform to the customs of one's
country, practice one's moral duties, and act upon matters on the
basis of probabilities without waiting for certainty. They could suspend
judgment on the question of whether such and such an obligation
is naturally and absolutely legitimate; but they did not suspend judgment on the question of whether it ought to be fulfilled on such and
such occasions. It is therefore only religion that has anything to fear
from Pyrrhonism. Religion ought to be based on certainty. Its aim, its
effects, its usages collapse as soon as the firm conviction of its truths
is erased from the mind. But this should not be a cause of uneasiness.
There never were, and there never will be more than a small number
of people who can be fooled by the arguments of the skeptics. The
grace of God in the faithful, the force of education in other men,

---

* [Remark C appears on p. 204.]
^c In remark B.

nor was he ever angry about anything.[f] No one was ever more completely persuaded than he of the vanity of things (F).[*] When he spoke, it did not matter to him whether anyone listened or not; and even if he saw that his audience went away, he nevertheless continued speaking. He kept house with his sister and shared even the smallest household chores with her. Those who say that he was honored with Athenian citizenship for having killed a king of Thrace are very much mistaken. Moreri has not committed many errors.

The equality he put between life and death has been praised by Epictetus, who otherwise had only the utmost contempt for Pyrrhonism.

and, even if you wish, ignorance[9] and the natural inclination to reach decisions, all these constitute an impenetrable shield against the arrows of the Pyrrhonists although this sect thinks it is more formidable today than it was in former times. We shall now see what this strange claim is based on.

About two months ago a very able man told me much about a discussion he had attended. Two *abbés*, of whom one knew only his duties and obligations and the other was a good philosopher, got into a fairly heated debate that almost became a full-fledged quarrel. The first had said rather bluntly that he could pardon the pagan philosophers for having drifted into the uncertainty of opinions but that he could not understand how there were still any miserable Pyrrhonists after the arrival of the light of the Gospel. "You are wrong," said the other, "to reason this way. Were Arcesilaus to return to this world, and were he to combat our theologians, he would be a thousand times more formidable than he was against the dogmatists of ancient Greece. Christian theology would furnish him with unanswerable arguments." All those present were much surprised to

---

[f] This should not be taken too strictly; no doubt he preferred good health to illness, and so on.

[*] [Remark F appears on p. 208.]

[9] It is a saying of Simonides that "those people are not clever enough to be deceived by a man like me." Balzac said the same thing about the girls of his village. Agesilaus complained about having to deal with opponents who did not understand enough about war, so that his stratagems were useless; he could not deceive troops who were inexperienced.

hear this, and begged the *abbé* to explain himself further, having no doubts that he had advanced a paradox that would only lead to his own confusion. Here is the answer he gave, addressing himself to the first *abbé:* "I will not make use of the advantages the new philosophy has given the Pyrrhonists. One hardly knew the name of Sextus Empiricus in our schools. The methods he had proposed so subtly for bringing about suspense of judgment were not less known than the *Terra Australis,* when Gassendi[10] gave us an abridgement of it, which opened our eyes. Cartesianism put the final touches to this, and now no good philosopher any longer doubts that the skeptics were right to maintain that the qualities of bodies that strike our senses are only appearances. Every one of us can justly say, 'I feel heat in the presence of fire,' but not, 'I know that fire is, in itself, such as it appears to me.' This is the way the ancient Pyrrhonists spoke. Today the new philosophy speaks more positively. Heat, smells, colors, and the like, are not in the objects of our senses. They are modifications of my soul. I know that bodies are not at all as they appear to me. They would have wished to exempt extension and motion, but they could not. For if the objects of our senses appear colored, hot, cold, odoriferous, and yet they are not so, why can they not appear extended and shaped, in rest and in motion, though they are not so?[11] Still further, sense objects cannot be the cause of my sensations. I could therefore feel heat and cold, see colors and shapes, extension and motion, even though there were no bodies in the universe. I have there-

---

10 In his work, *De fine logicae,* chap. 3, pp. 72ff., in his *Opera* (1658 ed.), Vol. I. [The *De fine logicae* is Book II of Part I of the *Syntagma philosophicum.* Bayle's *abbé* is wrong about the facts here. Sextus was published in Latin in the sixteenth century, and in Greek in 1621, several decades before the Gassendi work referred to here. See chap. 2 of R. H. Popkin, *History of Scepticism from Erasmus to Descartes* for the various sixteenth- and seventeenth-century editions, summaries, citations, etc., of Sextus, and the subsequent chapters for indications of the widespread knowledge of and interest in his works in the late sixteenth and early seventeenth centuries. Gassendi was certainly not one of the first to set forth Sextus' views, but he is one of those who made the most forceful and fruitful use of them after the appearance of the Greek edition of 1621.]

11 The Abbé Foucher proposed this objection in his *Critique de la recherche de la vérité.* Father Malebranche made no reply to it. He realized how strong it was. See footnote 12, following.

[Foucher's argument played a great role in the history of subsequent philosophy, especially through Bayle's use of it here. Berkeley and Hume took

fore no good proof of the existence of bodies.[12] The only proof that could be given me of this 'would be based on the contention that God would be deceiving me if he imprinted in my mind the ideas that I have of bodies without there actually being any.[13] But this proof is very weak; it proves too much. Ever since the beginning of the world, all mankind, except perhaps one out of two hundred millions, has firmly believed that bodies are colored, and this is an error. I ask, does God deceive mankind with regard to colors? If he deceives them about this, what prevents him from so doing with regard to extension? This second deception would not be less innocent, nor less compatible with the nature of a supremely perfect being than the first deception is. If he does not deceive mankind with regard to colors, this is no doubt because he does not irresistibly force them to say, 'These colors exist outside of my mind,' but only, 'It seems to me that there are colors there.' The same thing could be said with regard to

---

it over, apparently from this text, and from a somewhat similar discussion in the article "Zeno of Elea," remark G (p. 359), as the basis of their critiques of the distinction between primary and secondary qualities.

[Simon Foucher (1644–1696), canon of the Cathedral of Dijon, was a relatively obscure skeptic who took it upon himself to revive the skepticism of the Academy. He was a friend of Leibniz and Huet and the first critic of Malebranche. (Many of Leibniz' most important articles are answers to Foucher.) Bayle read Foucher's first attack on Malebranche in 1675 shortly after it appeared; and, though almost everyone else seemed to ignore it, Bayle apparently remembered it and incorporated it into a portion of his devastating critique of modern philosophy here and in the article "Zeno of Elea."

[On Foucher, see R. H. Popkin, "L'Abbé Foucher et le problème des qualités premières," *Dix-Septième Siècle,* No. 33 (1957), 633–647; and Richard A. Watson's article, "Foucher," in the forthcoming *Encyclopedia of Philosophy.* On the impact of Bayle's use of Foucher's argument, see R. H. Popkin, "Berkeley and Pyrrhonism," *Review of Metaphysics,* V (1951–1952), 223–226; and "Pierre Bayle's Place in 17th Century Scepticism," in *Pierre Bayle, Le Philosophe de Rotterdam,* ed. P. Dibon (Amsterdam, 1959), pp. 1–19, esp. pp. 4–5 and note 9 (this article deals at length with the arguments in "Pyrrho," remarks B and C); and R. A. Watson, "The Breakdown of Cartesian Metaphysics," *Journal of the History of Philosophy,* I (1963), 177–198.]

[12] Father Malebranche, in *Eclaircissement sur la recherche de la vérité,* shows that "it is extremely difficult to prove that there are bodies and that faith alone can convince us that bodies actually exist."

[13] Cf. chap. 28 of Arnauld's *Traité des vrayes & des fausses idées,* where he refutes the above-mentioned *Eclaircissement* of Father Malebranche, by reasons all based on this principle.

extension. God does not irresistibly force you to say, 'There is some,' but only to judge that you are aware of it and that it seems to you that there is some. A Cartesian has no more difficulty in suspending judgment on the existence of extension than a peasant has in forbearing affirming that the sun shines, that snow is white, and so on. That is why, if we deceive ourselves in affirming the existence of extension, God would not be the cause, since you grant that he is not the cause of the peasant's errors. These are the advantages that the new philosophers would give to the Pyrrhonists and which I will not use here."

Right afterwards, the philosophical *abbé* declared to the other that if one had any hopes of victory over the skeptics, one would have to prove to them first of all that truth is certainly recognizable by certain marks. These are commonly called the criterion of truth *(criterium veritatis)*. You could rightly maintain to him that self-evidence *(l'évidence)* is the sure characteristic of truth; for if self-evidence were not, nothing else could be.* "So be it," he will say to you. "It is right here that I have been waiting for you. I will make you see that some things you reject as false are as evident as can be. (1) It is evident that things which are not different from a third thing are not different from each other. This is the foundation of all of our reasonings, and it is on this that we base all our syllogisms. And nevertheless, the revelation of the mystery of the Trinity assures us that this axiom is false. Invent as many distinctions as you please, you will never be

---

* [In seventeenth-century discussions, *l'évidence* is the mark of truth, which, when present, makes it impossible to doubt a proposition. In Furetière's *Dictionnaire universel* (1727 ed.), the following entries are offered to explain the meaning of *l'évidence:*

> Manifest certainty, the quality of things that makes them clearly visible and knowable, as much to the body's eyes as to its mind. The consent which arises from *l'évidence* of a thing is more unshakeable than that which faith exacts (Huet). One has to accept *l'évidence* of a demonstration. The criterion of truth is *l'évidence*, which cannot be resisted as soon as it makes itself felt in us (Le Clerc). There is a kind of *évidence* attached to truth that cannot be resisted in any way whatsoever (Abbé de St. Réal). *L'évidence* is the essential and infallible mark of truth, and if an *evidently* true proposition were ultimately false, then God himself would be the cause of our error (Le Clerc). If *l'évidence* can deceive us, then there is no longer any characteristic that distinguishes truth from falsity (La Placette).

[In this passage Bayle is going beyond any previous skeptic in challenging the contention that *l'évidence* is the criterion of truth, by suggesting that a proposition can have *l'évidence* and yet be known to be false. Sextus

able to show that this maxim of logic is not denied by this great mystery. (2) It is evident that there is no difference between an individual, a nature, and a person. However, this same mystery has convinced us that persons can be multiplied without the individuals and the natures ceasing to be unique. (3) It is evident that for a man to be really and perfectly a person, it is sufficient if a human body is united with a rational soul. However, the mystery of the Incarnation teaches us that this is not sufficient. From this it follows that neither you nor I can be certain whether we are persons; for if it were essential that a human body and a rational soul united together constitute a person, then God could never make it the case that they, thus united, did not constitute a person. It must therefore be said that personality is accidental to this union. Now every accident can be separated from its subject in several ways. It is therefore possible for God to prevent our being persons in several ways, even though we are composed of bodies and souls. And who knows whether he is not employing some of these means to deprive us of personality. Is he obliged to reveal to us all the ways he affects us? (4) It is evident that a human body cannot be in several places at the same time and that its head cannot be penetrated with all the rest of its parts into an indivisible point. And

---

Empiricus, Gassendi, Huet, and others had not challenged the criterion per se but had questioned whether the criterion could actually be applied in given cases, and whether it was in fact a usable means of ascertaining if a proposition was true. Gassendi had asked if any one could be sure that *l'évidence* was really present in a given proposition, or if it just seemed to be. Others asked if any proposition had yet been found that had *l'évidence*. Bayle went much further by raising the possibility that a proposition could have *l'évidence* and yet be false. If this were so, then no criterion would remain for ever distinguishing truth and falsity. Some of Bayle's opponents— for example, Jean le Clerc and Jean la Placette—were staggered by the implications of his challenge and saw that the salvation of rationality depended upon rebutting the discussion in "Pyrrho," remark B. Cf. La Placette, *Réponse à deux objections qu'on oppose de la part de la raison à ce que la foi nous apprend sur l'origine du mal, et sur le mystère de la Trinité* (Amsterdam, 1707), esp. Chap. II; Jean le Clerc, review of C. M. Pfaff's *Dissertationes Anti-Baelianae*, in *Bibliothèque ancienne et moderne*, XV (1721), 176–198; and "Remarques sur la réponse pour M. Bayle au sujet du III & X article de la *Bibliothèque choisie*," *Bibliothèque choisie*, X (1706), 346–426. The discussion in Hume's *Treatise of Human Nature* (Bk. I, Pt. IV, sec. 1), "Of skepticism with regard to reason," seems to be an outgrowth of Bayle's view and the criticisms of it, plus, possibly, Jurieu's solution that *sentiment* replaces *l'évidence* as our way of telling what is true.]

nevertheless, the mystery of the Eucharist teaches us that these two things happen every day.[15] From whence it follows that neither you nor I can be certain whether we are distinct from other men, or whether we are at this moment in the seraglio at Constantinople, in Canada, in Japan, and in every city of the world, under different conditions in each place. Since God does nothing in vain, would he create many men when one, created in various places and possessing different qualities according to the places, would suffice? By this doctrine we lose the truths that we found in numbers, for we no longer know how much two and three are. We do not know what constitutes unity or diversity. If we judge that John and Peter are two men, it is only because we see them in different places and because one does not have all the properties of the other. But the basis for this distinction is destroyed by the doctrine of the Eucharist. Perhaps there is only one creature in the whole universe, produced many times in several places and with a diversity of qualities. We make great rules of arithmetic as if there were many distinct things.[16] All is illusory. Not only do we not know if there are two bodies; we do not even know if there is a body and a spirit. For if matter is penetrable, it is clear that extension is only an accident of bodies, and thus that body, according to its essence, is an unextended substance. It can then have all the attributes that we conceive of as belonging to spirit—understanding, will, passions, sensations. Therefore, there is no longer any standard for discerning if a substance is spiritual by nature or if it is corporeal. (5) It is evident that the modes of a substance cannot subsist without that which they modify. Nevertheless, we know by the

---

[15] Note that it is an *abbé* who is speaking. I am obliged to add this, in the second edition, because several Protestants have been shocked to see the mystery of the Trinity and that of the Incarnation put on the same level as the dogma of the real presence and that of transubstantiation. [Transubstantiation teaches that the whole body of Christ is in every host and every particle of every host in the world. As far as Bayle is concerned, this is philosophically inconceivable. Ironically enough, these impossibilities of Catholic doctrine are also the logical consequences of the most un-Catholic system of Spinoza; see remark N (p. 300).]

[16] Note that if a body may be produced in several places, every other being—spirit, place, accident, etc.—may be multiplied in the same manner; and thus there will not be a multitude of beings, but all will be reduced to one sole created being.

mystery of transubstantiation that this is false.[17] This confuses all our ideas. There is no longer any means of defining substance; for if the accidents can subsist without any subject, then substance in its turn can subsist dependent on another substance in the way accidents do. Mind could exist in the way bodies do, just as in the Eucharist matter exists in the way minds do. The latter could be impenetrable, just as matter becomes penetrable in the mystery.* Now, if in passing from the darkness of paganism to the light of the Gospel, we have learned the falsity of so many self-evident notions and so many certain definitions,[18] what will it be like when we pass from the obscurity of this life to the glory of paradise? Is it not very obvious that we will learn the falsity of thousands of things that now seem incontestable? Let us profit from the temerity with which those who lived before the Gospel tidings affirmed to us as true certain self-evident doctrines whose falsity has been revealed to us by the mysteries of our theology.

"Let us turn to ethics. (1) It is evident that we ought to prevent evil if we can and that we sin if we allow it when we can prevent it. However, our theology shows us that this is false. It teaches us that God does nothing unworthy of his perfections when he permits all the disorders in the world which he could easily have prevented. (2) It is evident that a creature who does not exist cannot be an accomplice in an evil action. (3) And that it is unjust to punish him as an accomplice of that action. Nevertheless, our doctrine of original sin shows us the falsity of these evident truths.† (4) It is evident that we ought

---

17 See above, footnote 15.

* [In the Eucharist matter supposedly gets condensed and thus is penetrable. Bayle is showing here how the notions of matter as an impenetrable substance, and mind as an unextended one, become completely confused if transubstantiation is accepted as a genuine process.]

18 Those who accept transubstantiation place the essence of matter in the faculty of receiving extension, and so of the essence of all things, nothing being actual. Every capacity is passive. Now this capacity may consist with spirit, etc., which confounds all definitions. [That is to say, the essence of matter is not an actual extension, but a faculty, capacity, or potentiality for having extension. Because this capacity is passive, something could have it without having extension. Thus, a spirit could possess the essense of matter; and this would confound the definitions of matter.]

† [The "creature who does not exist" that Bayle is referring to is an unborn man, who will suffer the consequences of Adam's sin even though he took no part in that sin.]

to prefer what is righteous to what is profitable; and that the more holy a being is, the less it is allowed to prefer what is profitable to what is righteous. Nevertheless, our theologians tell us that God, having to choose between a world perfectly regulated, adorned with every virtue, and a world like ours, where sin and disorder predominate, preferred ours to the other as suiting better the interest of his glory. You are going to tell me that the duties of the creator should not be measured by our standards. But, if you do this, you fall into the nets of your adversaries. This is where they want you. Their major aim is to prove that the absolute nature of things is unknown to us and that we can know them only relatively. We do not know, they say, if sugar is sweet in itself. We know only that it appears sweet when it is placed on our tongues. We do not know if a certain action is righteous in itself and by its nature. We only believe that with regard to such a person, with respect to certain circumstances, it has the appearance of righteousness. But it is something else in other respects and other relations. Behold then what you are exposed to when you say that the ideas we have of justice and righteousness admit of exceptions and are relative. Consider also that the more you elevate the power or right of God not to act according to our ideas, the more you destroy the one means you have left for proving the existence of bodies, namely, that God does not deceive us, and that he would if there were no corporeal world. To show a whole people a sight or spectacle that does not exist outside their minds would be a deception. You might wish to answer that one should distinguish two cases. If a king did it, it would be a deception; but if God does it, it is not; for the obligations of a king and of God are quite different. Besides this, if the exceptions you make to the principles of morality are based on the infinite incomprehensibility of God, then I can never be sure of anything. For I can never be able to comprehend the whole extent of the rights and privileges of God. And now I conclude. If there were a mark or characteristic by which truth could certainly be known, this would be self-evidence. Now, self-evidence is not such a mark since it is compatible with falsities. Therefore, etc."

The *abbé* to whom this long disclosure was directed could hardly forbear interrupting it. He listened to it with pain; and when he saw that no one else was speaking, he flew into a rage against the Pyrrhonists and did not spare the other *abbé* for mentioning the difficulties that he drew from the systems of theology. He was answered modestly

that one knew very well that these difficulties were sophisms and
trivialities, but that it would be good if those who were so haughty
to the skeptics were aware of what the state of things is. "You believed
up to now," he was told, "that a Pyrrhonist could not puzzle you.
Answer me, therefore; you are forty-five years old; you do not doubt
this. And, if you are sure of anything, it is that you are the same
person to whom the abbey of ——— was given two years ago. I will
show you that you have no good reason at all to be certain of this. I
shall argue from the principles of our theology. Your soul has been
created. God must therefore renew its existence every moment, for the
preservation of creatures is a continual creation. How do you know
that this very morning God did not allow that soul, which he continually created from the first moments of your life until now, to fall
back into nothingness. How do you know that he has not created another soul with modifications like the ones yours had?[21] This new
soul is the one that you have at the moment. Show me what is wrong
with my argument and let those present judge the merits of my case."
A learned theologian* who was present spoke up and acknowledged
that once creation was supposed, it was just as easy for God to create
a new soul at every moment as it was to reproduce the same soul; but
that nevertheless, the ideas of his wisdom, and still more the light that
we draw from his Word, are able to give us a legitimate certainty that
we have the identical soul today that we had yesterday, the day before
that, and so on. He concluded that it was wrong to waste time disputing with the Pyrrhonists or to imagine that their sophisms can be
easily eluded by the mere force of reason; that it was necessary above
all to make them feel the infirmity of reason so that this feeling might
lead them to have recourse to a better guide, which is faith. This is
the subject of the following remark.

≪←

C. *(It may . . . make men . . . implore help from on high and*
submit to the authority of faith.) A modern writer, who has
made a more detailed study of Pyrrhonism than of other schools of

---

21 That is, with the memories he would have reproduced had he continued to create the soul of the *abbé.*

* [In Bayle's last work, the *Entretiens de Maxime et de Themiste,* it is
revealed that this "learned theologian" is none other than Pierre Bayle
himself.]

philosophy, regards it as the one least opposed to Christianity and as the one "which can most docilely accept the mysteries of our religion." He offers some reasons to confirm his opinion, and then says, "It is not, then, without basis that we believe that the skeptical system, founded on a simple recognition of human ignorance, is the least contrary of all to our beliefs and the most appropriate for receiving the supernatural lights of faith. We are saying nothing here that does not conform to the best theology since that of St. Denis teaches nothing more expressly than the feebleness of the human mind and its ignorance about all things divine. It is thus that this great teacher explains what God himself has announced through the mouth of his prophets that he made his retreat in darkness. For, since that is the case, we cannot approach near him without entering into this mysterious darkness, from which we draw this important lesson: that he may only be known obscurely, replete with enigmas or clouds, and as the Schools say, by not knowing him. But as those who have always professed humility and ignorance accommodate themselves much better than others to this spiritual darkness, the dogmatists, on the other hand, who have never dreaded anything but appearing ignorant, lose themselves in it immediately; and their presumption of having enough light in their understanding to overcome every kind of obscurity makes them more blind the more they think they are advancing into the darkness that human nature cannot penetrate. However this may be, I find that skepticism is of great value to a Christian soul when it makes him give up those doctrinaire opinions that St. Paul detests so strongly." He develops this theme at greater length and with more clarity and more forcefulness in another book.[24]

When one is able to comprehend well all the tropes set forth by Sextus Empiricus for suspending judgment, one realizes that this logic is the greatest effort of subtlety that the human mind has been able to accomplish. But, at the same time, one sees that this subtlety is in no way satisfactory. It confounds itself; for if it were solid, it would prove that it is certain that we ought to be in doubt. There would then be some certitude; there would then be a criterion or sure rule of truth. Now this ruins that system, but do not fear that it will

---

[24] In Part II of the *Prose chagrine* by François de la Mothe le Vayer. [The quotation is from *De la vertu des païens* by the same author. La Mothe le Vayer (1588–1669) was the leading skeptic of this period, following in the tradition of Montaigne.]

come to this, the reasons for doubting being themselves doubtful. We must then doubt if it is necessary to doubt. How great a chaos, and how great a torment for the human mind! It seems therefore that this unfortunate state is the most proper one of all for convincing us that our reason is a path that leads us astray since, when it displays itself with the greatest subtlety, it plunges us into such an abyss. The natural conclusion of this ought to be to renounce this guide and to implore the cause of all things to give us a better one.* This is a great step toward the Christian religion; for it requires that we look to God for knowledge of what we ought to believe and what we ought to do, and that we enslave our understanding to the obeisance of faith. If a man is convinced that nothing good is to be expected from his philosophical inquiries, he will be more disposed to pray to God to persuade him of the truths that ought to be believed than if he flatters himself that he might succeed by reasoning and disputing. A man is therefore happily disposed toward faith when he knows how defective reason is. This is why Pascal and others have said that in order to convert the libertines they should make them realize the weakness of reason and teach them to distrust it. Calvin is admirable on this subject. Here is what he says in the liturgy of Baptism,[25] that is to say, here is how he begins his instructions for those who are to be initiated into the Christian religion. "In this[26] God then admonishes us to be humble and to be displeased with ourselves; and in this he prepares us to wish for and require his grace, by which all the per-

---

* [It is interesting to compare the calm, almost tepid character of this whole presentation of the debacle of reason and the need for faith with that in Pascal's *Pensées*, No. 434 (Brunschvicg ed.), where the same case is presented with burning religious passion. On the other side, various similar passages in Bk. I, Pt. IV of Hume's *Treatise* show the despair of the skeptic without faith. See, for example, the section in Hume's conclusion to Bk. I (Selby-Bigge ed., pp. 268–269). Pascal passionately leaps toward the answer; Hume desperately tries to overcome his total skepticism and cannot. Bayle unperturbedly reveals the disastrous failure of human reason seeking to know anything or seeking to doubt all. And then he just unemotionally states the fideistic answer. On this point, see R. H. Popkin, "Bayle and Hume," *Transactions of the XIIIth International Congress of Philosophy*, Mexico City, September 1963, forthcoming.]

25 Notice that this liturgy is in use in the churches of the Geneva Confession, and thus the maxims that it contains ought to be considered as the general view of these churches and not just the private opinion of John Calvin.

26 That is, by telling us that we must be reborn.

versity and curse of our basic nature may be abolished. For we are
not ready to receive it until we have first divested ourselves of all confidence in our own virtue, wisdom, and justice, and until we have
condemned everything that is in us. However, after showing us our
unhappiness, he also comforts us by his mercy, promising to regen-
erate us by his Holy Spirit into a new life, which may be to us as an
entrance into his kingdom. This regeneration consists of two parts,
namely, denying to follow OUR OWN REASON, our pleasure, and will;
but by ENSLAVING OUR UNDERSTANDING and our heart to the wisdom
and justice of God, we mortify whatever belongs to ourselves and to
our flesh; and then that we FOLLOW THE LIGHT OF GOD to comply with
and obey whatever pleases him, as he teaches us by his Word and
leads us by his Spirit." Be this as it may, there are some able men
who claim that nothing is more opposed to religion than Pyrrhonism.[27] "It is the total extinction not only of faith but of reason; and
nothing is more impossible than to rescue those who have carried
their wild meanderings to this extent. The most ignorant persons
can be taught. The most obstinate can be convinced, the most incredulous can be persuaded. But it is impossible, I will not say to convince a
skeptic, but to reason justly against him, since it is not possible to
employ any proof against him that is not a sophism, the greatest, in
fact, of all sophisms, that of begging the question. Actually no proof
can be conclusive without supposing that anything evident is true,
that is to say, without supposing the very thing in question. For Pyrr-

---

27 Jean la Placette, *Traité de la conscience*. [La Placette, a Calvinist minister in Copenhagen, had written several works attacking skepticism, claiming that it was an enemy of true religion. In his *De insanabili romanae
ecclesiae scepticismo* (1686) he argued that the theory of religious knowledge
of the Catholics and their doctrine of the Eucharist "introduces a universal
skepticism into the whole system of Christian religion." In another work,
Traité de l'autorité des sens contre la transubstantiation (1700), he again
argued that Catholicism led to, or was really a form of, complete Pyrrhonism, which is in total opposition to the foundations of religion. The work
Bayle cites carries on this same attack. After seeing Bayle's contentions (in
this article and in various defenses of it), La Placette wrote a detailed answer to Bayle in which he tried to refute Pyrrhonism and Bayle's use of it.
The work, *Réponse à deux objections qu'on oppose de la part de la raison
à ce que la foi nous apprend sur l'origine du mal, et sur le mystère de la
Trinité*, was almost finished when Bayle died, and it only appeared in 1707.
As a result, La Placette does not appear in the many discussions in Bayle's
last works dealing with the attempts by such thinkers as Le Clerc, Bernard,
and Jacquelot to answer Bayle's views about faith and reason.]

honism, properly speaking, consists only in not admitting this fundamental maxim of the dogmatists."[28] See Vossius, who, having said
that Pyrrhonism and Epicureanism are extremely opposed to the
Christian religion, confirms his view by a passage from Clemens
Romanus. . . .

Observe that La Mothe le Vayer excludes the Pyrrhonists from the
grace that he conceded in the case of several ancient philosophers.
What he is going to say to us includes several facts that belong in
this article. "I despair of Pyrrho's salvation and that of all his disciples who have held the same views as he about the deity. It is not
that they professed atheism, as some have believed. It can be seen in
Sextus Empiricus that they admitted the existence of gods as other
philosophers did, that they worshipped them in the customary manner, and that they did not deny their providence. But, in addition to
the fact that they never acknowledged a first cause, which might have
made them despise the idolatry of their time, it is certain that they
believed nothing about the divine nature but with a suspense of judgment, nor confessed any of the things mentioned above, except in a
doubtful way, and merely to accommodate themselves to the laws and
customs of the age and the country in which they lived. Consequently,
since they did not have the slightest ray of that implicit faith on
which we have based the hope for the salvation of some heathens who
have possessed it with an extraordinary grace from heaven, I cannot
see that there is any ground for believing that any skeptic or Pyrrhonist of that type was able to avoid the road to hell."[31]

≪←

   F. *(No one was ever more completely persuaded than he of the
   vanity of things.)* He especially despised human nature, and he
was forever repeating the words of Homer, where he compares men to
leaves. . . . According to Gassendi, he liked this parallel because it indicated the mortality of mankind and that inconstancy of their opinions, turning like leaves with every change of the wind. He greatly

---

28 This maxim was formerly more potent, as, for example, when used
by the Stoics. Since then one can offer an *ad hominem* objection to the theologians that some evident propositions are false. See remark B, above, for the
dispute of the two *abbés*.
31 La Mothe le Vayer, *De la virtu des païens,* p. 226.

enjoyed other passages in Homer, where men are compared to birds and flies, and where their infirmities and childishness are described. . . . I am surprised that we are not told that he had enormous esteem for this verse of Homer:

> *For, frail men's reason daily ebbs and flows,*
> *Just as almighty God his grace bestows.*
> Odyssey XVIII. 136–137.

This signifies that the minds of men are unstable and that God gives them their provision of reason as a kind of daily bread that he renews each morning. This fits wonderfully with the hypothesis of the Pyrrhonists. They were always searching, and they were always unsteady. At every moment they felt ready to reason in a different manner as things changed. A certain doctor of theology [Jurieu] does the same thing, if one can believe his adversary [Saurin]. Above all, the latter cannot forgive the former's changes of opinions and his perpetual contradictions. He shows him that he lays down principles according to his needs; and as soon as they get in his way, he replaces them with opposite ones. To use the adversary's words, he reproaches him for "reasoning from day to day," according to the passion "whose turn it is" to be in charge of his soul. Nevertheless this theologian is very positive. He denies, he affirms professorially and promptly. The skeptics were no more cautious on these occasions than he is bold. One should not encroach on their rights but should leave them the privilege of reasoning from day to day, a privilege they assumed in Cicero's presentation. For the rest, the inconstancy of human opinions and passions is so great that it might be said that man is a small republic that often changes its magistrates.

Rangouze, a French author during the reign of Louis XIV, is not known to me for any good qualities; for we cannot call a "good quality" the industry by which an author knows how to profit from his dedicatory epistles and his flatteries. This industry, though very bad morally, may hold a very high rank among what are called "good qualities," whether natural or acquired `(A). Rangouze possessed this industry to a very high degree, as will appear from my remarks below.

«←

A. *(Among what are called "good qualities," whether natural or acquired.)* All languages suffer from sterility, some more, some less. This applies principally to things that are deprived of the perfection they ought to have. If this perfection is a moral virtue, these things are termed "bad." If it is a physical virtue, one also gives them the name "bad." On the other hand, we use the term "good" indifferently for those things that possess the moral virtue of their kind and those that possess the physical virtue of their condition. An iniquitous judge is called a bad judge, an ignorant painter is called a bad painter. Someone is called a good judge if he is fair and wise, and someone is called a good painter if he makes beautiful pictures. We are aware in these cases that we are lacking in words since we have to designate by "good" and "bad" hundreds of things of quite different natures. One ought not then to be surprised that I have classed the industry of Rangouze among the good things after excluding it from the moral virtues. It is good in the same sense that we give this praise to memory, sight, hearing, smell, and the like, when these faculties are naturally perfect. Every subject, including how to play confidence games, is a kind of perfection. Acuteness of mind is a natural advantage, while stupidity and foolishness are disadvantages. Morally, the science of deceit is neither good nor bad; but, physically, it is a very good quality, it is an advantage, it is a perfection. A simplicity of mind which is not capable of either deceiving or avoiding being deceived is, physically, a defect, a bad quality. If one puts the art of deceiving into practice, it then becomes, morally, a very bad thing. This is a punishable crime. But when certain thieves, whose industry and other natural qualities had reached a supreme degree of perfection of their kind, are punished, being broken on the wheel, this does not stop us from admiring the physical good in them. We detest only the bad use they made of it. Let us say in general that the art of growing rich, whether by finance or by business, is a good thing and a natural advantage that ought to be esteemed when separated from the abuse men may make of it. The same must be said of the industry of an author who enriches himself by his pen and by the dexterity with which he handles dedicatory epistles and copies of his books, which are sent hither and yon. You cannot deny that such a man has a kind of genius, a type of sagacity, and a fine discernment, which constitute a natural perfection that ought to be admired in certain respects, save for the right to despise and blame it as a result of its abuses and consequences. Those who are equitable do not criticize this class of authors equally. They do not try to overwhelm, with all the satirical barbs that Furetière gathered together in his *Somme dédicatoire*, those who have a large family, no patrimony, no public pension, and no other way of subsisting than by the income from their pens. The multiplicity of their dedications is excused, and people are a good deal less astonished at the fact that each of their works is divided into several volumes dedicated to several different persons, that the second editions are dedicated to new Maecenases; people are less surprised at this than at the fact that they manage to earn an honorable subsistance for their wives and children from the work of their pens, and that this is the sole means they have for keeping a large family going. They extend in their favor a rule that a wit proposed for justifying those who apply themselves to trivial matters. Here are his words: "Who does not know that authors are sometimes obliged, for very solid reasons, to devote themselves to works that do not seem very solid, and that often a hidden and unknown duty prevails, without any injustice, over a public and conspicuous one? This writer whom you blame has perhaps found that in order to restore his ruined health, to defend himself from ill fortune, or to achieve the well-being of a family of which he is the sole support, it is more practical for him to compose songs than treatises of morality or politics. If this is the case, I will say bluntly that the very principles of morality and political philosophy will require him to compose songs, and that it is the greatest injustice to condemn the occupations of others when one knows neither the motives nor the circumstances which have given rise to them."[3]

---

[3] Pellison, *Discours sur les œuvres de M. Sarrazin.*

Rorarius, HIERONYMUS, nuncio of Pope
Clement VII at the court of Ferdinand,
king of Hungary, wrote a book that deserves to be read. He
undertook to show there not only that beasts are rational creatures, but also that they make better use of reason than men do.
The circumstance that led him to write this book is curious and
extraordinary. He was engaged in a discussion in which a learned
man remarked that Charles V was not the equal of the Ottos
or Frederick Barbarossa. It took no more than this to make
Rorarius conclude that beasts are more rational than men, and
immediately he began composing a treatise on the subject (A).
This was at the time that Charles V was at war with the
Schmalkaldic League. This book is not badly written and con-

≪←

A. *(He began composing a treatise on the subject.)* There are
two dedicatory epistles at the beginning of this work, the first
dated March 1, 1547, to the Bishop of Arras, the other to Cardinal
Christopher Mandrucio, Bishop of Trent. This writing lay buried for
almost one hundred years in the dark recesses of libraries. Finally
Naudé had it printed in France and dedicated it to the Messieurs du
Puy. His dedication is dated Paris, April 9, 1645. It has been reprinted
in Holland more than once. I do not know why it has been classed
among the medical books in *Lindenius renovatus.* I am sure that I
will be accused of sometimes providing unnecessary proofs, but it
would be unjust to say this with regard to what I have put forth
concerning the motivation of this work by Rorarius. If I did not cite
his own words, one would have grounds for thinking that I made up
an imaginary writer in order to divert my readers. For what can be
more fantastic than for a man to take up the pen to place mankind
below beasts, only because a learned man is unhappy that the Emperor
Charles V aspires to be the universal monarch without having the

tains a great many unusual facts about the ingenuity of beasts and the maliciousness of men. The facts concerning the capacity of animals very much puzzle both the followers of Descartes and those of Aristotle (B). The former deny that beasts have souls;

qualities of an Otto the Great or Frederick Barbarossa? It is therefore essential that I prove what I said above. "Most illustrious Prince," Rorarius says, "A few days ago I was in a place where the emperor was the subject of discussion. In this company there was a person, in other respects of great learning, who said that he could not conceive what grounds that monarch had for attempting to subdue the Christian world; and that he ought, at least, to possess the qualities that might make him worthy of being compared to Otto or Frederick Barbarossa. I will own that I was exasperated to hear a prince, worthy of immortality, esteemed less than others who, though very illustrious, nevertheless would be inferior to his greatness if both their qualities were compared. This suggested to me an opinion that brutes frequently make better use of their reason than men, and I have attempted to prove it in two books."[2] But he was not satisfied with making this single declaration. He had already said in the other dedication, "I had written two little books wherein I showed that brutes frequently make a better use of their reason than men: and I was prompted to this in order to repress the impudence or, rather, madness of some persons, whose eyes are not strong enough to behold the glories of Charles V, the greatest of all emperors."[3] If the reader looks at the rest of this dedication, he will find the author strongly prejudiced in favor of Charles V, and a great flatterer. Many other people have been and still are like him.

≪←

B. *(The facts concerning the capacity of animals very much puzzle both the followers of Descartes and those of Aristotle.)* No proof is needed with regard to the Cartesians. Everyone knows how difficult it is to explain how pure machines can accomplish what

---

[2] Rorarius, Dedicatory Epistle to Cardinal Mandrucio.
[3] Dedicatory Epistle to the Bishop of Arras.

while the latter maintain that they have souls endowed with sensation, memory, and passions, but not reason. It is too bad that Descartes' view is so difficult to maintain and so far from being probable; for it is otherwise of very great advantage to

animals do. Therefore let us only show that the Peripatetics find themselves in great difficulties when they have to justify their attitude. Every Peripatetic who hears that beasts are only automata, or machines, objects immediately that a dog who has been beaten for touching a dish of meat will not touch it again when he sees his master threatening him with a stick. But to show that this phenomenon cannot be explained by the one who introduces it, it is sufficient to say that if this dog's action is accompanied by knowledge, then the dog must necessarily reason: he must compare the present with the past and draw a conclusion from this. He must remember both the blows he has received and why he received them. He must know that if he leaped to the dish of meat that strikes his senses, he would commit the same action for which he had been beaten; and he concludes that in order to avoid being beaten again, he ought to abstain from this meat. Now is this not definite reasoning? Can we explain this situation by simply supposing a soul that is capable of feeling, but not of reflecting on its actions, but not of recalling past events, but not of comparing two ideas, but not of drawing any conclusion? Look carefully at the examples that have been compiled and are raised against the Cartesians, you will find that they prove too much; for they prove that beasts compare ends with means, and that they prefer on some occasions what is just to what is useful; in a word, that they are guided by the rules of equity and gratitude. Rorarius says that there have been horses who have refused to mate with their mothers or, having done this unknowingly, deceived by the tricks of a groom, have thrown themselves over a cliff when they realized what had taken place. "It is recorded that a certain herdsman, though he employed his utmost endeavors, could not get a horse of his to mate with his dam; and as both were extremely beautiful, he was obliged to have recourse to fraud, he blindfolded its eyes so that the dam might not be seen; but when the bandage was taken off afterwards, by which the horse discovered what he had done, he flew to a precipice and plunged headlong, conscious of the guilt he had committed. Such was the virtue of a male; and now follows a similar example by a female. In the terri-

the true faith (C), and this is the only reason that keeps some people from giving it up. It is not liable to the very dangerous consequences of the ordinary opinion. For a long time people

tory of Reate, a mare, after tearing to pieces a coachman who was the cause of its guilt, made a similar exit."[5] What he says, and what others report about how ardently some dogs have worked to help their masters, to avenge their deaths, and so on, are matters absolutely inexplicable by the Aristotelian hypothesis. Thus, all their disputes against the disciples of Descartes is wasted effort. Only the skill employed by Pereira is needed. "You admit," he used to say to his opponents, "that animals do several things which resemble those done by rational souls and that, nevertheless, their souls are not rational. Then why do you forbid me to maintain that they do several things that resemble those done by sensitive souls without their souls being sensitive? I am not surprised that neither Descartes nor his followers have not taken advantage of the passage in the Justinian Code in which it is said that beasts are incapable of committing a crime since they do not sense anything. It is obvious that the word *sensus* in this law ought to be taken as design and intelligence."

≪←

C. *(Descartes' view is . . . of very great advantage to the true faith.)* What leads the Cartesians to say that beasts are machines is that according to them all matter is incapable of thinking. They are not content to say that only spiritual substances are capable of reflecting and constructing a long chain of reasoning; but they maintain that all thought, whether it be called reflection, meditation, inference, whether it be called sensation, imagination, instinct, is of such a nature that the most subtle and the most perfect matter is incapable of it and that it can only exist in incorporeal substances. According to this thesis every man can be convinced of the immortality of his soul. Every man knows that he thinks, and consequently, if he reasons in the Cartesian way, he cannot doubt that what thinks in him is distinct from the body; from which it follows that he is immortal

---

5 Rorarius, Bk. II, p. 73. [This reference is probably to the Amsterdam edition of 1654 of *Quod animalia bruta ratione utantur melius homine.*]

have maintained that beasts do have a rational soul. The Schoolmen are quite mistaken if they persuade themselves that by
rejecting that position they will avoid the distressing conse-

in this respect; for the mortality of creatures consists only in that
they are composed of several parts of matter that separate from one
another. Here is a great advantage for religion; but it will be almost
impossible to preserve this advantage by philosophical reasons if
one admits that beasts have a material soul that perishes with
the body, a soul, I say, whose sensations and desires are the cause of
the actions that we see them do. See remark F [p. 225]. The theological
advantages of Descartes' view that beasts are automata do not stop
there. They extend to many important principles that cannot be
maintained with any strength once it is admitted that beasts have sensitive souls. If St. Augustine maintained these principles though he
admitted this kind of soul in beasts, and if he was not bothered about
the connection of these two things, then he was more happy than wise.
"From the principles that he carefully examined and solidly established it follows manifestly *that beasts do not have souls*, as Ambrosius
Victor[8] shows in the sixth volume of the *Christian Philosophy*."[9] The
author from whom I take these words supposes that "this holy teacher,"
knowing "too well how to distinguish the soul from the body to think
that there were corporeal souls," admitted a spiritual soul in beasts.[10]
Now here is a sample that he gives us of the principles which St. Augustine maintained and which are incompatible with that soul of beasts.
"Some of St. Augustine's principles are that a creature that has never
sinned can never suffer evil. Now, according to him, pain is the greatest evil, and beasts suffer pain. That the more noble thing cannot
have for its goal the less noble. Now, according to him the soul of
beasts is spiritual and more noble than the body, and nevertheless
they have no other goal than the body. What is spiritual is immortal;

---

8 This is the fictitious name used by one of the fathers of the Oratory.

9 Malebranche, *Eclaircissemens sur le VIe livre de la recherche de la
vérité*.

10 It is certain, no matter what Father Malebranche may say, that St.
Augustine believed the soul of beasts to be sensitive and corporeal. See chap.
4 of St. Augustine's *Cognito vitae seu, De cognitione verae vitae* [*Knowledge
of the True Life*]; see also chap. 23 of *De spiritu et anima*. [The first-named
work is presently attributed to Honorius Augustodunensis.]

quences of the opinion that endows beasts with a sensitive soul
(E). These thinkers lack neither the distinctions, the exceptions
nor the boldness to assert that the acts of this soul never go beyond certain limits that they have set. But all this confused and
unintelligible verbiage is of no use in establishing a difference
in species between human and animal souls (F), and it seems
hardly likely that they can ever invent a better explanation than
they have given up till now. The author who has given the best
refutation of Descartes on the theory of the soul of beasts would
have done us a great favor if he could have cleared up the difficulties involved in the ordinary view on this (G). Leibniz, one
of the greatest minds in Europe, being perfectly aware of these
difficulties, has offered some leads that ought to be followed up
(H).* I shall say something about his view if only to indicate
my own doubts. But to get back to Rorarius, I do not believe
I am mistaken in giving my opinion that he was born in Por-
denone in Italy. I wish I could have read the speech he made

and the soul of beasts, though spiritual, is subject to death. There are
many other such principles in St. Augustine's works from which it
can be concluded that beasts do not have such a spiritual soul as he
claims for them."[11] I am not too convinced that St. Augustine believed that the soul of beasts is an incorporeal substance; but, be this
as it may, the second principle given here as an example is incompatible with the view of this great teacher; for that which knows is more
noble than that which does not. Now St. Augustine attributes at
least sensation to the soul of beasts. He therefore believed it much
more noble than the body. He therefore maintained on the one hand
that the more noble cannot have for its goal the less noble, and on the
other hand that the soul of beasts, more noble than their body, has no
other goal than their body. This, you will say, is of little importance
for religion. You are mistaken, it will be answered, for all the proofs
of original sin drawn from illness and death to which little children
are subject collapse as soon as you suppose that animals have sensations. They are subject both to pain and death. They, however, have

---

* [Remarks E, F, G, and H appear on pp. 221, 225, 231, and 235, respectively.]
11 Malebranche, *Eclaircissemens.*

in favor of rats. It was printed in the country of the Grisons*
in 1548. There is something like this in the writings of Président
Chassanée. I shall here give my readers the remainder of the
compilation, the chief part of which appears in article
"Pereira."†

I have learned from several quarters that many people who
enjoy the history of theories have approved the compilation I
published in the remarks of this article. They have even declared they would be happy if I would publish others, if I came
across some new opinions. This had led me to take the liberty
of introducing some supplements here (K), although I am aware
that many readers will not care for them and will consider them
as excrescences. But they will have no reason to think this of the
remarks I wish to make on Leibniz' reflections (L)** that have
appeared in Basnage's journal; for these notes are a natural
and necessary consequence of one of the items in the first edition
of this article. I hope that they will prove the occasion to examine a matter no less difficult than important.

never sinned. Thus your reasoning is faulty when you say, "Young
children suffer evil and die; they are therefore guilty"; for you suppose a false principle that is contradicted by the condition of beasts,
namely, "that which has never sinned cannot suffer evil." This is
nevertheless a most evident principle. It follows necessarily from the
ideas we have of the justice and goodness of God. It agrees with the
immutable order, with that order from which we clearly conceive
God never departs. The soul of beasts conflicts with this order and
overthrows these very distinct ideas. It must then be granted that the
automata of Descartes favor greatly the principles by which we judge
about the infinite being and by which we maintain orthodoxy. Read
the following.

---

* [A canton in Switzerland, also known as Graubünden.]

† [In remark E of the article "Pereira" Bayle presented a catalogue of
views about the nature of the soul of beasts. He gave the original texts in
Latin or Greek, with some discussion of the various views. After several
columns of text Bayle notes that he fears that his readers might find him too
prolix, and so he will continue the matter elsewhere, namely, here in the
article "Rorarius."]

** [Remark K appears on p. 239, L on p. 245.]

"Religion was immediately drawn into this cause,[12] the anti-Cartesians hoping thereby to destroy the machines of Descartes; but it would be impossible to express the advantage that thus accrued to the followers of this philosopher. For they believe they have shown that, by ascribing a soul to beasts that is capable of knowledge, all the natural proofs of our soul's immortality are destroyed. They have shown that the most obstinate enemies of their view are impious thinkers and Epicureans; and that no greater damage can be done to these wicked philosophers than by disarming them of all the false arguments that they borrow from the soul of beasts in order to conclude that there is only a difference of degree between them and us. It is certain that there are no people who do more than impious thinkers to make beasts come near to the perfection of man. This is how the followers of Descartes have interested religion in their cause. But they have not been satisfied with this. They have raised themselves up to the nature of God to find invincible arguments against the knowledge of beasts, and it can be said that they have found some pretty good ones. The author of the *Recherche de la vérité* has given us them in outline in some parts of his works. Father Poisson of the Oratory has treated fully the one based on St. Augustine's principle that, 'since God is just, misery is a necessary proof of sin;' from which it follows that beasts, not having sinned, are not subject to misery. Now they would be subject to it if they had sensations. Therefore, they do not have sensations."[13] You will find after this passage the summary of a book[14] in which it is shown that if beasts had a knowing soul, "it follows (1) that God does not love himself, (2) that he is not constant, (3) that he is cruel and unjust."[15] He would not love himself, for he would have created "souls capable of knowledge and love without obliging them to love and to know him." He would have created them to be in a state of sin; and consequently he would have released them from the law of order, which is however the supreme and indispensible law. . . . According to common opinion, the souls of beasts are annihilated the instant the beasts cease to live. Where then is God's constancy? He creates souls and soon he destroys them.

---

12 That is to say, in the dispute against the Cartesians concerning the soul of beasts.

13 *Nouvelles de la République des Lettres,* March 1684 [by Bayle].

14 Entitled *La bête transformée en machine.* The author is Darmanson.

15 *Nouvelles de la République des Lettres,* March 1684.

He does not do the same thing with regard to matter, for he never destroys it. He therefore conserves the less perfect substances and destroys the more perfect. Is this acting like a wise agent? The soul of beasts has not sinned, and yet it is subject to pain and misery. It is subject to all the irregular desires of creatures who have sinned. How do we treat beasts? We make them tear each other apart for our pleasure. We kill them to nourish ourselves. We dissect their entrails while they are living to satisfy our curiosity, and we do all this as a result of the dominion God has given us over the beasts. How disordered this is that the innocent creature should be subject to the capricious temper of the criminal creature! No casuist believes that one sins by making bulls fight against mastiffs, and so on, and by employing thousands of ruses and violent means to destroy animals in hunting, fishing, and the like, or by diverting oneself by killing flies as Domitian did. Now is it not cruel and unjust to submit an innocent soul to so many evils? But all these difficulties are removed by Descartes' view. . . .

.   .   .   .

≪-

   E. (*The distressing consequences of the opinion that endows beasts with a sensitive soul.*) Nothing can be more diverting than to see with what authority the Schoolmen endeavor to set limits to the knowledge of beasts. They insist that beasts know only particular and material objects, and that they love only what is useful and pleasant, that they cannot reflect on their sensations and desires, nor infer one thing from another. It would seem that they have searched more successfully into the faculties and the acts of the soul of beasts than the most expert anatomists into the entrails of dogs. Their temerity is so great that even if they should find the truth by chance, they would not deserve praise or even pardon. But let us spare them criticism on this point and grant them whatever they say. What do they hope to show? Do they think that they will prevail by this means with any person who knows how to argue, and get him to agree that man's soul is not of the same type as that of a beast? This claim is altogether illusory. It is evident to anyone who knows how to judge things that every substance that has any sensation knows that it senses, and it would not be more absurd to maintain that the soul of man actually knows an object without knowing that it knows it than it is absurd to say that the soul of a dog sees a bird without seeing that it sees it. This shows that all the acts of the sensitive faculties are by their nature and essence reflexive on themselves. Father Maignan, who, in spite of all his brilliance, has fallen into the errors and gross ignorance of the Schools with regard to the soul of beasts, admits, however, that to perceive anything one must know the perception we have of it. "That which we call sensation is not without the knowledge of that thing that is called sensible; but as nothing external is sensible in itself but only by its action, this action must consequently be chiefly sensible. And, moreover, as we cannot be said to feel the action of any agent if at the time that it is performed in us it is entirely unknown to us, consequently that thing we call sensation is not without the knowledge of the action performed in us at the time we feel. Nay, because sensation implies in those that feel nothing besides that knowledge, consequently, sensation itself, considered in the being that feels, consists in its perceiving what it feels; which is the same as to know that an action is received in itself or its passion."[53] It must then be said that the memory of beasts is an act that makes them remember the past and makes them aware that they are remembering. How then can anyone dare say that they do not have the power to reflect on their own thoughts or to draw inferences? But, once again, let us not dispute on this matter. Let us permit these philosophers to build badly on their suppositions. Let us only make use of their teachings. They say that the soul of beasts perceives all the objects of the five external senses; that it judges among these objects that there are some that suit it and others that are harmful, and that as a result of this judgment it desires those that suit it and abhors the rest. And in order to enjoy the object it wishes, it carries its organs to the place where such an object is. To avoid the objects that it dislikes, it takes its organs away from where it is. I conclude from all this that if it does not produce other acts as noble as those of our soul, it is not its fault. It is not due to its having a nature less perfect than man's soul, but only that the organs that it animates are not like ours. I would like to ask these gentlemen if they would find it just to say that the soul of a man is of another species at the age of thirty-five than at the age of one month, or that the soul of a madman, an idiot, or a senile old man is not substantially as perfect as that

---

53 Emanuel Maignan, *Philosophia naturae*, Chap. XXIV, No. 2.

of a capable man. They would no doubt reject this view as a very
great error, and rightly so. For it is certain that the same soul that
only senses in children meditates and reasons in a solid way in a mature person, and that the same soul whose reason and wit are admired
in a great man would only dote in an old man, only talk wildly in an
idiot, and only have sensations in a child. Now it would be a gross
error if it were claimed that the soul of man is only susceptible to
such thoughts as are known to us. There is an infinitude of sensations,
passions, and ideas of which this soul is capable, though it may never
be affected by them during this lifetime. If it were to be united to
organs different from ours, it would think otherwise than it does
now; and its modifications might be far nobler than those we experience. If there were substances that, in organized bodies, had a series
of sensations and other thoughts more sublime than ours, could one
say that they are of a nature more perfect than that of our soul?
Doubtless, no; for if our soul should be transported into those bodies,
it would have that same series of sensations and other thoughts much
more sublime than ours. It is easy to apply this to the soul of beasts.
It is admitted that it senses bodies, that it discerns them, that it desires
some of them and abhors others. This is enough. It is therefore a substance that thinks, and thus is capable of thought in general. It can
therefore receive all sorts of thoughts. It can then reason; it can
know what is good, the universals, the axioms of metaphysics, the
rules of morality, and so on. For, from the fact that wax can receive
the impression of a seal it clearly follows that it is capable of receiving the figure of any seal. It must also be said that as soon as a
soul is capable of having one thought, it is capable of having every
thought. It would be absurd to argue as follows: "This piece of wax
has received the impression of only three or four seals; therefore it
cannot receive the impression of a thousand. This piece of pewter
never was a plate; therefore it cannot be a plate; and it is of a different nature than this pewter plate that I see there." They do not
reason any better when they assert, "The soul of a dog has possessed
nothing but sensations, and the like; therefore it is not capable of
ideas of morality or metaphysical notions." How does it happen that
one piece of wax bears the image of the prince and the other does
not? It is because of the seal that has been applied to one and not
the other. This piece of pewter which has never been a plate will
be one as soon as you cast it in the mold of a plate. Cast, in the same

way, this soul of a beast in the mold of universal ideas and notions of the arts and sciences; I mean, unite it to a well-chosen human body; and it will be the soul of a capable man, and no longer that of a beast.

One sees, therefore, that the Schoolmen are not able to prove that the soul of man and the soul of beasts are of a different nature. Let them say, and let them repeat thousands and thousands of times, "The soul of man reasons and knows universals and virtue; that of animals knows nothing about all this." We shall answer them: "These differences are only accidental and are no sign that there is a difference in the species of the subjects. Aristotle and Cicero at the age of one did not have more sublime thoughts than those of a dog; and if they had remained in infancy for thirty or forty years, the only thoughts in their souls would have been sensations and childish passions for playing and eating. It is then by accident that they have surpassed the beasts; it is because their organs, on which their thoughts depend, acquired such and such modifications, which do not happen to the organs of beasts. The soul of a dog in the organs of Aristotle and Cicero would have lacked nothing for acquiring all the knowledge of those two great men."

Here is a very false line of reasoning: such a soul does not reason and does not know universals; therefore it is of a different nature from the soul of a great philosopher. For if this line of reasoning were just, then it would be necessary to say that the soul of small children is not of the same species as that of mature men. What are you thinking of, you Peripatetic philosophers, when you dare to claim that if the soul of beasts does not reason, it is substantially less perfect than souls that do? You would first have to prove that the defect in reasoning in beasts is due to a real and internal imperfection in their soul, and not to the organic dispositions on which it depends. But you can never prove this; for it is clear that a subject capable of the thoughts that you give to the soul of animals is capable of reasoning and of all other thoughts; from which it follows that if it does not actually reason, this is due to certain accidental and external obstacles; I mean due to the fact that the Creator of all things has fixed to each soul a certain series of thoughts by making it dependent on the movements of certain bodies. This is what accounts for the fact that children at the breast, fools, and madmen do not reason.

We cannot think without horror of the consequences of this doctrine: "Man's soul and that of beasts do not differ substantially. They are of the same species. The one acquires more knowledge than the other, but this is only an accidental advantage and depends on arbitrary factors." This doctrine is the necessary and inevitable result of what is taught in the Schools regarding the knowledge of beasts. It follows from this that if their souls are material and mortal, the souls of men are so also, and if the soul of man is an immaterial and spiritual substance, the soul of beasts is so also. These are horrible consequences no matter which way one looks at them. For, if, in order to avoid the immortality of the soul of beasts, we suppose that the soul of man dies with the body, we thereby overthrow the doctrine of another life and undermine the foundations of religion. If, however, in order to preserve for our soul the privilege of immortality, we extend it also to the soul of beasts, then into what an abyss shall we fall? What will we do with so many immortal souls? Will there also be a paradise and a hell for them? Will they migrate from one body to another? Will they be annihilated in proportion as beasts die? Will God incessantly create an infinitude of spirits, to plunge them back again so soon into a state of nothingness? How many insects are there who live only a few days? Let us not imagine that it suffices to create only the souls of beasts we know of. Those that we are not acquainted with are still more numerous. The microscope reveals them to us by the thousands in one drop of liquid. We could find many more if we had more perfect microscopes. And let it not be said that insects are machines, for that hypothesis would better explain the actions of dogs than those of ants and bees. There is, perhaps, more genius and more reason in invisible animals than in grosser ones. We are now going to see how vainly the Schools try to establish a difference in species between the soul of the beast and that of man.

≪≪←

   F. *(A difference in species between human and animal souls.)*
   They say that the soul of beasts is a material form, but the soul of man is a spirit created immediately by God. But how do they prove this? I assume that they reason only on the basis of the principles of the natural light without having recourse to either Scripture or the doctrines of religion, and I ask them for a good proof that the soul of beasts is corporeal while ours is not. They will tell me of the beauty and extent of human knowledge, and the smallness, grossness, and obscurity of animal knowledge; and they will conclude that a

corporeal principle is capable of producing the knowledge of beasts, but not the reflections, the reasonings, the universal ideas, the ideas of virtue, which are in the soul of man. And consequently this latter soul ought to be of an order superior to matter. It ought to be spiritual. Let us no longer tell them that they are rash in claiming that the soul of beasts does not reason and that it has no idea of what is virtuous. Let us set this objection aside, and let us say only that it is a thousand times more difficult to see a tree than to know the act by which we see it. So that if a material entity is capable of knowing an infinitude of things that take place outside of it, it will be much more capable of knowing its own thoughts and comparing them together and multiplying them. Thus the reflections, conclusions, and abstractions of man do not require a more noble principle than matter. A very capable Peripatetic grants this. Let us hear him speak. His admission will be more persuasive than my objections. "If you once admit that whatever is most wonderful in the actions of beasts can be accomplished by means of a material soul, will you not soon come to say that all that takes place in men can be accomplished also by means of a material soul? . . . If you once grant that beasts without any spiritual soul are capable of thinking, of goal-directed action, of foreseeing what is to come, of remembering what has happened, of profiting from experience by the particular reflections they make on it; why will you not say that men are capable of performing their functions without any spiritual soul? After all, the operations of men are no different from those that you attribute to beasts. If there is any difference, it is only one of degree. And thus all you could say will be that the soul of man is more perfect than that of beasts because it remembers better than they do, thinks with more reflection, and foresees with more assurance. But in the end you cannot say that their soul is not always material. You will say perhaps that there are certain operations found in men that cannot be compatible with beasts, nor can they proceed from any other principle than that of a spiritual soul. The operations that cannot belong to beasts or to non-spiritual souls are those by which we gain universal or general knowledge—that is, the methods of reasoning by which we infer one thing from another; and the ideas we have of infinite and spiritual things that are not learned from the senses. But those who deny that there is any knowledge in beasts do not therefore deny that these thoughts and reasonings are in us since we ourselves are conscious of them.

Thus they always have the same right as you to prove the existence of the rational soul. But they add besides that all these operations that you find so extraordinary only differ in degree from those operations that you attribute to beasts; and certainly it seems that to engage in goal-directed activity, to learn from experience, to foresee events (which, according to you, are all possibilities for beasts) ought no less to proceed from a spiritual principle than what is found in men. For in the end what is universal knowledge, if not a knowledge that agrees with several similar things, like a portrait of a man that should agree with all the faces that resemble him? What is reasoning but a knowledge produced by another knowledge, as we see that a motion is often produced by another motion? It is definitely the case that if it is once admitted that thought, intention, and reflection can arise from a body animated by a material form, it will be very difficult to prove that reasoning and the ideas of men cannot arise from a body also animated by a material form."[55]

I beg my readers to take note of the unhappy situation in which the Scholastics find themselves with relation to the doctrine of the sensitive soul. They put forth against Descartes the most surprising actions of animals; they choose them purposely to confound him the more. But then they find that they have gone too far, and that they have furnished weapons to their adversary for destroying the difference in species that they wanted to establish between our soul and that of animals. They would much prefer that we forgot all those examples of cunning, planning, docility, knowledge of the future, that they have displayed with so much pomp to show that beasts are not automata. They would prefer that we thought only of the gross actions of an ox who does nothing but graze. But it is too late for this. The same weapons are used to confound them and to prove to them that if a material soul can do all these things, it can also accomplish what the human soul does. It would be required only to ascribe various degrees of refinement to the souls of beasts. Must it not be supposed that the soul of a dog or a monkey is less gross than

---

[55] Pardies, *De la connoissance des bêtes*. [Father Ignace Pardies, S.J., argued with many people, including Isaac Newton. He was suspected of being a crypto-Cartesian. On him, and on the soul of beasts controversy, see George Boas, *The Happy Beast in French Thought of the Seventeenth Century* (Baltimore: Johns Hopkins Press, 1933), and Lenora C. Rosenfield, *From Beast-Machine to Man-Machine* (New York: Oxford University Press, 1941).]

that of an ox? In a word, if nothing but a spiritual soul can produce the actions of a big clod of a peasant, I will maintain that nothing but a spiritual soul can produce the actions of a monkey. And if you say that a corporeal principle is capable of accomplishing all that monkeys do, I will maintain that a corporeal principle is capable of accomplishing all that stupid people do and that, provided that matter is subtilized and disengaged from what are called earthly particles, phlegms, and so on, it will be the cause of whatever able people do.

A question concerning the freedom of the soul of beasts. There are some authors who suggest that since the human soul has free will, and that that of beasts is destitute of freedom, there must be a difference in species between them, that the one must be spiritual and the other corporeal. In 1630 the Jesuit Théophile Raynaud published a small book entitled *Calvinismus Bestiarum Religio* [*Calvinism, the Religion of Beasts*]. His chief aim was to prove that the doctrine of the Dominicans reduces man to the condition of beasts by depriving him of free will.[57] "The Catholic claimed that Calvinism ought to be considered the religion of beasts, chiefly on this account, because according to Calvinist principles man is degraded to a level with beasts and divested of the degree and dignity of man. To prove this in a solid manner he thought it proper to lay down two propositions: one is that man is a man only by virtue of his liberty; the other, that liberty is destroyed by Calvinism." He supposes that the characteristic of man, I mean that which distinguishes him from the beast, is the liberty of indifference. For, as for the liberty that consists only in being free from constraint, or in *spontaneity,* no Schoolman can deny that it is found in animals. Let us show that it is completely false that a soul endowed with free will is another species than that of a soul without it. The soul of children and that of madmen is destitute of free will; and yet they are of the same species as the soul most amply provided with liberty. Add to this that the advocates of the liberty of indifference agree that it will cease after this life, and yet they acknowledge that the soul of man on earth is the same substance as in heaven or in hell. It is therefore obvious that the liberty of indifference is not an essential attribute of the human creature but is a concession or an accidental favor which the Creator confers upon it. And consequently such

---

57 He indeed disputes against Calvin; but it is in order to condemn in the Dominicans (whom he claims agree with Calvin in that doctrine) what he condemns in Calvin.

souls who do not obtain this concession are not on this account of a
different species or kind from those that do receive it. It is then very
bad reasoning to employ this argument: the soul of beasts is destitute
of free will, and the soul of man is not destitute of it; therefore, the
soul of beasts is material, and the soul of man spiritual. Let us push
this farther and say that those who admit a sensitive soul have no
good reaon to take liberty away from beasts. Do they not say that
beasts do hundreds of things with extreme pleasure and that they
are directed to do this as a result of the judgment they make about the
usefulness of objects, a judgment that has excited in them the desire
to be united with those objects? If liberty consists only in the absence
of constraint and in a *spontaneity* that must be preceded by a discernment of the objects, is it not absurd to deny that animals are free?
Has not a hungry dog the strength to abstain from a piece of meat
when he is afraid of being beaten if he does not abstain? Does this
not amount to having the power to act or not act? His abstinence no
doubt comes from his comparison of his hunger with the blows of a
stick, and his judgment that the latter are more insupportable than
is hunger. Notice that with regard to all the human actions that one
attributes to the liberty of indifference, you will find that man never
suspends them or chooses one of the contraries except because, having compared the reasons pro and con, he has found either more
motives for suspension than for action, or more for this action than
that one. Let us listen again to the Jesuit who wrote against the Cartesians. "It is thus difficult to separate reasoning from thought; and
it seems easy to prove that, when a substance is capable of thinking,
it is also capable of reasoning, that it is endowed with volition and
free will, and, in a word, that it can act like men. The ancient philosophers and even the Church Fathers have proven that we have free
will by this general argument: that everything that is capable of knowing may know good and evil, that is to say, that this is good for it, and
that bad; that consequently, by considering these two objects, he can
compare them together, he can deliberate, he can determine to choose
one of them and not the other; and it is in these items that the use of
our freedom consists. And this is so true that the definition of liberty
in general that we still retain is this: the faculty of acting with causal
knowledge. . . ."59

---

59 Pardies, *De la connoissance des animaux.* [Bayle has *animaux*; the
title should probably read *De la connoissance des bêtes.*]

One of the strongest proofs that is given of man's freedom is drawn from the punishment of evildoers. All societies agree in making examples of them in their punishments, and even in certain cases to extend this to punishing publicly their dead bodies. It is forbidden to bury them, and the bodies are exhibited as spectacles on the wheels and the gallows. If man did not act freely, if a fatal and unavoidable necessity determined a certain series of thoughts, then theft and murder should not be punished, and no benefit could be hoped for from the punishment of the guilty parties. For those who may see the body of a malefactor on a wheel would not be less subject than before to that superior force that makes them act and does not allow them to employ any freedom. This proof of free will is not as strong as it appears. For even though men are convinced that machines have no feeling, this does not stop them from giving the machines a hundred blows with a hammer when they are out of order if they think that by flattening a wheel or another piece of iron the machines will be repaired. They would then flog a pickpocket, even if they knew that he had no free will, provided that experience had taught them that by whipping certain people they restrain them from continuing certain actions. But in any case, if this proof of free will have any force, it obviously serves to show that beasts are not destitute of liberty.[60] They are punished every day, and their faults are thereby corrected. Ochino, at the beginning of his *Labyrinth*, examines all the reasons that convince us that we act freely; and he says among other things against the arguments drawn from the punishment of malefactors that if the judges were sure that by hanging a horse who had killed a man and leaving him hanging a long time on the highway this would stop other horses from doing evil, then they would employ this punishment every time a horse maimed or killed anyone by his kicking and biting.[61] Apparently he did not know that such spectacles are in use in some countries to intimidate wild beasts. Rorarius was an eyewitness to this. He saw two wolves hung on the gallows in the duchy of Juliers; and he observes that this makes a stronger impression on other wolves than branding with a hot iron, the loss of ears,

---

[60] [Bayle here cites the discussions in Franzius, *Hist. animal. sacra*, about God's punishment of animals, referring to Genesis 9:5, Exodus 10:28, Leviticus 20:15–16.]

[61] I do not have Ochino's book at hand at the moment, so I am citing what he says from memory. Perhaps I am not giving his words exactly, but I am sure I am giving his thought.

and the like does on a thief. He also says that in Africa lions are hung upon a cross to frighten the others, and that this works. "It is usual for the Africans to crucify lions whenever any of them is caught lying in wait near the towns, which they do when they reach old age, because they then no longer have the strength to hunt wild beasts; the dread of which punishment, though they are pinched with hunger, makes them refrain. As I was travelling on horseback from Cologne to Duren through that large forest I saw two wolves trussed up like two thieves hanging on a gibbet. This was to deter others from doing such mischief by the fear of a similar punishment. But every day there is seen among men some who, for their guilt, have been whipped, had their ears cut off, been burned in the cheek, had a hand cut off, an eye plucked out, and yet would not give up their wicked ways until a noose put an end to their lives."[62]

《《←

G. *(If he could have cleared up the difficulties involved in the ordinary view on this.)* There has been a great to-do, and with good reason, about a book whose title is *Le voyage du monde de Descartes*.[63] Very great difficulties against the Cartesians are there raised in an agreeable and lively fashion, and they are well pursued. Those concerning the soul of beasts considered as machines are the best that could be proposed, it seems to me. The author sincerely admits how poorly the Peripatetics at first opposed this great paradox of Descartes, and the advantages that the latter's followers gained from this. He cleverly makes use of the unfortunate consequences that can be drawn from this paradox; for he shows that the arguments of the Cartesians lead us to judge that other men are machines. This is perhaps the weakest side of Cartesianism, and this confirms a very judicious view about the nature of human knowledge. It seems that God, who dispenses it, acts like a common father of all the sects; that is, he will not allow one sect to triumph completely over the others and destroy them utterly. An overwhelmed sect, put to rout, and almost worn out, always finds the means to recover as soon as it

---

[62] From Rorarius' book.

[63] Father Daniel, a Jesuit, is thought to be the author of this work. [Gabriel Daniel, S.J., was the author; and the work was extremely popular, having been translated into English, Spanish, etc.]

gives up defending itself, creating a diversion by taking the offensive and retaliating. The combat between sects is always what it was for a while between the Trojans and the Greeks the night Troy was taken. They vanquish each other by turns as they change their ways of fighting. The Cartesian has no sooner overthrown, ruined, annihilated the view of the Scholastics concerning the soul of beasts, than he finds out that he can be attacked with his own weapons and can be shown that he has proven too much; and that if he reasons logically, he will give up views that he cannot give up without becoming an object of ridicule and without admitting the most glaring absurdities. For where is the man who would dare to say that he is the only one who thinks and that everybody else is a machine? Would such a person not be considered as more insane than those who are put in lunatic asylums or kept away from all human society? This consequence of the Cartesian theory is most upsetting. It is like a peacock's feet, whose ugliness mortifies the vanity that the brilliance of the plumage has inspired. Be this as it may, one must agree that the entire strength of Father Daniel's attack against the theory of Descartes consists in the objections he has raised, and not at all in the answers he has given to the objections of the Cartesians. He does not deny that they raise strange difficulties by their questions; but he maintains that they, in turn, are not in less difficulty as a result of the questions put to them, and that *good reprisals* can be made. You would search in vain in his book for the solution of the physical, moral, and theological difficulties that have been raised against the Peripatetics concerning the soul of beasts. He is content to reply that, if there are incomprehensible things in this view, there are some things of the same kind in Descartes' hypothesis. The definition of the beast's soul, "a substance capable of sensation," that is, of seeing, understanding, and the like, is as clear as the Cartesian definition of mind, "a substance that thinks and reasons." These are Father Daniel's words. He then proves them as well as possible. A little earlier he had said that the soul of beasts is neither matter nor spirit, but "a being between the two, capable neither of reasoning nor thought, but only of perception and sensation." The fact that he says nothing better than this should rather be blamed on the nature of the subject than on his abilities.

He will allow me to say that his hypothesis cannot be maintained, and it cannot solve any difficulties. These two terms "matter" and "mind" seem at first glance to be opposed in such a way as to admit of something in between. But when they are examined more carefully, we see that they can be reduced to a contradictory opposition. To show this it is only necessary to ask if the substance that is neither body nor mind is extended or not. If it is extended, it would be wrong to distinguish it from matter. If it is not extended, I would like to know on what basis it is distinguished from mind; for it is like mind in being an unextended substance, and we cannot comprehend how this classification can be divided into two kinds, since the specific attribute that may be given to one—that of being unextended—would never be incompatible with the other. If God can join thought[68] to one unextended being, he could also join it with another unextended being, there being nothing but extension that seems to us to make matter incapable of thought. At least, we clearly conceive that an unextended substance which can have sensation is capable of reasoning; and consequently, if the soul of beasts is an unextended substance capable of sensation, it is capable of reasoning. It is then of the same species as man's soul. It is then not a substance between body and mind. Here is a question raised by Father Daniel: "Will the Cartesians deny the possibility of there existing a type of being that is only capable of sensation? And where is that respect that their master tried to inspire in them for the omnipotence of a God, who, according to him, can make it such that a triangle not have three sides and that two plus two not equal four; and who nevertheless cannot make a being that only has sensations?" This question would puzzle a man who had taken a vow never to deviate from what Descartes said; but one does not encounter Cartesians who subject themselves to such slavery; and we may be sure that Descartes would never have dared to assert seriously that God can make two feet of wax capable of possessing three or four figures, but not capable of having any others. Whatever Descartes may have held on this matter, his disciples will never believe that they are lacking in the respect due to God if they say that a "being solely capable of sensation" is not more possible than a piece[70] of wax that can have only a square figure. As

---

68 I use this word in the Cartesian sense, that is, for a generic modification that includes sensations, reflections, reasoning, etc., as various species.

70 By a piece here is meant an assemblage of different particles. This is to prevent the difficulty of an atomist who believes that the shape of an atom is essentially immutable.

to that which concerns a "being who only had sensations," they will believe this to be very possible, just as it would be possible that a certain piece of matter would be always round if God wished eternally to prevent the material particles from changing place. It would not displease Father Daniel if I say that he was not aware that "a being solely capable of sensation" and "a being that only had sensations" are not the same thing. The possibility of the first is inconceivable; that of the second is obvious. But just as a piece of wax in which God perpetually prevents the change of position of the particles would be of the same species as a piece of wax, the change of whose extremities would continually produce a new figure, so let us say also that a substance that God always confines to sensations would be of the same species as a substance that might be elevated to reasoning.

It remains for me to show the inadequacy of the Jesuit's hypothesis. (1) A system is needed that establishes the mortality of the soul of beasts. Now this is not found in a being in between body and mind; for such a being is not extended; it is therefore indivisible, it can only perish by *annihilation*; diseases, fire, the sword cannot affect it. In this regard, it is then of the same nature and same condition as minds, as the soul of man. (2) We have need of a system that establishes a difference in species between the soul of man and that of beasts. Now we do not find this by this in-between being. For if the soul of beasts, being neither body nor mind, nevertheless has sensations, then man's soul could very well reason even though it were neither body nor mind but something in between the two. It is more difficult for a being destitute of sensation to reach the perception of a tree and the awareness of this tree than for a being endowed with sensation to reach the state of reasoning. (3) We have need of a system that explains the astonishing activities of bees, dogs, monkeys, elephants; and you only give us a soul of beasts with sensations, but which does not think,[71] which does not reason. Consider well, and you will realize that such a soul is inadequate to explain the phenomena. Father Daniel admits this in another part of his work, where he seems to give the Aristotelians only the advantage of being here first. For after having dealt with the difficulties in Cartesianism relating to beasts, he adds: "The Peripatetics also, doubtless, have their difficulties to resolve. But were these even greater than they are, yet so

---

[71] Here the word "thinking" is taken in the sense of a species of perception, and not according to the general notion of Descartes.

long as the Cartesians have nothing to say that is more satisfactory or intelligible, we ought to stick to the former view and argue on this particular point as a great minister of state did, twenty-five years ago, regarding all philosophy. He was advised not to let his oldest son learn ancient philosophy because, as he was told, there was nothing in that philosophy but puerilities and foolishness. 'I have also been told,' he replied, 'that there is much foolishness and illusion in the new philosophy. Thus,' he continued, 'having to choose between ancient and new foolishness, I ought to prefer the old to the new one.' "[72] Perhaps this is the way Nihusius reasoned.[73]

≪←

H. (Leibniz . . . has offered some leads that ought to be followed up.) He approves[74] of the view of some moderns that animals are organized in the seed; and he also believes that matter alone cannot constitute a true unity, and that thus every animal is united to a form that is a simple, indivisible, and truly unique being. Besides this he supposes that this form never leaves its subject; from which it follows that, properly speaking, there is neither death nor creation in nature. He makes an exception of the soul of man, leaving it out of the discussion, and so on. This hypothesis[78] removes part of our difficulties. There is no longer the problem of answering the weighty objections made to the Scholastics. The soul of beasts, they are told, is a substance distinct from the body. It must therefore be produced by creation and destroyed by annihilation. Heat,[79] therefore, must have the power to create souls and to annihilate them;[80] and what can one say that is more absurd? The answers of the Peripatetics to this

---

[72] Gabriel Daniel, Suite du voiage du monde de Des Cartes, pp. 105–106.

[73] See remark H in the article on him [p. 162].

[74] See the article of Leibniz inserted in the Journal des Savans, June 27, 1695. [This is the famous essay entitled "Système nouveau de la nature et de la communication des substances, aussi bien que de l'union qu'il y a entre l'âme et le corps" ("New System of Nature and of the Communication of Substances, as well as of the Union of Soul and Body").]

[78] Bernier, in his Relation des Gentils de l'Hindoustan, reports an opinion almost like this held by the philosophers of that country.

[79] Chickens are hatched by putting eggs in ovens, which are heated by degrees. This is practiced in Egypt.

[80] One can kill many kinds of animals by putting them in an oven that is a little too hot.

objection do not deserve to be reported or removed from the obscurity of the classroom, where they are declaimed to young scholars. They are only suitable for convincing us that the objection is invincible with respect to this position. They will not do any better when they are asked to make some sense out of, or to find some shadow of reason in, the continual production of an almost infinite number of substances that are totally destroyed a few days later, though they be much more noble and excellent than matter, which never loses its existence. Leibniz' hypothesis wards off all these blows, for it leads us to believe, (1) that God, at the beginning of the world, created the forms of all bodies and, hence, all the souls of beasts, (2) that these souls have existed ever since that time, inseparably united to the first organized body in which God placed them. This spares us of having recourse to the theory of metempsychosis [transmigration of souls], which otherwise we would have had to turn to. To see if I have really understood his thought, I include here a part of his discourse.[81] "It is here that the transformations of Messrs. Swammerdam, Malpighi, and Leeuwenhoeck, who are among the best observers of our time, have come to my aid and have made me admit more easily that animals and all other organized substances do not begin existing when we suppose they do and that their apparent generation is only a development and a kind of augmentation. Also, I have noticed that the author of the *Recherche de la vérité* [Malebranche], Régis, Hartsoeker, and other learned men have not been far from this view. But there remains the biggest question, namely, what becomes of these souls or forms when either the animal dies or the unity of the organized substance is destroyed? And it is this that is most puzzling, insofar as it does not even seem slightly reasonable for the souls to remain uselessly in a chaos of confused matter. This made me decide finally that there was only one reasonable view to adopt; and that is the theory of the conservation of not only the soul, but also of the animal itself and of its organic machine, even though the destruction of gross parts may have reduced it to a smallness that is as much beyond our sense observation as it was before being born. Therefore, no one can actually fix the exact time of death, as it can, for a long time, appear as a simple suspension of observable actions and basically is never anything else in simple animals; witness the resuscitations of drowned flies who are then buried

---

[81] *Journal des Savans,* June 27, 1695.

in pulverized chalk and several other similar cases that are enough to show us that there would be many more resuscitations if men were able to put the machine in order again. . . . It is therefore natural that animals, always having been alive and organized (as some persons of great perspicacity are beginning to see), continue to remain so. And since there is thus no first birth, nor an entirely new generation of the animal, it follows that there will be neither a final extinction nor complete death in a strictly metaphysical sense. Consequently, instead of the transmigration of souls, there will be only a transformation of the same animal, depending upon whether the organs are folded differently and are more or less developed."

I will observe, by the way, that there are many people who believe that the basic subject to which our soul is united departs with it from our bodies when we die. Poiret is not far from this view, and he even believes that Moses appeared on the day of the Transfiguration with the actual body that accompanied his soul when he departed from this life; that is, as he explains it, when that blessed soul left only the cover or envelope that covered the subtle body to which it was united. . . . He published some objections that were sent him from Sedan.* The objection was raised, among others, that the example of Moses proves nothing, because in order for that great prophet to be seen, much matter would have to be added to that which issued out of his body when the soul left it. Now if it were necessary to give him more than half of a different body, there is nothing wrong in saying that all the matter that was seen that day was different from the original. Poiret answered that subtle matter which leaves the body with the soul, is, in truth, too delicate to strike our gross senses. But we are able to see when God gives us extraordinary assistance. He was told that there are some Scholastics who admit a fifth essence to be the connection of the human soul with the organs formed of the four elements and to serve as its vehicle when death dislodges it. They also say that this vehicle is the subject of the torments that reprobates endure before the resurrection. . . . Poiret answered that he had nothing to do with the notions of the Schoolmen. . . .

There are some things in Leibniz' hypothesis that cause difficulties, though they indicate the extent and power of his genius. He believes, for example, that a dog's soul acts independently of its body; "that it has everything from within itself by a perfect *spontaneity* with re-

---

* [Bayle is the co-author of these objections to Poiret.]

gard to itself and nevertheless with a perfect conformity to things outside itself. . . . That its internal perceptions arise from its own original
constitution, that is to say, its representative nature (one capable of
expressing the beings that are outside itself with respect to its organs),
a condition which was given to it from the time of its creation and
which constitutes its individual character."[88] From which it follows
that it would feel hunger and thirst at such and such a time even
though there were no bodies in the universe, though *nothing be in
existence but God and that soul.* He has explained[89] his view by the example of the two clocks that are in perfect agreement; that is to say, he
supposes that according to the particular laws that activate the soul, it
ought to feel hungry at such a time; and according to the particular
laws that regulate the motion of matter, the body united to this soul
ought to be modified when the soul is hungry. Before preferring this
theory to that of occasional causes, I will wait until its able author has
perfected it. I cannot comprehend the chain of internal and spontaneous actions that would make a dog's soul feel pain immediately after
having felt joy, even though this soul were the only entity in the universe. I understand why a dog passes immediately from pleasure to pain
when, being very hungry and eating some bread, he is suddenly beaten
with a stick. But that his soul be constructed so that at the instant he
is hit, he feels pain and would so even though he were not hit and
even though he continued eating bread without trouble and without
being stopped—this is what I cannot understand. I also find the
spontaneity of this soul most incompatible with its having painful
sensations, and in general with its having unpleasant perceptions. In
addition, the reason why this learned man does not like the Cartesian system seems to me to involve a false supposition; for it cannot
be said that the theory of occasional causes requires that the action of
God occur miraculously, *deus ex machina,* in the reciprocal dependence of soul and body. For as God intervenes there only according to
general laws, it is not a question of his acting extraordinarily. Does
the internal and active power communicated to the forms of bodies
know, according to Leibniz, the sequence of actions that it is supposed to produce? Not at all. For we know by experience that we do
not know if we are going to have such and such a perception in an
hour. The forms must then be directed by some external principle in

---

88 *Journal des Savans,* July 4, 1695.
89 In the *Histoire des Ouvrages des Savans,* February 1696.

the production of their acts. Would this not be as much the *deus ex machina* as is involved in the theory of occasional causes?[91] To conclude, as he very justly supposes that all souls are simple and indivisible, it is inconceivable how they can be compared to clocks, that is, how by their original constitution they can diversify their operations by making use of the spontaneous activity that they receive from their Creator. It is clearly conceivable that a simple being will always act uniformly if not hindered by some external cause. If it were composed of several parts, like a machine, it would act diversely because the particular activity of each piece might change the course of that of the others at any moment. But in a unified substance, where can you find the cause of the change of its operation?

≪←

K. *(This has led me to take the liberty of introducing some supplements here.) Authors who have believed that the soul of beasts is rational.* Let us begin by indicating what authors have given beasts rational souls. I do not believe that anyone has been more extreme on this subject than the philosopher Celsus; for in desiring to combat what the Christians say—that all things have been made for man—he endeavors to show that the beasts are not less excellent than man and that they even surpass him. He attributes to them[96] a form of government and an observation of the rules of justice and charity. He claims that ants enter into conversations with one another. "When they meet," he says, "they converse together, by which means they never lose their way. They therefore have reason in all its gradations. They naturally have the ideas of certain universal truths. They have the faculty of speech. They have knowledge of accidental things, and

---

91 Consult the objection made to Leibniz by Monsieur S. F. [Simon Foucher] in the *Journal des Savans,* September 12, 1695. [Foucher, the Academic skeptic, was a personal friend of Leibniz and argued with him in correspondence and in print. Up until Foucher's death in 1696, many of Leibniz' best statements of his theory consisted in his replies to Foucher in the *Journal des Savans.* (For further data on Foucher, see "Pyrrho," remark B, note 11, on p. 197.) Then, with the appearance of Bayle's *Dictionary,* and especially the article "Rorarius," Leibniz found that he had been placed in the center of the intellectual stage and that he had a new skeptical opponent to argue with. Leibniz wrote several answers to Bayle, one of which is discussed in "Rorarius," remark L (p. 245). The best known of his answers, of course, is his *Theodicy.*]

96 To bees and to ants.

they are able to express them.''[98] He insists "that there are beasts who
know the secrets of magic, so that mankind cannot boast that this is
one of the advantages that they have over beasts. . . . After this, desiring to show at large that men should not pretend to be superior to
all mortal beings on the pretext that they know the deity since there
are animals having no reason who have a pure and distinct idea of
it, while the most subtle among both the Greeks and the barbarians
everywhere are having disputes about it he adds, 'If one claims to raise
man above the animals because he is capable of knowing the deity and
of receiving the idea and impression of it, let him know that there are
several species that can boast the same advantage, and not without
some basis. For what can be more divine than to foresee and to pre-
dict the future? Now the other animals, and especially the birds, are
the instructors of men in this; and the skill of diviners consists only
in understanding what these animals teach them. Birds, then, and the
other animals capable of divination, to whom God reveals the future,
show the deity to us by signs and symbols. This is a proof that they
naturally have more direct contact with the deity than we do, that they
surpass us in knowledge of it, and that they are dearer to God than
we are. The most learned men also say that these animals communicate with one another in a much more holy and noble way than we
do; and these people understand their language, as they show, when
after telling us that the birds say that they will go to such and such a
place and will do such and such a thing, they let us see that they do in
fact go there and perform such things. With regard to elephants, no
creature shows a more religious respect for oaths or adheres to God
with a more inviolable fidelity, which can only happen, doubtless,
because they know him.' ''[101] I shall not report what Origen answers
to all this. It suffices that I inform my readers that he refutes it in the
work he wrote against Celsus.

Saumaise ought to be ranked among the moderns who believed that
animals are endowed with reason. He has written that the examples
which could prove this would fill a book. Osiander disapproved of
this view. See his notes on Grotius' *De jure belli et pacis,* in the chapter
where he rejects Justinian's definition of natural law. . . . This definition established that men and beasts participate in natural law. Most
of those who accept this base their view on the hypothesis that beasts

---

[98] Origen, *Contra Celsum* IV.
[101] Origen, *Contra Celsum.*

are not deprived of the use of reason, but most of those who reject this idea of natural law base their view on the contrary hypothesis. . . . In 1641 Giovanni Antonio Capella, a Neapolitan doctor, published *Opusculum paradoxicum quod ratio participetur à brutis.* I have not read this book and so cannot say what turn the author took. I know the view of Willis better. He claims that the soul of beasts is composed of organs and that it is of the same size and shape as that of the body that it animates, but that it is not as thick, and that its parts are so thin that they cannot be seen, and that they would disperse easily if the animal did not hold them together. . . . He attributes a kind of reason to this soul. . . . He claims that there is a soul exactly like this in man, plus a spiritual soul, and he claims to explain the conflict we feel within ourselves by these two souls. Other philosophers explain this by the superior faculty and the inferior faculty of a simple, unified spiritual substance that they call the reasonable soul. Though I do not want to displease him, it is the case that this method of explaining the conflict of reason and the sensitive soul cannot be satisfactory. For each person experiences in himself that the principle that desires carnal pleasures is numerically identical to the principle that opposes this desire, and sometimes surmounts it and is most often surmounted by it. We would not observe this unity of principle if we really had two kinds of souls actually distinct from one another. If it is answered that one of them produces its sensations and passions in the other, I would reply that there would then be two substances in man that desire the same thing. Now no man has ever perceived these two distinct principles. In addition, if a corporeal soul could communicate a carnal desire to man's spiritual soul, the body would be able to do it as well; and hence entities would be unnecessarily multiplied in attributing to man a body, a sensitive soul, and a reasonable soul. But let us leave the dispute at this point and turn to another matter. Willis notes that Sir Kenelm Digby holds the same view as Pereira and Descartes regarding the soul of beasts. "Pereira . . . affirmed that beasts are entirely deprived of all knowledge or perception; and he has been closely followed by the most illustrious men in this age—Descartes, Sir Kenelm Digby, and others—who, using their utmost endeavors to distinguish the soul of beasts from that of men, declared that it was not only corporeal and divisible, but likewise merely passive."[111] A little afterwards the difference between Descartes and Digby is ex-

---

[111] Thomas Willis, *De anima brutorum,* Chap. I.

plained, and it is shown that the latter does not remove sensation or memory from beasts. Then it is not true that he follows both Pereira and Descartes. Then why does he say this? . . . Let us conclude that Sir Kenelm Digby ought not to be placed in the catalogue of those who take beasts for automata. Locke has declared himself against those who will not attribute reason to beasts. You will see in what the difference consists according to him: "The having of general ideas is that which puts a perfect distinction between man and brutes, and is an excellency which the faculties of brutes do by no means attain to; for it is evident we observe no footsteps in them for making use of general signs for universal ideas; from which we have reason to imagine that they have not the faculty of abstracting, or making general ideas, since they have no use of words, or any other general signs.[113] . . . And, therefore, I think we may suppose, that it is in this that the species of brutes are discriminated from man; and it is that proper difference wherein they are wholly separated, and which at last widens to so vast a distance; for if they have any ideas at all and are not bare machines (as some would have them), we cannot deny them to have some reason. It seems as evident to me that they do, some of them in certain instances, reason as that they have sense; but it is only in particular ideas, just as they received them from their senses. They are the best of them tied up within those narrow bounds and have not (as I think) the faculty to enlarge them by any kind of abstraction."[114]

Authors who have ascribed the actions of beasts to an external principle. The *Nouvelles de la République des Lettres*[115] has published a summary of a book entitled *Essais nouveaux de morale*, which was published in Paris in 1686. The author, denying on the one hand that beasts have a soul capable of reasoning, avows on the other that their actions are directed by an "external reason and that this reason and this wisdom that leads them is a more excellent and surer wisdom and reason than that of man. . . . The reason," he continues, "that operates in beasts is not in them, . . . it is, as St. Thomas and all of the ancient Fathers say, the supreme and eternal reason of the su-

---

113 John Locke, *Essay Concerning Human Understanding*, Bk. II, chap. 11, para. 10. This is an excellent work, and it deserved to be translated into French as well as has been done by Coste. [This text is slightly shorter than Locke's final revision. Coste was evidently following an incomplete version.]

114 *Ibid.*, para. 11.

115 For October 1686 [at which time Bayle was its editor].

preme Architect, who preserves his works and directs them to the ends for which he created them by means of the secret mechanisms that he has put in them, which are differently determined in each case to make a thousand different kinds of motions according to what is needed." Add to that these words of Bernard. "Those philosophers who are most inclined to believe that beasts are only simple machines ought to admit frankly that they commit diverse actions whose mechanism cannot be explained. It would be much simpler to say in general that God, who wished that their mechanism continue for some time, has by his infinite wisdom arranged their parts in accord with this intention. I think I have read somewhere the thesis 'God is the soul of beasts.' This may appear a bit harsh, but it can be given a plausible explication."[118] Grotius has said that certain acts in which beasts give up their own interests in favor of others, proceed from an external intelligence. . . . Gaspar Ziegler in his note on this section complains that Grotius did not explain more clearly his view about the nature of this external principle. If it is Divine Providence, he continues, then Grotius leaves himself open to the attacks of Doctor Huarte, who has shown that a philosopher should not explain phenomena by the immediate operation of God. He cites two authors who have attributed to natural instinct all of the skill of animals, and he approves of their view. Osiander goes to great lengths to refute Grotius and says among other things that this external principle ought to be either God, or an angel, or Averroës' universal form, but that none of these three possibilities ought to be accepted. A propos of Averroës, I ought to say here that he admits a principle external to human intelligence, which is common to all particular minds, and which also influences beasts and stones. But, since he acknowledged that this influence remained without results with regard to beasts and insensible creatures, due to the fact that it fell on poorly arranged matter, it cannot be concluded that he attributed to beasts more perfection than the Scholastics have. . . . De Vigneul Marville relates that there was a philosopher who, in order to explain in Rohault's conferences, how, being only automata, beasts "nevertheless act is if they had souls," had recourse to the Count of Gabilis' hypothesis and by extending it made it fit his purpose; that is to say, he supposed that there are certain elementary spirits who apply themselves "to making all animal machines operate according to the laws of mechanics." His

---

[118] *Nouvelles de la République des Lettres*, October 1700.

discourse was very ingeniously developed, and it deserved what Pequet said to its author, namely, that, "If this lovely system is not true, at least it is a pretty invention." I have no doubts that it will please several people; but if I were to dispute about it here, it could easily be shown that it is incapable of accounting for the phenomena, and in certain respects it is more puzzling than the view of Descartes. What is most awkward for the Cartesians is not that beasts move readily in a thousand different ways, but that they exhibit many signs of friendship, hate, joy, jealousy, fear, suffering, and the like. The theory about these elementary spirits is of no use in explaining this since it is claimed that they only set the mechanisms in operation in beasts to amuse themselves. They would not then be crazy enough to subject themselves to the feeling of hunger, of cold, or of the pain which comes from blows of a stick, and so on. It would then be necessary to suppose that none of these passions are found in beasts, and there would be all the difficulties again. Or else it would be necessary to say that these spirits are condemned to direct animal machines in order to expiate their sins by suffering all the passions that the Peripatetics attribute to beasts, which is counter to the Gabalist philosophy. I will pass over other difficulties as great as this that can be posed against this theory that is claimed to be a "pretty invention."

Authors who have maintained that beasts are only machines or who have written against this. One can see in the *Nouvelles de la République des Lettres*[126] that Vallade, author of a philosophical discourse on the creation and the arrangement of the world, has explained mechanically the most surprising actions of animals. The same journal[127] tells us that De la Bruyère has been criticized for holding "that beasts are nothing but matter." You will find an illustration in the fine work of Dom Francois Lami[128] on the knowledge of one's self, "in which it is shown that there is no solid reason for attributing knowledge or immortality to the soul of beasts, whereas we cannot reasonably deny either to man's soul." This illustration is worth reading, and especially because one finds therein the solution to the most perplexing difficulty in the theory of automata; for the author shows by very strong reasons that each person can convince himself that other men are not simple machines; and yet this is what

---

[126] For October 1700.
[127] For April 1701.
[128] A Benedictine of the Congregation of St. Maur.

the opponents try to infer from the theory that beasts are composed of such well-arranged organs that they can do without knowledge all that we see them do. If God could make such a machine, they say, he could also make others that could perform all the actions of men, and consequently we can only be certain of our own thought, and we ought to doubt whether other men think. . . .

. . . .

«←

L. (Of the remarks that I wish to make on Leibniz' reflections.)

I shall begin by asserting that I am very pleased with myself for the slight difficulties that I raised against the theory of that great philosopher, since they have led to responses that have made the theory clearer to me and have made me see more distinctly what ought to be admired in it. I now consider this new theory as an important conquest that enlarges the bounds of philosophy. We had only two hypotheses, that of the Schools, and that of the Cartesians; the first was "the way of influence" of the body on the soul, and of the soul on the body; the other was "the way of assistance," or of occasional causality. But here we have a new acquisition, which we, with Father Lami, call "the way of pre-established harmony." We are indebted to Leibniz for it; and there is nothing else we can imagine that gives so exalted an idea of the intelligence and power of the Author of all things. This, added to the advantage of setting aside all notions of miraculous conduct, would make me prefer this theory to that of the Cartesians, if I could conceive some possibility in the way of "pre-established harmony." I trust that one will note that in asserting that this way sets aside all considerations of miraculous conduct, I am not retracting what I said previously, that the theory of occasional causes does not make the action of God enter in a miraculous way.[136] I am

---

[136] See the memoir that Leibniz has inserted in the *Histoire des Ouvrages des Savans*, July 1698. [This is Leibniz' famous essay entitled, "Letter to the author of *L'Histoire des Ouvrages des Savans;* containing an explanation of the difficulties that Bayle has found in the new system of the union of the soul and the body." After the appearance of remark L, Leibniz wrote another answer, "Reply of Leibniz to the reflections contained in the second edition of Bayle's *Critical Dictionary*, article 'Rorarius,' on the system of the pre-established harmony."

[Leibniz was most happy to have Bayle for an opponent and was only

as much convinced as ever that for an action to be miraculous God would have to produce it as an exception to the general laws; and everything of which he is the author, in accordance with these laws, is distinct from a miracle, properly so called. But, being willing to remove from this dispute as many things as I possibly can, I will agree to saying that the surest means of removing all miraculous considera- tions is to suppose that created substances are actively the immediate cause of the effects of nature. I will omit therefore what I could reply to this part of Leibniz' response. I shall also refrain from raising all those objections that are no more against his view than that of some other philosophers. Hence I will not set forth the difficulties that op- pose the supposition that a creature could receive from God the power of moving itself. These difficulties are great and almost insurmount- able;[137] but Leibniz' theory is no more open to attack on this score than is that of the Peripatetics; and I do not know whether the Car- tesians would dare to assert that God cannot communicate to our soul the power of acting. If they assert this, then how can they declare that Adam sinned? And if they do not dare assert it, they weaken the arguments by which they want to prove that matter is not susceptible

---

sorry that Bayle was unwilling to write more and more attacks so that Leib- niz could write more and more answers. The battle with Bayle was, for Leib- niz, one of the most fruitful ways of thinking out and developing his theory. In the reply to remark L, Leibniz said that he enjoyed reading the philo- sophical articles in the *Dictionary* and was always surprised at the fecundity, the force, and the brilliance of Bayle's views. "Never will any Academic skeptic, not excepting Carneades, make the difficulties more apparent. Foucher, though very capable in these matters, did not approach this level. And I find that nothing in the world is more useful for overcoming these same difficulties. It is this which leads me to be extremely pleased by the objections of capable and moderate people; for I feel that this gives me new strength. . . ."

[And, in a tribute to Bayle when he died in 1706, Leibniz said that he had profited very much from arguing with him about the pre-established har- mony, and that he hoped to have Bayle's criticisms of further aspects of Leibniz' system. Even when Bayle's objections were specious, he wrote in a draft of a letter to Jacquelot, one of Bayle's liberal Calvinist opponents, "I take pleasure in seeing and examining them, for these kinds of objections always serve to clarify the matter at hand and to set it in a new light." Leibniz' many comments about Bayle's attacks on the Leibniz system and on everything else indicate that the arguments of the author of the *Dictionary* served as catalytic agents for the sage of Hanover.]

137 See Sturmius' answers . . . especially *Acta eruditorum* for 1697 and 1699, the latter in answer to Leibniz' piece in *Acta* for 1698.

of any sort of activity. Also, I believe it would be every bit as difficult for Leibniz as for the Cartesians or other philosophers to protect himself from the objection of fatal mechanism, the demolishment of human liberty. Let us then leave this, and let us speak only of what applies especially to the theory of "pre-established harmony."

I. My first observation is that it raises the power and intelligence of divine art above what we can conceive. Imagine a ship that has neither sensation nor knowledge, and that is not directed by any created or uncreated being and yet has the power of moving itself so well that it always has favorable winds, that it avoids the currents and the reefs, that it casts anchor whenever it is necessary, and that it brings itself into a harbor whenever it has to. Suppose that such a ship sails in this way for several consecutive years, always turned and situated as it ought to be with regard to the changes in the air and the various locations of seas and lands. You will agree that the infinity of God is not great enough to communicate to a ship such power, and you will even say that the ship's nature is not capable of receiving this power from God. However, what Leibniz supposes about the mechanism of the human body is more wonderful and more surprising than all this. Let us apply to the person of Caesar his theory of the union of soul and body.

II. According to this theory, it must be said that the body of Julius Caesar exercised its moving faculty in such a way that from his birth to his death it went through a continual series of changes that corresponded exactly to the continual changes of a certain soul that it did not know and that made no impression on it. It must be said that the rule according to which that faculty of Caesar's body was to produce its acts was such that he would go to the senate on such and such a day, at such and such a time, that he would there pronounce such and such words, and so on, even if it had pleased God to annihilate Caesar's soul the day after it was created. It must be said that this motive faculty changed and modified itself punctually according to the volubility of the thoughts of that ambitious spirit and that it gave itself one state rather than another because the soul of Caesar went from one thought to another. Can a blind force modify itself so exactly as the result of an impression communicated thirty or forty years earlier, and which has not been renewed since, and which force is abandoned to itself without ever knowing what it has to do? Is this not much more incomprehensible than the voyage I spoke of in the preceding paragraph?

III. What augments the difficulty is that a human machine contains an almost infinite number of organs, and that it is perpetually
exposed to the shock of the bodies which surround it[138] and which by
an innumerable diversity of shakings excite a thousand kinds of modifications in it. How will it be possible to understand that there will
never be any disorder in this "pre-established harmony" and that it
will always go on its course no matter how long the life of a man
may be, notwithstanding the infinite variety of the reciprocal actions
of so many organs on one another, surrounded on all sides by innumerable particles, sometimes cold, sometimes hot, sometimes wet, sometimes dry, always active, always stimulating the nerves this way or
that? I will take it for granted that the multiplicity of organs and
external agents may be a necessary instrument of the almost infinite
variety of changes of the human body. But can this variety have such
an exactness as is required here? Will it never disturb the correspondence between these changes and those of the soul? This is what
seems completely impossible.

IV. In order to maintain that beasts are only automata, it would be
vain to have recourse to God's power; it would be vain to claim that
God can make machines so artistically arranged that a man's voice,
the reflected light of an object, and the like will strike exactly where
necessary to make it move in such and such a manner. All men, except
for a group of Cartesians, reject this supposition; and no Cartesian
would want to admit it if it were extended to man, that is to say, if it
were to be maintained that God can make bodies that could do mechanically all that we see other men do. In denying this, one is not
claiming to set limits to the power and knowledge of God. It is only
intended to indicate that the nature of things does not permit the
faculties communicated to creatures to exist without certain necessary
limitations. The actions of creatures must necessarily be proportioned
to their essential state and be performed in accordance with the char-

---

138 Observe that according to **Leibniz** what is active in each substance
is a thing that ought to be reduced to a true unity. Because, therefore, the
body of each man is composed of several substances, every one of them
must have a principle of action really distinct from the principle of the
others. He insists that the action of every principle must be spontaneous.
Now this ought to vary their effects infinitely and disturb them, for the
shock of neighboring bodies should place some constraint on the natural
spontaneity of each of them.

acter belonging to each machine, according to the axiom of the philosophers—whatever is received is proportional to the capacity of the subject. Leibniz' hypothesis can then be rejected as impossible since it contains greater difficulties than that of automata. It supposes a perfect harmony between two substances that do not act upon one another. But if servants were machines and punctually did this or that every time they were ordered to, it could not be said that they did it without any real action on the part of their master upon them; for he would speak some words and make some signs that would really set in motion the organs of the servants.

V. Let us now consider the soul of Caesar. We will find even more impossibilities. This soul was in the world without being exposed to the influence of any spirit. The strength that it had received from God was the sole principle of the particular actions that it produced each moment. And if these actions differed one from another, this was not the result of some being produced by the concourse of some springs that did not contribute to the production of the others since man's soul is simple, indivisible, and immaterial. Leibniz admits this; and if he did not agree but, on the contrary, supposed with most philosophers and with some of the most excellent metaphysicians of our time[140] that a being composed of several material parts arranged in a certain way is capable of thinking, I would regard his hypothesis as absolutely impossible on that account; and there would be many other ways of refuting it, which I do not have to bring up here since he acknowledges the immateriality of our soul and builds upon this. Let us come back to the soul of Julius Caesar, and let us call it an immaterial automaton,[141] and let us compare it with one of Epicurus' atoms (I mean an atom surrounded by a vacuum on all sides, and which never comes in contact with any other atom). This comparison is very just; for on the one hand this atom has the natural power of self-movement and exerts this without being aided by anything else whatsoever and without being retarded or interfered with by anything; and on the other hand Caesar's soul is a spirit 'which has received a faculty of producing thoughts and which exerts this without the influence of any other spirit or body. Nothing helps it. Nothing

---

[140] Locke, for example.

[141] Leibniz makes use of this expression in his memoir inserted in the *Histoire des Ouvrages des Savans*, July 1698. "The soul," he says, "is a most perfect immaterial automaton."

hinders it. If you consult the common notions and the ideas of order, you will find that this atom would never stop, and that being moved the preceding moment it ought to move in this moment and in all those that will follow, and that the manner of its movement ought to be always the same. This is the consequence of an axiom approved by Leibniz, which is "that a thing always remains in the state it is in, if nothing happens that makes it change. . . ."[142] "We conclude," he says,[143] "not only that a body at rest will always be at rest, but also that a body in motion will always keep this motion or change, that is, the same velocity and the same direction, if nothing interferes with it." Everyone knows clearly that this atom, whether it moves itself by an innate power, as Democritus and Epicurus have insisted, or whether by a power received from the Creator, will always move forward uniformly, and also along the same line, without its ever happening to turn to the right or the left or go backwards. Epicurus was laughed at when he invented the movement of declination.[144] He gratuitously assumed its existence in order to extricate himself from the labyrinth of the fatal necessity of all things, and he could give no good reason for this new part of his theory. It clashes with the most evident notions of our mind. For one clearly conceives that in order for an atom that is assumed to have followed a straight line for two days to turn itself from its route at the beginning of the third, there has to be some obstacle or some desire to move it from its path, or there must be some inner springs that start operating at this moment. The first of these reasons is incompatible with empty space. The second is impossible since an atom has no power of thinking. The third is similarly impossible for an absolutely unified particle. Let us make some use of all this.

VI. The soul of Caesar is a being to which unity belongs in a rigorous sense. The faculty of producing thoughts is a property of the soul's own nature.[145] It has received this faculty from God both with regard to possession and exertion. If the first thought that it gives

---

142 Memoir inserted in the *Histoire des Ouvrages des Savans,* July 1698.

143 Leibniz, in the same place, insists that he assents to this axiom. "And I assert," he adds, "that it is most favorable to me since it is indeed one of the bases of my system."

144 See remark U of the article "Epicurus" [not included in these selections].

145 This is said according to the theory of Leibniz.

itself is a feeling of pleasure, then why is not the second one also this? For when the total cause of an effect remains the same, the effect cannot change. Now this soul at the second moment of its existence does not receive a new faculty of thought. It only retains the faculty that it had in the first moment and is as independent of the concourse of all other causes in the second moment as it was in the first. Therefore it ought to reproduce in the second moment the thought that it had just produced. If you answer me that it ought to be in a state of change and it would not be in the case that I have supposed, I reply to you that its change would be like the change of the atom; for an atom that moves continually along the same line acquires at each moment a new location, but one that is like the preceding location. A soul may therefore continue in its state of changing, if it gives itself a new thought like its preceding one. Let us not limit this soul so narrowly. Let us allow it a metamorphosis of thoughts; it would be necessary, as a minimum, that the transition from one thought to another include some reason of affinity. If I suppose that at a certain moment Caesar's soul sees a tree in flower and with leaves, I can conceive[146] that it may immediately wish to see one that has only leaves and then one that has only flowers, and that in this manner it will form for itself several images that will arise one from another. But one cannot set forth as possible the strange changes from black to white and from yes to no, or those tumultuous leaps from earth to heaven, which are common in man's thoughts. We cannot understand how God was able to put the principle I am going to speak about into the soul of Julius Caesar. No doubt it happened to him more than once that he was pricked with a pin while he was nursing. It would then have been necessary according to the theory being examined here that his soul modified itself with a sensation of pain immediately after pleasant sensations of the sweetness of milk, which it had had continuously for two or three minutes. By what mechanism was it determined to interrupt its pleasures and to give itself suddenly a sensation of pain when nothing had alerted it to prepare itself for this change and when no alteration took place in its substance? If you run through the life of this first Roman emperor, you will find material for an objection much stronger than this at each stage.

---

[146] I speak in this manner by way of concession; that is to say, I do not wish to take advantage of the reasons that prevent our believing that a created spirit can give itself ideas.

VII. This would be more comprehensible if we supposed that man's soul is not a spirit but rather a legion of spirits, each of which has its functions that begin and end precisely as demanded by the changes that occur in the human body. As a result of this it would be necessary to say that something analogous to a great number of wheels and springs, or to material that ferments, arranged according to the changes of our machine, wakes up or puts to sleep for such and such a time the action of each of these spirits. But then the soul of man would no longer be a substance. It would be a *being by aggregation,* a heap and collection of substances, just like material beings. We are seeking here for a single being that may form at one time joy, at another grief, and so on. We are not looking for several beings, one of whom produces hope, and another despair, and so on.

The above mentioned observations are only the development of those that Leibniz did me the honor of examining. I am now going to make some reflections on his answers.

VIII. He says[147] that "the law of change of the animal substance transports it from joy to pain the instant that it makes a 'solution of continuity' in its body because the law of the indivisible substance of this animal is to express what occurs in its body in the manner in which we experience it, and even to express in some fashion, and in relation to this body, all that happens in the world." These words are a very good explanation of the foundations of this theory. They are, as it were, the unraveling of, and the key to it. But at the same time they constitute the view of the objections of those who find this new hypothesis impossible. The law we are told of supposes a decree of God and shows in what way this theory agrees with that of occasional causes. These two theories come together at this point, that there are laws according to which the soul of man "ought to express what occurs in its body in the manner in which we experience it." But these theories disagree about the way in which these laws are put into execution. The Cartesians claim that God is the executor. Leibniz wants the soul to execute them itself. It is this that appears impossible to me, the soul not having the instruments that would be required for such an execution. Now, no matter how infinite the knowledge and power of God may be, he cannot make a machine that is missing a certain piece perform a function that requires the concourse

147 Leibniz' memoir inserted in the *Histoire des Ouvrages des Savans,* July 1698.

of this piece. He would have to supply this defect, and in that case it would be he, and not the machine, that would produce this effect. Let us show that the soul does not have the necessary instruments for the execution of the divine law we have been told of, and let us make use of this comparison.

Let us imagine arbitrarily an animal created by God and destined to sing incessantly. It will always sing; this is indubitable. But if God allots to it a certain musical score, it is absolutely necessary either that he put it in front of its eyes, or that he imprint it in its memory, or that he give it an arrangement of muscles that according to the laws of mechanics would make such and such a tone follow another precisely according to the order in the score. Without this we cannot conceive how this animal will ever be capable of following the whole series of notes as set down by God. Let us apply a similar plan to man's soul. Leibniz claims not only that it has received the faculty of continually giving itself thoughts but also the faculty of always following a certain order of thoughts that corresponds to the continual changes of the body's machine. This order of thoughts is like the score allotted to the animal musician we spoke of above. In order to change its perceptions or modifications at each moment according to this score of thoughts, would this soul not have to know the series of notes and actually think about them? Now experience shows us that it knows nothing about them. Would it not be at least necessary in the absence of such knowledge that there should be a series of particular instruments, each of which would be the necessary cause of such and such a thought? Would they not have to be placed in such a manner that the right one operated after another according to the pre-established correspondence between the changes in the body's machine and the soul's thoughts? Now it is quite certain that an immaterial, simple, and indivisible substance cannot be composed of this innumerable multitude of particular instruments placed one in front of the other according to the score in question. It is therefore not possible that the human soul executes this law.

Leibniz supposes that the soul does not distinctly know its future perceptions, "but that it perceives them confusedly, and that there are in every substance traces of everything that has happened to it and everything that will happen to it;[149] but this infinite multitude of

---

[149] This is what cannot be conceived of in an indivisible, simple, and immaterial substance.

perceptions prevents us from distinguishing them. . . . The present state of each *substance is a natural consequence of its preceding state.* . . . The soul, notwithstanding its simplicity, always has a sensation composed of several perceptions at one and the same time, which answers to our purpose as much as if it were composed of parts, like a machine. For every preceding perception has some influence on those that follow in conformity to a law of order that is in perceptions as well as in motions. . . . As the perceptions that are found together in the same soul at the same time include a numberless multiude of small indistinguishable sensations that may be unfolded later on, we must not wonder at the infinite variety of what is to result from it in time. All this is only a consequence of the soul that must express what happens and even what will happen in its body, and in some fashion in all the other bodies, by connection or correspondence of all the parts of the world." I have not much to reply to this. I will only say that this supposition, after it is carefully and completely worked out, will be the true means of resolving all difficulties. Leibniz, by the penetration of his great genius, has very well understood the entire extent and force of the objection and what ought to be the source of the remedy of the principal inconvenience. I am convinced that he will smooth out the rough places in his theory and that he will teach us some excellent things about the nature of spirits. No one is able to travel more usefully or more surely in the intelligible world than he. I hope that his beautiful clarifications will make all the impossibilities that have come to my mind so far disappear, and that he will resolve, in a solid way, my difficulties as well as those of Dom François Lami. And it is with these hopes that I have been able to say, without just trying to pay a compliment, that his theory ought to be considered as an important conquest.

It will not cause much of a problem that, instead of the Cartesian supposition that there is only one general law for the union of all minds with bodies, Leibniz claims that God gives a particular law to each spirit. From this it would seem to follow that the primitive constitution of each spirit is different in species from all the others.[154] Do not the Thomists say that in the angelic nature there are as many species as individuals?

---

[154] No two men ever had the same thoughts, I do not say for a month together, but not even for two minutes. The principle of thought therefore must have a rule and a particular nature in each one.

Rufinus, the favorite of the Emperor Theodosius, "was a Gaul from the province of Aquitaine, who came from a lowly condition but possessed an exalted mind of a supple, insinuating, and polished kind, fit to divert a prince and even capable of serving one. He came to the court of Constantinople; he made friends there as well as protectors; he became known to Theodosius; he pleased the latter. He made such good use of these beginnings of his fortune that soon he obtained considerable positions. The emperor gave him the post of high steward of his palace, admitted him into all his councils, honored him with his friendship and confidence, and finally made him consul with his son Arcadius. This man preserved his position as he had acquired it—by his cunning rather than his virtue. His ambition grew along with his fortune. He sought to enrich himself with the spoils of those whom he oppressed by his slanders. It was enough, in order to become his enemy, that one possess extraordinary merit and be able to challenge his exalted position. Nevertheless, since he feared losing the friendship of the prince if he did not keep his esteem, he appeared modest and disinterested. He covered his evil counsels with the specious pretense of justice or policy; and he knew so well how to set off his good qualities and hide his bad ones that the emperor, though wise, and though jealous of his authority, was often deceived and manipulated without realizing it. The chief lords of the court could not watch the rise of this favorite without being piqued. . . . They conspired together against him and resolved to destroy him,"[b] but their efforts only led to their own ruin or strengthened his authority. He was baptized with great pomp in 394. He so resented seeing Stilico above him after the death of Theodosius that he carried on the treasonable

---

[b] Flechier, *Histoire de Théodose,* Bk. IV.

255

enterprises that undid him. "He took advantage of his master's weakness, and he set at variance the empires and the emperors by his secret understandings with the Huns, the Goths, and the Alans," and he wanted "to make himself sovereign, or at least independent of both his masters and his enemies."[c] He was killed in 395.[d] See Moreri. His death put an end to the doubts that had troubled Claudian about the question of whether there is a Providence. He no longer doubted as soon as he saw the fall of this insolent and unjust favorite. I shall make some reflections on his words (C), and this will give me the occasion to examine if all of those who have maintained the orthodox view regarding Providence have observed the rules of disputation well. Naudé asserts something that is quite false, namely, that Rufinus has been praised by three or four famous historians.

≪←

    C. (*I shall make some reflections on Claudian's doubts.*) He declares that the beautiful order that reigns in nature led him to believe that it is directed by the very wise laws of an infinite God; but that the disorder that reigns among men, the prosperity of the wicked, the unhappiness of the virtuous led him to follow the Epicurean hypothesis that all things happened by chance and that the gods did not enter into the affairs of the world. "Finally," he said, "the punishment of Rufinus removed my doubts. I entirely absolve the gods. I no longer complain that the wicked acquired so much power, for they are only raised up so that they may fall farther." He will tell us this better himself.

> *Frequent my mind sad doubts has entertained,*
> *Whether the gods regard terrestrial things;*
> *Or (none presiding) they by chance are hurled.*
> *For, when my eyes beheld this beauteous frame,*
> *And all things moving in such glorious order;*
> *The swelling sea within its bounds restrained;*
> *The various progress of the rolling year;*
> *And the alternate change of day and night:*

---

[c] Ibid.
[d] According to Flechier this happened in 397.

I thence concluded, that a deity
Directed all with an almighty sway.
That he gave motion to the circling planets;
And bid the fruits in various seasons rise.
Bid the fair moon with borrowed luster shine,
And Phoebus glitter by his native rays.
Bid the proud waves extend to every shore,
And this round ball to hang on its own axis.
But when I saw all human things involved
In such deep gloom; the wicked flourish high,
And good men groan beneath a load of woe:
Religion's dictates soon forsook my bosom,
And I the famed hypothesis maintained,
Which wildly fancies that the seeds of things,
Confusedly hurled through the extended void,
Not by amazing art, but chance, produced
The unnumbered worlds that compass us around:
Which vainly thinks no deities exist,
Or that they proudly disregard vain mortals.
But now, the punishment Rufinus met with
Has cleared my anxious doubts and justified
The immortal gods. I now no more complain
To see the wicked raised to fortune's summit:
For such are lifted to a greater height
Only to make their sudden fall more dreadful.

(Claudian, *In Rufinum* I. 1–24)

I have promised in the article on the Maréchal d'Ancre,[7] to speak here of the reflections of Balzac on a thought of Malherbe that is similar to Claudian's. Now I will keep my promise. "It is true that one spoke this way before the Christian religion had reformed our speech. The gods were accused of all of the evil that men did. Divine Providence was impeached daily by someone who complained that the affairs of this world were not going on as he would have wished them to. 'This happy tyrant bears witness against god' is an ancient saying mentioned by Cicero. And there is nothing so common in the verses of the pagan poets as the crime of their gods and their fate. . . . 'Cynthia is sick; and if she dies of her illness,' says the poet who is

---

[7] See remark F of the article "Concini." [Not included in these selections. Concino Concini, the Maréchal d'Ancre, was the detested prime minister of France under the regency of Marie de Médicis. He was killed in 1617; and after his burial the corpse was disinterred, cooked, and eaten on the Pont-Neuf by the citizens of Paris. At the trial of his wife Leonora Galigai, the Concinis were accused of practicing Judaism and sorcery. After the trial Leonora Galigai was burned alive.]

in love with her, 'the death of such a beauty will be the crime of the god of medicine.' . . . Since the time of Constantine even, and under the children of Theodosius, there have been examples of this poetic blasphemy and profane liberty. If Rufinus had not been punished for his crimes, the gods would have been impeached as abettors and accomplices of Rufinus. . . . One of our poets has said something like this, but in a most excellent manner, and his copy surpasses the original works. I offer it to you as a masterpiece that can be compared with the most beautiful and most finished pieces of antiquity. The god of the Seine speaks to a favorite who was passing over the Pont-Neuf."[8] I shall not copy the verses of Malherbe cited by Balzac. You will find the conclusion of them in the article "Concini," remark F.* Let us add to the passage from Balzac one from Ménage. "By the way this thought, 'And heaven, accused of winking at thy crimes, resolves to clear up its mysterious conduct,' is not originally from Claudian. It appears in several authors before him. . . ." . . . Barthius has collected a great number of such sentences and has not omitted those appearing in Scripture. One could mention here all the passages of the ancients where Fortune is attacked as a blind, inconstant, vagabond, unjust being, an abettor of the unworthy.[13] One of the passages will serve as an example of all of them. I will take it from Pliny. "Mankind has invented, between these two opinions, a medium whereby the conjecture with regard to the existence of God is become more uncertain than before. For in every part of the world, in all places, and at all times, Fortune alone is invoked by all persons; is only named, accused, condemned, thought on, praised, censured, and adored with reproaches; fickle, and thought by most people to be

---

[8] Guez de Balzac, *Socrate chrétien.*

* [The verses in question are:

> *The life is near its end; prepare, prepare*
> *For mighty ruin, lo! thy fall's at hand:*
> *Once more behold me—once, then leave the world.*
> *Enough that five long years thy frantic pride,*
> *On waxen wing convey'd beyond the stars,*
> *Dared to contend for sway with potent kings.*
> *Fortune now calls thee to her splendid victims;*
> *And heaven, accused of winking at thy crimes,*
> *Resolves to clear up its mysterious conduct.*

Bayle gives a good deal of data about Concini and his wife in the two articles, "Concini" and "Galigai."]

[13] See remark H in the article "Pays" [Not included in these selections].

blind; inconstant, uncertain, various, and an abettor of the undeserving. To her all things given and received are ascribed, and she alone fills both pages in all human account books. And we are so greatly subject to chance that chance itself is looked upon as a god, whereby the existence of God is made uncertain."[14] It can be said that in all ages and in all countries, not excepting either our century or Christendom, the prosperity of the wicked has made people murmur against God and has inspired many doubts about Providence. On the other hand, this objection has been answered in all times and places. Therefore, since it has kept recurring notwithstanding all the replies made to it, we must conclude that it contains something very specious and possesses I know not what relation to our understanding which allows it to return there with no difficulty though it is thrown out with pitchforks. It might be said that one could attribute to it the lovely words said of the palm tree, "curvata resurgo," ["Having been bowed, I rise again"]; the replies may indeed make me bend a little, but I quickly straighten myself out.   It is not at issue to examine whether this point is solid; for we must be completely convinced that it is false, that it is worthless. But perhaps it will not be improper to ask if Claudian answered it well.

Considerations Concerning the Methods for Answering Doubts about Providence; Laws of Disputation.

There might be people who would say to him: "You have not taken the right path. The only answer you ought to have made to your difficulty was to consider the vast and immense idea of a supremely perfect being and to draw this consequence from it: he is the author of all things; he governs everything; then nothing happens that is not governed and conducted in an infinitely just and infinitely admirable way. This is certainly the right way to remove the doubts. Silence reason, and oblige it to submit to authority.[17] God said it, God did it, God has permitted it. It is therefore true and just, wisely done, and wisely permitted. If you want to descend into the detail of particular arguments, you will never see the end of it; and after a thousand disputes you will be constrained to have recourse to the reason of authority, to the immense idea of the supremely perfect being. But

---

14 Pliny, II. 5.

17 "I was dumb, I opened not my mouth; because thou didst it" (Psalms 39:9).

since we must come back to this, let us not leave it; let us adhere immovably and unshakably to it, putting our fingers on our mouths, imposing silence on our imperfect knowledge, persuaded that in these matters the best use of reason is not to reason at all." Let us make the motives for this kind of conduct be felt more forcefully. When one engages in a dispute one ought to claim that one will make his adversary see that he is wrong; but one should not expect him to yield to our first or our second replies. The laws of this sort of dispute require that each party reply to the other as many times as they oppose argument to argument until they have come to first principles. If I can show a man that his thesis is repugnant to common notions and that mine is the natural and necessary consequence of these notions, then I do not have to listen to him any more; and I can silence him with the axiom, "There is no disputing with those who deny the principles." But if I give only a probable solution to his objections, against which he can advance new doubts that are as probable, or almost as probable, as my solution, then I have no right to demand that he acquiesce to my answers. I must search for new solutions to his new difficulties; and if I do not find any evident ones, or ones that will not admit of a specious reply, then I am the one who ought to retire from the combat without claiming victory. Otherwise I would be like the Catholics who tried to convert the French Protestants. Around 1680 these gentlemen began offering to dispute about religion with their errant brethren. They promised to listen to their doubts, to enlighten them, to instruct them cordially. But after they had replied two or three times, they would no longer allow any contradiction; they wanted those whom they were enlightening to give in to them, otherwise they would declare that they were obstinate. It would have been much better if they had said this at the outset. It is ridiculous to enter into a discussion when one is not willing to suffer his adversary to answer hundreds and hundreds of times. . . . This is how disputes are conducted. Someone attacks your thesis. You answer. But your answer is quite often more open to difficulties than the thesis itself. It is then right for you to refute his reply. You answer again with I know not what, which gives rise to new doubts more plausible than the first ones. These then have to be examined, and so on to infinity, unless you can get the common notions[18] on your side, to

---

[18] By common notions here are understood, in general, all the principles that two contending parties agree on.

crush your antagonist with them. These are the laws of combat. If you do not intend to observe them, it is better not to enter the contest but say at once, "This must be believed without reasoning. God has said it, that ought to be sufficient."

This procedure would be unjust if the state of the question was, "Has God spoken?" But it is not unjust when one disputes with people who acknowledge the existence of a supremely perfect being, and who foment doubts on the pretext that the virtuous people are unhappy and the wicked prosper. The only response that ought to be given to these doubters is this: "You are convinced of the existence of a supremely perfect nature. Believe then that it governs all things perfectly well. For if you will not draw this conclusion from the principle you accept, you do not know the first rules of common sense. You would be capable of reasoning in this manner: The sun is incapable of producing shadows, therefore it has produced them." To show better why we should keep to that short response and that general principle of the existence of God, I am going to show what one gets into when one descends into the details of particular reasons. First of all, in such a case one surely is obliged to answer all the replies of an adversary until he can be offered a reason to which he has nothing to reply. These are the laws of dispute, as I have indicated above. In the second place, it is certain that your particular reasons will be fought to infinity by other reasons more or less equally specious. Let us show this by a small example. Our poet would have asserted to someone else the same reason that dissipated all of his doubts. He would have said to him, "Since Rufinus has been punished, there is a Providence that governs all things wisely and justly. The prosperity of that wicked man did not prove that Providence was asleep, but, on the contrary, that it was preparing little by little a more severe punishment. It lifted him up so that he could fall farther, that he would break all his bones; 'For such are lifted to a greater height only to make their sudden fall more dreadful.'" Our poet might have been answered, "If this is all that you know, though your solution be ever so old, it is not good. You get out of a great difficulty by raising a still greater one. Your particle *ut* ['so that'] strikes one with horror, and one cannot think of the idea without trembling. You ascribe to the supremely perfect being, and consequently one with an infinite goodness, a motive and a final cause that, far from containing any vestige of goodness, are the most tyrannical and the most demoniacal that can be conceived. It is as if one of our emperors, wishing to put some of his servants to death, should appoint them as governors of provinces and allow them to exercise every kind of violence until they suck the marrow of the populace's bones; it is, I say, as if he allowed this in order to punish them more severely. If you had dared to say of Theodosius what you say of God, that he raised Rufinus to the summit of his favor only to be able to crush him more surely and more severely and in order to show the populace his sovereign power of raising and lowering, he would have had you hanged as a satirical poet who had insolently defamed him." Claudian doubtless would have recognized the enormity of his *ut* and of his final cause, and would have asked that his words not be taken in so strict and criminal a sense. He would say that the design of Providence in heaping up such riches upon the infamous Rufinus was not to make his punishment greater, but rather was in hopes that this favorite would make good use of them. He would add that according to natural laws the fall of a body is much more violent when the place from which it fell is higher, and that thus Rufinus' elevation would aggravate his punishment when his continual abuse of the heavenly favors called out for his chastisement. Claudian will be answered: "This does not remove the difficulty. Hope has no place in the divine nature. It knows infallibly all that will happen. It certainly knew of the abuse that Rufinus would make of the heavenly favors. It therefore would have been better to have prevented the abuse than to tolerate his crimes for several years in order to inflict a punishment on him that cannot compensate for the evil he did, the oppression of so many innocent people, the death of so many persons, the ruin of so many families. It is a poor satisfaction for a province whose governor is desolating it for the people to be assured that he will be punished. It is still as miserable as before, while the arrest sometimes makes the criminal's condition more agreeable." I shall not go on with the replies the poet might make. There are a very great number of them, I do not doubt this at all. But the replies of his adversary would not be less numerous and would resemble those we have just seen, that is to say, they would be more proportionate to our mind's notions and to the ideas by which we judge the perfection of a government, than those of Claudian. I suppose that after a long dispute he would be told, "I believe as much as you that all that occurred in the Rufinus affair is just and perfect in relation to God; but not because of the reasons you

offer. They are more fit to give rise to doubts than to calm the irreso-
lution of the mind. Nevertheless, make use of them for those who will
be happy with them; but do not say a word about them to great reasoners. The idea of a supremely perfect being ought to and does suffice for them when they make good use of their reason. I have known
some people who have read Boethius' *The Consolation of Philosophy*
several times, and who remain surprised at the difference they have
always noticed between the objections and the responses of that
author. Boethius was both an able philosopher and a very good man.
Overwhelmed by the enormous weight of his disgrace and with his
soul plunged into sadness, he imagines that philosophy has come to
console him. He made several objections to it concerning Providence,
and philosophy answers as well as it can. But whereas the difficulties
posed by Boethius can be understood by the least penetrating minds
and reach the understanding of even the dullest persons, the answers
require the strongest attention and the utmost vivacity to grasp at all.
Philosophy cannot hide her diffidence. She asks always to be allowed
to proceed circuitously and to mount higher. And no matter how just
may be what she says, we unhappily cannot always understand her.
If she convinces us, it is almost always without enlightening us. This
is what some readers of Boethius say. They have pointed out to me that
a very subtle seventeenth-century professor has protected the honor of
philosophy more adroitly than Boethius did. For, after having introduced a pagan who propounds thousands of doubts about Providence,
he offers him no other expedient than the grace of the Holy Spirit.[22]

I must not end this remark before observing the injustice of certain
people who believe that, when one rejects the reasons given for a
doctrine, one also rejects the doctrine. There is the greatest difference
between these two things. Persons of an equitable and judicious turn
of mind will not fail to distinguish them and will very patiently allow,
without forming any bad suspicions, that one may oppose the temerity of the orthodox with regard to the weak arguments that have too
often been used to maintain the truth. Abuses can be committed in
this way. For example, the Pyrrhonists, under the pretext of only
combatting the reasons offered by the dogmatists for proving the existence of God, effectively undermine the doctrine itself. They declared
at the outset[23] that they followed the common opinion, without ad-

---

22 Claudius Berigardus, *In priores libros Phys. Aristot.*
23 Sextus Empiricus, *Pyrrhoniarum hypotoposeon* III. 1.

hering to any particular sect, that they agreed that there are gods, that they honored them; that they attributed a providence to them, but that they could not bear to have the dogmatists rashly reasoning about this. Then they propounded objections to them, which by overthrowing providence tended to overthrow the existence of God. See Sextus Empiricus, who instead of basing his doubts as Claudian did on the prosperity of the wicked, bases them on the adversity and evil that the world is full of. He presents the argument that has been better stated than refuted by Lactantius. See, on this, the article "Paulicians," remark E, footnote 16 [p. 169], and the words of a Jesuit who has observed that Arnobius admits that this argument is insoluble. . . .*

---

* [Bayle closes remark C with a quotation to this effect from the work *Theologia naturali* by the seventeenth-century Jesuit, Theophilus Raynaud.]

Sanchez, THOMAS, a Spanish Jesuit, born in Cordova in 1551, entered the order in 1567. The austerity of his life, his sobriety, his macerations, his application to study, his chastity were all prodigious, if what Alegambe and Southwell tell of him is true. He died at Granada on May 19, 1610, and was interred there magnificently. His learning was unquestionable. He gave public proof of it in the large volume that was printed in Genoa in 1592 and in the four folio volumes that appeared after his death. It would be desirable that the work printed in Genoa, and then in many other cities, gave as much proof of his good judgment as of his wit and learning; for his rashness in explaining an incredible number of obscene and horrible questions can produce great disorders. There have been bitter complaints, and all that has been said to justify him is weak (C), and yet there are casuists who continue to publish similar obscenities every day.[f] They have done this for a long time, and it is a deplorable thing to see that the courtiers who had filled their memoirs with all sorts of stories of that kind have cited as a repertory the *"Summa Bene-*

≪←

C. (*All that has been said to justify him is weak.*) The critics of this writer can claim two things. One is that he could not spread such great details of obscenities on paper without himself being an indecent person. "There are extant among others the writings of some Jesuits upon these subjects, in which such things are explained as

---

[f] See the censure of the book of Amadeus Guimenius made by the Faculty of Theology of Paris on February 3, 1665. Several propositions are there condemned which are only designated by their first words, and which one did not dare translate into French for fear of offending the modesty and decency of chaste ears.

dicti—[Benedictus] who is a Franciscan scholar, who wrote very well on all the sins and shows that he has seen and read a great deal."[g] This work of Benedictus has been translated into French. It was published in this language in Lyons in 1584, and in Paris in 1602, a service we could well have done without.

scarce the devil himself with his utmost imagination could suggest; and in these books they inquire into not only the several kinds, and species, but also all the ways, objects, subjects, and circumstances, so minutely, that no man in his senses can think these things proceeded from a pure and chaste mind. Among these writers, one of the most eminent is Thomas Sanchez, a Spanish Jesuit, in his large volume *De matrimonio*."[9] The other thing is that he could not communicate to the public the knowledge of so many monstrous irregularities without doing great harm to good manners, since it is certain that several persons are led to commit these abominations when they learn that they are practiced. A prudent man, zealous for the salvation of his neighbor, must then carefully avoid revealing the types of lewdness that he has learned of in the confessional, for it should be certain that those who know nothing about it will abstain much better from it than those who know the enormity and the turpitude of it.

Concerning the first of these two accusations, Sanchez' friends answer that he was a man of admirable virtue and perfect chastity. His immaculate virginity accompanied him to the grave, they say; and the day he was buried, everyone tried either to kiss or touch with their rosary his dead body, which was covered with flowers and shone with a virginal beauty.[10] . . . They refer us to some authors who praised the purity of his life. . . . This amounts to telling us that his mind and his imagination were filled with these impure matters, without his heart or his body being infected by the contagion. Many persons are convinced that that was hardly less difficult than to have been like the Hebrew children in the Babylonian furnace without being burned. But after all, it would not be impossible that the horror that might be conceived against these execrable abuses of marriage could have preserved the innocence of an author who should wallow in this filth;

g Brantôme, *Dames galantes*, Vol. I.

9 Andr. Rivet, *Explicat. Decalogi.*

10 Southwell, *Biblioth. Scriptor. Societ. Jesu;* and Theophilus Raynaud, *De bonis et malis libris.*

of an author, I say, whose age, temperament, and education would be powerful preservatives against the pollutions of the flesh. There is reason to believe that authors who spend too much time in explaining the *Priapeia* and the dirty portions of Catullus and Martial are not very chaste, and it is only too certain that there have been commentators who dwelt on these matters who only studied them and sifted them out of curiosity because they were lewd men. However, we ought not to make this a general rule, for the desire of showing a great amount of reading and erudition is very capable of engaging a humanist to comment amply on the poets I have spoken of. The first reading of their poems makes a strong attack upon virtue, especially on that of young people. Little by little they get hardened to it, and there are critics, who, after having read Catullus and Martial many times, either to find some enlightenment there about some ancient custom or illustrate them with a commentary, are no more moved by their obscenities than if they read an aphorism of Hippocrates. The same thing happens to these critics as happens to doctors and surgeons, who by being used to handling ulcers and finding themselves exposed to bad odors, become accustomed to them and are not bothered. God grant that confessors and casuists whose ears are the sewers for all the filth of human life may be able to boast of being so hardened! There are, no doubt, only too many of them who never achieve this, and whose virtue is shipwrecked by hearing the irregularities of their penitents. But this leads to no conclusion about any person in particular. That is why we would be very rash if we were to claim that Thomas Sanchez did not possess that insensibility and that he was infected by the stinking filth that he stirred so much. And after all he had an excuse that even the most chaste commentators on the *Catalecta* could not have; for he could say that he only put his hand to these obscenities in order to try to rid the world of them. It is in this way that they try to answer the second accusation which is much more perplexing than the first.

I have mentioned elsewhere[13] what was said to justify Albertus Magnus, who was in the same situation. His friends claim that there have to be books in which confessors can find necessary instructions against the disorders confided in them and that thus a great teacher, such as he, had to write on the matter. This is what has been answered in

---

[13] See remark **D** of the article "Albertus" [not included in these selections].

favor of Sanchez. The obscene questions and the enormous examples of lewdness that he examines so precisely, we are told, are of much use to the directors of conscience. We should not then be scandalized. Would anyone find it bad if a doctor, for the good of his patients, stirred their excrements? This consideration convinced the Jesuits not to remove from Sanchez' book the obscenities that people complained about. One of them said, among other things, that, having to judge one of the most impure matters there can be, he would never have been able to overcome the insurmountable difficulties that came up if he had not had the solutions of that author.[14] . . . The Abbé de Saint-Cyran, under the name of Petrus Aurelius, had refuted this bad argument in advance. He maintains that this work could cause a great deal of harm and could render only a little help. In exhibiting to public view an infinite number of infamous, lascivious acts that are committed in the marriage bed, pious souls are scandalized; and the curiosity of some and the lewdness of others are excited, and so on. However, if the directors of conscience have to say something about such matters, it is much better that they have recourse to the living voice of learned experts than to an easily available book in which it is very difficult to find the same case that may be in question, with exactly the same circumstances. It must be admitted that this observation is a very solid one. The Roman Catholics have been very wrong in not imitating the sects of ancient philosophy that never taught their entire system in writing. They reserved a part of it to be taught orally to their favorite disciples. This part was preserved only by tradition. The pope should have forbidden the casuists to publish anything concerning cases of lewdness. He should have taken care that the instruction of confessors, both with regard to questions and penances on that important subject, be communicated to one another privately, or at most by manuscript, kept under the seal of secrecy. . . .

The other arguments of Theophilus Raynaud are no better. He quotes long passages from St. Chrysostom that show that this Church Father has set forth the infamous impurities of his age in a lively and naïve manner. He shows that St. Epiphanius has described the obscenities of the Gnostics in the same way, and that St. Cyril employed the same liberty in describing those of the Manicheans. It is maintained that Hincmar, in the work on the divorce of Lotharius and

---

[14] Theophilus Raynaud, *Hoplotheca*.

Tetberga, has written more obscenely than Thomas Sanchez. He says that the excuses that St. Chrysostom, St. Ephiphanius, St. Cyril, and Hincmar have made to their auditors or to their readers can serve as an apology for his fellow Jesuit. He mentions what Raoul de Flavigni has observed against the false delicacy of those who condemn the lewd expressions Moses employed in Leviticus. But it is so easy to perceive the difference that exists between these examples and the conduct of the Spanish writer that I shall not devote any time to showing the weakness and uselessness of this comparison. Everyone easily sees that the same liberties that are allowed to those who know a fact that either has been shown by the researches of historians or by the proceedings of a court of law ought to be forbidden to those who are only aware of it through auricular confession. The ancient Fathers had the right to enjoy the liberty of making known the execrable irregularities of heretics. Hincmar was able to write an account of the extremely impure conduct of a repudiated queen; and when once vice is attested to either by history or by court record, authors have a right to mention it if it is pertinent. But, as for vices that are only revealed to confessors, they should be treated in another way. I shall leave aside what many people would not fail to say, namely, that there is no famous preacher today who would dare to take the same liberties in this matter as St. Chrysostom and St. Cyril have done, and that if some writer of the ancient Church ought to be imitated on this, it is Salvianus, from whom Theophilus Raynaud offers these fine words. "All these things are so scandalous that no person can explain or represent them consistently with modesty. For who, without offering violence to modesty, can relate those obscene expressions, and lewd motions and gestures? For how criminal they are appears from this, that they cannot be decently told. For even some of the greatest crimes may be mentioned and censured without disgrace to the reporter, such as homicide, theft, adultery, sacrilege, and other sins of that nature; but the impurities of the theaters are the only ones that cannot be modestly exposed and reprehended. Thus a new circumstance arises for him who censures those infamous practices, that though he undoubtedly is a modest man who would condemn them, yet he cannot represent or censure them without blemishing his modesty."[20] Salvianus' opinion concerning the impurities of the theater is that a man must have

---

[20] Salvianus, *De providentia* VI.

honor and modesty to condemn them, but he must be immodest to describe them.[21] This is the model that Sanchez and several other casuists ought to have copied. I say several others because he is not the first nor the last who has written in this way. . . . Let us conclude that it is a very blameworthy and deplorable matter that there exist so many books of this nature. But it is infinitely more deplorable that the obscenities contained in them are actual crimes. The Scholastics give themselves to making fine distinctions even in questions of morality; they have gotten agitated about very useless points and about cases that never occurred; and you find the casuists always distinguishing between theory and practice, and proposing metaphysical and imaginary cases. This is probably one of the reasons that led Rivet to think that the infamous things that he read in Thomas Sanchez had been invented by that author. That is why, once finding himself in Aix-la-Chapelle with a Jesuit, he said to him that he could only be greatly surprised that a man who had made a vow of continence could suppose abominations that were never practiced. "I plainly perceive," the Jesuit answered him, "that you have never sat in a confessional. More atrocious and lewder enormities than these are heard there, so that it is necessary that the confessors be furnished with a scale of things so that they can have rules for imposing penances." Rivet replied smiling, "It is indeed strange that you should take such pride in the holiness of your Church, since according to your admission things are practiced in it of which the pagans did not even know the names."[23]. . . We are not able to know the small domestic secrets of the ancient pagans as we know those of the lands where auricular confession is in use. Thus, we cannot tell if marriage was as brutally dishonored among the pagans as it is among the Christians; but it is probable at least that in this respect the infidels do not at all surpass many people who are convinced of all the doctrines of the Gospel. Those for whom Sanchez' book was written are people who confess and submit to the penances imposed on them by their confessors. Therefore they believe what Scripture teaches us about heaven and hell. They believe in purgatory and the other doctrines

---

21 Apply here the words of Cicero, *Philippic* II, against Mark Anthony, "You are the more free because you have been guilty of such crimes as cannot be mentioned by a modest adversary." See the use that has been made of these words in the *Cabale chimérique* [one of Bayle's answers to Jurieu].

23 Rivet, *In Decalog. ad Vers.* 13 in *Opera*, Vol. I.

of the Roman Communion. And there they are, notwithstanding these convictions, completely immersed in abominable filthy matters that cannot be named and that draw severe reproaches upon the heads of those authors who dare mention them. I point this out against those who are convinced that the corruption of manners proceeds from people's doubting or not knowing that there is another life after this one.

Simonides, one of the best poets of antiquity, was from Ceos, an island in the Aegean Sea. He was still flourishing at the time of Xerxes' expedition, that is, about the seventy-fifth Olympiad. He employed his talents in various kinds of poetry but succeeded chiefly in elegies. It is said that he was twice saved from mortal peril, and that this was a reward for his virtue. He is said to be the inventor of local memory.* He is one of those poets whose verve and memory lasted a long time, for at the age of eighty he competed for the poetry prize and won it, and he boasted of having a better memory than any other man. He lived yet ten more years. It is said that the destruction of his tomb by a general of the Agrigentines did not pass unpunished. The answer he gave to a prince who asked him for the definition of God is very famous (**F**). I

≪←

F. (*The answer he gave to a prince who asked him for the definition of God is very famous.*) Hiero, the tyrant of Syracuse, asked this poet to tell him what God is. The poet answered that this was not one of those questions that one answers immediately, and that he had need of a day to examine it. When this time was over, Hiero asked him for his answer, but Simonides begged him for two more days. This was not the last delay he requested. He was often summoned to answer, and every time he asked for twice as much time as before. The tyrant was surprised at this behavior and wanted to know its cause. "I act this way," Simonides replied, "because the more I examine this matter, the more it seems obscure to me.". . . [Cicero said of this answer], "But I am of the opinion, that Simonides (who was

---

* [Remark C (not present in these selections) goes into some detail; apparently, "local memory" is remembering things by the recollection of their locations and the relation of these to where other things are located.]

mean the one he gave to Hiero, the tyrant of Syracuse, to whose court he had gone, despite his old age. He regarded his avarice more than his years, for he loved money and knew of Hiero's generosity. There are some theologians who could not reprove the confession he made, that he could not give the definition of God (G).* His answer to a king of Lacedaemon had the same effect as Solon's to Croesus. Another answer is attributed to him, which is very much like that of the philosopher who boasted of carrying all his belongings about with him. His answer to a question of Hiero's wife does not have to be taken literally. It was more a jest than a serious declaration of his opinion. He acknowledged that he was incapable of deceiving fools. Certain verses, in which he criticized a maxim of Pittacus, seemed very difficult to understand. The discussion of that point shows that he was not one of those severe critics who praise only what appears perfectly good to them and find fault with anything that has the slightest defect. He was much more tractable. Human imperfections were treated with great le-

not only a pleasing poet but also is represented as a wise and learned man), when many acute and subtle things came into his mind, being doubtful which of them was true, despaired of all truth."[31] Take notice of these last words of Cicero. They strike home, they go to the heart of the matter. Simonides could have easily answered if he confined himself to popular ideas and to those lively impressions that one nowadays calls "proofs of feeling." But since he was dealing with an able prince who had refined his judgment by frequent discussions with learned men, Simonides was afraid of not satisfying him if he did not give him a precise answer; he was even afraid of risking his reputation. This is why he took time to examine the matter. He looked at it from all sides; and because his mind suggested refutations of answers sooner than it did answers, he found nothing solid. He found everywhere strengths and weaknesses and impenetrable depths. Therefore,

---

* [Remark G appears on p. 284.]
31 Cicero, *De natura deorum* I. 22.

niency by him. He was satisfied as long as a man was not too bad. "We would never get done," he said, "if we wished to criticize all those who are foolish. The number of madmen is infinite, and I am not looking on the earth for a man above reproach. There are none such, and I will never praise anyone on this score. It suffices for me if he be moderately good and free of serious crimes." He advised treating all the things of this life like a game, and not to take any of them too seriously. Though the principal characteristic of his poetry is a certain sweetness very proper for affecting tender passions, he also made himself formidable by some severe invectives. I do not find that anyone denies that he was an excellent poet; and when one considers that he was capable of pacifying two princes who were extremely upset, and who had taken arms against each other, one must agree that his merit did not consist solely in writing good verses. No doubt he had several other qualities which made him quite a considerable person, but we cannot excuse his avarice and the venality of his pen. His glory cer-

he was afraid of being wrong no matter what views he might advance to establish the definition of God. He no longer hoped to find the truth and so abandoned the quest. Someone of lesser intelligence would not have had so much delicacy. He would have allowed himself to be dazzled by the first hypothesis that came to mind. He would not have seen the difficulties in it and would have presented it magisterially as the fixed point of truth beyond which there would be nothing but impertinence and extravagance. There are even some men of great intelligence who readily advance their hypotheses as the only stand that one should take. They decide that it is evident and insult those who do not agree. A strong persuasion leads them to this conduct. Tertullian will furnish us with another example. He claims that this affair happened not at the court of Syracuse, but at that of Lydia. According to him, Croesus asked Thales for the definition of God and did not get it, no matter what delays he granted that philosopher for examining the question. "For what certain answer did Thales, the prince of natural philosophers, give to Croesus when he inquired concerning the deity, when after all his delays in examining

tainly diminishes because of this. I mean that there are shadows which, instead of setting off the beautiful parts of his portrait, obscure them and make them ugly. Of all of the sentences attributed to him, I shall only mention the following one: he used to say that necessity was the one thing the gods themselves did not wish to contest or joust with. His father Leoprepes deserves to be cited for the good advice that he gave two young men. No matter how good the collections of Giraldi are, they are not equal to those that Allatius has published concerning our Simonides. We find there the titles of all his poems that could be discovered from the monuments of antiquity remaining to us; but we do not find the *Egg of Simondes* mentioned by Blondel the architect. The latter is mistaken in this. He confused Simonides with Simmias of Rhodes. The reader will see in the next article* if I have anything to say against Moreri.

that point, he found himself disappointed? Every Christian workman both discovers and shows God and thence is able to satisfy others upon that important question, though Plato asserts that the maker of the universe is not easily discoverable nor, when discovered, easily describable to all men."[33] You see how this Father raises the knowledge of the lowest Christian workman above that of the most famous philosophers of paganism. All our workmen, he says, find God and show him, indicating effectively all that can be asked about the divine nature. This means that if Croesus or Hiero had asked the most ignorant of the Christians, "What is God, and what are his attributes?" they would have immediately received a categorical answer, so exact that nothing would have been lacking in it. Tertullian goes too fast, he lets his imagination lead him too quickly. He does not consider that the philosophers of paganism who admitted themselves incapable of satisfying the curiosity of those who asked them about what God was were only reduced to silence because they would not stop at popular notions, as an ignorant man would have done. Nothing would have been easier for them than to have an-

---

* ["Simonides, son of the daughter of the preceding person," not included in these selections.]

33 Tertullian, *Apologeticus* XLVI. 8–9.

swered, "God is an infinite being, and omnipotent, who formed the universe, and who governs it, who punishes and rewards, who is angry with sinners, and who is appeased by our sacrifices." This is how our workmen would have answered Hiero, while adding what we read in the catechism about the persons of the Trinity, about the death and passion of Christ, and so on. Once more, if Thales or Simonides had been satisfied with these general ideas, they would not have asked for time to prepare their answers. They would have answered the question on the spot. But, since they wished that all the terms in the required definition should be clear and incontestable, and since they found that all they could advance could be contested, they asked for delay after delay; and finally they did not know what to say. I think that Simonides imagined that his answer would be given for examination to all the bright people at the court of Syracuse and that he would be obliged to defend it by clarifying all their difficulties.

Here is apparently how he reasoned: "If I answer that God is distinct from all the bodies that make up the universe, I will be asked, has the universe always existed, at least with regard to its matter? Does this matter have an efficient cause? And if I answer that it has one, I am obliged to maintain that it was made out of nothing. Now this is a doctrine that I shall never be able to make King Hiero or the bright people in his court understand, and I do not understand it myself. Therefore I have reason to be uncertain whether this doctrine is true or not; for while it remains incomprehensible to me, I cannot rightly be sure of its status and nature. If I say that the matter of the universe does not have an efficient cause, I will be asked, where does the power come from that God has over it, and why does it not have as much power over God as God has over it? I would have to give good reasons why, of two beings independent of one another with regard to existence, both equally necessary and eternal, one has absolute power over the other without being reciprocally subject to the action of the other. It is not sufficient to say that God is distinct from the bodies that make up the universe. One will want to know if he resembles them with regard to extent, that is, if he is extended. If I answer that he is extended, one will conclude that he is corporeal and material; and I am not capable of making Hiero's court understand that there are two kinds of extension, one corporeal and the other incorporeal, one composed of parts and hence divisible, the other perfectly simple and hence indivisible. If I say that God is not extended, one will conclude that he is nowhere and can have no union with the world. How then does he move bodies? How does he act where he is not? Besides our understanding is not capable of conceiving of an unextended substance and a spirit entirely separated from matter. But if it should be once granted to me that God is an immaterial substance, unextended, an infinite spirit and omnipotent, how many new questions will I have to answer? Does not this spirit exist necessarily with respect either to its substance or its qualities? Is not its power an attribute as necessary as its knowledge? Therefore, it does not act freely, if we understand by freedom the power of acting or not acting. Everything it does is then necessary and inevitable. You thus overturn the whole system of religion, I will be told; for it is necessarily built on the hypothesis that God changes his conduct as men change their ways of living; and that, if men do not appease him by their prayers, he would do an infinite number of things that he refrains from doing on account of their devotions. If I avoid this troublesome difficulty by the hypothesis of the liberty of indifference, and conditional wills, then I have to show how this kind of liberty is compatible with a being who is not the cause of his own power,[36] and that an infinite series of conditional decrees is compatible with a cause infinitely wise and independent, which ought to have formed a fixed and immovable plan and which at bottom has no attributes more essential than immutability; for there is no property more evidently contained in the idea of a supremely perfect being than this." Here is, if I am not mistaken, a small part of the reasons that were turning about in Simonides' mind while he was looking for the requested definition, and this made him resolve to say nothing, for he feared so much to affirm things that were not true.

I may dare say that there is hardly anyone to whom it is less becoming to insult Thales and to compliment our workmen than Tertullian, for he would have not done well if he had been in the place of Thales or Simonides. Ardent and impetuous as he was, he would have immediately answered the question of Croesus or Hiero. But if you want to know how he would have answered, read these words of Daillé. "How strange is his philosophy concerning the nature of God, which he seems to represent as subject to passions like ours, to resent-

---

[36] The nature of God with all his attributes exists necessarily; his power and will therefore must be necessary; now necessity excludes indifference.

ment, hate, grief? He attributes to him a corporeal substance, not believing (as he says) that anyone would deny that God is a body, which
will make us wonder the less that he announces boldly that there is
no substance that is not corporeal."[37] Everyone sees that Tertullian
would have defined God as "a corporeal substance subject to passions." Paraphrasing his definition, he would have said that our sins
annoy God, that he hates vice, and that he feels a real pain when we
transgress his laws, but that he is easily appeased when we implore
his mercy. Could he have sustained this answer in the presence of
Simonides and the other learned men at Hiero's court? Would they
not have objected that every body is divisible, composed of parts, and
consequently that a supremely perfect being is not a body? Would they
not have said that sovereign happiness is essential to the divine nature, and that thus it is exempt from all passion, and that nothing can
afflict or trouble it? Would they not have said that it is immutable, and
consequently that it cannot move from love to hatred, nor from hatred
to love, nor from pity to anger, nor anger to pity? If he had resorted
to metaphors, he would have been told that Hiero did not ask for the
answer of an orator, but for an exact definition perfectly in agreement
with the laws of logic. One will say, I am sure, that Tertullian would
have done better to be silent, like the one whom he insulted. Let us
suppose that his Christian workman, whom he represents as so ingenious, should be asked by Hiero, and that he answers, "God is an immaterial, infinite, all-powerful being, perfectly good, perfectly holy,
perfectly just, who created all things according to the good pleasure
of his will." Can we think that Simonides, examining this response,
would not have said: "This occurred to me as well as to you; but I
dared not affirm it because it seemed to me that a being infinitely
powerful, infinitely good, infinitely holy, and who had created all
things with the sovereign liberty of indifference, would not have exposed men to the criminal and miserable state in which they live.
If he had left the soul the liberty of uniting itself to the body or not
doing so, it would never have entered into it; for that choice would
have shown that it was too foolish to be a product of an infinitely
perfect being. If it is he who unites our souls to our bodies, he must
have been urged by some natural and inevitable determination; for
if he had acted freely, that is, if he could have acted one way or another, then one cannot conceive that he would have chosen that course

---

[37] Daillé, *Du vrai usage des pères,* Bk. II, chap. 4, p. 354.

because the soul, by its union with the body, finds itself subject to a hundred shameful and absurd disorders and to an almost continual series of miseries." Let us not leave the Christian workman exposed to this attack. Let us introduce a theologian who presents to Simonides the entire system of grace and the whole economy of the decrees of predestination. The poet would certainly have answered him: "You lead me from one land of darkness to a still darker one. I cannot understand that, under a deity who has the attributes you name, it could ever be necessary to punish anyone; for the sovereign power of such a deity, joined to an infinite goodness and holiness, would never permit that any crime worthy of punishment should be committed in his dominions. A nature like this does not seem capable of linking his glory with the misery of another and making it depend on the eternal duration of the torments of hell. I conceive even a formal contradiction between these two things. Three persons, who are but one God, one of whom punishes, the other is punished, and yet it cannot be said, that he who is punished punishes and he who punishes is punished, though both of them are but one and the same substance, one and the same God. These three persons, I say, are a formal contradiction to me. Therefore, I prefer to have given no answer to the prince of Syracuse than to have given him such definitions of God."

But, it will be said, was Tertullian grossly mistaken when he put the ordinary Christian above the philosophers? I answer that his assertion can be very well corrected. It only has to be said that the poorest Christian workman firmly believes more things about the nature of God than the greatest philosophers of paganism were able to know. It only has to be asserted that with his catechism alone he will give so much detail that, for each item that they only partly affirm, he will affirm forty without any hesitation. This is what Tertullian might have said without being at all mistaken. But these Christians who are so knowledgeable in comparison to Thales and all the other philosophers of ancient Greece would say as little and be as silent as Thales if they were to say nothing but what they clearly and distinctly comprehended. And they owe their great knowledge only to the luck of having been raised in a Church where they have acquired a historical faith, and sometimes even a justifying faith of revealed truths. This convinces them of several things that they do not comprehend at all. Our greatest theologians, if they acted like Simonides, that is, if they would not assert anything about the nature of God except that which would, to the light of reason, appear incontestible, evident, and safe from all objections, would perpetually demand new delays of all the Hieros in the world. Add also that Simonides, if he had consulted and examined Scripture without the influence of either education or grace, would not have extricated himself from his labyrinth or his silence. Reason would have prevented him from denying the facts contained in Scripture and from not seeing something supernatural in the chain of these facts, but this would not have been sufficient to enable him to have come to a decision about this. The powers of reason and philosophical examination goes no further than to keep us in suspense and in fear of error, whether we affirm, or whether we deny.[39] It is necessary that either the grace of God or childhood education should come to their assistance. And observe that there is no hypothesis against which reason furnishes more objections than against that of the Gospel. The mystery of the Trinity, the Incarnation of the Word, his death for the expiation of our sins, the propagation of the sin of Adam, the eternal predestination of a small number of persons to the happiness of heaven, the eternal condemnation of almost all mankind to the endless torments of hell, the extinction of free will since the Fall of Adam, and the like, are matters that would have thrown Simonides into greater doubts than all that his imagination suggested to him. Let us consider St. Paul's words, not only that the Gospel was "a stumbling block to the Jews, and to the Greeks foolishness, but also that God saved men by the foolishness of preaching" (I Corinthians 1:23 and 21).

Here is a thought which, perhaps, ought not to be rejected. Simonides apparently found himself in difficulties concerning the genus of his definition. He did not dare say that God was a body. A hundred objections kept him from this. He did not dare say that God was a pure spirit, for he only conceived of things in terms of the idea of extension. Until Descartes, all our learned men, whether theologians or philosophers, had ascribed extension to spirits—an infinite one to God, and a finite one to angels and rational souls. It is true that they maintained that this extension is not material nor composed of parts and that spirits are completely in every part of space that they occupy (*toti in toto et toti in singulis partibus*). From this it followed that there are three kinds of local presence: the limited presence of bodies,

---

[39] Notice that the issue between Hiero and Simonides is not that of the existence of God but of his exact definition.

the definite presence of spirits, and the omnipresence of God. The Cartesians have overthrown all these doctrines. They say that spirits have no kind of extension, nor local presence. But their view is rejected as absurd. Let us say then that even today almost all our philosophers and all our theologians teach, in conformity with popular views, that God is diffused throughout infinite spaces. Now it is certain that this amounts to destroying with one hand what was built by the other. In effect, the materiality of God is restored after it had been removed. You say that he is a spirit. Well and good! This gives him a nature different from matter. But at the same time you say that his substance is diffused everywhere; you say, therefore, that it is extended. Now we do not have any idea of two kinds of extension. We conceive clearly that all extension whatsoever has parts that are distinct, impenetrable, and separable from one another. It is monstrous to contend that the soul is entirely in the brain and entirely in the heart. It is not conceivable that divine extension and material extension can be in the same place. This would constitute a real penetration of dimensions that our reason cannot conceive. Besides this, things that are penetrated by a third object are penetrated by one another;[41] and thus the heavens and the sphere of the earth are penetrated by one another; for they would be penetrated by the divine substance, which according to you, has no parts. From this it follows that the sun is penetrated by the same being as the earth is. In a word, if matter is only matter because it is extended, it follows that all extension is matter. You are challenged to name any other attribute that makes matter matter. The impenetrability of bodies comes only from extension. We can conceive of no other basis for it. And thus you ought to say that if spirits were extended, they would be impenetrable. They would then not differ from bodies at all by penetrability. After all, according to the ordinary view, divine extension is neither more nor less penetrable or impenetrable than that of bodies. Its parts, call them virtual as much as you please, its parts I say, cannot be penetrated by one another; but they may so be by the parts of matter. Is this not what you say of the parts of matter; they cannot be penetrated by one another, but they can be penetrated by the virtual parts of divine extension? If you carefully consult common sense, you will see that when two extensions are penetratively in the same place, one

---

41 It is by this axiom that those are refuted who say that a continuous body consists of mathematical points.

is as penetrable as the other. It cannot therefore be said that the extension of matter differs from any other kind of extension by impenetrability. It is thus certain that all extension is matter, and consequently you take away from God only the name of body and leave all the reality of it in him when you say that he is extended. Since it is impossible for you to do otherwise, you should not find it strange that Simonides did not dare deny that God was a body; he did not dare affirm it either. He preferred to keep quiet. Let us remember that the most subtle Cartesians maintain that we have no idea at all of a spiritual substance. We know only by experience that it thinks, but we do not know what the nature of a being is whose modifications are thoughts. We do not know what is the subject, nor what is the substratum in which thoughts inhere. Simonides was perhaps led by this not to risk asserting that God was a spirit. He had no idea at all of what a spirit was.

For the rest, a Jesuit [Lescalopier], who has commented on Cicero's *De natura deorum,* does not condemn the caution of Simonides; and he wishes that the ancient philosophers and poets and the heretics had imitated it. What he says concerning the incomprehensibility of God deserves to be transcribed. "What Tertullian imputes to ignorance, others ascribe to modesty. And I wish the ancient philosophers and poets, and the heretics who followed them, had been as modest in this point as Thales or Simonides. They certainly would not have falsely ascribed so many absurd, impious, and blasphemous things to the divine nature, nor even have fallen into the grossest errors, which we see with great regret that presumptuous men have run into. We are all possessed with a strong desire for knowledge, but with a much greater desire of knowing God; whence we may infer that God is willing to be known by us, but within certain prescribed limits, between pillars, upon which he inscribed with his own finger, *ne plus ultra.* For there are in divine things some secret recesses into which almighty God would not have us penetrate. But if any person influenced by rashness and pride proceeds farther and attempts to break into this sacred recess, the farther he advances, the thicker is the darkness he encounters, so that he may, if he be wise, confess the unfathomable majesty of God and the weakness of the human mind and be obliged to confess with Simonides, 'The longer I consider this, the more obscure it appears to me.' . . ."[42] He then cites a fine passage from St.

[42] Lescalopier, *Cicero, De natura deorum,* Bk. I, pp. 84–85.

Augustine on this. A French author [La Mothe le Vayer] has regarded the behavior of Simonides as an act of piety, and has used this as an occasion to condemn the confidence of the Eunomians. "Remember the pious modesty of Simonides," he says, "who having asked King Hiero for only one day to prepare to discuss the divine essence before him, then asked two days, then three, protesting that the more he thought about it, the more difficulties he found in keeping his promise. For my part, I do not doubt that this humble profession of ignorance was more pleasing to the supreme being, pagan though Simonides was, than the insolence of a Eunomius and that sect of his Arian followers, who boasted of knowing God exactly as he is able to know himself."[44] Du Plessis Mornay in the chapter in which he proves both by authorities and arguments that it is impossible to know God does not forget the reply of Simonides. He remarks, without giving any citation, that this poet "very justly taught that God is wisdom itself." He also says that "Aristotle in his *Metaphysics* cites and praises the common response of Simonides to Hiero, that this says in substance that it belongs only to God to be a metaphysician, that is, to speak of things that are beyond nature." In looking over Aristotle's *Metaphysics*, I could not find this passage. However that may be, this thought is a very good one and amounts to the same thing.

When I said that I could not find the passage Du Plessis [Mornay] cites in the work of Aristotle, I had reference to the circumstances by which the passage was characterized, namely, that it was an answer of Simonides to Hiero that was praised by Aristotle. The words of *Metaphysics* (Bk. I, chap. 2) . . . amount to this, that the knowledge of first principles is so sublime that it may justly be said that it does not belong to man to possess it, that this was the reason why, according to Simonides, this possession is the privilege of God alone. But it would be an unbecoming thing for man not to seek to know himself, or to neglect the knowledge that relates to him. I imagine that if I had lived in Aristotle's time, I would have found his reflection clearer than I do. But, be that as it may, I find nothing that leads me to believe that he praises or approves of the opinion of Simonides, and I have seen commentators who say expressly that he refutes it. Fonseca, making a paraphrase note on this passage in Aristotle, labels it in the margin, "Refutation of the words of Simonides." Here is what he says: "It is so well known that this knowledge does not belong to man that this

---

[44] La Mothe le Vayer, Letter CXVI, Vol. XII, p. 26.

gave occasion for the error of the poet Simonides. For he declared that
men ought only to apply themselves to such sciences as were suitable
to a man's situation; and consequently, that the science that deals
with divine beings should be left to God and divine things because it
is above human capacity. In opposition to this absurd advice, which
is unworthy of the dignity of a manly soul, Aristotle answers, 'that a
man ought not neglect the science that is most suitable to the understanding'; for that is not to be thought foreign to human nature, the
chief part of which is the mind itself."[49] . . .

.   .   .   .

⫷

G. (*There are some theologians who could not reprove the confession he made, that he could not give the definition of God.*)
One can see proof of this in the preceding remark. But here is an
author who speaks still more categorically. It is the famous Pierre
Charron, Prebendary of Condom. "Since the deity," he says, "is so
high and so distant from us and from our capacities that we do not
know at all what he is, either far off or near, it is on the one hand a
very great and mad presumption to decide and determine about him,
as the atheists do, who in all their objections argue about him as
something very definite, circumscribed, and necessarily of such and
such a character, saying that if there be a God, he must be such and
such: and being such, he would, should, might do this and this,
which is not so, *ergo*. On the other hand, it is an error to think of finding any reasons which are sufficient and demonstrative enough to
prove and establish evidently and necessarily what deity is. We ought
not to be surprised at this, but we should rather be surprised if such
reasons could be found. For it is not possible that the powers of
human nature or the capacities of creatures can go that far. . . . Deity
is that which cannot be known or even perceived. From the finite to
the infinite there is no comparison, no transition. Infinity is totally
inaccessible, even imperceptible. God is the one, true, and only infinite. The greatest genius and the greatest effort of the imagination
approach no nearer to it than does the lowest and weakest conception.
The greatest philosopher and the most learned theologian do not

---

[49] Fonseca, *Arist., Metaphys.*, Bk. II, chap. 2, pp. 99–100.

know God any more, or any better, than the lowliest workman. Where there is no avenue or route, then there can be neither far nor near. . . . God, deity, eternity, omnipotence, infinity, these are only words thrown into the air, and nothing more to us. These are not things subject to human understanding. . . . If all that we say and profess about God were judged rigorously, it would be nothing but vanity and ignorance. Therefore, a great and ancient sage said that to speak of God, even saying true things, is very dangerous. The reason for this saying is that, in addition to the fact that such sublime truths are corrupted in passing through our senses, our minds, and our mouths, we still do not know, and cannot be certain, that what we say is true. It is by chance that we come across such 'truths,' for we are completely in the dark and do not know either what God is or what he does. Now to speak of God dubiously and uncertainly, as if groping in the dark and by conjecture, is dangerous; and we do not know if God approves. It is only that we trust in his goodness, that he will take well what we say of him with good intention and with a view to honoring him as best we can. But who knows if this trust is pleasing to him, and if divine goodness is such that it takes kindly to that which is done with good intention and in order to do him honor? This is what human, created, and finite goodness is like. But who knows if the divine, uncreated, infinite one is of the same stripe? Even with regard to human goodness, there is no universal agreement as to its rules and duties. . . . This is why the best course that a man can take, who wishes to think about and conceive the deity, is for his soul, after a universal abstraction from all things, raising itself above all, as in an indeterminate and infinite vacuum, with a profound and pure silence, an astonishment full of awe, an admiration full of fearful humility, should imagine that it is in a luminous abyss, without bottom, without sides, without height, without depth, without holding on to anything that comes to it from its imagination, and should lose itself, be drowned, and swallowed up in this infinity. The following old sentences of the saints amount very nearly to this. The true knowledge of God is a perfect ignorance of him. To approach God is to know an inaccessible light, and to be absorbed by it. The best we can do is to feel that he is above all, that he cannot be known; then, to praise him eloquently we should be silent with astonishment and awe, and adore him silently in the soul. But because it is very difficult, and almost impossible, for the soul to be able to remain in so uncertain and indeterminate an infinity (for it would be completely perplexed, and racked), like a man who all dizzy from spinning around, not knowing where he is, falls down, and even if the soul could do it, being stupefied, unable to move, and ravished with awe and admiration, it would not be capable of communicating in any manner with God, praying to him, invoking him, acknowledging him, honoring him, which are the basic and principal features of religion. For in all these activities it is a necessary requirement that God be conceived as having some quality—good, powerful, wise, intelligent, accepting our good intentions. It is necessary, and cannot be otherwise in the present condition of life, that everyone should paint for himself an image of the deity that he may regard, address, and adhere to, and that may, as it were, be his God. The soul does this by raising its imagination above all things, and conceiving with all its strength a supreme goodness, power, and perfection. For the utmost and highest degree to which anyone can rise by the greatest effort of his conception is his God and serves as his image of God, an image always false, that is to say, lacking something and imperfect. For, since the deity is, as is said, unimaginable and infinite, since the soul cannot approach it near or far by any conception, nor can it form any true image of, any more than of a thing that it knows nothing at all of, it is sufficient that it make the conception the least false, the least vicious, the highest, and the purest that it can."[56] Thousands and thousands of readers who will see these lines of a sublime genius in this dictionary would never have known of them if I had not quoted them. This is why I have inserted them in this note.

It will be said, perhaps, that Charron is a theologian who is too suspect* to deserve that his views be taken seriously. Let us parry this objection, and let us observe that Arnobius expressed himself in a

---

[56] Pierre Charron, *Des trois veritez,* Bk. I, chap. 5.

* [Pierre Charron (1541-1603) was a leading Catholic preacher and theologian of the sixteenth century, who became the friend and, ultimately, the intellectual heir of Montaigne. His two major works are *Les trois veritez* (1594), a massive attack on atheism, non-Christian religions, and especially Calvinism; and *De la sagesse* (1601), a skeptical examination of human rational abilities and achievements, leading to an appeal for an acceptance of religion on faith alone, and an advocacy of living by natural morality until grace is received. His views, especially those of *De la sagesse,* were widely read and admired by both orthodox and so-called *libertin* thinkers in France during the seventeenth century. However, he was accused by the fanatical Father François Garasse and others of being a secret

manner that strongly justifies Simonides' answer. Has he not said that
our words cannot signify anything about the nature of God, and that
we must be silent if we want to conceive of him, and that in order
that our vague conjectures may provide some clues in the shadows
around us, we ought to keep our mouths closed? "O great and supreme creator of things invisible! O thou unseen being, who art never
comprehended by any other beings! . . . Thou art the first cause, the
place of things and the space, the foundation of all things that exist,
infinite, unbegotten, immortal, perpetual, alone, whom no corporeal
form can describe, no boundaries determine, void of quality, quantity,
without situation, motion, and habit, of whom nothing can be said
or expressed by the language of mortals; to understand whom, we
must be silent, and to the end that wandering conjecture may search
thee out under a cloud, we must entirely enjoin ourselves to silence."[57]
Someone would be very ignorant if he told me that this passage ought
to be ranked among the errors of Arnobius, for all those who have
consulted the commentators on him have been able to see that the
most orthodox Church Fathers have confirmed his view. Just read a
little of the commentators on these words of Minucius Felix, "Our
capacity is too narrow to understand; and therefore we esteem God
rightly when we say that he is inestimable. I will speak as I think, he
lessens the majesty of God who thinks he knows Him; whoever is not
desirous to lessen it acknowledges that he does not know Him.
Neither do you seek for a name of God." You will find that the commentators give an infinite number of references to passages where
the Church Fathers agree with Arnobius on this point. And observe
that the Jesuit Lescalopier cites these very words of Minucius Felix
to confirm the remark he had just made, that the wisest and most
modest philosophers admit everywhere that God is not only invisible
and inexpressible but also unintelligible. . . .

---

atheist. Garasse called *De la sagesse* "the breviary of the libertines" and contended that Charron, contrary to his public avowals, was an insincere Christian whose aim was to destroy religious belief rather than to defend it.
Bayle, in his lengthy article "Charron," contends that Charron's views are
really orthodox and offers a fideistic interpretation of his theology.

[The argument about the proper interpretation of Charron's views has
gone on from the seventeenth century up to the present. For a discussion of
his thought and how it has been evaluated, see R. H. Popkin, *History of
Scepticism,* chaps. 3 and 4.]

[57] Arnobius, I.

Spinoza, BENEDICTUS DE, a Jew by birth, and afterwards a deserter from Judaism, and lastly an atheist, was from Amsterdam. He was a systematic atheist who employed a totally new method, though the basis of his theory was the same as that of several other ancient and modern philosophers, both European and Oriental. With regard to the latter, it is only necessary to read what I reported in remark D of the article "Japan" [not included in these selections], and what I shall say below about the theology of a Chinese sect (B). I have not been able to learn anything special about Spinoza's family, but there are grounds for believing that they

≪≪

B. *(What I shall say . . . about the theology of a Chinese sect.)* The name of that sect is *Foe Kiao.* It was established by royal authority among the Chinese in the year 65 of the Christian era. Its first founder was the son of the king *In Fan Vam,* and was at first called *Xe* or *Xe Kia,* and then, when he was thirty years old, *Foe,* that is to say, "not man." The Prolegomena of the Jesuits prefacing the edition of Confucius that they published in Paris treats amply of this founder. We find there, "that he, having retired into the desert when he reached his nineteenth year and having put himself under the discipline of four Gymnosophists in order to learn philosophy from them, remained under their instruction until he was thirty years old, when, rising one morning before daybreak and contemplating the planet Venus, the mere sight of it gave him at once a perfect knowledge of the first principle, so that being full of divine inspiration, or rather of pride and madness, he undertook to instruct men, represented himself as a god, and attracted eighty thousand disciples. . . . At the age of seventy-nine, finding himself near death, he told his

were poor and not very important. He studied Latin under a physician[a] who taught it at Amsterdam, and he applied himself at an early age to the study of theology, to which he devoted several years. After this he devoted himself completely to the study

disciples that, for the forty years he had preached to the world, he had not told the truth to them; that he had concealed it under a veil of metaphors and figures of speech; but that it was time to tell it to them. 'It is,' he said, 'that there is nothing to seek, nor anything to put one's hopes on, except the nothingness and the vacuum that is the principle of all things.' "[26] Here is a man very different from our freethinkers; they cease combating religion only at the end of their

---

[a] Named François Van der Ende. Note that Kortholt, in the Preface to the second edition of his father's *De tribus impostiborus*, says that a young woman taught Spinoza Latin, and that she later married Keckering, who was her student at the same time Spinoza was. [Recent examination of the seventeenth-century theological and philosophical manuscripts of the Spanish and Portuguese Jewish community of Amsterdam convinces the translator that a knowledge of Latin was not unusual in this group at that time, especially since many of the leaders—Morteira, Orobio de Castro, etc.—were graduates of Catholic universities in Spain and Italy and had taught or worked there. The Spinoza commentators who have made much of the contention that the Amsterdam Jewish community was cut off from the Latin world, and that Spinoza had to leave the community, in order to obtain Latin materials and a knowledge of the language; are, possibly, very much mistaken about both the local situation of the time and the personal background of the leaders of Amsterdam Jewry then. Many of the manuscripts preserved in Amsterdam indicate that the Jewish leaders were *au courant* with materials published in Latin, French, Spanish, Italian, etc., in theology, philosophy and science; and that they were, or had been, in personal contact with Christian theologians, philosophers, and scientists. Since most of the leading figures of Amsterdam Jewry at that time had been Marranos, that is, crypto-Jews, in Spain and Portugal, they had lived for some time at least in a non-Jewish world where Latin was the intellectual language. Some of them (including Menasseh ben Israel) had published works in Latin. And they were most concerned with intellectual issues in the theological, philosophical, and scientific spheres of Christendom. In terms of the rich body of materials that still exists in Amsterdam, it will be necessary to re-evaluate Spinoza's intellectual relationship to the Jewish community of the time, and many of the traditional myths on this subject will have to be abandoned. The publication by Professor I. S. Révah, of Paris, *Spinoza et Juan de Prado* (The Hague: Mouton, 1959), is the first important indication of this.]

[26] *Bibliothèque universelle*, VII, 403–404, in the extract [or resumé] of the same book of Confucius.

of philosophy. Since he had a mathematical mind and wanted to find a reason for everything, he soon realized that rabbinical doctrine was not for him. As a result, it was easily seen that he disapproved of Judaism in several respects; for he was a man who was averse to any constraint of conscience and a great enemy of dissimulation. This is why he freely set forth his doubts and his

lives. They give up their libertinism only when they believe that time for leaving the world is at hand. But *Foe* finding himself in this state began to announce his atheism. . . . His method was the reason why his disciples "divided their doctrine into two parts, one exterior, which is the one that is publicly preached and taught to the people, the other interior, which is carefully hidden from the common people and made known only to the initiates. The exterior doctrine, according to the bonzes, is 'only like the frame on which the arch is built, and which is later taken away when one has completed the building. It consists in teaching: (1) that there is a real difference between good and evil, justice and injustice; (2) that there is another life in which one will be punished or rewarded for what one will do in this one; (3) that happiness can be attained by means of thirty-two figures and eighty qualities; (4) that *Foe* (or *Xaca*) is a deity and the saviour of mankind, that he was born out of love of them, taking pity on the disorder in which he saw them, that he expiated their sins, and that by this expiation they will obtain salvation after death, and will be reborn happier in another world.' " To this are added five moral precepts and six works of mercy, and damnation is threatened to those who neglect these duties.

"The interior doctrine that is never revealed to the common people because they have to be kept in their place by the fear of hell and other stories of that kind, as these philosophers say, is, according to them, however, the solid and true doctrine. It consists in laying down as the principle and goal of all things a certain *vacuum* and *real nothingness*. They say that our first parents came forth from this vacuum and that they returned there after death; that it is the same with all men, who are changed back into this principle by death; that we, all the elements, and all creatures make up part of that vacuum; that thus there is but one and the same substance, which is different in particular beings only by the shapes and qualities or interior configuration, somewhat like water, which is always essentially water,

beliefs. It is said that the Jews offered to tolerate him, provided that he would conform outwardly to their ceremonial practices, and that they even promised him an annual pension, but that he could not submit to such hypocrisy. However, he estranged himself little by little from their synagogue; and perhaps he would have kept up some degree of contact with them for a longer

though it take the form of snow, hail, rain, or ice." If it is monstrous to maintain that plants, animals, men are really the same thing and to base this on the claim that all particular beings are not distinct from their principle, it is still more monstrous to assert that this principle has no thought, no power, no virtue. This is nevertheless what these philosophers say. They make the sovereign perfection of that principle consist in inaction and absolute rest. . . . Spinoza has not been so absurd. The only substance he admits always acts, always thinks; and he could not by his most general abstractions divest it of action and thought. The foundations of his theory cannot let him do this.

Quietism taught and practiced by the Chinese. Note in passing that the followers of *Foe* taught quietism; for they say that all those who seek true happiness ought to allow themselves to be so absorbed in profound meditations that they make no use of their intellect, but, by a complete insensibility, sink into the rest and inaction of the first principle, which is the true means of perfectly resembling it and partaking of happiness. They assert also that after one has reached this state of quietude, he should follow the ordinary course of life outwardly and teach others the commonly received doctrine. It is only in private and for his internal use that it is necessary for one to practice the contemplative institute of beatific inaction. . . . Those who attached themselves most ardently to the contemplation of this first principle formed a new sect called *Vu Guei Kiao*, that is to say, the sect of the idle or of the do-nothings. It is thus that among the monks those who are most concerned with the strictest observance form new societies or a new sect. The greatest lords and the most illustrious persons allowed themselves to become so infatuated with this quietism that they believed that insensibility was the road to perfection and happiness, and that the more one approached the nature of a stump or a stone, the more one made progress, the more one became like the first principle to which one would one day return. It was not enough to be without any bodily movement for several hours; it was also neces-

time had he not been treacherously attacked by a Jew who struck him with a knife when he was leaving the theater. The wound was minor but he believed that the assassin's intention was to kill him. After this event he broke off from the Jewish community, and this was the cause of his excommunication. I have looked into the circumstances of it without having been able to dig them out.[c] He wrote an apology in Spanish for his quitting the synagogue. This work has never been published. However,

sary that the soul be immobile and that one lose all sensation. . . . A follower of Confucius refuted the impertinences of this sect and proved very amply the Aristotelian maxim that nothing comes from nothing; however, the sect went on and grew, and there are many people today who attach themselves to these vain contemplations. If we did not know of the extravagances of our quietists, we would believe that the writers who tell us about these speculative Chinese have not understood well and have not reported well what was going on. But after what takes place among the Christians, it would be wrong to be incredulous about the insanity of the sect *Foe Kiao* or *Vu Guei Kiao*.

I am willing to believe either that what those men mean by *Cum hiu* is not exactly expressed or that their ideas are contradictory. It is claimed that these Chinese words signify "vacuum and nothingness," *vacuum et inane*, and this sect was attacked by the axiom that nothing comes from nothing. Therefore it must be that it is claimed that they taught that nothing is the principle of all beings. I cannot convince myself that they took the word "nothing" in its strict sense, and I imagine that they understood it as people do when they say that there is nothing in an empty chest. We have seen that they ascribe attributes to the first principle that suppose that they conceive it as a liquor.[38] It is therefore probable that they divested it only of what is gross and sensible in matter. On this basis the disciple of Confucius would have been guilty of the sophism called *ignoratio elenchi*; for he would have understood by *nihil* ("nothing") that which has no existence, and his adversaries would have understood by the same word that which has no properties of sensible matter. I believe that they understood by that word something very much like what modern thinkers under-

---

[c] This is taken from a memoir sent to a bookseller.

[38] "Pure," "limpid," "subtle" are terms that they use.

it is known that he put many things in it that later appeared in his *Tractatus theologico-politicus*,[d] published in Amsterdam in 1670, a pernicious and detestable book in which he slips in all the seeds of atheism that were plainly revealed in his *Opera posthuma*. Stoupp unjustly insults the ministers of Holland for not having answered the *Tractatus theologico-politicus*. What he says is not always pertinent (E). When Spinoza turned to philosophical studies, he quickly became disgusted with the usual theories and was wonderfully pleased with that of Des-

stand by the term "space"; the modern thinkers, I say, who, not wishing to be either Cartesians or Aristotelians, maintain that space is distinct from bodies and that its indivisible, impalpable, impenetrable, immobile, and infinite extension is something real. The disciple of Confucius could have proven easily that such a thing cannot be the first principle if it be otherwise destitute of activity, as the contemplative Chinese claim. An extension as real as you please cannot serve for the production of any particular being if it is not moved; and if it be supposed that there is no mover, the production of the universe will be equally impossible, whether there be an infinite extension or whether there be nothing. Spinoza would not deny this thesis; but he does not get into such perplexities since he does not contend for the inaction of the first principle. Abstract extension, which he ascribes to it in general, is only the idea of space, properly speaking; but he adds movement to it; and thus the varieties of matter can arise.

≪←

E. *(What he says is not always pertinent.)* Does he not say that according to Spinoza religions have been invented to lead men to apply themselves to virtue, not on account of the rewards of the next world, but because virtue is excellent in itself, and because it is advantageous during this life? Is it not certain that this atheist never thought of this and could never have reasoned so without making himself ridiculous? All the religions of the world, the true one as well

---

[d] See the book of Van Til, minister and professor of Dortrecht, entitled *Het Voorhof der Heidenen voor de Ongeloovigen geopent*. The *Journal of Leipzig* for 1695 speaks of it.

cartes. He felt such a strong passion to search for truth that to some extent he renounced the world to be better able to carry on that search. He was not content with having removed himself from all sorts of affairs; he also left Amsterdam because his friends' visits interrupted his speculations too much. He retired to the country, he meditated there at his leisure, and he worked on microscopes and telescopes there. He kept up this kind of life after he settled in The Hague; and he gained so much pleasure from meditating, from putting his meditations in order, and from communicating them to his friends, that he allowed very little time for mental recreation; and sometimes he let three whole months go by without setting foot outside his lodgings. This retired life did not hinder the spreading of his name and reputation. Freethinkers came to him from all over. The court of the Palatinate wanted him and offered him a chair as professor of philosophy at Heidelberg. He turned it down as a post that would be little compatible with his desire to search after truth without any interruption. When he was a little more than forty-four years old, he sank into a long illness that ended his life on February 21, 1677. I have heard it said that when the

as the false ones, turn on this great pivot, that there is an invisible judge who, after this life, punishes and rewards the actions of mankind, both exterior and interior. It is from this that the principal value of religion is supposed to flow. It is the principal motive that would have influenced those who might have invented it. It is evident enough that in this life good actions do not lead to temporal well-being, and that bad ones are the most usual and the surest means of making one's fortune. To prevent a man, then, from plunging himself into crime, and to lead him to virtue, it would have been necessary to propose to him some punishments and rewards after this life. This is the strategem that the freethinkers attribute to those that they claim were the first authors of religion. This is what Spinoza should have thought, and it is doubtless what he did think. Thus Stoupp has not understood him on this point and has interpreted him as holding the opposite view. I am surprised that this mistake has been left in the supplement to Moreri, in an article bearing the name of Simon.

Prince de Condé was at Utrecht, he asked him to come and see
him. Those who were acquainted with him, and the peasants of
the villages where he had lived in retirement for some time, all
agree in saying that he was sociable, affable, honest, obliging,
and of a well-ordered morality. This is strange; but, after all, we
should not be more surprised by this than to see people who
live very bad lives even though they are completely convinced
of the Gospel. Some people claim that he followed the maxim,
"Nobody grows very bad suddenly," and that he only fell into
atheism gradually and that he was far from it when he published
the geometrical demonstration of Descartes' principles. He is
as orthodox in this work about the nature of God as Descartes
himself; but it must be said that he did not speak thus on account of his own convictions. It is not wrong to think that the
ill use he made of some of this philosopher's maxims led him
to the precipice. There are some people who consider the pseu-
donymous tract *De jure ecclesiasticorum,* which was published
in 1665, as a precursor of the *Tractatus theologico-politicus.*
All those who have refuted the *Tractatus theologico-politicus*
have found in it the seeds of atheism, but nobody has developed
this point as clearly as Johannes Bredenbourg (M). It is not as

Observe that those who deny the immortality of the soul and Providence, as the Epicureans did, are those who maintain that men should
apply themselves to virtue on account of its excellence and because
one finds enough advantage in the practice of morality in this life
not to have anything to complain about. This is undoubtedly the doctrine Spinoza would have put forth if he had dared to dogmatize
publicly.

≪←

   M. *(All those who have refuted the* Tractatus theologico-politicus *have found in it . . ., but nobody has developed this point
as clearly as Johannes Bredenbourg.)* . . . Let us speak of Johannes
Bredenbourg. He was a citizen of Rotterdam, who published a book

easy to deal with all the difficulties contained in that work as
to demolish completely the system that appeared in his *Opera
posthuma;* for this is the most monstrous hypothesis that could
be imagined, the most absurd, and the most diametrically op-

in 1675, entitled *Joannis Bredenburgii enervatio tractatus theologico-
politici, una cum demonstratione, geometrico ordine disposita*
NATURAM NON ESSE DEUM, *cujus effati contrario praedictus tractatus
unice innitur.*[80] He has put forth there in the fullest light what Spinoza had tried to wrap up and disguise, and he refuted it solidly. The
world was surprised to see that a man who was not a scholar by profession and who had very little learning[81] had been able to penetrate
so subtly into the principles of Spinoza and overthrow them with
such success after having reduced them by a just analysis into such a
state from which they could best appear with all their strength. I have
heard a rather remarkable fact mentioned. I have been told that this
author, having reflected for a very long time about his answer and
about the principle of his adversary, finally found that this principle
could be reduced to a demonstration. He then undertook to prove
that there is no other cause of all things but a nature that exists necessarily, and which acts by an immutable, inevitable, and irrevocable
necessity. He kept completely to the geometrical method; and after
having constructed his demonstration, he examined it from all imaginable sides; he tried to find some defect in it and was never able to
find any means of destroying it or even of weakening it. This caused
him much vexation. He groaned about it; he sighed about it. He
stormed against his reason, and he begged the most learned among
his friends to help him in the search for the defect in this demonstration. However, he would not let anybody make a copy of it. Francis
Cuper furtively copied it, contrary to the promise he had made.[82] This
man, who was perhaps filled with the jealousy of an author (for he
had written against Spinoza with much less success than Johannes

---

80 It is a quarto of one hundred pages.

81 He admits in his Preface that, because he did not feel himself capable
of expressing himself in Latin, he had composed his book in Flemish and
then had it translated into Latin.

82 I have just learned that Cuper always denied this and always pro-
tested, as his friends still do, that he found the demonstration among Har-
tighvelt's papers, which he inherited.

posed to the most evident notions of our mind (N).* It might
be said that Providence has punished the audacity of this author
in a peculiar way by blinding him in such manner that, in order
to avoid some difficulties that can cause trouble to a philosopher,

Bredenbourg), made use, some time afterwards, of this copy to accuse
Bredenbourg of being an atheist. He published this in Flemish, along
with some reflections. The accused defended himself in the same
language. Several writings appeared on each side, which I have not
read, for I do not understand Flemish at all.† Orobio, a very clever
Jewish doctor,[83] and Aubert de Versé[84] got into this quarrel and took
Cuper's part. They maintained that the author of the demonstration
was a Spinozist, and consequently an atheist. As far as I have been
able to understand the matter by hearsay, Bredenbourg defended
himself by putting forth the usual distinction between faith and reason. He claims that just as the Catholics and the Protestants believe
in the mystery of the Trinity, though it is opposed by the natural light,
so he believes in free will, although reason furnishes him with strong
proofs that everything happens by an inevitable necessity and con-

---

* [Remark N appears on p. 300.]

† [Though Bayle lived in Holland for a quarter of a century, he did not
learn Flemish or Dutch.]

83 I have seen the treatise he published in Amsterdam, entitled *Certamen
philosophicum propugnatae veritatis divinae ac naturalis adversus J. B.
principia, etc.* It is in Latin and Flemish. [Orobio de Castro is an extremely
interesting figure, who had been professor of metaphysics and theology at
the University of Salamanca, in Spain. After being arrested by the Inquisition for secretly practicing Judaism, he escaped to France, where he became
professor of pharmacy at the University of Toulouse. Then, desiring to
practice Judaism openly, he went to Amsterdam where he became a medical
practitioner and polemicist, fighting against various Christian theologians,
as well as Spinoza and Juan de Prado. He also debated with Philip Limborch on the subject of the truth of the Christian religion, a debate that
was published in 1687, the year Orobio died. John Locke either attended
the debate, or was well acquainted with all the details, and seems to have
been quite influenced by it. There are a great many manuscript works of
Orobio in Amsterdam that have never been published. The work against
Bredenbourg and Spinoza was published in Latin, though apparently written originally in Spanish. It was reprinted in the early eighteenth century
in Fénelon, *Refutation des erreurs de Benoît Spinoza* (Brussels, 1731).]

84 I have something of what he has published in the same year, under the
name of Latinus Serbaltus Sartensis. It is in Latin and Flemish.

he threw himself into other perplexities infinitely more inexplicable and so obvious that no balanced mind could ever be unaware of them. Those who complain that the authors who have

sequently that there is no religion. It is not easy to force a man out of such an entrenchment. One may cry out that he is not sincere; and that our mind is not made in such a way, that it can accept as true that which a geometrical demonstration shows is completely false. But is this not setting yourself up as a judge in a case in which it can be objected that you are not competent? Have we any right to decide what goes on in another's heart? Do we know the human soul sufficiently to declare that such and such a combination of views cannot be found in it? Have we not many examples of absurd combinations that are much closer to being contradictory than the one that John Bredenbourg sets forth? For it must be observed that there is no contradiction between these two things: (1) The light of reason teaches me that this is false; (2) I believe it nonetheless because I am convinced that this light is not infallible and because I prefer to submit to the proofs of feeling and to the impressions of conscience, in short, to the Word of God, than to a metaphysical demonstration. This is not at all the same as believing and not believing the same thing at the same time.* That combination is impossible, and nobody ought to be allowed to offer it as his justification. However that may be, the man of whom I am speaking showed that the feelings of religion and the hope of another life had maintained their ground in his soul against his demonstration; and I have been told that the indications he gave during his last illness do not allow his sincerity to be doubted. The Abbé de Dangeau[85] speaks of certain people who have religion in their minds but not in their hearts. They are convinced of its truth without their consciences being affected by the love of God. I believe that one can also say that there are people who have religion in their

---

* [In the last English edition of 1734–1741 a crucial mistranslation occurs at this point, where a negative is left out so that the sentence reads, "This is the same as believing and not believing the same thing at the same time." Some lines were left out of what follows, practically inverting Bayle's sense here, where he gives an excellent and clear statement of his views of the relationship of faith and reason.]

[85] See his *Third Dialogue,* or the extract of it in the *Nouvelles de la République des Lettres,* August 1684.

undertaken to refute him have not succeeded confound things. They would like to have the difficulties he succumbed to completely removed (O),* but it ought to suffice for them that his

hearts, but not in their minds. They lose sight of it as soon as they seek it by the methods of human reasoning. It escapes from the subtleties and the sophisms of their dialectic. They do not know where they are while they compare the pro and con. But as soon as they no longer dispute, and as soon as they listen only to the proofs of feeling, the instincts of conscience, the weight of education, and the like, they are convinced of a religion; and they conform their lives to it as much as human weakness permits. Cicero was like this. We can hardly doubt this when we compare his other books with that of the *De natura deorum* where he makes Cotta [the skeptic] triumph over the other interlocutors who maintained that there are gods.

Those who would like to know better the replies and equivocations that Spinoza made use of to avoid showing his atheism plainly, have only to consult the work of Christian Kortholt, *De Tribus Impostoribus*,[86] printed in Kiel in 1680. The author has there collected several passages from Spinoza and set forth all the poison and artifice there is in them. This is not the least curious part of the history and character of that atheist. Among other items, he cites his nineteenth letter,[88] in which he complains of the report being spread about that he had a book in the process of being published proving that there is no God at all.

---

* [Remark O appears on p. 314.]

[86] Namely, Edward, Lord Herbert of Cherbury; Thomas Hobbes; and Benedictus de Spinoza. [This is not the more famous work of the same title that portrays Moses, Jesus, and Mohammed as the three imposters. This latter work is much discussed in seventeenth-century literature, by Bayle among others; and grave doubts are raised as to whether it existed at that time. In the eighteenth century many manuscripts appeared as well as published copies. The work purports to be from the Middle Ages, and the first printed title page gives the date 1598. For information about it and its possible histories, see the recent edition, *De Tribus Impostoribus Anno MDIIC, Von den Drie Betrügern 1598*, translated by Rolf Walther, edited with an Introduction by Gerhard Bartsch (Berlin, 1960); and also the appendix, "De Tribus Impostoribus," in Don Cameron Allen, *Doubt's Boundless Sea* (Baltimore: Johns Hopkins Press, 1964), pp. 224–243.]

[88] Written to Oldenburg in 1675.

hypothesis has been completely overthrown as has been done by even the weakest of his adversaries. It must not be forgotten that this impious man did not know the inevitable consequences of his theory, for he made fun of the apparition of spirits, and there is no philosopher who has less right to deny it (Q). He ought to have recognized that everything in nature thinks, and that man is not the most enlightened and intelligent modification of the universe. He ought then to have admitted demons. The whole dispute by his followers about miracles is merely playing with words (R) and only serves to show even more the inexactitude of his ideas. He died, they say, completely convinced of his atheism, and he took precautions to keep any last-minute lapse from his principles from being found out, should it occur. If he had reasoned logically, he would not have treated the fear of hell as chimerical (T).* His friends claim that for modesty's sake he wished not to give his name to a sect. It is not true that his followers have been very numerous. Very few persons are suspected of adhering to his theory; and among those who are suspected of it, there are few who have studied it; and among the latter group, there are few who have understood it and have not been discouraged by the perplexities and the impenetrable abstractions that are found in it.ᵐ But here is what hap-

《←

N. *(The most monstrous hypothesis . . . the most diametrically opposed to the most evident notions of our mind.)* He supposes⁹⁰ that there is only one substance in nature, and that this unique substance is endowed with an infinity of attributes—thought and extension among others. In consequence of this, he asserts that all the bodies that exist in the universe are modifications of this substance in

---

⁹⁰ Among his posthumous works see the one entitled *Ethics.*

* [Remarks Q, R, and T appear on pp. 317, 318, and 320, respectively.]

ᵐ It is for this reason that some persons think that it is not necessary to refute him. See the *Nouvelles de la République des Lettres,* June 1684, Article VI [by Bayle].

pens. At first sight, all those are called Spinozists who have
hardly any religion and who do not do much to hide this. It is
in this way that in France all those are called Socinians who are
thought to be incredulous about the mysteries of the Gospel
although most of these people have never read either Socinus
or any of his disciples. Besides, the same thing happened to
Spinoza that is inevitable for those who construct systems of
impiety. They defend themselves from certain objections, but
they expose themselves to other more perplexing difficulties.
If they cannot submit to orthodoxy, if they are so fond of disputing, it would be much more comfortable for them not to
become dogmatists. But of all the hypotheses of atheism, Spinoza's is the least capable of misleading anybody; for, as I have
already said, it opposes the most distinct notions in the human
mind. Objections arise in crowds against him, and he can only
make answers that are more obscure than even the thesis itself
that he is obliged to maintain.[n] Thus his poison carries with it
its own antidote. He would have been more formidable if he
had employed all his strength to clarify a theory that is much
in vogue among the Chinese (X),* and very different from the
one of which I have spoken of in the second remark of this article. I have just learned a curious item, which is that after he had

so far as it is extended, and that, for example, the souls of men are
modifications of this same substance in so far as it thinks; so that God,
the necessary and infinitely perfect being, is indeed the cause of all
things that exist, but he does not differ from them. There is only one
being, and only one nature; and this nature produces in itself by an
immanent action all that we call creatures. It is at the same time both
agent and patient, efficient cause, and subject. It produces nothing that
is not its own modification. There is a hypothesis that surpasses all
the heap of all the extravagances that can be said. The most infamous
things the pagan poets have dared to sing against Venus and Jupiter
do not approach the horrible idea that Spinoza gives us of God, for

---

[n] Consult his letters. You will see that his letters almost never have anything to do with the point at issue.

* [Remark X appears on p. 323.]

renounced the profession of Judaism, he openly professed the Gospel and attended the meetings of the Mennonites or those of the Arminians of Amsterdam. He even approved of a confession of faith that one of his intimate friends communicated to him.

What is said of him in the continuation of the *Menagiana* is so false that I am surprised that Ménage's friends did not perceive this. De Vigneul-Marville would have made them suppress it if he had had a share in the edition of that book, for he has told the public "that there is reason to doubt the truth of that fact." The reasons he sets forth for his doubt are very just. He would not have gone too far if he decisively insisted upon the negative. We will take note of a mistake he made on the same page. Let us say something about the objections I have proposed against Spinoza's theory. I could add a very ample supplement to them if I did not think that they were already too long, in view of the nature of my work. Here is not the place to engage in a regular dispute. It will suffice for me to set forth some general observations that attack the foundations of Spinozism, and that show that it is a system that is based on so strange a supposition that it overthrows most of the common notions that serve to regulate philosophical discussions. To attack this

at least the poets did not attribute to the gods all the crimes that are committed and all the infirmities of the world. But according to Spinoza there is no other agent and no other recipient than God, with respect to everything we call evil of punishment and evil of guilt, physical evil and moral evil. Let us touch on some of the absurdities of his system.

That according to Spinoza God and extension are the same thing. I. It is impossible that the universe be one single substance; for everything that is extended necessarily has parts, and everything that has parts is composite; and since the parts of extension do not subsist in one another, it must be the case either that extension in general is not one substance, or that each part of extension is a particular substance distinct from all the others. Now, according to Spinoza extension in general is the attribute of one substance. He admits, along with all other philosophers, that the attribute of a substance does not

system by its opposition to the most evident and most universal axioms we have had up to now is no doubt a very good way of combatting it, although it is perhaps less fit for curing the old Spinozists than if it were made known to them that the propositions of Spinoza contradict one another. They would feel the weight of prejudice much less if they were forced to agree that he is not always in agreement with himself, that he proves poorly what he ought to establish, that he leaves items unproven that need to be established, that his conclusions do not follow logically, and so on. This method of attacking him by pointing out the absolute defects[q] of his work and the relative defects of the different parts of it compared with each other has been very well employed in some of the refutations of him. I have just learned that the author of a small Flemish book printed a few days ago has used this method forcefully and adroitly. But let us speak of the supplement that I am going to give. It consists of a clarification of the objection I have developed from the immutability of God (CC) and of the examination of the question whether it is true, as I have been told that several people claim, that I have not understood Spinoza's theory at all (DD).* This would be very strange since I have only endeavored to refute the proposition which is the foundation of his system and which he ex-

differ actually from that substance. Therefore he must acknowledge that extension in general is a substance. From which it necessarily follows that each part of extension is a particular substance, which destroys the foundations of the entire system of this author. He cannot say that extension in general is distinct from the substance of God; for if he said that, he would teach that this substance in itself is not extended. Then, it could never be able to acquire the three dimensions except by creating them, for it is obvious that extension can never arise or emanate from an unextended subject except by way of creation. Now Spinoza did not believe that nothing could be made

---

q What is meant by this term are the errors that are not due to Spinoza's maintaining things contrary to the maxims that are generally received as true by other philosophers.

* [Remark CC appears on p. 325, DD on p. 329.]

presses with the greatest clarity. I have confined myself to opposing what he clearly and precisely sets forth as his first principle, namely, that God is the only substance that there is in the universe and that all other beings are only modifications of that substance. If one does not understand what he means by this, it is no doubt because he has given to the words a completely new signification without warning the reader. This is a capital way of becoming unintelligible by one's own doing. If there be any term which he has taken in a sense new and unknown to philosophers, it is apparently that of "modification." But in whatever sense he takes it, he cannot avoid being confounded. That is what can be seen in a remark in this article.[aa] Those who will carefully examine the objections I have proposed will easily perceive that I have taken the word "modification" in the sense in which it ought to be taken and that the consequences I have drawn and the principles I have used to combat these consequences accord exactly with the rules of reasoning. I do not know whether it is necessary that I say that the place that I attack and that has always appeared to me to be the weakest is the one that Spinozists care least to defend (EE).* I shall finish by saying that several persons have assured me that

from nothing. It is even more obvious that an unextended substance by its nature can never become the subject of three dimensions, for how would it be possible to place them on a mathematical point? They would therefore subsist without a subject. They would then be a substance; so that, if this author admitted a real distinction between the substance of God and extension in general, he would be obliged to say that God would be composed of two substances distinct from one another, namely his unextended being and extension. We see him thus obliged to recognize that extension and God are only the same thing; and since, in addition, he maintains that there is only one substance in the universe, he has to teach that extension is a simple being, as exempt from composition as the mathematical points. But is it

---

[aa] Remark DD [p. 329. To designate this and footnote bb, Bayle used the letters a and b.]

* [Remark EE appears on p. 338.]

his theory, even considered apart from the concerns of religion, has appeared very contemptible to the greatest mathematicians of our time.[bb] This will be easily believed if two things are remembered; one, that there are no persons who ought to be more convinced of the multiplicity of substances than those who apply themselves to the consideration of extension; the other, that most of these people admit a vacuum. Now there is nothing more opposed to Spinoza's theory than to maintain that all bodies do not touch each other; and there have never been two systems more opposite than his and that of the Atomists. He is in agreement with Epicurus in what concerns the rejection of Providence, but in all the rest of their systems they are like fire and water.

I have just read a letter in which it is claimed that "he [Spinoza] lived for some time" in the city of Ulm; "that the magistrate made him leave because he spread his pernicious doctrine there," and "it is there that he began his *Tractatus theologico-politicus*." I greatly doubt all this. The author of the letter adds that "his father, while he was still a Protestant, was a good friend of Spinoza, and that it was as a result of his attentions that that extraordinary genius left the sect of the Jews."

not a joke to maintain this? Is this not to fight against the most distinct ideas we have in our minds? Is it not more evident that the thousandth number is composed of a thousand unities than even that a body of a hundred inches is composed of a hundred parts actually distinct from one another, each having one inch of extension?

That extension is composed of parts which are each a particular substance. Let no one come and urge objections to us against the imagination and the prejudices of the senses; for the most intellectual notions, and the most immaterial ones, make us see with complete evidence that there is a very real distinction between things, one of which possesses a quality and the other of which does not. The Scholastics have perfectly well succeeded in showing us the characteristics

---

[bb] Among others, those mentioned to me are Huygens, Leibniz, Newton, Bernoulli, and Fatio.

and the infallible signs of distinction. When one can affirm of a thing, they tell us, what one cannot affirm of another, they are distinct; things that can be separated from one another with regard to time or place are distinct. Applying these characteristics to the twelve inches of a foot of extension, we will find a real distinction between them. I can affirm of the fifth that it is contiguous to the sixth, and I deny this of the first, the second, and so on. I can transpose the sixth to the place of the twelfth. It can then be separated from the fifth. Observe that Spinoza cannot deny that the characteristics of distinction employed by the Scholastics are very just; for it is by these marks that he recognizes that stones and animals are not the same modality of infinite being. He admits then, I will be told, that there is some difference between things. It is most necessary that he admit it since he was not enough of a madman to believe there was no difference between himself and the Jew who struck him with a knife, or to dare to say that in all respects his bed and his room were the same being as the emperor of China. What then did he say? You are about to see. He taught not that two trees were two parts of extension, but two modifications. You will be surprised that he worked so many years constructing a new system, since one of its principal pillars was the alleged difference between the word "part" and the word "modification." Could he promise himself any advantage from this change of words? Let him avoid as much as he wants the word "part"; let him substitute as much as he wants the word "modality" or "modification"; what does this accomplish? Will the ideas attached to the word "part" vanish? Will they not be applied to the word "modification"? Are the signs and characteristics of difference less real or less evident when matter is divided into modifications than when it is divided into parts? Poppycock! The idea of matter still continues to be that of a composite being, that of a collection of several substances. Here follows what will prove this.

Incompatible modalities require distinct subjects. Modalities are beings that cannot exist without the substance they modify. It is therefore necessary that there be substance everywhere for modalities to exist. It is also necessary that it multiply itself in proportion as incompatible modifications are multiplied among themselves, so that wherever there are five or six of these modifications, there are also five or six substances. It is evident, and no Spinozist can deny it, that a square shape and a round one are incompatible in the same piece of

wax. It must necessarily then be the case that the substance modified
by a square shape is not the same substance as that modified by a
round one. Thus, when I see a round table and a square one in a room,
I can assert that the extension that is the subject of the round table is
a substance distinct from the extension that is the subject of the
other table; for otherwise it would be certain that a square shape and
a round one would be at the same time in one and the same subject.
Now this is impossible. Iron and water, wine and wood, are incompatible. Therefore they require subjects distinct in number. . . . All
this shows that extension is composed of as many distinct substances
as there are modifications.

   *The immutability of God is incompatible with the nature of exten-
sion. Matter actually allows for the division of its parts.* II. If it is
absurd to make God extended because this would divest him of his
simplicity and make him consist of an infinite number of parts, what
will we say when we consider that this is reducing him to the condition of matter, the lowest of all beings, and the one that almost all the
ancient philosophers placed immediately above nonbeing? He who
speaks of matter speaks of the theater of all sorts of changes, the battlefield of contrary causes, the subject of all corruptions and all generations, in a word, the being whose nature is the most incompatible with
the immutability of God. The Spinozists, however, maintain that it
allows for no division, but they support this claim by the most frivolous and lowest chicanery that can be imagined. They contend that
for matter to be divided it is necessary that one of its portions be
separated from the others by empty spaces, which never happens. It
is most certain that this is a very bad way of defining division. We are
as actually separated from our friends when the interval that separates
us is occupied by other men ranged in a file as if it were full of earth.
One overthrows, then, both our ideas and our language when one
asserts to us that matter reduced to cinders and smoke is not divided.
But what will they [the Spinozists] gain if we give up the advantage
that their false way of defining the divisible gives us? Would we still
not have enough proofs of the mutability and corruptibility of Spinoza's God? All men have a very clear idea of the immutable. They
understand by this term a being that never acquires anything new,
that never loses anything that it once had, that is always the same, both
in its substance and in its ways of being. The clarity of this idea shows
that we comprehend very distinctly what mutable being consists in.

It is not only a nature whose existence can begin and end, but a nature that, always subsisting in terms of its substance, can acquire successive modifications and lose accidents or forms that it has sometimes had. All the ancient philosophers have recognized that this continual series of generations and corruptions that is seen in the world neither produces nor destroys any portion of matter, and it is from this that they say that matter is "ingenerable" and "incorruptible" in terms of its substance while it is the subject of all the generations and corruptions. . . . It is the most obvious and most suitable example, however, that can be given of a mutable being, subject actually to all sorts of variations and interior changes. . . . The forms produced in matter are united to it internally and penetratively. It is their subject of inherence; and according to sound philosophy, there is no other distinction between them and matter than that which there is between modes and the thing modified; from which it follows that the God of the Spinozists is a nature actually changing, and which continually passes through different states that differ from one another internally and actually. It is therefore not at all the supremely perfect being, "with whom is no variableness, neither shadow of turning" (James 1:17). Observe that the Proteus of the poets, their Thetis, and their Vertumnus, the images and examples of inconstancy, and the foundation of the proverbs that denote the most bizarre fickleness in the heart of man would have been immutable gods if the God of the Spinozists was immutable; for it was never claimed that any change of substance occurred in them, but only new modifications. . . .

God cannot be the subject of inherence of man's thoughts since these thoughts are contrary to one another. III. We are going to see still more monstrous absurdities by considering the God of Spinoza as the subject of all the modifications of thought. The combining of extension and thought in a single substance is already a great problem; for it is not a question here of an alloy like that of metals, or a mixture like that of water and wine. That requires only *juxtaposition;* but the alloy of thought and extension ought to be an *identity;* thinking and being extended are two attributes *identified* with the substance. They are therefore *identified* with each other by the fundamental and essential rule of human reasoning.[96] I am sure that if Spinoza had found such a perplexity in another sect, he would have judged it unworthy of his attention; but he did not regard this to be so in his own cause,

---

[96] Things equal to the same thing are equal to each other.

so true is it that those who most contemptuously criticize the thoughts of others are most indulgent to themselves. He no doubt ridiculed the mystery of the Trinity; and he marveled that an infinity of people dared to speak of a Being terminated by three hypostases, he, who properly speaking, gives to the divine nature as many persons as there are persons on the earth. He regards as fools those who, admitting transubstantiation, say that a man can be at the same time in several places, alive in Paris, dead in Rome, and so on; he who maintains that the extended, unique, and indivisible substance is everywhere at the same time, cold here, hot elsewhere, sad here, elsewhere gay, and so on. This should be said in passing, but consider attentively what I am about to say. If there is anything certain and incontestable in human knowledge, it is this proposition, . . . two opposite terms cannot be truly affirmed of the same subject, in the same respect, and at the same time.[97] For example, it cannot be said without lying, "Peter is well, Peter is very sick: he denies this, and he affirms it," assuming that the terms always have the same relation and the same meaning. The Spinozists destroy this idea and falsify it in such a way that one can no longer know where they will be able to find the mark of truth; for if such propositions were false, there would be none that one could guarantee as true. One could then hope for nothing in a dispute with them; for if they are capable of denying this, they will deny any other argument that is offered them. Let us show that this axiom is completely false in their system, and let us assume at the outset as an incontestable maxim that all the names that are given to a subject to signify either what it does or what it suffers apply properly and physically to its substance and not to its accidents. When we say that iron is hard, iron is heavy, it sinks in water, it splits wood, we do not intend to say that its hardness is hard, that its heaviness is heavy, and so on. That language would be very extravagant. We intend to say that the extended substance of which it is composed resists, is heavy, sinks in water, divides wood. In the same way, when we say that a man denies, affirms, gets angry, caresses, praises, and the like, we ascribe all these attributes to the substance of his soul itself, and not to his thoughts as they are either accidents or modifications. If it were true then, as Spinoza claims, that men are modalities of God, one would speak falsely when one said, "Peter denies this, he wants that, he affirms

---

97 See the logic of Coimbra, *In cap. X Aristotelis de praedicamentis*, and that of Burgerdicius, Bk. I, chap. 22.

such and such a thing"; for actually, according to this theory, it is God who denies, wants, affirms; and consequently all the denominations that result from the thoughts of all men are properly and physically to be ascribed to God. From which it follows that God hates and loves, denies and affirms the same things at the same time; and this according to all the conditions required to make false the rule mentioned above concerning opposite terms; for it cannot be denied that, taking all these terms with all possible rigor, some men love and affirm what other men hate and deny. Let us proceed further. The contradictory terms of willing and not willing belong at the same time to different men. It must be the case in Spinoza's system that they belong to that single and indivisible substance called God. It is God then who, at the same time, forms an act of will and does not form an act of will with regard to the same object. Two contradictory terms are then true of him, which is the overthrow of the first principles of metaphysics.[99] I know indeed that in the disputes about transubstantiation, a cavil is employed that may here be of help to the Spinozists. It is said that if Peter wills something at Rome that he does not will at Paris, the contradictory terms "willing" and "not willing" would not be true with regard to him; for since it is supposed that he wills at Rome, one would lie in saying that he does not will. Let us allow them this vain subtlety. Let us say only that just as a square circle is a contradiction, so also is a substance when it loves and hates the same object at the same time. A square circle would be a circle and not be one. There is a complete contradiction. . . . I say as much of a substance that hates and loves the same object. It loves it, and it does not love it, which is a direct contradiction. . . . Our man could not bear the slightest obscurities either in Aristotelianism, Judaism, or Christianity; and yet he embraced with all his heart a theory that unites together two terms as opposite as "square figure" and "circularity," and by which an infinity of discordant and incompatible attributes and all the variety and antipathy of the thoughts of the human race are true at one and the same time of a single, most simple, and indivisible substance. It is commonly said, "So many men, so many opinions." But according to Spinoza all the opinions of all men are in a single head. Simply to report such things is to refute them, is to show the contradictions clearly; for it is obvious either that nothing is impossible, not even

---

[99] Two contradictories cannot be simultaneously true. The same thing cannot be and not be in the same respect. See Aristotle, *Metaphysics* IV. 3–4.

that two plus two equals twelve, or that there are in the universe as many substances as subjects that cannot be designated in the same way at the same time.

Another proof of what is said above, drawn from the wickedness of man's thoughts. IV. But if it be, physically speaking, a prodigious absurdity that a simple and single subject be modified at the same time by the thoughts of all mankind, it is an execrable abomination when this is considered from the point of view of morality. What then? The infinite being, the necessary being, the supremely perfect being would not be steady, constant, and immutable! Why did I say immutable? He will not be the same for a moment. His thoughts will succeed one another ceaselessly and without end. The same medley of passions and feelings will not recur twice. This is hard to digest, but here is something much worse. This continual mobility will retain much uniformity in this sense, that for one good thought the infinite being will always have a thousand foolish, extravagant, impure, and abominable ones. It will produce in itself all the follies, all the dreams, all the filthiness, all the iniquities of the human race. It will not only be the efficient cause of them, but also the passive subject, the subject of inhesion. . . . Several great philosophers, not being able to comprehend how it is consistent with the nature of the supremely perfect being to allow man to be so wicked and miserable, have supposed two principles, one good, and the other bad;[100] and here is a philosopher who finds it good that God be both the agent and the victim of all the crimes and miseries of man. Let men hate one another, let them murder one another in a forest, let them meet in armies to kill one another, let the conquerors sometimes eat the vanquished; this may be understood, because it is supposed that they are distinct from one another and that the *mine* and *thine* produce contrary passions in them. But that there should be wars and battles when men are only the modifications of the same being, when, consequently, only God acts, and when the God who modifies himself into a Turk is the same God in number as the God who modifies himself into a Hungarian; this is what surpasses all the monstrosities and chimerical disorders of the craziest people who were ever put away in lunatic asylums. Observe carefully, as I have already said, that modes do nothing; and it is the substances alone that act and are acted upon. This phrase, "the

---

[100] See the articles "Manicheans," "Marcionites," and "Paulicians." [The second article here mentioned is not included in these selections.]

sweetness of honey pleases the palate," is only true in so far as it signifies that the extended substance of which the honey is composed pleases the tongue. Thus, in Spinoza's system all those who say, "The Germans have killed ten thousand Turks," speak incorrectly and falsely unless they mean, "God modified into Germans has killed God modified into ten thousand Turks," and the same with all the phrases by which what men do to one another are expressed. These have no other true sense than this, "God hates himself, he asks favors of himself and refuses them, he persecutes himself, he kills himself, he eats himself,[101] he slanders himself, he executes himself; and so on." This would be less inconceivable if Spinoza had presented God as an assemblage of distinct parts; but he has reduced him to the most perfect simplicity, to unity of substance, to indivisibility. He asserts therefore the most infamous and most monstrous extravagances that can be conceived, and much more ridiculous than those of the poets concerning the gods of paganism. I am surprised either that he did not see them, or if he did, that he was so opinionated as to hold on to his principle. A man of good sense would prefer to break the ground with his teeth and his nails than to cultivate as shocking and absurd a hypothesis as this.

Another proof of what is said above, drawn from the misery of man.
V. Two more objections. There have been some philosophers impious enough to deny that there is a God. But they have not pushed their extravagances as far as to say that if he existed, he would not be of a perfectly happy nature. The greatest skeptics of antiquity have said that all men have an idea of God according to which he is a living being, happy, incorruptible, perfect in felicity, and not susceptible of any evil.[102] . . . Happiness was the most inseparable property contained in the idea of him. Those who deny him the authority over, and the direction of, the world at least leave him felicity and immortal beatitude. Those who made him subject to death at least say that he was happy all his life. It was no doubt an extravagance bordering on madness not to unite immortality and happiness in the divine nature. Plutarch refutes this absurdity of the Stoics very well.[104] . . . But no matter how foolish this dream of the Stoics was, it did not deprive the gods of their happiness during their lifetime. The Spinozists are per-

---

[101] The fable of Saturn devouring his own children is infinitely less unreasonable than what Spinoza asserts.

[102] Sextus Empiricus, *Adversus mathematicos* IX. 33.

[104] Plutarch, *Moralia*, "De Stoicorum repugnantiis."

haps the only ones who have reduced the divinity to misery. Now what misery? Sometimes so great that it is thrown into despair, and it would annihilate itself if it could; it tries; it deprives itself of anything it can; it hangs itself; it jumps over precipices, not being able to bear the frightful grief any longer that devours it. These are not just declamations. This is an exact and philosophical language; for if man is only a modification, he does nothing. It would be an impertinent, comical, jocular way of expressing things to say, "Joy is merry, sadness is sad." In Spinoza's system, to say, "Man thinks, man afflicts himself, man hangs himself, and so on," would be expressing oneself in the same way. All these propositions ought to be said of the substance of which man is only a mode. How can it be imagined that an independent being who exists by himself and who possesses infinite perfections might be subject to all the miseries of mankind? If some other being forced it to vex itself, to feel pain, we would not find it so strange that it turned its own activity to making itself unhappy; we should say, "It must be obeying a *force majeure*; obviously it is giving itself the stone, colic, high fever, and madness in order to avoid a greater ill." But it is the only being in the universe. Nothing orders it, exhorts it, begs it. It is its own nature, Spinoza will say, that leads it to give itself in certain circumstances great vexation and very severe pain. But, I will reply to him, did you not find something monstrous and inconceivable in such a fatality? . . .

·   ·   ·   ·   ·   ·   ·   ·   ·   ·   ·   ·   ·   ·

The hypothesis of Spinoza would make all his conduct and his discourse appear ridiculous. VI. If I did not remember that I am not writing a book against this man, but merely a few brief remarks in passing, I would show many other absurdities in his system. Let us finish with this one. He has embarked on a hypothesis that would make all his work ridiculous, and I am very sure that on each page of his *Ethics* one could find some pitiful nonsense. First, I would like to know what he means when he rejects certain doctrines and sets forth others. Does he intend to teach truths? Does he wish to refute errors? But has he any right to say that there are errors? The thoughts of ordinary philosophers, those of Jews, and those of Christians, are they not modes of the infinite being, as much as those of his *Ethics*? Are they not realities that are as necessary to the perfection of the universe as all his speculations? Do they not emanate from the necessary cause? How then can he dare to claim that there is something to rectify? In the second place, does he not claim that the being of which they are modalities acts necessarily, that it always goes on its course, that it cannot turn aside, cannot stop, nor, since it is the sole entity in the universe, can any external cause ever stop it or correct it? Then, there is nothing more useless than the lectures of this philosopher. Is it right for him, being only a modification of substance, to prescribe to the infinite being what he must do? Will this being hear him? And if he hears, could he profit from this? Does he not always act according to the entire extent of his powers, without knowing either where he is going or what he is doing? A man like Spinoza would sit absolutely still if he reasoned logically. "If it is possible," he would say, "that such a doctrine might be established, the necessity of nature would establish it without my book. If it is not possible, all of my writings would accomplish nothing."

≪←

O. *(They would like to have the difficulties Spinoza succumbed to completely removed.)* We will not be mistaken, it seems to me, if we suppose that he only threw himself over this precipice by not having been able to comprehend either that matter is eternal and different from God, or that it has been produced from nothing, or that an infinite and supremely free mind, creator of all things, could produce a work such as the world. A matter that necessarily exists, and that nevertheless is destitute of activity and subject to the power of another principle, is not something that agrees with reason. We see no harmony between these three qualities. The idea of order opposes such a combination. A matter created from nothing is inconceivable, whatever efforts we make to form an idea of an act of will that might convert into a real substance that which was formerly nothing. This principle of the ancients, "Ex nihilo nihil fit," "From nothing, nothing comes," continuously presents itself to our imagination and shines there in so brilliant a manner that it stops us short in case we have begun to form any notion about the creation. Finally, that an infinitely good, infinitely holy, infinitely free God, being able to make creatures always holy and happy, should have preferred that they should be eternally criminal and miserable is something that troubles reason, and all the more so since reason cannot reconcile the free will of man[107] with the quality of a being produced from nothing. Now it would be incomprehensible that man could deserve any punishment under a free, good, holy, and just Providence, without reconciling these two items. These are three difficulties that obliged Spinoza to look for a new system in which God would not be distinguished from matter and in which he acts necessarily and in accordance with the full extent of his powers, not outside of himself, but in himself. It follows from this supposition, that this necessary cause, setting no limits to its power and having as a rule of its actions neither goodness, nor justice, nor knowledge, but only the infinite force of his nature had to modify itself according to all possible realities; so that errors and crimes, pain and vexation, being modalities as real as truths, and virtues, and pleasures, must be contained by the universe. Spinoza thought that by this means he could satisfy the objections of the Manicheans against one principle. They are forceful only against the supposition that a unique principle acts by choice, that it can act or not act, and that it limits its power in accordance with the rules of its goodness and equity, or in accordance with malicious instinct. Supposing this, one asks, "Where does evil come from if this unique principle is good?" Spinoza would reply, "Since my unique principle has the power to do evil and good and does all that it can do, it is completely necessary that there be good and evil in the universe." Weigh, I beg you, on an impartial balance the three difficulties that he wished to avoid and the extravagant and abominable consequences of the hypothesis that he adopted. You will find that his choice is not that of a good man or of a man of judgment. He gave up some things, of which the worst that can be said is that the weakness of our reason does not allow us to know clearly if they are possible, and he embraces others the impossibility of which is manifest. There is a great deal of difference between not understanding the possibility of a thing and understanding the impossibility of it. Now see the injustice of readers. They claim that those who write against Spinoza are obliged to show them with the utmost clarity the truths which he [Spinoza] could not understand, the difficulties of which forced him into another theory. And because they do not find this in the anti-Spinoza writings, they announce that these works are unsuccessful. Is it not enough that the edifice of this atheist has been overthrown? Good sense tells us that

---

[107] That is to say, the liberty of indifference.

custom ought to be maintained against the undertakings of innovators unless the latter produce better laws. Their views ought to be rejected from the fact alone that they are not better than the established opinions even though they be not worse than the abuses they fight against. Submit to custom, these people ought to be told, or offer us something better. With much greater reason it is just to reject the system of the Spinozist since it only gets us away from some difficulties in order to get us into much more inexplicable perplexities. If the difficulties were equal on both sides, the common system ought to be maintained since, in addition to the privilege of possession, it would also have the advantage of promising us great benefits for the future and giving us a thousand consolations for the miseries of this life. Is it not some consolation in misfortune to flatter oneself that the prayers that are addressed to God will be answered and that in any case he will reward us for our patience and will furnish us with a magnificent compensation? It is a great consolation to be able to flatter ourselves that other men will have some regard for the dictates of their conscience and the fear of God. This means that the ordinary theory is at the same time truer and more convenient than the theory of impiety.[110] To have good grounds for rejecting Spinoza's hypothesis, it would suffice then to be able to say, "It is open to no fewer objections than the Christian hypothesis." Thus, every writer who shows that Spinozism is obscure and false in its first principles and perplexed with impenetrable and contradictory absurdities in its consequences ought to be considered as having well refuted it, even though he does not answer all the objections clearly. Let us reduce the whole matter to a few words. The ordinary hypothesis, compared with that of the Spinozists, in those matters that are clear has more evidence of truth. And when it is compared with the other with regard to the obscure matters, it seems less opposed to the natural light; and besides, it promises us an infinite happiness after this life and brings us a thousand consolations in this one, whereas the other promises us nothing beyond this world and deprives us of confidence in our prayers, and in the remorse of our neighbors. The ordinary hypothesis is then preferable to the other.

---

110 I have already said in the article "Socinus, Faustus," remark I, that it is in the interest of each individual person that all the others be conscientious and God-fearing. [The article "Socinus" is not included in these selections.]

≪←

Q. *(There is no philosopher who has less right to deny the apparition of spirits.)* I have said elsewhere[130] that when it is supposed that a supremely perfect spirit has produced creatures from
his bosom out of nothing without being determined to it by his nature,
but by a free choice of his will, it can be denied that angels exist.[131]
If you ask why such a creator did not produce other spirits than the
soul of man, you will be told that such was his pleasure. . . . You cannot make any reasonable answer to this unless you can prove the
fact, namely, that there are angels. But when it is supposed that the
creator has not acted freely and that he has used up all his power without choice or rule, and that, in addition, thought is one of his attributes, it would be ridiculous if one were to maintain that there are
no demons. It ought to be believed that the creator's thought is
modified not only in the bodies of men, but also throughout the universe, and that in addition to the animals we know there are an infinite number we do not know, and which surpass us in knowledge
and malice as much as we surpass dogs and cattle in these respects.
For it would be the most unreasonable thing in the world to imagine
that the mind of man is the most perfect modification that an infinite being could produce, acting in accordance with the full power
of his forces. We do not perceive any natural connection between the
understanding and the brain. That is why we ought to believe that a
creature without a brain is as capable of thinking as a creature organized as we are. What then could have led Spinoza to deny what is said
about spirits? Why did he believe that there is nothing in the world
capable of exciting in our machine the sight of a specter, of making
some noise in our room, and of causing all the magical phenomena
that are mentioned in books? Was it because he believed that, in order
to produce all these effects, it would be necessary to have a body as
bulky as man's; and that in this case, demons could not subsist in air,

---

[130] In remark D of the article "Ruggeri" [not included in these selec-
tions].

[131] If we put aside the authority of Scripture and only reason philosophically.

or enter our houses, or disappear from our sight? But this idea would be ridiculous. The mass of flesh of which we are composed is less an aid than an obstacle to the mind and its powers; I mean its mediate powers, or the faculty it has of applying the instrument most capable of producing the greatest effects. This is the faculty that gives rise to the most surprising actions of man. We are shown this by thousands of examples. An engineer, who is as small as a dwarf, lean and pale, accomplishes more than two thousand of the strongest savages could do. An animated machine, much smaller than an ant might be capable of producing greater effects than an elephant. It could find the invisible parts of animals and plants and place itself on the first springs of our brain and open the valves there that would result in our seeing phantoms, hearing noises, and so on.[133] If doctors knew the basic fibers and combinations of parts in vegetables, minerals, and animals, they would also know what instruments would put them out of order; and they could apply these instruments as would be necessary to produce new arrangements that would convert good meats into poison, and poisons into good meats. Such doctors would be incomparably more capable than Hippocrates; and were they small enough to enter the brain and the viscera, they could cure whom they wished and could also cause the strangest illnesses that have ever been imagined whenever they wished. All this reduces to this question, "Is it possible that an invisible modification may have more knowledge and more wickedness than man?" If Spinoza takes the negative, he does not know the consequences of his own hypóthesis and proceeds rashly and without principles. A long dissertation might be written on this subject, examining and obviating all his subterfuges and objections. . . .

≪←

R. (*The dispute by the* Spinozists *on miracles is merely playing with words.*) The common opinion of orthodox theologians is that God produces miracles immediately, whether he makes use of

---

[133] Note in passing that nothing can be more improper than to dispute whether angels who appear form their own bodies or borrow those of some dead men. All this is useless. It suffices that they move the optical and acoustical nerves in the same way the light reflected from a human body and the air that comes out of a human mouth moves them.

creatures, or whether he does not. Both these methods constitute incontestable proof that he is above nature; for if he produces anything
without employing other causes, he can get along without nature; and
in the second method he never employs other causes in a miracle unless he has turned them from their normal course. This shows that
they depend on his will, that he suspends their power when he sees fit,
or that he applies it in a different manner from their usual determination. The Cartesians who make him the immediate cause of all the
effects of nature suppose that when he performs miracles, he does not
observe the general laws he has established. He makes an exception to
them, and he deals with bodies completely differently than he would
have done if he had followed the general laws. On this they say that
if there were general laws by which God had pledged to move bodies
according to the desires of angels, and if an angel had wished that the
waters of the Red Sea be parted, then the passage of the Israelites
could not be properly called a miracle. This consequence, which follows necessarily from their principle, prevents their definition of a
miracle from having all the advantages that might be desired. It would
have been better then if they had said that all of the effects contrary
to the general laws known to us are miracles; and by this means, the
plagues of Egypt and all the other extraordinary events reported in
Scripture would be miracles, properly speaking. Now, to show the
insincerity and illusions of the Spinozists on this subject, it is sufficient
to observe that when they reject the possibility of miracles, they offer
this reason, that God and nature are the same entity, so that if God
did something contrary to the laws of nature, he would have done
something against himself, which is impossible. Speak clearly and
unequivocally; say that the laws of nature have not been produced by
a free lawgiver who knew what he did but were the result of a blind
and necessary cause, and that therefore nothing can happen that is
contrary to those laws. You will then be offering your own thesis
against miracles. This would be a *petitio principii* [begging the ques-
tion]; but at least you will be speaking frankly. Let us get them down
from these generalities. Let us ask them what they think of the miracles
reported in Scripture. They will absolutely deny everything about
them that they cannot attribute to some clever contrivance. Let us
set aside the effrontery involved in listing facts of this nature as false.
Let us direct the attack against their principles. Have you not said
that the power of nature is infinite? And would it be so if there were

nothing in the universe that could restore a dead man to life? Would
it be so if there were only one way of making men, that of ordinary
generation? Have you not said that nature's knowledge is infinite?
You deny that divine understanding, in which, in our view, the knowledge of all possible beings is reunited. But by dispersing that knowledge, you do not at all deny its infinity. You ought to say that nature
knows all things, in about the same way that we say that man understands all languages. One single man does not understand them all;
but some understand one, some another. Can you deny that the universe does not contain anything that understands the construction of
our body? If that were the case, you would fall into a contradiction.
You would no longer recognize that the knowledge of God was divided
in an infinite number of ways. The manner in which our organs are
constructed would not be known to him. Admit then, if you want to
reason logically, that there is some modification that knows it. Admit
that it is quite possible for nature to revive a dead body, and that your
master got himself mixed up in his ideas and did not know the consequences of his theory when he said that if he had been able to convince himself of the resurrection of Lazarus, he would have broken
his system into pieces and would have embraced without difficulty the
ordinary faith of Christians.[136]

This suffices to prove to these people that they deny their hypotheses when they deny the possibility of miracles, that is, so that there
will be no ambiguity, the possibility of the events recorded in Scripture.

≪⋲

T. (*If he had reasoned logically, he would not have treated the
fear of hell as chimerical.*) Let a person believe as much as he
would like that this universe is not the work of God, and that it is not
directed by a simple, spiritual nature, distinct from all bodies. He must
at least admit that there are certain things that have intelligence and
will, and that are jealous of their power. They exercise their power
over other things, command them to do this or that, punish them,
mistreat them, and avenge themselves with severity. Is the earth not
full of these types of things? Does not each man know this by experi-

---

136 I have been assured that he said this to his friends.

ence? To think that all the beings of this kind are only on the earth, which is merely a point in comparison to the world, is certainly an entirely unreasonable view. Is it likely to be the case that reason, intelligence, ambition, hate, cruelty, be on the earth rather than elsewhere? Why? Could any good or bad reason be given for this? I do not believe so. Our eyes lead us to be convinced that the immense spaces we call the heavens, in which there are such rapid and active movements, are as capable as the earth of producing men and as worthy as the earth of being divided into several dominions. We do not know what goes on there; but if we only consult reason, it would be necessary for us to believe that it is very probable, or at least possible, that there are thinking beings there who extend their empire as well as their light on our world. The fact that we do not see them is no proof that we are unknown or indifferent to them. We are perhaps a part of their dominions. They make laws, and reveal them to us by means of the light of conscience, and are extremely angry with those who transgress them. It suffices that this be possible in order to make the atheists anxious; and there is only one good means of escaping from fear, that is, by believing that the soul is mortal. They would escape in this way the anger of these spirits, for otherwise they could be more formidable than God himself. I will explain myself. There are some people who believe in a God, a paradise, and a hell; but they deceive themselves into thinking that the infinite goodness of the supremely perfect being does not allow him to torment his own creatures for eternity. He is the father of all men, they say. He therefore paternally punishes those who disobey him; and after having made them see the error of their ways, he restores them to his good graces. This was the way Origen reasoned. Others suppose that God will deprive rebellious creatures of their existence, and that with the plea, "What end of labors do you grant, O great King?"[143] he will be appeased and moved to pity. They carry their illusions so far that they think that the eternal punishments that the Bible speaks of are only warnings. If such people did not know that there is a God, and by reasoning about what goes on in our world, they would convince themselves that elsewhere there are beings who are concerned about the human race; they would only liberate themselves from anxiety about dying if they believed in the mortality of the soul. For, if they believed it to be immortal, they might be afraid of falling into the hands of

---

143 Virgil, *Aeneid* I. 241.

some savage master who had conceived some resentment against them because of their actions. It would be in vain that they might hope to escape after a few years of torment. A limited being may have no kind of moral perfection. It could easily resemble our Phalarises and our Neros, people capable of leaving their enemies in a dungeon forever if they were capable of possessing eternal authority. Will they hope that the evil-doing beings will not last forever? But how many atheists are there who claim that the sun never had a beginning and will never have an end? This is what I meant when I said that there are beings who might seem more formidable than God himself. One can have some hopes when considering a God who is infinitely good and perfect, and one might fear everything from an imperfect being. One cannot tell whether his wrath will last forever. Everyone knows the choice of the prophet David.[144]

To apply all this to a Spinozist, let us remember that he is obliged by his theory to admit the immortality of the soul since he considers himself as a modification of an essentially thinking being. Let us remember that he cannot deny that there are some modifications that get angry at other ones, who torture them, and who make their torments as great as they can, who send them to the galleys for the rest of their lives, and who would make this punishment eternal if death did not prevent it. Tiberius, Caligula, and a hundred others, are examples of these kinds of modifications. Let us remember that a Spinozist would make himself ridiculous if he did not admit that the universe is filled with ambitious, vexatious, jealous, and cruel modalities. For since the earth is filled with them, there is no reason to think that the air and the heavens are not likewise full of them. Let us remember, lastly, that the essence of human modifications does not consist in being clothed in large pieces of flesh. Socrates was Socrates the day of his conception, or a little afterwards.[145] All that he was at that time could subsist in its entirety after a mortal malady had made the circulation of the blood and the motions of the heart stop in the matter in

---

144 Having to choose either to be defeated by his enemies or to be afflicted by some scourge sent by God, he replied to the prophet Gad, "I am in a great strait; let us fall now into the hand of the Lord; for his mercies are great; and let me not fall into the hand of man" (II Samuel 24:14).

145 Spinoza, who was a maker of microscopes, ought to have believed that man is organized and alive in the seed, and that thus Socrates was Socrates before his mother conceived him.

which he was enlarged. He is therefore after his life the same modification that he was during his lifetime, considering only the essential features of his person. He does not at all escape justice then by death or
avoid the caprice of his invisible persecutors. They can follow him
wherever he goes and mistreat him in all the visible forms that he may
assume.

These considerations could be employed to the practice of virtue to
lead even those who stagnate in the impious views of similar sects, for
reason desires that they chiefly fear having violated the laws revealed
to their consciences. Such faults are the ones in which those invisible
beings would be most likely interested in punishing.

《《←

X. *(He would have been more formidable if he had employed
all his strength to clarify a theory that is much in vogue among
the Chinese.)* A Church Father made an admission that perhaps
would not be pardoned today if offered by a philosopher. It is that
even those who deny the deity and providence set forth probabilities as
much for their cause as against their adversaries. "Some deny that there
are gods; others say that they are doubtful whether there are any; but
others assert that they exist but do not care about human affairs;
and others affirm that they interpose in the affairs of mortals and ad-
minister them. As this is the case, and as but one of these opinions is
true, they all oppose one another with arguments; and each of them
has something probable to urge, either in defense of his own opinion,
or in opposition to those of others."[146] If he were right, it would perhaps be chiefly with regard to those who suppose that there are a
great number of souls in the universe distinct from one another, each
one of which exists by itself and acts by an internal and essential
principle. Some have more power than others, and so on. This is what
the atheism that is so generally spread among the Chinese consists in.
Here is how it is thought that they have little by little obscured the
true ideas.[147] "God, that most pure and perfect being, at most has
become the material soul of the whole world, or of its most beautiful
part, the heavens. His providence and his power have become no more

---

[146] Arnobius, *Adversus gentes*.
[147] La Loubère, *Relation de Siam*.

than a limited power and providence, although, however, much more extended than the power and prudence of men. . . . The doctrine of the Chinese has always ascribed spirits to the four parts of the world, to the stars, the mountains, rivers, plants, cities and their moats, houses and their hearths, and, in a word, to all things. And they do not think that all the spirits are good. They acknowledge that some of them are wicked and are the immediate causes of the evils and disasters to which human life is subject. . . . Therefore, since the soul of man was, in their opinion, the source of all the vital actions of man, they thus ascribed to the sun a soul that is the source of its qualities and motions. And on this principle, souls were diffused everywhere, causing in all bodies the actions that appear natural to those bodies. Nothing further is needed on this theory, to explain the whole economy of nature and to take the place of the omnipotence and infinite providence that they do not admit is in any spirit, not even that of the heavens. In truth, since it seems that man, using natural things for his food or for his comforts, has some power over natural things, the ancient opinion of the Chinese giving a proportionately similar power to all souls supposed that that of the heavens could act upon nature with a prudence and strength incomparably greater than human prudence or strength. But, at the same time, this theory recognized an internal force in the soul of each thing, independent by its nature of the power of the heavens, and which might sometimes act contrary to the designs of the heavens. The heavens governed nature in the manner of a powerful king. Other souls owed it obedience. It almost always forced them to give in, but sometimes some of them disobeyed.'' I admit that it is absurd to suppose several eternal souls, independent of one another, and unequal in strength. But this supposition appeared true to Democritus, to Epicurus, and to several other great philosophers. They admitted an infinite number of tiny bodies of different size and shape, uncreated, self-moving, and the like. This view is still very common in the Levant.[149] Those who contend that matter is eternal are never more reasonable than when they claim there is an infinite number of atoms; for if there can be two co-eternal and independently existing beings, there can be one hundred billion of them, and so on to infinity. They even ought to say that there actually is an infinity of them because matter, no matter how

---

[149] See the anonymous work published in Amsterdam in 1690, entitled *Philosophia vulgaris refutata*.

small it is, contains distinct parts. And note carefully that all ancient thinkers were ignorant of the creation of matter, for they never departed from the axiom, "From nothing, nothing comes." They therefore did not know that it was absurd to acknowledge an infinite number of coeternal substances existing independently of one another. No matter how absurd that hypothesis may be, it is not subject to the dreadful difficulties that destroy Spinoza's. The former would account for many phenomena by assigning an active principle to each thing, a stronger one to some, a weaker one to others. Or, if they were all equal in strength, it would be necessary to say that those which are victorious have formed a more numerous alliance. I do not know whether there has ever actually been a Socinian who has said or believed that man's soul, not being produced out of nothing, exists and acts of and by itself. Its liberty of indifference would obviously flow from that.

«‹‹

CC. (*A clarification of the objection I have developed from the immutability of God.*) You will find this objection above in remark N, paragraph II [p. 307, above]. It is necessary to defend it, since there are some people who assert that, to see that there is nothing to it, it is only required to note that no change ever happens to Spinoza's God in that it is a substance that is infinite, necessary, and so on. Let the whole universe change its face every moment, let the earth be reduced to ashes, let the sun be obscured, let the sea become light; there would only be a change of modifications. The one and only substance would still equally be an infinite, extended, thinking substance, and so on, with all the other substantial or essential attributes. In saying this, they set forth nothing but what has already been refuted;[157] but to show their error more clearly, I must point out here that they argue against me as if I had maintained that according to Spinoza the deity annihilates and reproduces himself successively. This is not at all my objection when I claim that he subjects the deity to change, and that he deprives him of his immutability. I am not, as they are, overthrowing the ideas of things and the meaning of words. What I understand by change is what the whole world has meant by this word since

---

[157] See remark N, paragraph II [p. 307, above].

reasoning began. I mean, I say, not the *annihilation* of a thing, its total destruction, or its reduction to nothing; but its passage from one state to another, the subject of the accidents that it ceases to have and those that it commences to acquire remaining the same. The learned, the ordinary people, mythology and philosophy, poets and scientists, have always been in agreement on this idea and this locution. The fabulous metamorphoses so much sung by Ovid and the actual generations explained by the philosophers both equally supposed the conservation of substance and retained it immutably as the successive subject of the old and the new form. Only the unfortunate theological disputes in Christendom have confused these concepts, and furthermore it must be admitted that even the most ignorant missionaries get back on the right track as soon as the question is no longer about the Eucharist. Ask them in any other case what is meant by the change of one thing into another, the conversion, the transelementation, and the transubstantiation of one thing into another; and they will answer, "This means, for example, that from wood fire is made, that from bread blood is made, from blood flesh is made, and so on." They are no longer thinking of the improper language consecrated to the controversy over the Eucharist, that bread is converted and transubstantiated into the body of our Lord. This way of speaking is not at all suitable to the doctrine that one wishes to explain by it. It is as if one should say that the air in a cask is transformed, changed, converted, and transubstantiated into the wine that is poured into the cask. The air goes somewhere else, and the wine follows it in the same place. There is not the slightest indication of metamorphosis from one into the other, nor is there any more in the mystery of the Eucharist, as explained by the Roman Catholics. The bread is annihilated with respect to its substance. The body of our Lord puts itself in the place of the bread and is not the subject of inherence of the accidents of that bread, which are preserved without their substance. But, once more, this is the only case in which the missionaries misuse the words "change," "conversion," or "transelementation," of one being into another. On all other occasions, they suppose, along with the rest of the human race: (1) that it is of the essence of transformations that the subject of the destroyed forms subsists under the new forms, (2) that this conservation of the subject in everything essential to it does not prevent it from undergoing an internal change, which is both properly so called and is inconsistent with immutable beings. Let the Spinozists therefore cease to think that they are permitted to create a new language contrary to the concepts of all mankind. If they have any residue of sincerity, they will admit that in their theory God is subject to all the vicissitudes and all the revolutions that the prime matter of Aristotle is subject to in the theory of the Peripatetics. Now, what can be more absurd than to maintain that by supposing Aristotle's theory, matter is a substance that never undergoes any change?

But, to embarrass the Spinozists greatly, it is only necessary to request that they define what change is. They will have to define it in such a way that it will be in no way different from the total destruction of a subject, or that it will apply to that one and only substance they call God. If they define it in the first way, they will make themselves more ridiculous than the transubstantiators; and if they define it in the second way, they will let me win.

I shall add that the argument they use to escape from my objections proves too much. For if it were sound, they would have to claim that there has not been, and there never will be, any change in the universe, and that all change, the very greatest or the very smallest, is impossible. Let us prove this consequence. "The reason why," they say, "God is immutable is because, as a substance and as an extension, nothing ever happens to him, and no change can ever happen to him. He is extended substance under the form of fire, as well as under the form of wood, which is turned into fire, and so on with regard to other cases." I am going to prove to them by this argument that the modifications themselves are immutable. Man is, according to them, a modification of God. They admit that man is subject to change since he is, for example, sometimes gay, and sometimes sad, sometimes willing something, sometimes not. This is not change, I will say to them, for he is no less a man in sorrow than in joy. The essential attributes of man remain immutable in him, whether he wills to sell his house, or whether he wills to keep it. Let us consider the most inconstant of men. . . . At random let us suppose someone who has given his heart and lips in turn to all the religions in less than two years, who has tasted all of the conditions of human life, who has gone from being a merchant to being a soldier to being a monk, and then has gotten married and divorced, and after that worked in the registry office, in financial affairs, and then ecclesiastical ones, and so on. Let the Spinozists go and tell him, "You have been very inconstant." "Who me?" he will answer them. "You are being funny. I have never changed. A mountain has not continued more invariably to be a mountain than I to be a man from the moment of my birth." What can they reply to this *ad hominem* argument? Is it not completely evident that the entire essence of the human species subsists in man whether he wishes the same thing, or whether he hates today what he loved yesterday and changes his inclination more often than his shirt?

Let us use an example that is most proper for a country where people have sea legs. Let us suppose that a Spinozist returning from Batavia reports that his voyage lasted longer than usual because the winds changed almost every day. "You are mistaken," he would be told. "The winds never change. You can rightly say that they blow sometimes from the north, sometimes from the south, and so on, but they always retain the essence of wind. They do not change, then, as wind; and they are as immutable as your one and only substance of the universe; for according to you, it is immutable because it never changes state in relation to its essential properties. No more does the wind ever change its state in relation to its quality as wind. It always retains the entire nature and essence of it. It is therefore as immutable as your deity."

Let us go on, and let us say that even when a man is burned alive, no change happens to him. He was a modication of divine nature when he was alive. Is he not so in the flames, or in the form of ashes? Could he lose the attributes that constitute a modification? As a modification, could he undergo any change? If he changed in this respect, would it not be necessary to maintain that the flame is not a mode of extension? Could Spinoza hold this view without contradicting himself and without destroying his theory? This is enough to show the error of those who claim that I have not sufficiently proven that this theory subjects God to change. One cannot avoid my argument without establishing that the modifications themselves are immutable, and that no change ever occurs, neither in the thoughts of man, nor in the dispositions of the body, which is completely absurd and contrary to the doctrines the Spinozists cannot avoid accepting. For they do not dare deny that the modifications of infinite substance are subject to corruption and generation.

Let us ask them to grant for a moment, without conceding anything, that, for the sake of argument, they let us consider Socrates a substance. Then they would have to say that each particular thought of Socrates is a modification of the substance. But, is it not true that Socrates, in passing from affirmation to negation, changes his thought, which is a real internal change, and properly so called? However, Socrates remains always a substance, and an individual of the human species, whether he affirms, whether he denies, whether he desires or whether he rejects this or that. It cannot then be concluded that he is immutable because he does not change at all as a man; and in order to be able to say that he is mutable and that he actually changes, it is sufficient that his modifications are not always the same. Let us give back to the Spinozists what they have lent us, and let us grant them in turn, for the sake of argument, that Socrates is only a modification of the divine substance. Let us grant them, I say, that his relation to this substance is like the relation of the thoughts of Socrates to the substance of Socrates in the ordinary view. Then, in view of the fact that the change of these thoughts is a sound reason for maintaining that Socrates is not an immutable being, but rather a changeable one, and a moveable substance that varies a great deal, it must be concluded that the substance[160] of God undergoes a change and a variation, properly called, every time that Socrates, one of his modifications, changes state. It is therefore a thesis of an evident truth that, in order for a being to pass actually and really from one state to another, it suffices that it change in respect to its modifications. And, if more be demanded, that is to say, that it should lose its essential attributes, this would grossly confuse *annihilation* or total destruction, with alteration or change. . . .

≪

DD. *(Whether it is true, as I have been told that several people claim, that I have not understood Spinoza's theory at all.)* I have heard this from several quarters, but nobody has been able to tell me what those who make this judgment base it on. Thus, I cannot answer them precisely, or examine if I ought to give in to their arguments since they are unknown to me. I can only justify myself in a general way; and I think that I can say that, if I did not understand the proposition I undertook to refute, it is not my fault. I would speak with less confi-

---

160 Note that Aristotle, in *Categories* V, has placed among the properties of substance that of remaining the same in number under contrary qualities.

dence had I written a book against Spinoza's entire system, following it page by page. No doubt, it would have happened more than once that I did not understand what he intended; and it is improbable that he completely understood himself and could make all the consequences of his hypothesis intelligible in great detail. But, since I stopped at one single proposition which is stated in very few words, which seems to be clear and precise, and which is the foundation of the entire structure, it must be the case either that I have understood it or that it contains some ambiguities entirely unworthy of a system-builder. In any case, I can console myself that I have given the same sense to Spinoza's proposition that his other adversaries have given it and that his followers can give no better answer than to say that he has not been understood. This reproach did not hinder the last person who wrote against him from understanding the proposition in question just as I did, an evident sign that their accusation is groundless.

But, to say something less general, here is what I suppose in my objections. I attribute these teachings to Spinoza: (1) that there is only one substance in the world; (2) that this substance is God; and (3) that all particular beings with corporeal extension—the sun, the moon, plants, animals, men, their motions, their ideas, their imaginings, their desires—are modifications of God. I now ask the Spinozists, has your master taught this, or has he not? If he did teach this, it cannot be said that my objections suffer from the defect called *ignoratio elenchi* (ignorance of the state of the question); for they suppose that such was his doctrine and attack it only on these grounds. I am then safe, and one would be wrong every time it was claimed that I refuted what I did not understand. If you say that Spinoza did not teach the three doctrines stated above, I ask you why, then, did he express himself exactly as would men who had the greatest passion in the world to convince the reader that they taught these three things? Is it fair or commendable to employ the common language, without attaching the same ideas to words that other men do and without announcing the new sense in which they are to be taken? But, to discuss this a little, let us see where the misunderstanding may be. I have not been mistaken with regard to the word "substance," for I have not opposed Spinoza's view on this point. I have admitted what he supposes, that for something to deserve the name of substance, it must be independent of all causes, or exist by itself eternally and necessarily. I do not believe that I could have been mistaken in imputing

to him the view that God alone has the nature of a substance. I believe, then, that if there were any mistake in my objections, it would
consist only in that I have understood by "modalities," "modifications," and "modes" something different from what Spinoza intended
by these words. But, once again, if I were mistaken on this point, it
would be his fault. I took these terms in the sense that they have always been understood, or at least in the sense that all the new philosophers understand them;[165] and I had the right to assume that he took
them in this same sense since he had not warned the world that he
took them in some other sense. The general doctrine of the philosophers is that the idea of being contains, immediately under it, two
species—substance and accident—and that substance subsists by itself
. . . , and an accident subsists in some other being. . . . They add that
"to subsist by itself" signifies only "not being dependent on any subject of inhesion"; and since this agrees, according to them, with matter, angels, man's soul, they admit two kinds of substance, one uncreated, the other created; and they subdivide created substance into
two species. One of these two is matter, the other is our soul. With
regard to accidents they all agreed, before the wretched disputes that
divided Christendom, that they depend so essentially on their subjects of inhesion that they cannot exist without them. This was their
specific characteristic, which differentiated them from substances. The
doctrine of transubstantiation overthrew this whole idea and forced
philosophers to say that an accident can subsist without its subject.
They had to say this since they believed, on the one hand, that after
consecration the substance of the bread of the Eucharist no longer
subsisted, and they saw, on the other hand, that all the accidents of
the bread subsisted as before. They therefore admitted a real distinction between a substance and its accidents, and a reciprocal separa-
bility between those species of beings, which would result in the fact
that each of them could exist without the other. But some of them
continued to say that there were accidents whose distinction from
their subject was not real, and which could not subsist outside of it.
They called these accidents "modes."[166] Descartes, Gassendi, and, in

---

[165] I employ this restriction because of the difference that exists between
the theory of the modern Aristotelians and that of the Cartesians, Gassen-
dists, etc., concerning the nature of accidents. This difference is significant,
but it amounts to the same thing with respect to the objections against
Spinoza.

[166] Of this kind are union, duration, and ubiquity.

general, all those who have abandoned Scholastic philosophy, have denied that an accident is separable from its subject in such a way that it could subsist after its separation, and have ascribed to all accidents the nature of those that are called "modes" and have employed the term "mode," "modality," or "modification," rather than that of "accident." Now, since Spinoza had been a great Cartesian, it is reasonable to suppose that he ascribed to these terms the same sense that Descartes did. If this is the case, by "modification of a substance" he only understood a way of being that has the same relation to substance as shape, motion, rest, and location have to matter, and as pain, affirmation, love, and the like, have to man's soul. For these are what the Cartesians call "modes." They acknowledge no others than these, from which it appears that they have kept the old idea of Aristotle according to which accidents are of such a nature that they are no part of their subject, that they cannot exist without it, and that the subject can lose them without prejudicing its existence. All this agrees with roundness, motion, rest, with relation to a stone, and does not agree any less with respect to pain and affirmation with regard to man's soul. If our Spinoza has joined the same idea to what he calls "modification of substance," it is certain that my objections are just. I have attacked him directly according to the true sense of his words. I have rightly understood his theory, and I have refuted it in its actual sense. In short, I am safe from the accusation I am examining. But if he had the same conception as Descartes of matter (or extension) and the human soul, and if, however, he did not want to ascribe the status of substance either to extension or to our souls, because he believed that a substance is a being that does not depend on any cause, I admit that I have attacked him without grounds, have attributed to him a view that he does not hold. This is what remains for me to examine.

Having once set forth that substance is that which exists by itself, as independently of every efficient cause as of every material one or every subject of inhesion, he could not say that either matter or men's souls were substances. And since, according to the usual view, he divided being into only two species, namely substance and modification of substance, he had to say that matter and men's souls were only modifications of substance. No orthodox person will disagree with him that, according to this definition of substance, there is only one single substance in the universe, and that substance is God. It will only be a question of knowing whether he subdivides the modification of substance into two species. In case he makes use of this subdivision and means that one of those two species is what the Cartesians and other Christian philosophers call "created substance," and the other species what they call "accident" or "mode," there will be only a dispute about words between him and them; and it will be very easy to bring his whole system back to orthodoxy and to make his sect vanish; for a person is only inclined to be a Spinozist because he believes that Spinoza has completely overturned the Christian philosophers' system of the existence of an immaterial God governing all things with a perfect liberty. From which we can conclude in passing that the Spinozists and their adversaries agree completely about the meaning of the phrase "modification of substance." They both believe that Spinoza employed this term only to designate a being that has the same nature as what the Cartesian philosophers call "modes," and that he never understood by this term a being that had the properties or nature of what we call "created substance."

Those who should insist strongly that I have been mistaken might suppose that Spinoza only rejected the designation, "substance," given to beings dependent on another cause with respect to their production, their conservation, and their operation . . . as is said in the Schools. They could say that, while retaining the entire reality of the thing, he avoided using the word, because he thought that a being so dependent on its cause could not be called . . . "a being subsisting by itself," which is the definition of substance. I reply to them, as I did above, that there will then be only a pure logomachy, or dispute about words, between him and the other philosophers, and that I will admit my mistake with the greatest pleasure in the world if it is the case that Spinoza actually was a Cartesian but had been more careful than Descartes in employing the word "substance," and that all of the impiety attributed to him consists only in a misunderstanding. He meant to say nothing else, it will be added, than what is found in the books of the theologians, namely that the immensity of God fills heaven and earth and all the imaginary spaces to infinity,[168] that consequently his essence penetrates and locally surrounds all other beings, so that it is in him that "we live and move" (Acts 17:28), and that nothing has been produced outside of him. For, since he fills all spaces, he can place a body in himself only, in view of the fact that outside of him

---

[168] Note that the Cartesian theologians explain the immensity of God in another way.

there is nothing. Besides, we know that all beings are incapable of existing without him. It is then true that the properties of Cartesian modes agree with what are called "created substances." These substances are in God and cannot subsist outside of him and without him. It must not then be found strange that Spinoza called them "modifications"; but on the other hand, he did not deny that there was a real distinction, and that each of them constituted a particular principle of either actions or passions in such a manner that one does what the other does not do, and that when it is denied of one what is affirmed of the other, this is done in accordance with the rules of logic, without anyone being able to object to Spinoza that it follows from his principles that two contradictory principles are true of one and the same subject at the same time.

All this discourse has no purpose, and if one wants to get to the point, one ought to answer this precise question: Does the true and proper characteristic of a modification belong to matter with respect to God, or does it not? Before answering me, wait until I explain to you, by examples, what a characteristic of a modification is. It is to be in a subject in the way in which motion is in a body, and thought is in man's soul, and the form of a bowl is in a vase that we call a bowl. It is not sufficient to be a modification of the divine substance to subsist in the immensity of God, to be penetrated with it, to be surrounded by it on all sides, to exist by virtue of God, and not to be able to exist without him or outside him. It would also be necessary that the divine substance be the subject of inherence of a thing, just as in the ordinary view, the human soul is the subject of inherence of feeling and desire, pewter is the subject of inherence of the form of the bowl, and the body is the subject of inherence of motion, rest, and shape. Answer me now; and if you say that according to Spinoza the substance of God is not in that way the subject of inherence of that extension, or motion, or human thoughts, I will admit to you that you make him an orthodox philosopher who did not deserve to have the objections made against him that have been offered, and who only deserved to have been reproached for having gone through so much trouble to embrace a view that everyone knows and for having constructed a new system that is only built on the ambiguity of a word. If you say that he claimed that divine substance is the subject of inherence of matter and of all the varieties of extension and thought, in the same sense that according to Descartes extension is the subject of inherence of motion and man's soul is the subject of inherence of sensations and passions, then I have all that I ask for. That is exactly how I understood Spinoza, and it is on this that I based all my objections.

To sum up all this, it is a question of fact concerning the true sense of the word "modification" in Spinoza's system. Must it be taken for the same thing that is commonly called "created substance," or must it be taken in the sense it has in Descartes' system? I believe that the latter is correct, for in the other sense Spinoza would have acknowledged creatures distinct from divine substance and who have been made either out of nothing or from a matter distinct from God. Now it would be easy to prove by a great number of passages in his books that he admits neither of these two things. Extension, according to him, is an attribute of God. It follows from this that God is essentially, eternally, and necessarily an extended substance, and that extension is as proper to him as existence. From which it follows that the particular varieties of extension, which make up the sun, earth, trees, bodies of beasts, bodies of men, and so on, are in God in the way in which the School philosophers suppose that they are in prime matter. Now, if these philosophers supposed that prime matter is a simple and perfectly unique substance, they would conclude that the sun and the earth are really the same substance. It must be the case then that Spinoza came to the same conclusion. If he did not say that the sun is composed of divine extension, he would have to admit that the sun's extension has been made from nothing; but he denies creation, and he is therefore obliged to say that the substance of God is the material cause of the sun, is what composes the sun. . . , and, consequently, that it is not distinct from God[170] but is God himself and God entirely, since according to him God is not a being composed of parts. Let us suppose for a moment that a mass of gold has the strength to convert itself into plates, dishes, candlesticks, bowls, and the like. It would not be at all distinct from these dishes and plates. And if one adds that it is a simple mass, not composed of parts, it will be certain that it is entirely in each dish and in each candlestick, for if it were not entirely there, it would then be composed of parts, which is contrary to the supposition. Then these reciprocal or convertible propositions would be true, "The candlestick is the mass of gold, the mass of

---

[170] Matter, Aristotle says in *Physics* I. 9, remains in the effect that it produces.

gold is the candlestick. The candlestick is the entire mass of gold, the entire mass of gold is the candlestick." This is the picture of the God of Spinoza; he has the power to change or modify himself into earth, moon, sea, tree, and so on, and he is absolutely one and not composed of any parts. It is then true that it can be asserted that the earth is God, that the moon is God, that the earth is God entirely, that the moon is also, that God is the earth, that he is the moon, that God entirely is the earth, that God entirely is the moon.

There can only be three ways in which the modifications of Spinoza are in God, but none of these ways is that which the other philosophers say of created substance. It is in God, they say, as in its efficient and transitive cause, and consequently, it is actually and totally distinct from God. But according to Spinoza, creatures are in God either as an effect is in its material cause, or as an accident is in its subject of inhesion, or as the form of a candlestick is in the pewter of which it is composed. The sun, moon, and trees, in that they are three dimensional, are in God as in the material cause of which their extension is composed. There is then an identity between God and the sun, and so on. The same trees, in so far as they possess a form that distinguishes them from a stone, are in God as the form of a candlestick is in the pewter. To be a candlestick is only one of the pewter's ways of being. The motion of bodies and the thoughts of men are in God as the accidents of the Peripatetics are in a created substance; they are entities inherent in their subjects, and which are not composed of them and are not part of them. See below, footnote 171.

I am not unaware that an apologist for Spinoza[172] maintains that this philosopher does not attribute a corporeal extension to God, but only an intelligible extension,* which cannot be imagined. But if the

---

171 Note this difference, that the accidents of the Aristotelians are really distinct from their subject of inhesion, and that Spinoza cannot say this of the modifications of divine substance, for if they were composed of it, they would be made out of nothing. Spinoza would admit this. He would not cavil as the Peripatetics do when it is proven to them that the accidents would be created if they were distinct from their substance. See the *Journal de Trevoux,* June 1702.

172 Kuffalaer, *Artis ratiocinandi.* Observe that he carries on very much against Blyenberg, who had said that Spinoza attributed corporeal extension to God. Note also that he refutes a certain Adrian Verwer, who had said something against Spinoza's theory.

* [This is Malebranche's term to denote the kind of conceptual reality that exists in the mind of God.]

extension of bodies that we see and imagine is not God's extension, then where does it come from, and how has it been made? If it has been made from nothing, then Spinoza is orthodox, and there is no novelty in his system. If it has been produced from the intelligible extension of God, it is still a real creation; for intelligible extension, being only an idea and not really possessing three dimensions, cannot furnish the stuff or the matter of the extension formally existent outside the understanding. Besides this, if two species of extension are distinguished, one intelligible that belongs to God, the other imaginable that belongs to bodies,* it would be necessary to admit two subjects of these extensions, distinct from one another; and then the unity of substance is overthrown; and the entire edifice of Spinoza falls to the ground. Let us say then that his apologist does not resolve the difficulty and creates still greater ones.

The Spinozists could take advantage of the doctrine of transubstantiation; for if they will consult the writings of the Spanish Scholastics, they will find an infinite number of subtleties there to give some answer to the arguments of those who say that the same man cannot be a Mohammedan in Turkey and a Christian in France, sick in Rome and healthy at Vienna. But I cannot tell, after all, if they will not find themselves obliged to compare their theory with the mystery of the Trinity in order to extricate themselves from the contradictions with which they are overwhelmed. If they do not say that the modifications of God, Plato, Aristotle, this horse, this monkey, this tree, this stone, are so many personalities, which, although *identified* with the same substance, can each be a particular and determinate principle, and distinct from the other modifications, they can never parry the blow that can be struck against them concerning the principle that "two contradictory terms cannot belong to the same subject at the same time." Some day perhaps they will say that just as the three persons of the Trinity, without being distinct from the divine substance, according to the theologians, and without having any absolute attribute that is not numerically the same in all of them, do not fail to have, each one of them, properties that can be denied of the others, so nothing stops Spinoza from admitting an infinite number of modalities or personalities in the divine substance, one of which does

---

* [The contrast here seems to be between something that can be intellectually understood and something that is just an image in the imagination, which is understood here as a lesser faculty of the mind.]

something that the others do not do. This will not be a real contradiction, since the theologians acknowledge a virtual distinction . . . with respect to the susceptibility of the two terms that are contradictory. But as the subtle Arriaga judiciously remarks, on the subject of the metaphysical degrees,[173] which some men would maintain are capable of receiving two contradictory propositions: to undertake to transfer to natural things what Revelation teaches us about the nature of God would be to ruin philosophy completely; for this would open the door to proving that there is no real difference between creatures.[174]. . . Here is the great debt we owe to Spinoza: he takes away from us, with all the force he commands, the most necessary of all principles. For if it were not certain that at the same time the same thing cannot be such and such and not such and such, it would be useless to meditate or to reason. See what Averroës said.[176]

≪←

EE. *(The place that I attack . . . is the one that Spinozists care least to defend.)* I have attacked the supposition that extension is not a composite being, but one unique substance numerically; and I have attacked this rather than any other part of the system because I know that the Spinozists say that it is not here that the difficulties lie. They think they are much more perplexed when they are asked how thought and extension can be united in one and the same substance. There is something strange in this; for if it is certain from the concepts in our minds that extension and thought have no affinity with one another, it is even more obvious that extension is composed of parts actually distinct from one another; and yet they are more aware of the first difficulty than the second and treat the latter as a bagatelle compared to the other. I then believed that it was necessary to give them occasion to have the following thought, "If our system is so hard to defend in a part that we thought had no need of help, how then will we repel the attacks of the weak parts?"

---

173 This is what they call the attributes that constitute the nature of man: being, substance, body, living, animal, rational. It is agreed that they are not distinct one from the other, but really one and the same entity.

174 Arriaga, *Disput. V Logica*, Sec. II, no. 29.

176 Cf. Fonseca, *In metaphys. Aristotel.*, Bk. IV, chap. 3.

Takiddin, a Mohammedan author. I will only mention one thing about him, which is that he said that the Caliph Almamon would indubitably be punished by God for having disturbed the religious devotion of the Moslems by the introduction of philosophical studies. There is nothing special in this view. It has been set forth in all countries of the world and in all ages; and even today one finds a great number of people who complain about Descartes and some other great modern philosophers as the cause of the contempt that so many people show for religious devotion and for the Christian mysteries. This could provide the occasion for a lengthy commentary (A).

≪←

A. *(This could provide the occasion for a lengthy commentary.)*
A thousand things could be said about this, both on the question of fact, and on the question of right. However, I shall be very brief, for I already have more copy than is required to complete this volume. With regard to fact, I shall only say that philosophers have always been suspected of having hardly any religion. The ancient rhetoricians, after having said that among probable propositions some were based on what happens almost all the time and others were based on common opinion, then offered these two examples: Mothers love their children; and philosophers do not believe that there are gods. "That is probable which commonly comes to pass or is generally believed.

. . . A probability of the first kind, namely, of those things that commonly come to pass, is this: If she be a mother, she loves her son; if he be covetous, he disregards his oath. But probabilities of the second kind, namely, of those things that are generally believed, are these: Punishments are prepared below for the wicked; those who apply themselves to philosophy do not believe the existence of the gods."[1] Apuleius observes that almost all the ancient philosophers had been accused either of denying that the gods exist or of practicing magic. "These things are, through a common mistake of ignorant persons, objected to philosophers; that one group of them, who search into the primary and simple causes of bodies, are thought to be irreligious and to deny the existence of the gods, as Anaxagoras, and Leucippus, and Democritus, and Epicurus, and other patrons of nature; and another group of them, who are more curious in investigating the conduct of providence in the world and more zealously worship the gods, are vulgarly styled magicians, as if they knew how to do those things that they find to be done, as formerly Epimenides, and Orpheus, and Pythagoras, and Osthanes."[2] Our Takiddin would not have delivered to divine justice the great Almamon, that supporter of the sciences, that introducer of philosophical studies, had he not observed the bad effects of these studies. They had raised doubts in people's minds. They had opened the eyes of many people to the foolishness of the Mohammedan sect; and because of this, the public worship, piety, and devotion had all undergone a prodigious weakening. There are theologians who maintain that the Arabian philosophers were only Mohammedans in appearance, and that they actually made fun of the Koran because they found things in it that were contrary to reason. You cannot get a great many people to stop believing that Descartes and Gassendi were as little convinced about the Real Presence as about the fables of Greece. You would have the same difficulty in convincing people that the followers of these two great philosophers are good Catholics and that, if they received permission to teach their principles publicly, they would not soon undermine all the foundations of the Roman Catholic religion. The Protestants do not have any better opinion of the doctrines of Descartes. Generally speaking,

---

[1] Cicero, *De inventione* I. 29. 46.
[2] Apuleius, *Apologia*.

the Cartesians are suspected of irreligion; and their philosophy is believed to be very dangerous to Christendom, so that, according to the
view of a great many people, the same men who in our century have
dispelled the shadows that the Scholastics had spread throughout
Europe have multiplied the number of freethinkers and opened the
door to atheism, or to Pyrrhonism, or to the disbelief of the greatest
mysteries of Christianity. But it is not only the study of philosophy
that is blamed for irreligion. The study of literature is also accused;
for it is claimed that atheism only began to appear in France during
the reign of François I, and that it only began to appear in Italy when
the humanities began to flower there again. "The less foreign learning we have," a Catholic author says, "the more submission we show
to the faith; and the most learned ages, Baronius says, have often been
the most unbelieving. The Aladinists only appeared during the reign
of Almansor, who was the most learned monarch of his time; and I do
not find any atheists in our country before the reign of François I,
nor in Italy, until after the last conquest of Constantinople, when
Argyropilus, Theodore of Gaza, and George of Trebizond, along with
the most famous men of Greece, retired to the court of the dukes of
Florence."[4] What is certain is that most of the brilliant men and
learned humanists who shone in Italy when literary studies began to
be revived, after the capture of Constantinople, had hardly any religion. But, on the other hand, the revival of the study of learned languages and literature prepared the road for the Reformers, as the
monks and their partisans had foreseen when they ceaselessly clamored
against Reuchlin and Erasmus and other opponents of barbarianism.
Thus, while the Roman Catholics have a basis for deploring the consequences of the study of literature, the Protestants have a reason for
praising and glorifying God for it.[5] They do not have reason to feel
the same way about the new philosophy, which so demonstratively
overthrows transubstantiation and all its consequences; for the same

---

[4] Clavigny de Sainte Honorine, *Discernement & usage des livres suspects.*
Note that I do not offer what he sets forth as a certain fact.

[5] See the reflections of Jurieu, *Apologie pour les reformat. . . . ,* on what
Maimbourg in *Histoire du calvinisme* had said, to the effect that the means
employed by François I "to revive learning in his kingdom . . . were, by a
misfortune he did not foresee, those which allowed heresy to enter his
domain."

weapons have been abused to attack the most essential doctrines. In a word, man's fate is so bad that the knowledge that delivers him from one evil throws him into another. Eliminate ignorance and barbarism and you destroy superstition and the foolish credulity of the people, which is so profitable for their leaders, who afterwards misuse their gain by plunging themselves into idleness and debauchery. But by enlightening men about these disorders, you inspire them with a desire to examine everything. They sift and analyze so much that they find nothing that satisfies their wretched reason.

However that may be, I have heard it said by very wise men that there is no prudence in the too common affectation of imputing impiety to the philosophers; for what a scandal it would be to ignorant people if they took the trouble to consider the matter carefully and to see that, according to the claims of many theologians, faith is hardly to be found among the great philosophers, that devotion is mainly to be found among the most humble people, and "that those who have most examined the divine characteristics of Holy Scripture are usually the least pious and the least devout."[6] It would be much more edifying to teach with Plutarch[7] that philosophy is the cure for impiety and superstition, and with Origen that without philosophy no one can be really pious. . . . The mixture of good and evil found in all human affairs shows itself here most distinctly. The Arabian philosophers came to know by their philosophy that the Koran was worthless. But, on the contrary, several Jews have abandoned their religion in order to embrace pagan philosophy, which showed them, they said, that Moses had prescribed superfluous laws for them. "This opinion was formerly maintained so firmly by many Jews that at the beginning of the Saracen empire they revolted to the pagan philosophy because not a few of the laws seemed useless and superfluous to them."[9] Thus,

---

6 Jurieu, cited by Saurin in *Examen de la théologie*. See the reflections Saurin made on this statement.

7 See Plutarch, *Moralia*, "Isis and Osiris."

9 Johannes Spencerus, *De legibus Hebraeorum*, Bk. II, chap. 3, sect. 1. He reinforces this with the testimony of Guillaume de Paris. [This episode is discussed at greater length in Bayle's earlier work *Commentaire philosophique*, Pt. I, chap. 1, in *Œuvres diverses*, II, 370, where the reasoning of the Jews in question is analyzed as a basis for considering the relation between natural light and revelation.]

the same principle that is sometimes of service against error some-
time renders a disservice to truth.*

---

* [One of the striking features of this passage is that Bayle here contrasts
Mohammedanism as error with Judaism as truth. Throughout the *Dictionary* what Bayle calls the true religion is always Christianity. He is willing to
play havoc with the Old Testament, but never with the New Testament.
There are many facetious articles about the heroes of Judaism, but only one
insignificant article ("St. John the Evangelist") on any figure in the four
Gospels or the Book of Acts. But at the same time, Bayle's views, as exhibited in many of these selections, show that his attitude toward Judaism is
far from that of most of his contemporaries, and very far from that of
Enlightenment figures such as Anthony Collins and Voltaire, who were to
make Judaism the evil cause of all that they considered wrong with Christianity. Bayle's tolerance of Judaism was far in advance of his contemporaries, even including John Locke. And in view of the disputations and
polemical writings appearing in the Netherlands in the latter half of the
seventeenth century, between members of the Spanish-Portuguese Jewish
community and Calvinist theologians, about whether Judaism *or* Christianity was the true religion (a debate Bayle was aware of, since he had read
Locke's account, in Le Clerc's *Bibliothèque universelle,* of the disputation between Philip Limborch and Orobio de Castro on just this point), the fact
that Bayle would classify Judaism as the truth here is the more startling.
[Also, Bayle was aware that Nicholas Anthoine, a Catholic turned Protestant who became a Jew, and the last man burned at the stake in Geneva
(1632), had maintained that Judaism, and *not* Christianity, was the true religion. (Bayle mentions Spanheim's answer to Anthoine in article "Spanheim," remark D.) Though some French Protestant leaders were willing to
defend Anthoine's character and oppose burning him, they were not willing
to defend his views. And the usual Protestant explanation of how Anthoine
could have come to his strange theory that Judaism was the true religion
was that he had a weak mind or was crazy. In view of all this, Bayle's statement here seems very odd and unusual for its time.]

Tiraqueau, ANDRÉ (in Latin Tiraquellus), one of the most learned men of the sixteenth century, was born at Fontenai-le-Comte, a city of Poitou. I have only a few things to add to what Teissier and Moreri have said of him. I shall only say that there is no probability that he had as many children as some have claimed. They make the total reach forty-five; and they say that, had he drunk wine, he would have been much more fruitful both with the productions of his pen and the productions of his marriage (A). He died at a very old age in 1588. Some plagiarized much more from him than he did from others. I have cited a passage elsewhere in which it is observed that he inserted a great many obscenities into one of his books.

≪←

A. *(They make the total number of children reach forty-five; and they say, etc. . . . .)* Not long ago I read in a thesis, *De aquae calidae potu* [On Drinking Hot Water], sustained at Helmstedt . . . in 1689, that although Tiraqueau drank only water, he was the father of forty-five children and as many books. It is said of him, "The fruitful and eloquent Tiraqueau, who was a water-drinker, was father of five and forty books and as many children; and if he had not abated his fire by his abstemiousness in drinking water, he would have filled the world with the offspring of his mind and body." I am sure this is exaggerated. De Thou would not have been ignorant of a fact so extraordinary as this, and he would have mentioned it if he thought it true. Now he was satisfied to say that each year Tiraqueau gave a book and a child to the public. Other writers have been more specific about the number, but they limit it to thirty. Tiraqueau "was no less fruitful in producing children of his mind than of his body, for during a thirty-year period there did not pass a single year in which he did not give a book and a son to the public. Thus, if on the one hand he extended his name and family by a great number of children —all excellent persons—whom he had by a virtuous wife, he gained as much glory by the great number of books with which he enriched the public. What makes this more amazing is that he was so fecund though he drank only water."[2] Teissier . . . also limits himself to the number thirty. One cannot go as high as forty-five if one follows the common observation of the writers who mention this, that Tiraqueau had only one wife and that all his children were legitimate. I do not wonder that this fecundity appears most amazing to those who reflect that this learned man drank only water. But maybe this even contributed to his prolificness. Perhaps his natural heat would have reached an excessively high degree had he the use of good wines; in this state he would not have been so capable of generation. For it is said that some marriages are barren because of too great a lustfulness on the part of the parties concerned. However that may be, Tiraqueau's wife did not have to fear the attacks of jeerers, as she would have had to if she had been rarely pregnant. Her husband loved study to an excess. His writings speak strongly that he spent entire days among his books. We find in them a prodigious amount of reading, much labor, and research requiring great effort. When it is known that a man spends that kind of day, it is assumed that he is worn out and has need of much rest at night. . . . It is supposed that he has dissipated his spirits by meditating, composing, and reading, and that he tries to renew his spirits by a sound sleep instead of by new dissipations. Therefore, some would make jests at his wife in company, some would pity her, some would give her insincere condolences. But if she can show a house full of children, she is protected from these jests. As everything has two sides, it is the case that a husband-author, buried all day long in his papers and books, can be either an easy or a troublesome husband. This depends on the wife he has. If she is a coquette and not too virtuous, then he is an easy husband. For while he studies twelve hours or more each day, she has free rein to do as she likes. But if she is resolved to do her duty, he is not a good husband in all respects. He forces her sometimes to wish she were a book. He goes to bed completely fatigued from his studies, with his head full of some

---

[2] Pierre de St. Romuald, *Abrégé du thrésor chronolog.*, III, 324, for the year 1558.

chapter he could not finish. Everyone knows the inconveniences of this disposition of mind and body. Observe that everything has its exceptions. We discover by reading the lives of learned men that there are a great many who had large families. Some temperaments are so strong and so well constituted that they suffice for everything.

.   .   .   .

Weidnerus, PAUL, a Jewish doctor of the six-
teenth century, was called from
Udino, a city in Italy, to practice medicine in Carinthia. He
lived there for six years and received a handsome pension from
the public. During this time, he entertained some doubts about
his religion, which obliged him to compare the Old and New
Testaments and to examine carefully the commentaries of the
rabbis. And since he realized from these studies that Jesus
Christ is the Messiah, he resolved to embrace the Christian faith
openly. He wavered for a whole year, even though fully convinced; and he carefully hid his thoughts. He was not unaware
of the dangers to which he would be exposed (A) if he let the
Jews know the state of his soul. But finally the importance of
his salvation won out over considerations of the flesh. He left
Carinthia and moved to Vienna; and there he had himself
solemnly baptized with his wife and four children in St.
Stephen's Church on August 21, 1558. He was made professor
of Hebrew at the University of Vienna, and he published something on the motives for his conversion and in order to refute
Judaism.

≪

A.* *(He was not unaware of the dangers to which he would be
exposed.)* To believe firmly that a religion is true, to resolve to
profess it, and to undergo many struggles within one's soul before
executing such a resolution are not incompatible attitudes. It must

---

* [The discussion in this note seems to be autobiographical and may well
indicate what happened to Bayle during the period of his temporary conversion to Catholicism while he was attending the Jesuit college at Toulouse.]

not then be thought that Weidnerus' narration is lacking in fidelity. There are few projects whose execution is more thwarted than that of changing religion. For, not to mention other obstacles, does not the prospective convert know that he will anger those whom he loves and those whom he respects the most? Is he not aware that he will become odious and infamous to his relatives. I say infamous; for every society may rightfully attach the idea of infamy to the action of a man who forsakes its religion. Not satisfied with calling him a rebel and an apostate, they also call him a renegade.[1] They maintain that his desertion is a disgrace to his family, and I have known a pious lady who used to say quite seriously that she would have preferred that her sisters take on the profession of prostitution than that she see them going to Mass. These horrid ideas are necessary for the temporal wellbeing of a community, and that is why they are fomented. A casuist will not find it bad that a father disowns his sons who become apostates, and that in a similar case, a brother will no longer see his own brother, and a husband will abhor his wife, or a wife will desert her husband. If the Protestants reproach the Catholics for this kind of persecution, the Catholics, on their side, accuse the Protestants of the same thing.[2] Be this as it may, it is certain that this practice often serves as a bogey to scare those who are convinced that they ought to leave the Church in which they have been raised. Let us cite Arnauld: "There is something so astonishing," he says,[3] "in a person's plan to change his religion that sometimes it is difficult to execute, even when one is resolved to do so. . . . I know that a young lady, daughter of a very zealous Huguenot, concealed from her father for seven years the fact that she was a Catholic, and that during all that time, she accompanied him to sermons, abstaining herself only from taking Communion, from fear that it would grieve him to death. She got someone to consult me on this matter; and having heard that I did not approve of this dissimulation, she resolved to reveal her status, though with great reluctance. . . . There may also be some, as in St. Augustine's time, who are convinced of the truth of the Catholic

---

[1] This name was used in some French cities by the Protestants to designate those who embraced papism.

[2] See the book by Brueys entitled *Réponse aux plaintes des protestans;* it is mentioned in the *Nouvelles de la République des Lettres,* August 1686, Article I [by Bayle].

[3] Arnauld, *Apologie pour les catholiques,* Pt. II, chap. 12.

religion, but yet are not able to break the chains of habit that pull them to Protestant sermons, nor able to expose themselves to the reproaches they fear that their change would bring from their relatives or their partisan friends. They are not in condition to follow very easily the truth that they are aware of, unless some other human consideration opposite those already mentioned would constitute a counterweight to the impression the first have made upon their hearts." There are some communities that believe themselves so completely disgraced by the apostasy of a meritorious monk and fear that it will prove to be a fatal shock to the faith of simple people and too great a triumph for the other side, that they will do everything against anyone who shows any signs of wanting to desert. The Jews have the same attitude. Did they not want to destroy Spinoza by assassination,[4] and did they not try to eliminate our Weidnerus after his conversion? "Further," the latter says,[5] "when there was no possibility of concealing this affair any longer, I immediately had apprehensions of great danger from such of my brethren according to the flesh, as might suspect my design for turning Christian. And alas! I am so unfortunate as to see, and know by experience, that those dangers still threaten me." Let us not forget a terrible kind of persecution, of those who change religions. They are overwhelmed with libels and slanders.[6] Their entire lives are picked over; and if any blemishes are found, they are given out to the public with every kind of exaggeration. The most minor faults of their youth are not forgiven. If they have written any confidential letters that can be used to blacken their reputation, they are published. In a word, for the community's interest, and to discredit the authority of this change of religion, the public will not scruple to make great crimes of those very actions that would not have stopped it from having esteem and affection for someone had he remained in his religion. . . .

---

[4] See the text of article "Spinoza," [p. 288].

[5] Weidnerus in his Dedicatory Epistle to the Emperor Ferdinand.

[6] Compare this with Pierre Charron's words which I quoted in remark P of the article on him [not included in these selections].

Zeno, of Elea, one of the major philosophers of antiquity, flourished in the seventy-ninth Olympiad. He was the disciple of Parmenides and was even, according to some, his adopted son. He was a handsome man. Some writers claim that he was loved by his teacher more than he should have been. You will find in Moreri that he was the inventor of dialectic. One ought to find there that he also endeavored to free his country, which was oppressed by a tyrant, and that, when this undertaking was discovered, he suffered the most rigorous tortures with extraordinary courage. This affair is related with thousands of variations, as will be seen in our remarks. I have only two sins of commission with which to reproach Moreri.* Moreover, the views of Zeno of Elea were almost the same as those of Xenophanes and Parmenides concerning the unity, the incomprehensibility, and the immutability of all things. I cannot believe that he maintained that there is nothing in the universe (E); for how could he have said that he himself, who

≪←

E. *(I cannot believe that he maintained that there is nothing in the universe.)* I therefore distrust Seneca who attributes this view to him. Justus Lipsius is also dubious about the matter. "Hear the evils that flow from too much subtlety, and how pernicious it is to truth. Protagoras says that a man may dispute on any subject, and take either side of the question with equal advantage, and may even dispute on this question, whether any subject is disputable on either side. Nausiphanes says that in things that seem to exist there is no difference between existence and nonexistence. Parmenides says that nothing exists

---

* [In remark D (not included in these selections) Bayle discusses two small factual errors in Moreri's citations from Diogenes Laertius.]

maintained such a doctrine, did not exist? How could he, who sought only to perplex everybody by his arguments pro and con, perplex them, I say, in such a way that they would have no place

of whatever is seen in the universe. Zeno of Elea rejects the existence of all things and says that there is nothing. The Pyrrhonists, the Megarians, the Eretricians, and the Academics entertain the same way of thinking and introduced a new science, that we know nothing. But all of these notions ought to be ranked in the class of superfluous learning. The former [Zeno] declares that learning will be of no use to me, and the latter [the Pyrrhonists, etc.] deprive me of the hopes of ever acquiring any; but it is better to be the master of superfluous learning than of none at all. The former does not offer a light to guide me to the paths of truth, the latter put my eyes out. If I believe Protagoras, all things in nature are doubtful; if Nausiphanes, the only thing certain is that nothing is certain; if Parmenides, there is but one being in nature; if Zeno, there is not so much as one. What then are we? And what are those things that surround, nourish, and support us? The whole circle of nature is a shadow, a nothing, an illusion. I could not easily say whether I am most angry with those who affirm that we know nothing or with those who will not even allow that we know nothing."[41] I have given Seneca's words at some length so that one might see all the degrees of skepticism, among which there is nothing as outlandish as the view of our Zeno. If he had actually held such a paradoxical theory, he did it either as a diversion, or he did not take the word "nothing" as others understand it, or else he was talking nonsense. But there is no sign of insanity in the rest of his views. It would be better then to have recourse either to the hypothesis of a play on words, or that of a peculiar meaning of the word "nothing." Let us say the same thing about the book in which Gorgias of Leontini maintained three theses:[42] the first, that nothing exists; the second, that if something did, man cannot comprehend it; and third, then even if he could comprehend it, he could not express it. Let us see Justus Lipsius' view on the passage from Seneca: "There is a saying that Zeno of Elea freed us from all uneasiness and inquiry, he maintaining that there is nothing. But this is a wonderful and wise saying, or a silly one,

---

41 Seneca, *Epistulae morales* LXXXVIII. 43–46.
42 See Sextus Empiricus, *Adversus mathematicos* VII. 65ff.

to turn to, had he been willing to commit himself to such a position? Did he not see that it was easy to confound him by asking if something that is nonexistent can argue? He argued

and incomprehensible to me. If it is offered as an indication of the contempt for things, that all sublunary things are nothing (not that there is nothing in the world), I not only assent to but applaud the saying. But if otherwise, and if he was speaking of the very existence of things, he was mad. By the way, Zeno of Elea says nothing like this in Diogenes Laertius, where many of his opinions are related; nor do I remember having met with this elsewhere. Let Seneca look to this."[43] It will be doubtless brought up against me what Plutarch reports concerning the character of Zeno. "Pericles," he says,[44] "was likewise for some time the auditor and disciple of Zeno the philosopher, a native of the city of Elea, who taught natural philosophy after the manner of Parmenides; but he professedly contradicted everyone and stated so many objections in disputation that he so puzzled his antagonist that the latter did not know what to answer nor what to resolve, as Timon of Phlius declares in the following words:

> *Great was his eloquence and strength of art,*
> *When Zeno argued either pro or con;*
> *Still contradicting all who dared oppose him."*

A philosopher of this stripe, I will be told, was quite capable of quibbling up to the point of maintaining that all things are nothing. I answer that it is not at all probable that so clever a disputant as he would have carried things so far that it does not seem possible that he could have extricated himself.

But no matter how incredible this may seem, nevertheless let us observe that the consequences of Pyrrhonism have been able to lead people to maintain many outlandish things; and let us moderate a little the affirmations that I have just listed.[45] Let us observe also that perhaps our Zeno only maintained that there is nothing while arguing about those principles he wanted to oppose. It may be that people concluded that he taught this positively and absolutely from an *ad*

43 Lipsius, *Manuduct. ad stoic. philos.*, Bk. II, Disc. 4.
44 Plutarch, *Lives*, "Pericles" IV.
45 See the Clarification concerning the Pyrrhonists, footnote 3 [p. 423].

strenuously against the existence of motion. Some of his objections on this have been preserved for us in the writings of Aristotle (F); but it is probable that he proposed several others

hominem argument he used, although he only offered this as a doctrine that resulted from the hypothesis that he had undertaken to refute.

.   .   .   .

≪←

F. (*Some of his objections against the existence of motion have been preserved for us in the writings of Aristotle.*) Read Aristotle's *Physics.* You will find there an examination of the four objections of Zeno.[48]

Here is the first:[49] If an arrow that points toward a certain place were to move, it would be simultaneously both at rest and in motion. Now this is contradictory, and therefore it does not move. The consequence of the major is proven in the following way. The arrow is at every moment in a space equal to itself. It is therefore at rest there, for a thing is not in a space when it has left it. Therefore there is no moment in which it moves; and if it were to move in some moments, it would be both at rest and in motion. In order to understand this objection better, it is necessary to take notice of two undeniable principles; the first, that a body cannot be in two places at the same time; and the other, that two time intervals cannot coexist. *Time is not divisible ad infinitum.* The first of these two principles is so evident even when we do not pay attention to it, that there is no need that I explain it. But, since the other requires a bit more contemplation in order to be understood, and since it contains the entire strength of the objection, I will make it more obvious by an example. Thus I say that what suits Monday and Tuesday with regard to succession suits every part of time whatsoever. Since it is thus impossible that Monday and Tuesday exist together, and since it must be the case necessarily that Monday cease before Tuesday begins to exist, there is no other part of

---

48 Bk. VI, chap. 9.

49 I rank it as the first because Aristotle sets it forth and answers it at the beginning of the chapter; but in the following sections, he places it third.

that were, perhaps, the same as those that will be seen below (G), some of which oppose the existence of extension and seem much stronger than all the arguments that the Cartesians could set forth. I am speaking of some Cartesians who publicly maintain, even in the countries that have an Inquisition, that one can only know by revelation that there are bodies. The senses deceive us, they say, with regard to the qualities of matter; we then ought to distrust their evidence with regard to the three dimensions. It is not necessary, they add, that there be bodies. Without them, God can communicate to our souls all that they feel and all that they know; and, consequently, the proofs that reason furnishes us of the existence of matter are not evident enough to furnish a good demonstration on this point (H). As for the objections that can be based upon the distinction between a plenum and a vacuum and can be very perplexing for the modern philosophers, I am sure that he did not forget them (I).* Since he was not a contemporary of Diogenes the Cynic, it

time, whatever it may be, that can coexist with another. Every one has to exist alone. Every one must begin to exist, when the other ceases to do so. Every one must cease to exist, before the following one begins to be. From which it follows that time is not divisible to infinity, and that successive duration of things is composed of moments properly so called, of which each is simple and indivisible, perfectly distinct from the past and the future, and contains only the present time. Those who deny this conclusion ought either to be left to their stupidity or their insincerity, or to be given up because they are dominated by prejudices. Now if you once grant that time is indivisible, you will be forced to admit Zeno's objection. You cannot find an instant in which an arrow leaves its place. For if you found one, the arrow would be at the same time in that place and not in that place. Aristotle is satisfied with answering that Zeno supposes very falsely the indivisibility of moments.

Zeno's second objection is this: If there were motion, it would be necessary that the moving object go from one place to another, for all motion includes two extremities, *terminus a quo, terminus ad*

---

* [Remarks G, H, and I appear on pp. 359, 373, and 377, respectively.]

was not his lecture that was refuted by Diogenes' walking up and
down. Everyone admires the method Diogenes employed to
overthrow the arguments of the philosopher he had heard dog-
matizing on the denial of motion. He walked up and down in
the lecture hall and felt that this was sufficient to prove the
falsity of all that the professor had just said. But it is definitely
the case that an answer like this is more sophistic than the arguments of our Zeno (K).* I do not think that he taught, as some
allege, that matter is composed of mathematical points. Rather,
I should believe that he maintained that matter could not be so
composed. I must not omit that he submitted to slanders with
less patience than to the cruelties inflicted on his body. He got
very angry at a man who insulted him; and when he realized
that people were surprised by his indignation, he replied, "If
I were insensible to insults, I would also be so to praise." This
answer is not worthy of a philosopher.

quem, the place from which one sets out and the place that one goes to.
Now these two extremities are separated by spaces that contain an
infinity of parts, since matter is divisible to infinity. It is therefore
impossible for the moving object to go from one extremity to the
other. The intermediate space is composed of an infinity of parts that
must be traversed successively one after the other, without our ever
being able to touch that part which comes first at the same time we
touch the one that is beyond it; so that, in order to traverse a foot of
matter, I mean to arrive from the beginning of the first inch to the end
of the twelfth inch, an infinite time is required; for, since the spaces
that must be traversed successively between these two limits are infinite in number, it is clear that they can only be traversed in an infinity of moments unless it be admitted that an object is in several places
at the same time, which is false and impossible. Aristotle makes a very
poor answer to this. He says that a foot of matter, being only potentially infinite, may very well be traversed in a finite time. Let us give
his answer with the clarity that the Commentaries of Coimbra have
given it. "Aristotle declares that he had answered that objection before, having taught in this book that a body infinite in division, that

---

* [Remark K appears on p. 385.]

is, a body not actually but potentially infinite, may be traversed in a finite time. For as time is formed of a continuity of parts that are infinite in like manner, time and magnitude or body will reciprocally answer one another by the same law of infinity and the like division of parts. Nor is it repugnant to the nature of such an infinite body to be traversed in this manner."[51] You see two things in this: (1) that each part of time is divisible to infinity, which has been totally refuted above; (2) that the continuum is only potentially infinite. This means that the infinity of a foot of matter consists in the fact that it could be divided without end, and incessantly, into smaller and smaller parts, but not in that it can actually be divided infinitely. It is ridiculous to make use of this theory; for if matter is divisible to infinity, it actually contains an infinite number of parts. It is then not a potential infinite; it is an infinite that really and actually exists. The continuity of parts does not prevent their actual distinction. Consequently their actual infinity does not at all depend on division. It subsists equally in continuous quantity and in that which is called "discrete." But even if one should grant this potential infinity, which would become an actual infinite by the actual division of its parts, one would not lose any ground; for motion has the same property as division. It touches one part of space without touching the other and touches them all one after the other; now is this not to distinguish them actually? Is this not the same as a geometer would do on a table by drawing lines that would designate all the half inches? He does not break the table into half inches; but he nevertheless makes such a division in it that indicates the actual distinction of the parts. And I do not believe that Aristotle would have denied that if an infinite number of lines were to be drawn on an inch of matter, a division would there be introduced that would make that an actual infinite, which according to him was only a potential infinite. Now what would be done with respect to the eye by drawing these lines on an inch of matter, motion surely does with respect to the understanding.[52] We conceive that a moving object, as it touches the parts of space successively, marks them out and determines them, just as chalk marks could do. But further, when we say that the division of an infinite entity has been achieved, have we not an actual infinity? Do not Aristotle and his followers say that

---

[51] Coimbra, *Commentaries on Aristotle's Physics*, Bk. VI, chap. 9.

[52] Confirm this by what the geometers say about the production of lines and surfaces. See Clavius, *Euclid*, Bk. I, nos. 2 and 5.

an hour contains an infinity of parts? Then when it is past, it must be said that an infinity of parts have actually existed one after the other. Is this a potential infinite? Is it not an actual infinite? Let us then say that his distinction is null and void and that Zeno's objection retains all its strength. An hour, a year, a century, and so on, are a finite time; a foot of matter is an infinite space. There is then no moving object that could ever get from the beginning of a foot to the end. We shall see in the following remark if this objection could be eluded by supposing that the parts of a foot of matter are not infinite. Let us be satisfied here with observing that the subterfuge of an infinity of parts of time is of no use; for if there were an infinite number of parts in an hour, it could never begin nor end. All its parts must exist separately; two never exist together and cannot be together. They therefore must be comprised between a first and and last unity, which is incompatible with an infinite number.

The third objection was the famous argument called "Achilles." Zeno of Elea was the inventor of it according to Diogenes Laertius, who nevertheless says that Phavorinus attributes it to Parmenides and to several others. This objection has the same basis as the second one, but it is more suitable for declamations. Its aim was to show that a faster moving body pursuing a slower one could never reach it. . . . Let us suppose a tortoise twenty paces ahead of Achilles, and let us limit the speed of this hero to twenty times that of the tortoise. While he goes twenty paces, the tortoise will go one. It will then still be ahead of him. While Achilles goes the twenty-first pace, the tortoise will move a twentieth part of the twenty-second pace; and while he achieves this twentieth part, it will traverse the twentieth part of the twentieth part, and so on. Aristotle refers us to what he answered to the second objection. We can refer him to our reply. See also what will be said in the following remark with regard to the difficulty of explaining in what the speed of motion consists.

Let us go on to the fourth objection, whose aim is to show the contradictions of motion. Imagine a table of four ells, and take two bodies of four ells also, one of wood, the other of stone.[56] Let the table be immovable and let it support the piece of wood with the length of two ells to the west. Let the piece of stone be to the east, and let it only

---

[56] Any other material would do as well. Wood and stone are used here only as examples.

touch the edge of the table. Let it move on this table toward the west, and let it travel two ells in a half hour. It will then become contiguous to the piece of wood. Let us suppose that they only meet at their edges, and in such a way that the motion of the one toward the west does not hinder the motion of the other toward the east. At the moment that they become contiguous, let the piece of wood begin to move eastward, while the other [i.e., the stone] continues to move westward. Let them move at equal speeds. In half an hour the piece of stone will have traversed the entire table. It will then have traversed a space of four ells in an hour, that is the entire surface of the table. Now the piece of wood in half an hour has gone through a similar space of four ells, since it has touched the edges of the entire extension of the piece of stone. It is therefore the case that two bodies, which move with equal speed, traverse the same distance, one in half an hour, the other in an hour. Therefore, an hour and a half an hour are equal times, which is contradictory. Aristotle says that this is a sophism, since one of these bodies is considered in relation to a space that is at rest, that is, the table, and the other is considered in relation to space that is moving, that is, the piece of stone. I admit that he is right to observe this difference, but this does not remove the difficulty. For there still remains the problem of explaining one item that seems incomprehensible: It is that in the same time that a piece of wood traverses four ells on its southern side, it only traverses two by its lower side. Here is a less puzzling example. Take two folio volumes of equal length, each two feet long. Place them on a table one in front of the other. Move them at the same time one over the other, the one toward the east, the other toward the west, until the eastern edge of one and the western edge of the other touch. You will find that the edges by which they used to touch are four feet distant from one another, and yet each of these books has only traversed a space of two feet. You can fortify this objection by supposing whatever body you please in motion in the midst of several others that are moving in different directions, and with various speeds. You will find that this same body will have traversed in the same time various sorts of spaces, double, triple, and so on, one more than the other. If you think carefully about this, you will find that it can only be explained by arithmetical calculations, which are only ideas in our minds; but in the bodies themselves, it does not seem practicable,[57] for these three essential properties of motion must be remembered: (1) A moving body cannot touch the same part of space twice successively; (2) it can never touch two parts of space at the same time; (3) it can never touch the third before the second, nor the fourth before the third, and so on. Whoever can physically reconcile these three things, with the distance of four feet existing between two bodies that have only traversed two feet of space,[58] will not be an incompetent man. Observe carefully that these three properties apply as necessarily to a body that moves through spaces, whose motion is contrary to it, as to a body that might move through spaces where nothing opposed it.

⫷

G. *(The same as those that will be seen below.)* It seems to me that those who would like to revive Zeno's opinion ought to argue at the outset in the following manner:

Objections Against the Existence of Extension

I. There is no extension; therefore there is no motion. The inference is valid; for what has no extension occupies no space; and what occupies no space cannot go from one place to another, nor consequently move. This is not open to question. The only difficulty then is to prove that there is no extension. Here is what Zeno could have put forth. Extension cannot be made up of either mathematical points, atoms, or particles that are divisible to infinity; therefore its existence is impossible. The consequence seems certain since we can conceive of only these three types of composition in extension. It is therefore only a question of proving the antecedent. It will take me only a few words to establish the case with regard to mathematical points; for persons of the slightest depth can comprehend with complete certainty, if they give the matter a little attention, that several nonentities of extension

---

[57] The same difficulties may be raised from the small wheels of a coach going over the same space of ground as the large ones in the same number of turns around their center. The same may be said of two wheels attached to the same axle, one very small, the other very large.

[58] For example, the folio volumes that have been mentioned.

joined together will never make up an extension.[59] Consult the first course of Scholastic philosophy that you come across; and you will find there the most convincing arguments in the world, supported by many geometrical demonstrations, against the existence of these points.[60] Let us speak no more about this, and let us look upon it as impossible or at least inconceivable that the continuum is composed of these points. It is not any less impossible or inconceivable that it be composed of Epicurean atoms, that is to say of extended and indivisible corpuscles; for every extension, no matter how small it may be, has a right and a left side, an upper and a lower side. Therefore it is a collection of distinct bodies. I can deny concerning the right side what I affirm about the left side. These two sides are not in the same place. A body cannot be in two places both at the same time, and consequently every extension that occupies several parts of space contains several bodies. I know, besides, and the atomists do not deny it, that because two atoms are two beings, they are separable from one another. From which I conclude with the utmost certainty that since the right side of an atom is not the same entity as the left side, it is separable from the left. The indivisibility of an atom is thus illusory. If there is any extension then, it must be the case that its parts are divisible to infinity. But, on the other hand, if they cannot be divisible to infinity, we would have to conclude that the existence of extension is impossible, or at the very least, incomprehensible.

Infinite divisibility is the hypothesis that Aristotle embraced, and it is the one of almost all philosophy professors in all universities for several centuries. It is not that they understand it or can answer objections made to it; but that having understood clearly the impossibility of points, be they mathematical or physical, they found this the only course to take. Besides, this hypothesis furnishes great comfort; for when its distinctions have been used up, without having been able to make this theory comprehensible, one can take refuge in the nature itself of the subject and claim that, since our mind is limited, no one

---

[59] See [Nicole and Arnauld,] *L'Art de penser (Port-Royal Logic)*, Pt. IV, chap. 1; and remark D of the following article, "Zeno the Epicurean" [p. 389].

[60] See, among other works, that of Libertus Fromondus, professor at Louvain, entitled *Labyrinthus seu de compositione continui*. This work is much stronger than the answer that Jacques Chevreuil (Capreolus), professor of philosophy at Paris, made in 1636 to two questions of Cardinal Richelieu, in *De demonstratione magnitudinis in puncto, etc.*

ought to find it odd that we cannot resolve what concerns infinity, and that it is the essence of such a continuum that it be surrounded by difficulties that are insurmountable to human beings. Observe that those who espouse the atomic hypothesis do not do so because they understand that an extended body can be simple, but because they conclude that the two other hypotheses are impossible. Let us say the same about those who admit mathematical points. In general, all those who argue concerning the continuum only come to a decision about choosing a hypothesis on the basis of this principle: "If there are only three ways of explaining something, the truth of the third necessarily follows from the falsity of the other two." They do not, therefore, believe that they can be mistaken in choosing the third when they have understood clearly that the other two are impossible. They are not disturbed at all by the insurmountable difficulties of the third. They console themselves about this either because retorts can be made to these difficulties, or because they are convinced that their hypothesis is true after all, since the other two are not. The subtle Arriaga, having proposed an insoluble objection to his own theory, insisted that he would not give up his view because of this; for, he said, the other sects do not resolve it any better. "I see that these objections are still raised to the above-mentioned argument; but I have not met with anyone who could solve them, nor do I presume to do so. Moreover, since they apply to all opinions concerning the structure of the continuum, there is no reason why any man should abandon his own opinion because of these objections.[61] . . . Notwithstanding that there are some other great difficulties in Aristotle's opinion, ones we cannot solve, yet we are not therefore obliged to give it up; for this subject is involved in so many difficulties that everywhere we are confronted with some inexplicable things. I would rather openly admit that I do not know how to solve an objection than offer such a one as possibly nobody could understand."[62]

A Zenoist could say to those who choose one of these three hypotheses, "You do not reason well, you make use of this disjunctive syllogism:

"The continuum is made up of either mathematical points, or physical points, or parts that can be divided ad infinitum:

---

[61] Arriaga, *Disput. XVI Phys.*, Sec. XI, no. 241.
[62] *Ibid.*, Sec. XII, no. 256.

"But it is not made up of . . . , or of. . . .[63]

"Therefore it is made up of. . . .

"The defect in your argument is not in its form but in its matter. You ought to give up your disjunctive syllogism and employ this hypothetical one:

"If extension existed, it would be made up of either mathematical points, or physical points, or parts that are divisible ad infinitum:

"But it is not made up of either mathematical points, or physical points, or parts that are divisible ad infinitum.

"Therefore, it does not exist."

There is no defect in the form of this syllogism. The sophism of insufficient enumeration of parts does not occur in the major premise. The conclusion is then necessary, provided that the minor is true. But we need only weigh the arguments with which these three sects confound one another and compare them with the answers. We need only do this, I say, to perceive the obvious truth of the minor. Each of these three sects, when they only attack, triumphs, ruins, and destroys; but in its turn, it is destroyed and sunk when it is on the defensive. To realize their weakness, it is sufficient to recall that the strongest, that which quibbles best, is the hypothesis of infinite divisibility. The Schoolmen have armed it from head to toe with all the distinctions that their great leisure was able to allow them to invent. But this served only to furnish their disciples with a jargon to use in public disputation, so that their relatives would not have the mortification of seeing them silent. A father or a brother goes home much happier when the student distinguishes between the "categorematical" infinite and the "syncategorematical" infinite, between the "communicating" and the "noncommunicating" parts, "proportional" and "aliquot," than if he had made no response. It was then necessary that the professors invent some jargon. But all the trouble they have gone to will never be capable of obscuring this notion that it is as clear and evident as the sun: "An infinite number of parts of extension, each of which is extended and distinct from all the others, both with regard to its being and to the place that it occupies, cannot be contained in a space one hundred million times smaller than the hundred thousandth part of a grain of barley."

---

63 To abridge this, the rejection and the admission are not expressed; for according to the laws of logic, we may proceed here from the rejection of any two parts, to the admission of the third.

Infinite divisibility would prevent all contiguity. Here is another difficulty. An extended substance that might exist should necessarily allow for the immediate contact of its parts. According to the hypothesis of the vacuum, there would be several bodies separated from all the others; but there would have to be several others that touch immediately. Aristotle, who does not accept this hypothesis, is forced to admit that there is no part of extension that does not immediately touch several others with all its exterior. But this is incompatible with infinite divisibility: for, if there is no body that does not contain an infinity of parts, it is evident that each particular part of space is separated from all the others by an infinity of parts, and that the immediate contact of two parts is impossible. Now when a thing cannot have all that its existence necessarily requires, it is certain that its existence is impossible. Since, then, the existence of extension necessarily requires the immediate contact of its parts, and since this immediate contact is impossible in an extension that is divisible to infinity, it is evident that the existence of this extension is impossible, and that this extension thus exists only in the mind. We must acknowledge with respect to bodies what mathematicians acknowledge with respect to lines and surfaces, about which they demonstrate so many lovely things. They frankly admit[64] that a length and breadth, without depth, is something that cannot exist outside our minds.* Let us say the same of the three dimensions. They can only exist in our minds. They can only exist *ideally.* The human mind is a certain terrain where a hundred thousand objects of different color, different shape, and different location are brought together; for we can see at once from a hilltop a vast plain dotted with houses, trees, flocks, and the like. But it is far from being the case that all these things are of such a nature as to be able to be disposed in this plain. Not even two of them could find room there. Each requires an infinite space, since it contains an infinity of extended bodies. It would be necessary to leave infinite intervals around each since between each part and every other there is an infinity of bodies. Let it not be said that God can do anything. For if the most devout theologians dare to say that in a straight line twelve inches long, God cannot make it so that the first and third

---

[64] Compare this with what is said in the following article, "Zeno the Epicurean," remark D [p. 389].

* [This section is the basis for some of Hume's discussion in his *Treatise of Human Nature*, Bk. I, Pt. II, on mathematics, especially secs. 1–4.]

inches be immediately contiguous, I may be allowed to say that he cannot make it so that two parts of extension touch immediately when an infinity of other parts separate them from one another. Let us then say that the contact of the parts of matter is only ideal; it is in our minds that the extremities of several bodies can be brought together.

Infinite divisibility would lead to the penetration of dimensions. Let us now present a completely contrary objection. The penetration of dimensions is impossible, and yet it would be inevitable if extension existed. It is therefore not true that extension could exist. Place a cannon ball on a table, a ball, I say, coated with some wet paint. Make the ball roll on this table, and you will see that it will draw a line by its motion. You will then have two strong proofs of the immediate contact of this ball and the table. The weight of the ball will teach you that it immediately touches the table; for if it did not touch it in this way, it would remain suspended in the air; and your eyes will convince you of the contact by the line made by the ball. Now I maintain that this contact is a penetration of dimensions, properly called. The part of the ball that touches the table is a determinate body, and really distinct from the other parts of the ball that do not touch the table. I say the same about the part of the table that is touched by the ball. These two parts that touch each other are each divisible to infinity in length, breadth, and depth. Therefore they mutually touch one another according to their depth, and consequently they penetrate one another. This is daily objected to by the Peripatetics in public disputations. They defend themselves by a jargon of distinctions that are only‚suitable for preventing the disappointment the student's relatives might have had if they had seen him reduced to silence. But, as to other uses of these distinctions, they have only served to show that the objection is unanswerable. Here then we have a very peculiar circumstance. If extension existed, it would not be possible for its parts to touch one another, and it would be impossible for them not to penetrate one another. Are not these very evident contradictions enclosed in the existence of extension?

The modes of suspending judgment employed against the existence of extension. Add to this that all the means of suspending judgment that overthrow the reality of corporeal qualities also overthrow the reality of extension. Since the same bodies are sweet to some men and bitter to others, one is right in inferring that they are neither sweet nor bitter in themselves and absolutely speaking. The "new" philoso-

phers, although they are not skeptics, have so well understood the
bases of suspension of judgment with regard to sounds, smells, heat,
cold, hardness, softness, heaviness and lightness, tastes, colors, and the
like, that they teach that all these qualities are perceptions of our soul
and that they do not exist at all in the objects of our senses. Why should
we not say the same thing about extension? If an entity that has no
color appears to us, however, with a determinate color with respect to
its species, shape, and location, why could not an entity that had no
extension be visible to us under an appearance of a determinate,
shaped, and located extension of a certain type? And notice carefully
that the same body appears to us to be small or large, round or square,
according to the place from which it is viewed; and let us have no
doubts that a body that seems very small to us appears very large to
a fly. It is not then by their own real or absolute extension that bodies
present themselves to our minds. We can therefore conclude that they
are not extended in themselves. Would you dare to reason in this way
today, "Since certain bodies appear sweet to one man, sour to another, bitter to a third, and so on, I ought to affirm that in general they
are savory, though I do not know what savor belongs to them absolutely and in themselves?" All the "new" philosophers would hoot at
you. Why then would you dare to say, "Since certain bodies appear
large to one animal, medium to another, and very small to a third,
I ought to affirm that in general they are extended, though I do not
know their absolute extension?" Let us look at the admission of a
celebrated dogmatist.[66] "One can indeed know by the senses that a
given body is larger than another body; but one cannot know with
certainty what is the true and natural size of each body; and to understand this, we have only to consider that if everybody had never
looked at external objects but through eyeglasses that enlarged them,
it is certain that they would only have conceived of bodies, and all the
measures of bodies, in terms of the size by which they would have been
represented to us by these glasses. Now our eyes themselves are glasses;
and we do not know precisely if they diminish or enlarge the objects
we see, and whether the artificial glasses, which we think diminish or

---

[66] Nicole [and Arnauld], *L'Art de penser (Port-Royal Logic)*, Pt. IV, chap.
1. See also Rohault, *Traité de physique*, Pt. I, chap. 27, no. 6, where he
speaks of the different appearance of the same colors. [Bayle usually attributes the *Port-Royal Logic* to Nicole rather than to Nicole and Arnauld.
Rohault was a leading Cartesian of the later seventeenth century.]

augment them, do not, on the contrary, exhibit them in their true size. Therefore, one does not know with certainty the absolute and natural size of any body. Also one does not know if we see objects of the same size as other men do; for even though two persons, on measuring them, agree, for example, that a certain body is only five feet long; nevertheless, what one of them thinks of as a foot is not perhaps the same as the other; for each thinks of what his own eyes inform him about. Now the eyes of the one, perhaps, do not inform him of the same thing that the eyes of others make known to them because of the way his glasses are constructed." Father Malebranche[67] and Father Lami, the Benedictine, will supply you with excellent detail on this, which is capable of making my objection very strong.

Use of geometrical demonstrations against the existence of extension. My last difficulty will be based on the geometrical demonstrations that are displayed so subtly in order to prove that matter is infinitely divisible. I maintain that they serve no other use but to show that extension exists only in our understanding. In the first place, I notice that some of these demonstrations are employed against those who say that matter is composed of mathematical points. It is objected to them that the sides of a square would be equal to the diagonal, and that among concentric circles the smallest would be equal to the largest. This consequence is proven by showing that the perpendicular lines that can be drawn from one opposite side of a square to the other will cross the entire diagonal, and that all the straight lines that can be drawn from the circumference of the large circle to the center will find a place on the circumference of the smallest circle. These objections are not more forceful against a continuum composed of points than against a continuum divisible to infinity; for if the parts of extension are not greater in number in the diagonal line than in the sides, nor in the circumference of the smallest concentric circle than in the circumference of the largest, it is clear that the sides of the square are equal to the diagonal, and that smallest concentric circle is equal to the largest. Now all the perpendicular lines that may be drawn from one of the sides of a square to the opposite one, and from the circumference of the largest circle to the center, are equal to each

---

[67] Malebranche, *Recherche de la vérité*, Bk. I, chaps. 6ff. [This discussion and the one in remark H of this article influenced both Hume and Berkeley. On Berkeley, see R. H. Popkin, "Berkeley and Pyrrhonism," *Review of Metaphysics*, V (1951–1952), 223–246.]

other. They must then be considered as aliquot parts, I mean, as parts of a certain magnitude and of the same type. Now it is certain that two extensions, in which the aliquot parts of the same size—as inch, foot, pace—are equal in number, do not exceed one another. It is therefore certain that the sides of the square would be as long as the diagonal, if the diagonal could not be intersected by more perpendicular lines than the sides could be. Let us say the same about the two concentric circles. In the second place, I maintain it is certainly true that if circles existed, it would be possible to draw as many straight lines from the circumference to the center as there are parts in the circumference; it follows that the existence of a circle is impossible. Everyone will grant me that every being that can exist only by containing properties that cannot exist is impossible. Now a round extension can only exist by having a center in which as many straight lines terminate as there are parts in the circumference, and it is certain that such a center cannot exist. One should then say that the existence of this round extension is impossible. I will prove evidently that such a center cannot exist. Let us suppose a round extension whose circumference is four feet long. It will contain 48 inches, each of which contain 12 lines (at $\frac{1}{12}$-inch intervals). It will then contain 576 lines: and this is the number of straight lines that may be drawn from the circumference to the center. [Apparently, Bayle means lines drawn with an actual physical ruler.] Let us draw a circle very close to the center. It could be so small that it could contain only 50 lines (at $\frac{1}{12}$-inch intervals). It could not then have room to allow the 576 straight lines to pass through. It will then be impossible for the 576 lines that have begun to be drawn from the circumference of this round extension to reach the center; and yet if this extension existed, it would be necessary that these 576 lines could reach the center. What remains then to say if not that this extension cannot exist, and that thus all the properties of circles, squares, and so on, are based upon lines without breadth, which can exist only *ideally*? Observe that our reason and our eyes are equally deceived in this matter. Our reason clearly conceives: (1) that the concentric circle closer to the center is smaller than the circle that surrounds it; (2) that the diagonal of a square is larger than the side. Our eyes see this without a compass and even more surely with a compass; and nevertheless mathematicians teach us that as many lines can be drawn from the circumference to the center as there are points on the circumference and that from the side of a square as many perpendicular lines can be drawn to the other side as there are points on this side. And besides, our eyes show us that there is not one point on the circumference of the small concentric circle that is not a part of a straight line drawn from the circumference of the big circle and that the diagonal of the square has no point that is not a part of a perpendicular line drawn from one of the sides to the opposite one. How can it be, then, that this diagonal is larger than the sides?

There is what concerns the first proof that I suppose Zeno could have used to refute the existence of motion. It is based on the impossibility of the existence of extension. Another reason for this same impossibility will be seen below.[69] I am willing to believe that the last of the above arguments he might have used—those based on geometrical demonstrations—is easy to refute by the same means. But I am strongly convinced that the arguments borrowed from mathematics[70] to prove infinite divisibility prove too much; for, either they prove nothing, or they prove the infinity of the aliquot parts.

II. Zeno's second objection might have been the following: I will grant for the sake of argument that there is extension outside our minds. I will not give up maintaining that it is immovable. Motion is not essential to it. It is not contained in the idea of it, and several bodies are sometimes at rest. It is therefore an accident. But is it distinct from matter? If it be distinct, from what will it be produced? From nothing, no doubt; and when it ceases to exist, it will be reduced to nothing. But do you not know that nothing comes from nothing, and nothing returns to nothing?[72] Further, must it not be the case that motion is diffused on and in the moving object? Motion will then be as extended as the object, and of the same shape. There will then be two equal extensions in the same space, and, consequently, a penetration of dimensions. But when three or four causes move a body, will it not be necessary that each produce its motion? Will it not be necessary that these three or four motions be penetrated all together, both with the body and among one another? How then can each produce its effect? A ship moved by the winds, the currents, and the rowers de-

---

[69] In remark I [p. 377].

[70] There are some very fine ones in *L'Art de penser (Port-Royal Logic)*, Pt. IV, chap. 1. See also Rohault, *Traité de physique*, Pt. I, chap. 9.

[72] Zeno could boldly say this, since all the ancient philosophers accepted this maxim of Lucretius, "A thing . . . cannot be created from nothing, nor can generated things be called back to nothingness" (Lucretius, I. 265–266).

scribes a line that partakes of these three actions, either more or less, depending upon their relative strengths. Would you dare to say that insensible entities, both penetrated among themselves and with the entire ship, would respect each other this much, and not quarrel at all? If you say that motion is a mode that is not distinct from matter, then you would have to say that what produced it is the creator of matter; for without producing matter, it is not possible to produce a being that is the same thing as matter. Now would it not be absurd to say that the wind that moves a ship produces a ship? It does not seem that these objections could be answered except by assuming, as the Cartesians do, that God is the sole and immediate cause of motion.

III. Here is another objection. We cannot say what motion is; for if you say that it is going from one place to another, you will be explaining something that is obscure by something more obscure. I would first ask you what is understood by the word "place"? Do you mean a space distinct from bodies? But in this case you would fall into an abyss from which you will never be able to get out.[74] Do you mean the location of a body among those that surround it? But in this case you would define motion in such a way that it would on thousands and thousands of occasions apply to bodies at rest. It is certain that up to now the definition of motion has not been found. Aristotle's definition is absurd; Descartes' is pitiful. Rohault, after having sweated greatly to find one that would rectify Descartes', has produced a description that could apply to some bodies that we very distinctly conceive not to move.[75] And because of this Régis felt himself obliged to reject it.[76] But the one he has given is not capable of distinguishing motion from rest.[77] God, the only mover according to the Cartesians, has to do the same thing with regard to a house as with regard to the air that moves away from it during a high wind. He has to create this air at every moment, with new local relations in terms of that house. He also has to create this house at every moment, with new local relations in terms of that air. And certainly, according to these gentlemen's principles,

---

[74] See remark I [p. 377].

[75] "Motion," he says in *Traité de physique,* Pt. I, chap. 10, no. 3, "consists in the successive application of all the external parts of a body to the different parts of those immediately near it."

[76] See his *Physique,* Bk. I, Pt. I, chap. 1.

[77] "Motion," he says in *Physique,* Bk. I, Pt. I, chap. 1, "is the successive active application of all the external parts of a body to different parts of the bodies that immediately touch it."

no body is at rest if an inch of matter is in motion. Then all they can say ends in explaining apparent motion, that is to say, in explaining the circumstances that make us judge that a body moves and another does not. This effort is useless. Everyone is capable of judging appearances. The problem is to explain the nature of the things that exist outside us; and since in this respect motion is inexplicable, it might as well be said that it does not exist outside our minds.

IV. I am now going to propose an objection that is much stronger than the preceding one. If motion can never begin, it does not exist. Now it can never begin, therefore. . . . This is how I prove the minor premise. A body can never be in two places at the same time. Now it can never begin to move without being in an infinite number of places at the same time; for no matter how little it advanced, it would touch a part that is infinitely divisible and consequently corresponds to some infinite parts of space; therefore. . . . Besides this, it is certain that an infinite number of parts does not contain any one that would be the first; and yet, a moving object can never touch the second before the first; for motion is essentially a successive entity of which two parts can never exist simultaneously. That is why motion can never begin if the continuum is infinitely divisible, as it doubtless is, if it happens to exist. The same argument demonstrates that a moving object, rolling on an inclined table, can never fall off the table, for before falling it has to touch necessarily the last part of that table. And how could it touch it, since all the parts that you might consider to be the last contain an infinite number of parts, and that infinite number has no part that might be the last? This objection forced some School philosophers to suppose that nature has mixed some mathematical points in with the infinitely divisible parts to serve as connections between them and to make up the extremities of bodies.* They believed by this they could also answer the objection about the penetrative contact of two surfaces, but this subterfuge is so absurd that it does not deserve to be refuted.

V. I shall hardly insist on the impossibility of circular motion although this could furnish me with a powerful objection. I will say in a couple of words that if there were a circular motion, there would be a whole diameter[78] at rest, while the remainder of the entire sphere

---

* [Hume uses this line in his *Treatise* (Selby-Bigge edn.; Oxford, 1941), Bk. I, pt. II, sec. 4, p. 44.]

[78] Namely, the axis.

would move rapidly. Conceive this, if you can, in a continuum. The Chevalier de Meré did not neglect this objection in his letter to Pascal.[79]

VI. To conclude, I say that if there were motion, it would be equal in all bodies. There would be no Achilleses and tortoises. A greyhound would never overtake a hare. Zeno made this objection, but it seems that he based it only on the infinite divisibility of the continuum; and perhaps, I may be told, he would have set aside this objection if he had had to deal with adversaries who admitted either mathematical points or atoms. I reply that this objection strikes equally at all three theories. Suppose a road made up of indivisible particles. Set the tortoise one hundred points ahead of Achilles. He will never catch up if the tortoise moves forward. Achilles will advance only one point each moment since if he advanced two, he would be in two places at the same time. The tortoise will advance one point each moment. This is the least that he can accomplish as there is nothing less than a point.[81] The true reason for the velocity of motion is inexplicable. The happiest view on this is to say that no motion is continuous and that every body that appears to us to be moving stops by intervals. A body that moves ten times faster than another stops ten times to the other's hundred. But no matter how well conceived this subterfuge appears, it is worthless. It is refuted by several solid arguments in all the philosophy courses.[82] I will content myself with that which is drawn from the motion of a wheel. You could make a wheel with a diameter so large that the parts of the spokes that are farthest from the center would move a hundred times faster than those set in the hub. However, the spokes would always remain straight; a manifest proof that the lower part would not be at rest while the upper part is

---

79 I will speak about this letter in remark D [p. 389] of the following article, "Zeno the Epicurean."

81 As it is plain that Epicurean atoms, since they have three dimensions, are divisible ad infinitum; and that no one would dare deny this with regard to the space they occupy; I therefore did not apply this objection to them.

82 See Arriaga, *Disp. 16 Physic.*, sec. 11. He accepts the hypothesis of "morules," or interruptions of motions. He answers the objections poorly and admits that that of the wheel is insoluble. Oviedo, in his *Cours de Philosophie*, makes great efforts to resolve it and believes he can give a new solution to it.

moving. The infinite divisibility of the parts of time, rejected above[83] as obviously false and contradictory, would be of no use against this sixth argument. You will find some other rather subtle objections in Sextus Empiricus.[84]

What use ought to be made of the preceding dispute. We can suppose that it was thus that our Zeno of Elea combatted motion. I would not wish to say that his arguments convinced him that nothing moves. He could have had another conviction even though he believed that no one refuted his arguments or eluded their force. If I were to judge about him by myself, I would affirm that he believed, just as others do, in the motion of extension; for even though I myself feel completely incapable of resolving all the difficulties that have just been presented, and it seems to me that the philosophical answers that can be made to them are far from solid, nevertheless I do not fail to follow the common opinion. I am even convinced that the exposition of these arguments can be of great service to religion, and I say here about the difficulties concerning motion that which Nicole [and Arnauld] have said about those concerning infinite divisibility. "The value that can be gained from these speculations is not simply that of acquiring this sort of knowledge, which is pretty sterile in itself; but it is in learning to know the limits of our mind and in making it admit, in spite of itself, that there are things that exist though it is not capable of understanding them. For this reason it is good that we wear it out with these subtleties in order to check its presumption and to keep it from ever being foolhardy enough to oppose its feeble light to the truths that the Church proposes to it on the pretext that it cannot understand them. For since all the strength of the mind of man is forced to succumb to the smallest atom of matter and admit that it sees clearly that the atom is infinitely divisible without being able to understand how this can be the case; is it not manifestly sinning against reason to refuse to believe in the marvelous effects of the almighty power of God, which is incomprehensible in itself, because our mind cannot understand them.[85]

---

[83] In remark F of this article, first objection [p. 353].

[84] Sextus Empiricus, *Pyrrhoniarum hypotoposeon* III. 8.

[85] Nicole [and Arnauld], *L'Art de penser (Port-Royal Logic)*, Pt. IV, chap. 1. Compare this with what has been said in the article "Pyrrho," remark C [p. 204].

«<

H. (*The proofs that reason furnishes us of the existence of matter are not evident enough to furnish a good demonstration on this point.*) There are two philosophical axioms that teach us: the one, that nature does nothing in vain; and the other, that it is useless to do by several methods what may be done by fewer means with the same ease. By these two axioms the Cartesians I am speaking of can maintain that no bodies exist; for whether they exist or not, God is equally able to communicate to us all the thoughts that we have. It is no proof at all that there are bodies to say that our senses assure us of this with the utmost evidence. They deceive us with regard to all of the corporeal qualities, the magnitude, size, and motion of bodies not excepted;[88] and when we believe them about these latter qualities, we are also convinced that there exist outside our souls a great many colors, tastes, and other entities that we call hardness, fluidity, cold, heat, and the like. However it is not true that anything like these exists outside our minds. Why then should we trust our senses with regard to extension? It can very easily be reduced to appearance, just like colors. Father Malebranche, after having set forth all the reasons for doubting that there are bodies in the world, concludes in this way: "In order to be completely certain of the external existence of bodies, it is therefore absolutely necessary to know God who gives us the sensation of them, and to be aware that since he is infinitely perfect, he cannot deceive us. For if the Intelligence that gives us the ideas of all things wished, as it were, to divert himself by making us know bodies as actually existing, even though there actually be none, it is plain that this would not be difficult for him to do."[89] He adds that Descartes has not found any other unshakable foundation than the argument that God would deceive us if there were no bodies. But he claims that this argument cannot pass for a demonstrative one. "To be fully convinced there are bodies," he says,[90] "it is necessary that it be demonstrated to us not only that there is a God, and that God is no deceiver, but also that God has assured us that he has actually created bodies, which I do not find proven in the works of

---

[88] See Malebranche. Also see above, footnotes 66 and 67 [pp. 365–366].
[89] Malebranche, *Eclaircissemens sur le Iᵉ livre de la recherche de la vérité.*
[90] *Ibid.*

Descartes. God speaks to the mind and obliges it to believe in only two ways, by self-evidence and by faith. I agree that faith obliges us to believe that there are bodies; but with regard to self-evidence, it is certain that it is not complete, and that we are not invincibly led to believe in the existence of anything other than God and our mind." Notice that when he affirms that God does not prompt us invincibly by self-evidence to conclude that there are bodies, he wants to teach us that the error we might hold in this respect should not be imputed to God. This is rejecting Descartes' proof, that is to say, that God would in no way be a deceiver even though no bodies might exist in reality.

A Sicilian named Michaelangelo Fardella published a logic book in Venice in 1696, in which he maintains the same doctrines as Father Malebranche. Here is a summary of that book.[91] "He tries especially to prove that it is quite possible that objects do not conform to the ideas we have of them. He says that he conceives very clearly that the author of nature could dispose our senses in such a way that they represent to us objects as existing that do not exist at all. However,[92] when he defined sensation in the second part, page 96, he said that sensations arise in the mind on the occasion of the impression that external bodies make on the extremity of the nerves. When it is objected to him that if the evidence of the senses is not infallible, Jesus Christ was making fun of the disciples when, in order to convince them that he had a real body, he said to them, 'Handle me, and see, for a spirit hath not flesh and bones'; he replies that the methods of arguing that the Scripture usually employs are drawn from a logic adapted to the capabilities of the common man rather than a true logic; from which he concludes that Jesus Christ, in order to convince the apostles that he was not a phantom but a real man, made use of the logic best adapted to the capacity of ordinary people, by which

---

[91] *Journal des Savans,* July 30, 1696.

[92] The author of the *Journal* is mistaken here. He erroneously claims that Fardella is guilty of contradicting himself; but it is not a contradiction to affirm that there really are bodies, and that it is possible that there might be none at all, and that nonetheless we might have the same sensations as we do have. The author of the *Journal* could have made a more firmly grounded objection, namely, that, supposing that Jesus Christ accommodated himself to ordinary logic, one could not prove at all by Scripture that there are bodies. How then will one be assured by faith that there are bodies?

people are used to being convinced that things exist. He adds that God is not obliged to teach us infallibly that there are bodies that exist; and if we have more than a moral certainty of this, it is only by faith that we have obtained it." Father Malebranche's arguments are doubtless very strong, but I will venture to say that they are far less so than those presented above.[93] I should be glad to know how Arnauld would have refuted this. No one was more capable than he of finding an answer. In examining Father Malebranche's doctrine, he showed that he understood the art of attacking through the foundations. He struck at the basis of his adversary's views; for he showed that if there are no bodies, we are "forced to admit in God things that are completely contrary to the divine nature, such as being a deceiver, or being subject to other imperfections that the natural light shows us clearly cannot be in God."[94] He makes use of eight arguments. Father Malebranche calls them "good proofs, but very bad demonstrations."[95] "I believe," he continues, "that there are bodies; but I believe it as well proven, and badly demonstrated. I even believe it as demonstrated, but by presupposing faith." He sets forth an objection that he bases on the "vicious and impious thoughts" of the soul,[96] and then he gives an answer to it. He answers that it is certain that the body does not act immediately on the mind, and that thus it is God alone who places in the mind all its good and bad thoughts; just as it is he who moves the arm of an assassin and an impious person, as well as the arm of the person who gives alms; and that the only thing that God does not do is the sin or grant the consent of the will. It is indeed true that God only places useless and bad thoughts in men's minds in consequence of the laws of the union of soul and body and of the sin that changed that union into dependence. But how will Arnauld 'demonstrate' (and I mean 'demonstrate') that he did not commit some sin ten or twenty thousand years ago, and that as a punishment for that sin, he has those troublesome thoughts by which God punishes him and will make him deserve his reward by combating what he calls the impulses of concupiscence? Will Arnauld demonstrate that God—who could permit sin and all its consequences, which oblige him, as a result of the natural laws he has established, to place so many

---

93 In remark G, where objection I is set forth [p. 359].
94 Arnauld, *Traité des vraies et des fausses idées.*
95 Malebranche, *Réponse au livre des vraies et fausses idées.*
96 *Ibid.*

obscene thoughts and impious feelings in men's minds—could not have allowed him to sin twenty thousand years ago? Will he demonstrate that God cannot give him the thoughts that trouble him unless he has a body, and could not have done so in keeping with the laws of the union of soul and body that he foresaw and can follow, without having formed any body? But though he argues as much as he likes, I can easily break the chain of his demonstrations by saying to him that God might have had plans that he has not told him about."[97] Arnauld answered many things, and especially this, that in Father Malebranche's answer there are "some outlandish propositions, which, if taken strictly, tend to establish a very dangerous Pyrrhonism."[98] His proof can be seen in the following passage.[99] "I beg him to tell me what he meant when he granted that one could take this proposition for a self-evident principle: *God is no deceiver, and it is not possible that he would want to take pleasure in deceiving me.* Did he claim that the self-evidence of this principle is absolute; or did he think that it was limited by this condition, *unless I had committed some sin ten or twenty thousand years ago,* in punishment of which God might take pleasure in deceiving me? If he says that it is absolute, then what he says about the sin I might have committed ten or twenty thousand years ago is entirely beside the point. And if he should say that it is not absolute, but limited by this condition, then nothing would be easier than to make him see that this cannot be said without overthrowing both divine faith and all human knowledge. For he maintains that not only divine faith but also all that we know by reasoning is built on the principle *that God is no deceiver.* . . .[100] Now this principle, that God is no deceiver, would be of no use if he who employed it were obliged to demonstrate first that he did not commit some sin ten or twenty thousand years ago. I will not say any more about this, the consequences of this quibbling being so horrible and impious that it is even dangerous to consider them too much. . . .[101] Is it necessary *that God should have told us of all his plans* to be sure that he can never have intended to deceive us? If this is the case, nobody could be sure of it; and thus there would be no more divine faith, no more

97 *Ibid.*

98 Arnauld, *Défense contre la réponse au livre des vraies et des fausses idées.*

99 *Ibid.*

100 *Ibid.*

101 *Ibid.*

human knowledge, according to the author himself, as I have just shown."

For several reasons I was obliged to set forth some pieces of the dispute between these two famous authors, and to insert, in general, all that is found in this remark. For in the first place, I was obliged to prove that there are still much stronger objections than those of Father Malebranche. Indeed, if it were true that the real existence of extension contained contradictions and impossibilities,[102] as is claimed above,[103] it would be absolutely necessary to have recourse to faith to be convinced that there are bodies. Arnauld, who had found other asylums, would be obliged to have recourse to only this one. In the second place, it was suitable that the article on Zeno of Elea should contain an extension of the difficulties that this philosopher could have proposed against the hypothesis of motion. Thirdly, it is useful to know that a Father of the Oratory, as illustrious for his piety as for his philosophical knowledge, maintained that faith alone can truly convince us of the existence of bodies. Neither the Sorbonne, nor any other tribunal, gave him the least trouble on that account. The Italian inquisitors did not disturb Fardella, who maintained the same thing in a printed work. This ought to show my readers that they must not find it strange that I sometimes point out that, concerning the most mysterious matters in the Gospel, reason gets us nowhere, and thus we ought to be completely satisfied with the light of faith. Lastly, a good part of the things that I have inserted in this remark can serve as a supplement to another place in this dictionary.[104]

≪

I. (*I am sure he did not forget* the objections that can be based upon the distinction between a plenum and a vacuum.) Melissus, who had studied under the same master as he, [105] admitted no motion and employed this proof: If there were motion, it would be necessary that there be a vacuum;[106] now there is no vacuum; therefore, etc. This shows us that at the time of Zeno there was a great philosopher

---

102 That is, according to the light of philosophy, it might seem that it contained contradictions and impossibilities.

103 In remark G, objection I, above [p. 359].

104 Article "Pyrrho," remark B [p. 194].

105 That is, under Parmenides.

106 Aristotle, *Physics* IV. 7.

who did not believe that motion and the plenum were compatible
together. Thus, since Zeno rejected the vacuum, I cannot but think
that he would have made use of the same proof as Melissus employed
against those who admitted motion. He made it his business to oppose
them, and to do this he employed several arguments. Would he have
forgotten the argument that the adherents of the vacuum have so
often put to use? He would have turned it otherwise than they did,
but not in a less specious manner. If there were no vacuum, they said,
there would be no motion; now there is motion, therefore there is a
vacuum. He would have argued in a contrary manner, while agreeing
with them about this principle, that motion cannot exist if everything
is a plenum; for from the thesis common to him and them, he would
have drawn a consequence diametrically opposed to theirs. Here is
what his syllogism should have been: If there were motion, there
would be a vacuum; now there is no vacuum, therefore there is no
motion. Observe that when I said that his manner of reasoning would
not be less specious than theirs, I meant this only with reference to
some philosophers completely capable of understanding the arguments
against the vacuum. I know very well that as far as ordinary people
are concerned it is almost as strange a paradox to deny the vacuum
as to deny motion. Anaxagoras found the common people so prejudiced in favor of the existence of the vacuum that he had recourse to
some trivial experiments in order to destroy this false prejudice. Aristotle,[108] in the chapter in which he observes this, sets forth some of
the arguments that have been used to prove the vacuum. They are
not strong, and he refutes them well enough in the following chapter.
Gassendi has given all the strength he possibly could to the experiments and reasons that favor the Epicurean hypothesis concerning the
vacuum,[109] but he has said nothing that is convincing, and the weakness of what he said is shown in *L'Art de Penser*.[110] I nevertheless believe that our Zeno was formidable on this subject. A dialectician, as
subtle and ardent as he, was quite capable of shuffling the cards on
such a topic, and it is not likely that he neglected this subject.

But if he had known what is said today by several excellent mathematicians,[111] he would have been able to create great havoc and

---

108 Aristotle, *Physics* IV. 7.
109 Gassendi, *Phys.*, Sec. I, bk. 2, chap. 3, in *Opera*, Vol. II.
110 Pt. III, chap. 18, no. 4.
111 Huygens, Newton, etc.

assume an air of triumph. These men say that it is absolutely necessary that there be a vacuum. Without one, the motions of the planets, and what follows from this, would be inexplicable and impossible. I have heard a great mathematician, who had profited greatly from the works and the conversations of Newton, say that it is no longer a problematical matter "whether, if everything were a plenum, everything could move." He claimed that the falsity and impossibility of this proposition had not only been proved, it has been mathematically demonstrated. Henceforth, to deny the vacuum will be to deny a completely evident fact. He affirmed that the vacuum takes up incomparably more space than bodies in the heaviest matter, and that thus, in the air for instance, there are not more particles than there are large cities on earth. *Arguments against the vacuum.* We are no doubt much indebted to mathematics. It demonstrates the existence of a thing that is contrary to the most evident notions we have in our understanding. For if there is any nature, the essential properties of which we know clearly, it is extension. We have a clear and distinct idea of it that makes us know that the essence of extension consists in the three dimensions and that the inseparable properties or attributes are divisibility, mobility, and impenetrability. If these ideas are false, deceitful, chimerical, and illusory, is there any notion in our minds that we ought not to consider as a vain phantom, or a thing we ought to distrust? Can the demonstrations that prove that there is a vacuum reassure us? Are they more evident than the idea that shows us that a foot of extension may change its place and cannot be in the same place as another foot of extension? Let us search as much as we please in the recesses of the mind, we will not find there any idea of an immobile, indivisible, and penetrable extension. However, if there were a vacuum, it would be necessary that an extension exist that had these three attributes essentially. It is no small difficulty to be forced to admit the existence of a nature of which we have no idea and which is repugnant to our clearest ideas. But here are many other inconveniences. Is this vacuum, or this immobile, indivisible, and penetrable extension a substance or a mode? It must be one of the two, since the adequate division of being includes only these two possibilities. If it is a mode, then it would be necessary that we be given the definition of its substance; and this is what can never be done. If it is a substance, I ask, is it created or uncreated? If it is created, then it can perish without the bodies, from which it is really distinct, ceasing to exist.

Now it is absurd and contradictory to think that the vacuum, that is to say, a space distinct from bodies, should be destroyed, and nonetheless the bodies should be distant from one another, as they might be after the destruction of the vacuum. If this space distinct from bodies is an uncreated substance, it would follow either that it is God, or that God is not the only substance that exists necessarily. Whichever side of this alternative one takes, one will be confounded. The latter is a formal impiety, the former is at least a material impiety. For every extension is composed of distinct parts, and consequently they are separable from one another; from which it follows that if God were extended, he would not be a simple, immutable, and properly infinite being, but an assemblage of beings, . . . each of which would be finite, even though all of them together would be unlimited. He would be like the material world, which, in the Cartesian theory, has an infinite extension. And as for those who want to claim that God could be extended without being material or corporeal and would give his simplicity as an explanation, you will find a solid refutation of them in a work by Arnauld. I will only cite these words: "So far ought we to be from believing, because of God's simplicity, that he may be extended, that all theologians after St. Thomas have acknowledged that it is a necessary consequence of God's simplicity that he cannot be extended."[112] Will anyone say with the Scholastics that space is at most no more than a privation of body, that it has no reality, and that, properly speaking, the vacuum is nothing? But this is so unreasonable an assertion that all the modern philosophers who are partisans of the vacuum have abandoned it, no matter how convenient it might be in other respects. Gassendi was careful not to have recourse to such an absurd hypothesis.[113] He preferred to plunge into a dreadful abyss, that of conjecturing that all beings are neither substances nor accidents, and that all substances are neither spirits nor bodies, and of putting the extension of space among the beings that are neither corporeal, nor spiritual, nor substance, nor accident. Locke, not having believed that he could define the vacuum, nevertheless has made it clear that he took it for a positive being.[114] He is too wise not to see

---

112 Arnauld, *Défense contre la réponse au livre des vraies et des fausses idées.*

113 Gassendi, *Phys.*, Sec. I, bk. 2, chap. 1.

114 Locke, *Essay Concerning Human Understanding*, Bk. II, chap. 13.

that nothing cannot be extended in length, breadth, and depth. Hart-soeker has grasped this truth very well. "There is no vacuum in nature," he says;[115] "this ought to be accepted without difficulty because it is completely contradictory to conceive of a pure nonentity having properties that can only belong to something real." But if it is contradictory that nothing, or nonentity, have extension or any other quality, it is no less contradictory that extension be a simple being, since it contains items of which we may truly deny what we may truly affirm of some other features that it does include. The space occupied by the sun is not the same one as that occupied by the moon; for if the sun and the moon filled the same space, these two heavenly bodies would be in the same place, and would be penetrated by one another, since two things cannot be penetrated by a third without being penetrated by one another. It is most evident that the sun and the moon are not in the same place. It can truly be asserted of the space of the sun, that it is penetrated by the sun; and this can be truly denied of the space penetrated by the moon. There are then two portions of space that are really distinct from one another since they receive contradictory denominations, being penetrated and not being penetrated by the sun. This plainly refutes those who dare to say that space is nothing other than the immensity of God; and it is certain that the divine immensity could not be the place of bodies, without leading to the conclusion that it is made up of as many actually distinct parts as there are bodies in the world. It would be in vain for you to claim that infinity has no parts, which must necessarily be false with respect to all infinite numbers, since number includes essentially several unities. You would be no more right to come to tell us that incorporeal extension is entirely in its space, and entirely in each part of its space.[118] For not only is this something of which we have no idea and which clashes with the ideas we have of extension; but it would also prove that every body occupies the same space, since each could not occupy its own, if divine extension were entirely penetrated by each body, numerically the same in its penetration by the sun and the earth. You will find in Arnauld

---

115 Hartsoeker, *Principes de physique.*
118 *Tota in toto et tota in singulis partibus.* This is what the Scholastics assert about the presence of the soul in the human body, and the presence of angels in certain places.

a solid refutation of those who attribute to God a diffusion of himself in infinite spaces.[119]

From this sample of the difficulties that can be raised against the vacuum, my readers can easily see that our Zeno would be much more formidable today than he was in his own time. It can no longer be doubted, he would say, that if there were a total plenum, motion would be impossible. This impossibility has been proven mathematically. He would be far from disputing against these demonstrations, but would have accepted them as indisputable. He would endeavor only to show that a vacuum is impossible, and to make his opponents fall into absurdities. He would keep them on the run no matter which way they might turn. He would throw them into perplexity after perplexity by his dilemmas. He would make them retreat from whatever ground they had moved back to. And if he did not quite silence them, he would at least force them to admit that they do not know or understand what they are talking about. "If anyone ask me," Locke says, "*what* this *space* I speak of *is*, I will tell him when he tells me what his *extension* is. . . . They ask: Whether it be body or spirit? To which I answer by another question: Who told them that there was, or could be, nothing but solid beings. . . . If it be demanded (as usually it is) whether this *space*, void of *body, substance* or *accident,* I shall readily answer I know not, nor shall be ashamed to own my ignorance, till they that ask show me a clear distinct *idea* of *substance*."[121] Since so great a metaphysician as Locke, after having so long meditated on these matters, finds himself reduced to answering the questions of Cartesians only by questions that he thinks are more obscure and more perplexing than theirs, we ought to conclude that the objections raised by Zeno cannot be resolved; and we can safely conjecture that he would address his adversaries in the following way: "You fly to the vacuum when you are driven from the hypothesis of motion and a plenum; but you cannot hold on to the vacuum, the impossibility of which is demonstrated to you. Learn a better means of extricating yourself. The one you have chosen is to avoid one precipice by throwing yourself over another. Follow me, and I will show you a better

---

[119] Arnauld, Letters 8 and 9 to Father Malebranche. The reader may also consult the book by Pierre Petit, a Parisian doctor, *De extensione animae,* and De la Chambre's answer to him.

[121] Locke, *Essay Concerning Human Understanding,* Bk. II, chap. 13, secs. 15–17.

way. Do not conclude from the impossibility of motion in a plenum
that there is a vacuum. Conclude, rather, from the impossibility of a
vacuum, that there is no motion, that is to say, any real motion; but
at most there is an appearance of motion, or an ideal and intelligible
motion."[122]

Let us gather together here some corollaries.

I. The first is that Zeno's dispute could not be entirely unfruitful,
for if he did not succeed in his chief undertaking—that of proving that
there is no motion—he would still have the advantage of strengthen-
ing the hypothesis of acatalepsia, or the incomprehensibility of all
things. The demonstrations of our new mathematicians that there is
a vacuum have made them realize that motion in a plenum is incomprehensible. They then have accepted the supposition of a vacuum.
It is not that they did not find it involved in several inconceivable
and inexplicable difficulties; but, having to choose between two theories, both incomprehensible, they preferred the one that repelled
them the least. They chose to satisfy themselves in mechanical matters
rather than metaphysical ones; and they even neglected the physical
difficulties that fell in their way, like this one: It is not possible to
explain the resistance of air and of water if there is so little matter
and so much vacuum in these two portions of the world. Other mathematicians[123] still reject the vacuum. It is not through unawareness of
the difficulties that obliged others to admit it, but that they were
more struck by the dreadful perplexites found in this supposition.
They did not believe that because of these difficulties one should renounce the clear ideas we possess of the nature of extension. Note that
some philosophers of the first rank[124] do not believe that we know
either what extension is or what a substance is. They cannot express
themselves otherwise as long as they believe in the vacuum. A great
triumph for Zeno and all the other acataleptics! For as long as a dispute is going on about whether we know or do not know the nature
of substance and of matter, this will be an indication that we do not
understand anything, and that we can never be certain that we shall

---

[122] Aristotle, *Physics* IV. 7, where it is pointed out that the ancients were
so perplexed by the dispute about the vacuum that some of them asserted
that vacuum and place were the matter of bodies.

[123] Leibniz; and De Volder, the famous mathematician and philosopher
of Leiden.

[124] Locke; see the quotation on the preceding page.

reach this goal, or that the objects of our minds are like the idea that we have of them.

II. *Spinoza's system is incompatible with the vacuum.* I shall say in passing that the theory of the vacuum is the best adapted in the world for destroying Spinoza's system. In essence, if there are two kinds of extension—the one simple, indivisible, and penetrable; the other composite, divisible, and impenetrable—then it must be the case that there is more than one substance in the universe. This would follow even more from the fact that the impenetrable substance would not be a complete continuum, but a collection of particles, each entirely separated from the others and surrounded by a large incorporeal space. The Spinozists would not deny that each of these particles was a particular substance distinct from the substance of all the others. And thus, by their own axioms they would abandon their system, if they once admitted that there is a vacuum.

III. The last consequence I shall draw is that the disputes about the vacuum have provided a specious reason for denying that extension has a real existence outside our understanding. It has been understood, in disputing against the Cartesians who deny the possibility of a vacuum, that extension is a being that can have no limits. Then it is necessary either that there are no bodies in nature, or that there are an infinite number of them. One cannot be destroyed without annihilating all the rest, nor can the smallest be preserved without preserving all the rest. However, we know by evident ideas that when two things are really distinct, one can be preserved or destroyed without the other being so; for whatever is really distinct from a thing is accidental to it; and since every thing can be preserved without that which is accidental to it,[125] it follows that body *A,* which is really distinct from body *B,* can remain in existence, even though *B* does not subsist, and that the preservation of body *A* does not entail the preservation of *B.* This consequence, which appears so clear and in such agreement

---

125 Porphyry, *Isagoge* V. If this is true of accidents that are the modes of a substance, as Porphyry understands it here, it is much more true of a substance, accidental with regard to the other ones, in that it is distinct from their [the other ones] essential attributes. Observe that the Scholastics raise a great difficulty here, under the pretext that blackness cannot be separated from an Ethiopean. This is why they have recourse to the distinction between mental separation and real separation. Pure illusion! For the subject of the blackness of an Ethiopean is matter that would not perish, even though the body of this man were calcined.

with common notions, does not fit the problem at issue; and you cannot suppose that all the bodies contained in a room perish and that
the four walls are preserved; for in that case there would remain the
same distance between them as before. Now this distance, the Cartesians say, is nothing but a body. Their theory then seems to oppose
the sovereign liberty of the Creator and the complete dominion he
has over his works. He ought to enjoy the complete right of creating
few or many of them, depending on his wishes, and of destroying or
preserving this one or that one, as he may think fit. The Cartesians
can reply that he can destroy each particular body, provided he makes
another of the same size. But is this not putting limits on his freedom?
Is this not imposing a kind of servitude on him that obliges him necessarily to create a new body every time he wishes to destroy one? These
are the difficulties that cannot be warded off by supposing that extension and body are the same thing; but they may all be thrown back
against those who propose them to Descartes, if they acknowledge a
spatial extension really existent and distinct from matter. This extension cannot be finite. One part of it cannot be destroyed without re-
producing another, and so on. Now if the nature of penetrable or impenetrable extension is necessarily attended with such great draw-
backs, the simplest thing is to say that it can exist only in our minds.

《《‹

    K. *(An answer like that of* Diogenes *is more sophistic than the*
arguments of our Zeno.) "After a certain person told him that
there was no such thing as motion, he rose up and walked."[126] That
is all we find on this subject in Diogenes Laertius. As you see, it is
very simply reported there. Modern authors have amplified it a bit.
"It is also commonly reported that Diogenes, hearing Zeno deny local
motion, instantly rose up and walked backwards and forwards several
times with great speed; and being asked what sudden enthusiasm had
seized him, he replied, 'I am refuting Zeno.' "[127] They have named the
philosopher who denies motion; they have embellished the circumstances of the practical answer; they have made it the subject of dec-

---

[126] Diogenes Laertius, VI. 39.
[127] Libertus Fromondus, *De compositione continui.*

lamations for the use of young rhetoricians. I am surprised that Sextus Empiricus did not deign to name the person who refuted in this way the objections against the existence of motion. What is not vague in what he tells us is that a Cynic employed this means of refuting the arguments. . . . It were better to name no one than to assert that Diogenes the Cynic and Zeno of Elea were the actors on this occasion. This chronological error is inexcusable.[130] The Jesuits of Coimbra have attributed it to Simplicius without refuting it. They have fallen into the common error in this respect. . . . They have not committed the other error that is so common; they did not believe that the Zeno who denied motion, and whose arguments Aristotle examined, was the leader of the Stoics. . . . Here is a passage that is full of errors: "Zeno, the head of the Stoic philosophers, asserted constantly in opposition to Aristotle that matter consisted of indivisible parts; he was followed in this particular by the philosophers Democritus and Leucippus, and, among the old theologians, by May, Gerardus, and Aegidus, the disciple of St. Thomas."[133] There is no room for doubting that the author in this passage intended the same Zeno whom Aristotle refuted in *Physics* VI. 9. Now, it does not seem that Zeno of Elea taught that the continuum was composed of indivisible parts. He contented himself with taking advantage of the contrary doctrine, to show that motion is impossible. He even said that an indivisible body does not differ from a nonentity, and we will show below that he did not admit any composition in the universe. However, he is regarded as the founder of the sect that maintains that the continuum is made up of mathematical points.[135] It would be more reasonable to attribute this view to Pythagoras and Plato as Derodon has done.[136]. . . But what a blunder it was to make the founder of the Stoics the guide of Democritus and Leucippus! He [Oviedo] ought to have known that Leucippus preceded Democritus, and that both of them lived several Olympiads before the leader of the Stoics. Besides that, their atoms made up a

130 Diogenes the Cynic lived a long time after Zeno of Elea.

133 Franciscus de Oviedo, *Physic.*, Controvers. XVII.

135 Arriaga and a hundred other Spanish Scholastics call "Zenoists" those who assert that the continuum is composed of indivisible and unextended parts, a view that is very different from that of the Atomists.

136 Derodon, *Disp. de atomis*. He cites Sextus Empiricus and Aristotle. [David Derodon (1600–1664), a philosopher and theologian, was born a Calvinist, became a Catholic, and then returned to Protestantism. He was an ardent Aristotelian.]

system that is quite different from the one that is attributed to the Zenoists, regarding the composition of matter.

Be that as it may, the answer of Diogenes the Cynic to the philosopher who denies motion is the sophism that the logicians call *ignoratio elenchi*. It is departing from the state of the question, for this philosopher does not reject apparent motion. He does not deny that to men it seems that there is motion. But he maintains that in reality nothing moves, and he proved this by some very subtle and perplexing arguments. Here is what Sextus Empiricus said of the skeptics, "There is motion apparently, but not according to philosophy."[137] To what purpose then is walking around or jumping? Does this prove anything other than the appearance of motion? Is this what the question was about? Did the philosopher deny it? Not in the least. He was not fool enough to deny the phenomena of the eyes, but he maintained that the testimony of the senses ought to be sacrificed to reason. Consult Aristotle, who will tell you that some ancient philosophers, having found reasons for entirely rejecting the plurality of parts, the divisibility and the mobility of the world, had afterwards considered the information from the senses as nothing. . . . Parmenides and Melissus are the ancient philosophers he speaks of. . . . The author of *L'Art de penser*, as we have seen in the article "Xenophanes" [not in these selections], has criticized Aristotle in favor of Parmenides and Melissus. For a long time people have been trying to justify them by giving their view a favorable interpretation and a semblance of conformity with the orthodox doctrine about the nature of God. But in all probability Aristotle does not deserve any blame here. He has well understood and reported what they taught, and consequently we ought to believe that their theory is a species of Spinozism. There is no basis for imagining[142] that they expressed themselves by enigmas or symbols, for the specific doctrine of the unity and immutability of all things was a consequence of several clear and evident principles. See the article "Xenophanes." It was therefore in earnest, and as a doctrine of a system and not as a jest, that they denied motion and that they maintained that its existence was only mental. . . .

From all this it follows that Diogenes' answer was sophistic, even though it was proper to obtain the applause of the audience. This was

---

137 Sextus Empiricus, *Pyrrhoniarum hypotoposeon* III. 8.
142 However, the Jesuits of Coimbra do this.

a scoffing answer, but I think as well that the philosopher who was concerned with it only despised it. He might perhaps laugh at it, and to
his heart's content make fun of it, in which he was a thousand times
more fortunate than the Sophist Diodorus who did not find himself
in a position to laugh when he was attacked with a malicious irony for
his lectures against the existence of motion. He had dislocated his
shoulder, and he went to find the doctor Herophilus to ask him to
set it. "You do not know what you are talking about," Herophilus answered him. "What! Your shoulder is dislocated? This cannot be. For
it cannot have left either the place where it was or where it was not."
This was one of the arguments of this sophist to oppose motion. If a
body moved, he used to say, it would move either in the place where
it is or in the place where it is not. But it does not move, neither in
the place where it is, nor in the place where it is not. But it does not
move, neither in the place where it is (for if it is there, it is not moving
anywhere), nor in the place where it is not, for it cannot do anything
where it is not. Therefore, Diodorus was at this time not in condition
to appreciate this logic and begged Herophilus not to remember his
discourse any longer, but to do something to remedy his condition.[145]

---

[145] Sextus Empiricus, *Pyrrhoniarum hypotoposeon* II. 22. 245.

Zeno, an Epicurean philosopher, born in Sidon, gloriously upheld the honor of his sect and thereby acquired a great reputation. Among his disciples were Cicero and Pomponius Atticus, from which we may judge when he lived. Vossius is mistaken about this. This Zeno has been portrayed as a philosopher who treated his opponents with great contempt and bitterness. There is hardly anything that better shows how bold he was than the work he wrote against mathematics (D). We possess neither this book nor the one Posidonius wrote to refute it. There are some people who more regret the loss of these two books than that of twenty or thirty plays, or that of the best historians of antiquity.

≪←

D. *(The work he wrote against mathematics.)* This we learn from Proclus, who adds that Posidonius refuted him. . . . Huet, after saying that Epicurus rejected geometry and the other branches of mathematics because he thought that, since they were built on false principles, they could not therefore be true, then adds that Zeno attacked mathematics another way. This was by alleging that in order for it [mathematics] to be certain, some things would have to be added to its principles that have not so been adjoined. . . .[22] Of all human knowledge mathematics is the most evident and certain, and yet it has had opponents. If our Zeno had been a great metaphysician and had followed principles other than those of Epicurus, he would have been able to write a work that would have been difficult to refute and that would have given geometers a harder task than they imagine. All branches of knowledge have their weak side. Mathematics is not exempt from this defect. It is true that few people are capable of fighting

---

[22] Huet, *Demonst. evang.* (Leipzig, 1694), Preface no. 3, p. 6.

well against mathematics; for to succeed in such a combat, one would have to be not only a good philosopher but also a very profound mathematician. Those who have this latter quality are so enchanted by the certitude and evidence of the subject that they do not think of examining whether there is something illusory in it, or if the basis of it has been well established. They rarely think of suspecting that something is lacking. One thing that is certain is that there are a great many disputes among the most famous mathematicians. They refute one another; replies and rejoinders multiply among them the same as among other learned men. We find this among modern mathematicians, and it is certain that the ancients were not any more unanimous.[23] This is an indication that one comes to several shadowy paths on this road and that one goes astray and loses the track to the truth. This must necessarily happen to one or the other disputant since one side asserts what the other denies. It will be said that it is the fault of the artist and not of the art that all these disputes are due to the fact that there are mathematicians who mistakenly accept as demonstrations what are not actually so. But even this shows that there are obscure things in this branch of knowledge. Besides, this explanation can be used to account for the disputes among other learned men; one can say that if they would follow exactly the rules of logic, they would avoid the bad conclusions and false theses that lead them to err. Let us admit that, due to the lack of self-evidence* in the object being considered, there are many philosophical matters concerning which the best logicians are incapable of coming to completely certain conclusions. This difficulty does not occur with mathematical objects. Granted, this may well be so. There is, however, an irreparable and most enormous difficulty with mathematical objects —they are chimeras that cannot exist. Mathematical points and, therefore, lines and geometrical surfaces, globes, and axes are fictions that can never have any existence. They are therefore inferior to the fictions of poets, for these latter usually contain nothing impossible; they have at least some probability and possibility. Gassendi made an ingenious observation. He says that mathematicians, and especially geometers, have established their domain in the land of abstractions and ideas. There they can wander as they will. But when they want to descend into the land of realities, they soon find insurmountable

---

23 Cf. Huet, *ibid*, Axiom 4, pp. 28–29.
* [See footnote * on p. 199.]

difficulties. "The mathematicians, and especially the geometers, by abstracting quantity from matter, have thereby made a certain kingdom for themselves, where they enjoy complete freedom, since they do not encounter any obstacle from the heaviness or stubbornness of matter. For this reason they came to suppose that there could be, in this world of abstract quantity, such things as a point with no parts, a line formed by a moving point, which would have neither length nor breadth, and so on. . . . And these are the suppositions by which the mathematicians, from within the separate kingdom of pure and abstract geometry, have woven their renowned demonstrations. . . ."[24] In a word, it is the mathematicians, who, in this their kingdom of abstractions, imagine those indivisible things which have no parts, without length or breath, and that multitude and division of parts which goes on ad infinitum. But it is not the same with the scientists, who cannot take such liberties since they have to deal with the realm of matter."[25] He gives an example of the vanity of their alleged demonstrations, namely, that subtle mathematicians [Cavalieri and Torricelli] . . .[26] had just proven that a finite quantity and an infinite quantity are equal. Others prove that there are infinite quantities limited on each side.[27] If they find any self-evidence in this sort of demonstration, should it not appear suspect to them since, after all, it does not surpass the self-evidence with which common sense teaches us that the finite can never be equal to the infinite, and that the infinite, being infinite, cannot have limits? I add that it is not true that self-evidence can accompany these men wherever they go. I shall quote a person who understands mathematical refinements very well. "One would wish," he says,[28] "that the analysis of infinitesimals, which is supposed to be so wonderfully fruitful, could convey in its demonstrations the evidence desired, and which is rightfully expected in geometry. But when one reasons about the 'infinite,' 'the infinite of the infinite,' 'the infinite of the infinite of the infinite,' and so on, without finding any final terms, and then applies these 'infinities of infinities' to finite magnitudes; those whom one wants to instruct or convince do

---

24 Gassendi, *Phys.*, sec. 1, bk. 3, chap. 5, p. 264, in *Opera*, Vol. I.

25 *Ibid.*, p. 265.

26 *Ibid.*, p. 264.

27 See chap. 12 of Father Maignan's *Physics*, page m.295, twelfth proposition.

28 *Journal de Trévoux* (Dutch edn., May–June 1701), Article 33, p. 423.

not always have the necessary acuteness to see clearly into such deep abysses. . . .[29] Those who are accustomed to the traditional ways of geo-metrical reasoning do not wish to give them up for such abstract pro-cedures. They prefer not to take up these procedures where they would find themselves on new paths of 'the infinite of the infinite of the in-finite,' where one does not always see clearly enough around oneself, and where one can easily get lost without realizing it. It is not enough in geometry to draw conclusions. One must see evidently that one draws right conclusions."

A good enough reason for being against mathematics is that Pascal scorned the subject even before he devoted himself to a life of piety. He had been passionately fond of mathematics and had made extraor-dinary progress in that field. Moreover, he had very good judgment. Few people knew better than he the worth of things. It was not by his conversion to the unique source of truth that he became disgusted with the subjects that had charmed him. The examination of them and the reflections he made on the discourse of a layman cured him of his prejudices. We would be too naïve if we thought that the Chevalier de Meré attacked them with pious thoughts. He no doubt employed only philosophical considerations. Let us see what effect they had and quote the beginning of the letter he wrote Pascal: "Do you remember having told me once that you were no longer so con-vinced of the exalted status of mathematics? You write me now that I have entirely disabused you of the subject and that I have made you see things that you never would have if you had not known me. I do not know, however, sir, if you are as obliged to me as you think. For you still have a habit, which you developed from that subject, of not judging of anything except by your demonstrations, which are most often false. These long tedious chains of logic hinder you at first with regard to a higher knowledge that is never deceptive . . . but you still remain in the errors in which the false demonstrations of geometry have cast you, and I shall not believe that you are entirely cured of mathematics so long as you maintain that these tiny bodies, about which we were disputing the other day, can be divided ad infinitum."[30] The Chevalier de Meré then proposes several objections to him con-cerning this infinite divisibility of the continuum. Some of these are

---

29 *Ibid.,* p. 430.
30 Chevalier de Meré, Letter 19 (Dutch edn.), p. 60.

good; and others very bad, seeming more like jokes than arguments. It is astonishing to see the same letter filled with such unequal things. Nevertheless, the author boasts of a marvelous ability in mathematics. . . . Observe that it is very proper that those who endeavor to show the weakness of mathematics should tell the public that they understand the subject, have studied it, know its value, and have no intention of diminishing its just worth. The learned Bishop of Avranches [Huet], whom I cited above, did this, after having made several fine observations about the uncertainty and the illusory character of this branch of knowledge.

Here is another passage from the Chevalier de Meré's letter: "May I advise you that besides the natural world, of which we have sense knowledge, there is another, invisible one; and that it is in this one that you can attain the highest knowledge. Those who deal only with the corporeal world usually come to common and wrong conclusions, as did Descartes, whom you esteem so highly, who only knew about space by means of the bodies that fill it. . . . But without stopping to convict him of this error, know that in this invisible and infinitely extended world we can discover the reasons and principles of things, the most hidden truths, the fitness, the exactness, the proportions, the archetypes, and the perfect ideas of all that one looks for."[35] This is the conclusion of his letter to Pascal. Let me say that it is hard to tell whom he is determined to refute, and that his views need some support since he expresses himself in so vague a way that one could come to an opinion opposite to what he wished to say. His aim was to cure Pascal entirely of his passion for mathematics. Hence, he wished to point out to him a different object of study and point it out to him as the source and location of the truths we aspire to. However, he describes an object to him that very much resembles mathematics, for this object is not contemplated in this "world of which we have sense knowledge," but in "this invisible and infinitely extended world" where one can discover "the exactness, the proportions," and so on. I believe that he intended to recommend the idealist philosophy, the most refined metaphysics, which aims only at the contemplation of spirits and the intelligible world that is in the mind of God. But care has not been taken to distinguish the characteristics of this study from that of mathematics . . . whose chief property is the consideration of

---

[35] Chevalier de Meré, Letter 19, pp. 68–69.

extension apart from matter and every sensible quality. . . . We learn from several passages of Aristotle that quantity separated from everything that is sensed is the object of mathematics. Most mathematicians admit that this object does not exist outside our minds. Dr. Barrow objected to their admitting this.[41] He was criticizing particularly the Jesuit Blancanus, and Vossius. But Blancanus is certainly right; and he ought to be criticized only for claiming that the existence of the globe, the triangle, etc., of the geometers is possible. "Lastly it may be said that these entities are possible, for who will deny that they may be produced by an angel or God?"[42] A long argument is not needed to show that it is impossible that this globe, triangle, etc., really exist. We have only to remember that such a globe, placed on a plane, would only touch it at one indivisible point, and that if it were rolled on this plane, it would always touch it at only one point. It would follow from this that it would be completely composed of unextended parts. Now this is impossible and contains clearly the contradiction that an extension would exist and would not be extended. It would exist according to the supposition; and it would not be extended since it would not be distinct from an unextended being. All philosophers agree that the material cause is not distinct from its effect. Therefore, what would be composed of unextended parts would not be distinguished from them. Thus, that which is the same as an unextended being is necessarily an unextended thing. When our theologians teach that the world has been produced from nothing, they do not mean that it is composed of nothing. The word "nothing" does not signify the material cause of the world, but rather the state antecedent to the existence of the world. . . . They realize that if the word "nothing" were taken in the first sense, then it would be absolutely impossible that the world was made from it. It is no more ridiculous to assert that the world was made of nothing, as its material cause, than to assert that a foot of extension is composed of unextended parts.[43] It is therefore not possible that either an angel or God himself could ever produce the triangle, the plane, the circle, the globe of the geometers; and thus Blancanus deserves some criticism.

I leave my readers to judge whether my critique of the last passage from the Chevalier de Meré is well founded.

---

[41] Isaac Barrow, Lecture V, p. 85.

[42] Blancanus, *De natura mathematicarum*, p. 7.

[43] Add to this what was said in remark G [p. 359] of the article "Zeno of Elea."

Clarifications about certain matters spread throughout this Dictionary, and which can be reduced to four general headings: (I) *The praise paid to persons who deny either providence or the existence of God,* (II) *The arguments attributed to the Manicheans,* (III) *The arguments attributed to the Pyrrhonists,* (IV) *The obscenities.*

A general and preliminary observation.

In putting this work together, I noticed that some rather free reflections that do not accord very much with usual opinions slipped into it. But I did not foresee that anyone might be shocked by this. I supposed that men whose judgment serves as a model or corrective to that of others would take note of several things that could furnish me with an apology.

I. I hoped in the first place that the nature of this dictionary would be considered. It is an enormous compilation, necessarily crowded with many critical details which are distasteful and tedious to the last degree for those who are not involved in such matters; and it has been necessary that I maintain in this mass of all sorts of things a dual personality, that of historian and that of commentator. There was no possible way of protecting the work from the contempt of many people, except by introducing into it many items that were unusual. Those who hardly care about the disputes of grammarians or the adventures of a minor individual are not small in number, and they deserve that one pay some regard to their taste. An author is therefore allowed to behave so that his book appears worthwhile to them in some respects; and if this author writes as an historian, he ought to report not only what heretics have done, but also what are the strong and weak aspects of their views. He ought to do this mainly if he is himself the commentator on his reports, for it is in his commentary that he ought to discuss matters and compare the arguments for and against something, with all the impartiality of a faithful reporter.

II. I hoped, in the second place, that notice would be taken of the air and the manner in which I reported certain views. It is not at all with the tone of those who want to dogmatize, nor with the obstinacy of those who are looking for followers. These are thoughts spread throughout at random and incidentally, and I am willing that they be taken as witticisms, and that they be rejected as one sees fit, with even more liberty than I would take. It is easy to recognize that an author who behaves in this manner has no bad intentions, and that he is not laying snares, and that if some reflection should come from him that would be dangerous under another form, it is hardly necessary to take offense at it.

III. I hoped, in the third place, that notice would be taken of the circumstances in which an error is to be feared or not. Its consequences ought to be dreaded when it is taught by persons whose relations to the populace furnish them with the opportunity of gaining authority and of forming a party. An error ought to be carefully followed, watched, and restrained when a man of venerable character, a pastor, a professor of theology, spreads it either by his sermons, his lectures, his small systematic tracts or catechisms, and by emissaries who go from house to house recommending the reading of his writings, and requesting people to attend secret religious meetings where the author explains his arguments and methods in more detail.[1] But if a man who is completely a layman like myself, and without status, should relate, among vast historical and literary collections, some error about religion or morality, one should not be disturbed at all about it. It is not in such works that a reader looks for a reformation of his faith. No one takes as a guide in that matter an author who only speaks about it in passing and

---

1 Observe that I place all these things together without claiming that we ought only to attack those who do all this. A portion of the items can supply sufficient motive.

incidentally, and who, by the very fact that he acts as if he were tossing off his views like a pin in a field, makes it well enough known that he does not care to have followers at all. The errors of such a writer are of no consequence and should not make anyone uneasy. This is how the faculties of theology in France behaved with regard to the book of Michel de Montaigne. They allowed all this author's maxims to pass, he who without following any system, any method, any order, heaped up and stirred together all that came into his mind. But when Pierre Charron, a priest and prebendary, bethought himself to relate some of the views of Montaigne in a methodical and systematic treatise on morality,[2] the theologians did not remain tranquil.[3]

IV. I hoped, in the fourth place, and this was the chief basis of my confidence, that it would be easy to distinguish these two points: (1) that I never set forth as my own particular opinion any doctrine that is in conflict with the articles of the confession of faith of the Reformed Church in which I was born, and which I profess; (2) that when I report, in the capacity of a historian, what can be objected to and replied to the orthodox, and when I confess that all the difficulties of unbelievers cannot be resolved by the natural light, I always make a digression in order to draw a conclusion favorable to the principle that reformers continually oppose to the Socinians, namely, that our reason, being as weak as it is, ought not to be the rule or measure of our faith.

These are the reasons that made me believe that it would not be taken amiss if I sometimes made use of what is called the liberty of philosophizing. I would not have made use of it had I foreseen that the public would not take into consideration the matters I have just set forth.

---

[2] Compare this with remark O of the article on him. [That is, the article "Charron." In some eighteenth-century editions a reference to the article "Montaigne" has been given by mistake; there is no such article. The article "Charron" does not appear in these selections.]

[3] See remark F of article "Charron." [This reference to the nonexistent article "Montaigne" also often appears in various eighteenth-century editions.]

But events did not correspond to my hopes. There have been murmurs and outcries against such passages in my dictionary. I have never been convinced that these were just. Nevertheless, I am sorry to have said anything that one might find bad, and I have always been perfectly prepared to remedy in the second edition anything that gives qualms. After complaints had been pointed out to me, it seemed to me that it would be easy to remedy them either by suppressing a few pages, by changing some expressions, or by some clarifications that show matters in their proper perspective. I undertook to do this without the least reluctance, as all authors ought to do who are not infatuated with their own thoughts and who are willing to sacrifice them for the reader's edification. I hope that everyone is content with my conduct, both with regard to what has been suppressed, and with regard to those matters that I am going to clarify; and it seems to me that I have reason to assure myself that everyone will be satisfied. I have given myself this task and have tried very hard to accomplish it.

FIRST CLARIFICATION

*The observations that have been made about the good morals of some people who professed no religion cannot be of any prejudice to the true faith and can do no damage to it.**

THOSE who have been scandalized by what I said about there having been atheists and Epicureans whose moral conduct surpassed that of most idolaters are requested to reflect carefully on all the considerations that I am about to set forth. If they do this, their shock will evaporate and disappear entirely.

I. The fear and love of God are not the sole springs of human actions. There are other principles that make people act; love of praise, fear of infamy, temperamental dispositions, punishments and rewards proposed by magistrates have much influence on the human heart. If anyone doubts this, he must be unaware of what goes on within himself and what the ordinary course of human events can show him at any moment. But there is no likelihood that anyone is so stupid as not to know this. What I have set forth about the other springs of human actions can then be placed among the common notions.

II. The love and fear of God is not always a more active principle than all the others. The love of glory, the fear of infamy or death or torments, the hope of a post act with more

---

* [The *Dictionary* does not seem particularly guilty of this charge, which is harder to substantiate than the other three brought against it. Whereas the Consistory's notes of the proceedings against Bayle name specific articles containing remarks on Pyrrhonism or Manicheanism that could be branded as dangerous, no single article is ever cited in the matter of atheism. The charge was obviously documented in only a general way. Significantly, it was on just this accusation that Jurieu succeeded in stripping Bayle of his professorship in 1692. It is likely that Jurieu had his allies repeat the accusation of atheism when they attacked Bayle again five years later.]

force on certain men than the desire to please God and the fear of violating his commandments. If anyone doubts this, he does not know part of what is going on within himself and is unaware of what is going on every day on the surface of the earth. The world is full of people who prefer to commit a sin rather than displease a prince who can make or break their fortunes. People every day sign formularies of faith against their conscience in order to safeguard their wealth or to avoid jail, exile, death, or the like. A military man who has given up everything for his religion, and who finds himself in the dilemma of either offending God if he avenges himself for a blow, or of appearing to be a coward if he does not avenge himself, will not let himself rest until he has been righted for this affront, even at the risk of killing or being killed in a state that will be followed by eternal damnation. There is no likelihood that anyone is so stupid as to be unaware of these facts. Let us place among the common notions this moral aphorism, *The fear and love of God are not always the most active principles of human actions.*

III. Since this is the case, it should not be considered a scandalous paradox but rather as something quite possible— that there are irreligious people who may be more strongly impelled toward a virtuous life by the springs of temperament accompanied by the love of praise and sustained by the fear of dishonor, than others are impelled by the dictates of conscience.

IV. It ought to be considered much more scandalous when it is noticed that so many people convinced of the truths of religion are yet immersed in crime.

V. It is even stranger that the idolaters of paganism have performed good actions than that atheistic philosophers have lived as virtuous men, for these idolaters should have been impelled to crime by their own religion. They should have believed that in order to live like their gods—which is the end and the kernel of religion—it was necessary that they be knaves, jealous people, fornicators, adulterers, pederasts, and the like.

VI. From this it can be concluded that the idolaters who lived virtuously were directed only by ideas of reason and of virtue, or by the desire for praise, or by temperament, or by such other principles as can all be found among the atheists. Why then should we expect to find more virtue in pagan idolatry than in the absence of religion?

VII. Please notice carefully that in speaking of the good morals of some atheists, I have not attributed any real virtues to them. Their sobriety, their chastity, their probity, their contempt for riches, their zeal for the public good, their inclination to be helpful to their neighbor were not the effect of the love of God and tended neither to honor nor to glorify him. They themselves were the source and end of all this. Self-love was the basis, the boundaries, and the cause of it. These were only glittering sins, *splendida peccata,* as St. Augustine has said of all the fine actions of the pagans. The prerogatives of the true religion are thus in no way damaged by saying of some atheists what I wrote concerning them. It remains true that good works can only be produced within the confines of true religion. And what difference does it make that the worshippers of false gods are no more prudent in their actions than those who profess no religion? . . .

VIII. If those who have been shocked claimed that one cannot praise the good conduct of Epicurus without claiming, with respect to the good life, that to have no religion at all or to profess any religion whatsoever amounts to the same thing, they do not know the art of drawing consequences and have not understood at all what is at issue. I have never compared atheism with anything but paganism. Thus the true religion is not involved. It is only a question concerning the religions introduced and fomented by the devil. The question is to find out whether those who have professed a religion as infamous in its origin and in its development as this have regularly behaved better morally than atheists. I take it for granted, as an indubitable and completely settled point, that there is not only more virtue in the true religion than elsewhere, but that there is no true virtue at all outside this religion, nor any "fruits of righteousness." To what purpose is it, then, to make a show of fearing lest I might offend that true religion? Is it in any way concerned with the bad things that can be said about the false one? And should one not be apprehensive that this great zeal that is shown may scandalize persons of good sense, who will see a tenderness exhibited in favor of a religious sect detested by God and produced by the devil, as is acknowledged by all our doctors of divinity?

IX. I could not justly have found fault with the complaints had I written a novel in which the characters were virtuous and irreligious; for, since I would have been the master of their actions and their words, I would have been free to paint them in accordance with the taste of the most scrupulous readers. But my dictionary is a historical work. I have no right at all to represent people as they ought to have been. I must represent them as they were. I cannot suppress either their defects or their virtues. Since, then, I set forth only those matters concerning the conduct of some atheists, which the authors I have cited report about them, no one has any reason to be shocked by what I have done. To make my critics realize this, it is only necessary to ask them if they believe that the suppression of verified facts is the historian's duty. I am sure that they would never subscribe to such a proposition.

X. I have no doubt that there are people ingenuous enough to assert that a factual truth ought to be hidden by a historian when it is capable of diminishing the horror of atheism, and the veneration that one should have for religion in general. But I most humbly entreat them to permit me to continue to believe that God has no need of these rhetorical artifices, and that though this can be allowed in a poem or an oration, it does not follow that I ought to adopt this policy in a historical dictionary. They will permit me to say that it suffices to work for the right religion, for everything that is done for religion in general would be of service as much to paganism as to Christianity.

XI. I would have been all the more culpable for suppressing

the truths about which they are complaining because, in addition to the fact that this would have acted against the fundamental laws of historical scholarship, I would have blotted out things that are fundamentally of great advantage to the true system of grace. I have shown elsewhere[1] that nothing is more suitable for proving the corruption of the human heart—that corruption which is naturally unconquerable and only surmountable by the Holy Ghost—than to point out that those who have no share in the supernatural aid are as wicked in the practice of a religion as those who live in atheism. I add here that one cannot make the Pelagians happier than by saying that the fear of false gods has been able to lead the pagans to give up some vice. For if the fear of drawing down the curses of heaven upon themselves had been able to make them abstain from evil, they could also be led to commit virtuous actions by the desire for spiritual rewards, and in order to obtain God's love; that is to say, they would have been able not only to fear, but also to love God, and to act on the basis of this good principle. The two levers by which man is moved are fear of punishment and desire of reward. If he can be moved by the former, he can also be by the latter. One cannot simply admit one of these and reject the other.

XII. If some persons of a more equitable and more intelligent outlook than is usually the case should offer as the sole reason for their taking offense the affectation with which it seems to them that I pointed out the virtuous lives of atheists to my readers, then I would beg them to consider that in the present case this affectation is very excusable, and that it may even be considered as a subject for edification. To understand this fully, it is only necessary to recall an episode in my treatise on comets. The real goal of this work was to refute by means of a theological argument what is ordinarily said about comets being omens.[2] The necessity of fortifying this argument led me to

---

[1] See the *Pensées diverses sur la comète* and the *Addition aux pensées diverses.*

[2] See the Preface to the third edition [of *Pensées diverses sur la comète*].

draw a parallel between atheism and paganism; for, without this, my proof would have been exposed to an objection which would have made it unfit to make convincing what I had to demonstrate. It was then necessary either to leave this gap or to refute the arguments of those who say that the idolatry of the pagans was not as great an evil as atheism. The whole success of the combat greatly depended on the outcome of this attack; and thus, according to the rules of disputation and according to all the rights belonging to an author, I could and was obliged to take advantage of all that logic and history were capable of furnishing me in order to repel this assault. It was not at all, then, either from a gaiety of heart or from audacity that I reported the facts which tended to convince people that atheists are not necessarily more dissolute in their morals than idolaters. The laws of disputation and the right that each person has to repel objections to which he sees his thesis is exposed indispensibly imposed this conduct upon me. Great clamors have been made against this portion of my work, and attempts have been made to portray it as dangerous. I was then obliged to maintain it as far as reason and truth could permit me; and consequently, no one should be shocked if I inform my readers, whenever an occasion presents itself, that history teaches us that such and such persons who denied either the existence or the providence of God, or the immortality of the soul, have nevertheless lived virtuous lives. This affectation, which perhaps might justly be considered scandalous in another book, should not at all be so considered in mine. On the contrary, it can serve to edify my readers because it shows that I have not set forth a paradox because of vanity, but because it is fundamentally quite true and only appeared false to those who had not examined it. Nothing is more shocking than a man who, in order to gain some distinction, rashly attempts to leave the beaten path; and if there are writers who have become suspect on this account, through no fault of their own, but because readers were not sufficiently acquainted with the matter, then nothing can be more edifying than to see such authors justify themselves.

XIII. To remove entirely all suspicions of a vicious affectation, I took care to mention the bad morals of atheists as often as I could.[3] If I have not done so more often, it is only because I lack materials. The public knew that I requested that examples be pointed out to me.[4] No one has taken the trouble to do this, and I have not yet been able to find any through my researches. I am not trying to deny that in all countries and all times there have been persons who have stifled the explicit faith in the existence of God by their debauchery and by long criminal habits. But since history has not preserved their names, it is impossible to speak about them. It is probable that among those bandits and hired assassins who commit so many crimes there are some who have no religion at all. But the contrary is still more probable, since of the many criminals who pass through the hands of the public executioner there are none found to be atheists.[5] Those who prepare them for death always find them sufficiently disposed to wish for the joys of paradise. As for those profane people, sunk in gluttony, who, in the opinion of Father Garasse and several others, are downright atheists, I was not obliged to include them in the list; for it is not a question of those who are called practical atheists—people who live with no fear of God, but not without some conviction of his existence. It was only a question of the theoretical atheists, as, for example, Diagoras, Vanini, Spinoza, and their sort— people whose atheism is attested to either by the historians or by their own writings. The question turns only on the morals of this class of atheists. It is with regard to them that I have wished that people would give me indications of their evil life. If I had found any, I would have given them ample mention. Nothing is easier to find in history than certain villains whose abominable

---

[3] As in the articles "Bion, Borysthenite" and "Critias" [not included in these selections].

[4] See the *Addition aux pensées diverses.*

[5] I speak this way because I do not recall having read any accounts in which this sort of person is said to have died an atheist, nor have I heard of any such.

actions almost make the reader tremble, but their very impious and blasphemous behavior is a proof that they believed in God. This is a natural consequence of the constant view of the theologians that the devil, the most wicked of all creatures, but himself incapable of atheism, is the promoter of all the sins committed by the human race. Hence, it must be the case that the most outrageous wickedness of man has the same characteristic as that of the devil, namely, that it is joined with a conviction of the existence of God. A maxim of the philosophers confirms this argument.[6]

XIV. If what I have just said is capable of edifying tender consciences, since they will see that a thesis that terrified them happens to accord very well with the most orthodox principles, they will not find a lesser subject of edification in what I am going to propose, namely, that the worst villains are not atheists, and that most atheists whose names have come down to us have been virtuous according to ordinary standards, and that this state of affairs is an indication of the infinite wisdom of God and an occasion for admiring his providence. He desired to set limits to man's corruption so that there could be societies on earth; and if he has only favored a small number of people with a sanctifying grace, he has everywhere spread a *restraining*[7] grace, which like a strong dike holds back the flood of sins as much as is requisite to prevent a general inundation that would destroy all monarchic, aristocratic, democratic, and other states. It is commonly said that the means that God has used to attain this end was to preserve in the human soul the idea of virtue and vice, and the awareness of a Providence that takes notice of everything, that punishes evil-doing and rewards good behavior. You will find this view in the commonplaces of theology and

---

[6] "The cause which prompts something to partake of a certain quality always partakes of that quality to a greater extent" (Aristotle, *Posterior Analytics* I. 2, and *Metaphysics* II. 1).

[7] I learned from a theologian that this is the word to use when one speaks of the providence of God, insofar as it has not allowed crimes to be carried so far as to destroy societies.

in an infinite number of other orthodox works. What is the natural consequence of this proposition? Is it not that, if there are some persons whom God does not abandon so much as to allow them to fall into the philosophy of Epicurus or the atheists, they are chiefly those ferocious souls whose cruelty, audacity, avarice, fury, and ambition would be capable of soon destroying all of a large country? Is it not that if he abandons certain people to the point that he allows them to deny either his existence or his providence, these are chiefly people whose dispositions of temperament, education, liveliness of ideas of virtue, love of glory, or dread of dishonor serve as a strong enough brake to keep them within the bounds of their duty? These are two consequences that naturally flow from the theological principle I stated above. Now, since, in informing my readers in certain sections of this dictionary that the greatest villains have professed some religion, and that persons who had none at all have lived in conformity with the laws of virtue, I have said nothing that does not accord with these two consequences, one has no longer any reasonable basis for being shocked.

XV. It will be much more legitimate to consider the finger of God and the admirable conduct of his providence as operating in this. He brings about the same end by various means. The *restraining* principle, so necessary for the preservation of societies, as the theologians teach, exerts its power with the brake of idolatry, by temperament in certain countries and in certain people, or by the liveliness of ideas and a taste for moral virtue in some others. The Greeks, who were ingenious and sensual, and thereby prone to the commission of a frightful series of crimes, had need of a religion that would obligate them to an infinite number of observances. They would have had too much time to devote to evil practices if the multitude of ceremonies, sacrifices, and oracles had not created enough distractions, and if superstitious terrors had not alarmed them. The Scythians, a crude people, who did not have much in the way of dress or food, had need only to despise sensual pleasures, or to be unaware of them. This alone supported their republic and kept them from doing wrong to one another. They were made in such a way that each was content with his lot. They had no need of a legal code or a list of what they should and should not do.

These are the fifteen considerations that seem to me sufficient to remove the stumbling block that some people have found in some sections of my dictionary. They could serve as the subject of a large work. I have contented myself with just setting them forth, since I have dealt with them elsewhere[10] in a little more extended fashion, or I will deal with them amply in a work that I have promised to write.[11]

---

10 In the *Pensées diverses sur la comète.*
11 See the Preface to the third edition of the *Pensées.*

SECOND CLARIFICATION

How what I have said about the objections of the Manicheans should be considered.

THOSE who are scandalized by certain things I have observed in the articles in which I have dealt with Manicheanism would have no excuse at all if they based this on the fact that I said that the question of the origin of evil is a very difficult one; all the Church Fathers frankly admitted this; and there is no orthodox theologian today who would not make the same admission. Therefore I believe that it is not in this that people have found a stumbling block, and I am convinced that they have only found it in the fact that I claimed that the objections of the Manicheans are unanswerable so long as they are examined only before the tribunal of reason.

This could not fail to be shocking to those whose great zeal for the evangelical truth convinces them that it triumphs in all kinds of disputes, no matter what arms are employed. They get so much pleasure from reading a book in which the doctrine of transubstantiation is knocked down, be it that it is opposed by sense evidence and by the principles of philosophy, or that it is opposed by Scripture and by the tradition of the first centuries; they get so much pleasure, I say, in such a complete victory that they easily convince themselves that all the disputes concerning orthodoxy are of the same kind. Happily charmed by such a sweet conviction, they are irritated and annoyed when they see someone affirm that all the articles of the Christian faith, maintained and opposed by the weapons of philosophy alone, do not emerge in good shape from the battle, and that there are some that give way and are forced to retire to the fortresses of Scripture and to request that in the future they have permission to arm themselves in a different way, for otherwise they would refuse to enter the fray.

Those who get angry at finding themselves thus harassed in their possession of an image of complete triumph are also afraid that in admitting a kind of inferiority, religion is exposed to a total defeat, or at least a notable lessening of its certainty, and that the cause of the enemies of the Gospel is aided.

An offense based on this has two favorable circumstances; the one, that it arises from a good principle; and the other, that it can easily be removed. It is the love of truth that produces it, and it is only necessary to go back to a consideration of the characteristics of the Gospel truths in order to be completely free of this uneasiness. For, it will be seen that, far from being a property of these truths that they conform to philosophy, it is, on the contrary, of their essence that they are incompatible with its dictates.[2]

Since the mysteries of the Gospel are above reason, it follows that the objections of unbelievers cannot be answered by the natural light. The Roman Catholics and the Protestants are at war over an innumerable number of articles of religion, but they are in agreement on this point, that the mysteries of the Gospel are above reason. There have even been theologians who have asserted that the mysteries denied by the Socinians are contrary to reason. I do not wish to take advantage of this assertion. It suffices for me that it is unanimously acknowledged that they are above reason; for it follows necessarily from this that it is impossible to solve the difficulties raised by philosophers; and, consequently, a dispute in which only the natural light will be employed will always end to the disadvantage of the theologians; and they will find themselves forced to give ground and take refuge under the protection of the supernatural light.

It is obvious that reason can never attain to what is above

---

[2] Restrict this to the Gospel truths in which the mysteries are contained, for it must be admitted that the moral precepts of Jesus Christ can easily be reconciled with the natural light.

itself. Now if it could furnish answers to the objections that are opposed to the doctrine of the Trinity and that of the hypostatic union, it would rise to the height of these two mysteries; it would subject them to herself; it would govern them and bend them until they could be measured by her first principles or the aphorisms that arise from common notions, and until it could at last conclude that they agree with the natural light. It would then do that which is beyond its strength. It would rise above its own limits, which is a downright contradiction. It must therefore be said that it cannot furnish at all answers to its own objections, and thus the objections remain victorious as long as one does not have recourse to the authority of God and the necessity of subjecting one's understanding to the obedience of the faith.

Let us try to make this clearer. If some doctrines are above reason, they are beyond its reach. If they are beyond its reach, it cannot rise to them. If it cannot rise to them, it cannot understand them. If it cannot understand them, it cannot discover any idea or principle that might be a source of a solution; and consequently the objections that it will have raised will remain unanswered, or, which is the same thing, they will be answered only by some distinction that is as obscure as the thesis itself that was attacked. Now it is very certain that an objection that is based on very clear notions remains equally victorious whether you make no response to it or whether you make a response that no one can understand. Can the match be equal between a man who objects to you on what you and he very clearly comprehend, and you who can only defend yourself by answers which neither you nor he can understand at all?

What the goal of a philosophical dispute is, and that this cannot be achieved when it turns on the mysteries. Every philosophical dispute supposes that the contesting parties agree on certain definitions, that they accept the rules of the syllogism and the signs by which bad arguments can be recognized. After that, the rest consists in examining whether a thesis conforms mediately or immediately to the agreed-upon principles,

whether the premises of a proof are true, whether the conclusion is properly derived, whether a syllogism with four terms
has been used, whether some fallacy or other has been committed, and so on. The victory is gained either by showing that
the subject under dispute has no connection with the principles
that were agreed upon, or by reducing an opponent's position
to an absurdity. Now the latter can be accomplished either by
showing that the consequences of his position are contradictory
or that he is forced to make only unintelligible answers. The
goal of this kind of dispute is to clarify obscurities and to find
something self-evident; and on this basis, during the course of
disputation, victory goes more or less to the sustaining party,
or the opposing one, according to whether there is more or less
clarity in the propositions of one than in the propositions of
the other; and at the end there is agreement that victory declares itself fully against the one whose answers are such that
they cannot be understood, and who admits that they are unintelligible. . . .

What has to be concluded from this is that the mysteries of
the Gospel, being of a supernatural kind, cannot and should
not be at all subject to the laws of the natural light. They were
not made to stand the test of philosophical disputations. Their
grandeur, their sublimity, does not permit them to submit to
it. It would be contrary to the nature of things for them to
emerge victorious from such a combat. Their essential characteristic is to be an object of faith and not an object of knowledge. They would no longer be mysteries if reason could resolve
all the difficulties concerning them. And thus, instead of finding
it strange that someone admits that philosophy can attack them
but not repel the attack, one ought to be scandalized if someone
said the opposite.[3]

If those whose scruples I desire to remove do not yield to
these considerations, perhaps finding something too abstract

---

[3] Observe that there is no desire here to condemn those who try to reconcile these mysteries with philosophy. Their motives can be good, and their
work can sometimes be beneficial, if it has God's blessings.

in them, I beg them to have recourse to some reflections which
are within everyone's grasp. I beg them to study a little the
spirit that reigns in the New Testament and in the mission of
the apostles.

Considerations about the way in which Jesus Christ, the
apostles, and the Church Fathers have taught. The disputative
spirit is that which seems to be least approved of in the Gospel
dispensation. The first thing Christ ordains is faith and submission. This is his usual beginning, and that of his apostles,
"Follow me,"[4] "Believe, and thou shalt be saved."[5] Now, this
faith that he demanded was not acquired by a series of philosophical discussions and a long series of reasonings. It was a
gift of God, a pure grace of the Holy Ghost, which ordinarily
descended only on ignorant persons.[6] It was not even produced
in the apostles by the effect of reflecting on the holiness of the
life of Jesus Christ and on the excellence of his doctrine and
his miracles. It was necessary that God himself reveal to them
that the person of whom they were disciples was his eternal
son.[7] If Jesus Christ and his apostles sometimes descended to
reasoning, they did not look for their proofs in the natural light,
but in the books of the prophets, and in miracles; and if St.
Paul sometimes made use of some *ad hominem* argument against
the gentiles, he did not insist on it very much. His method was
entirely different from that of the philosophers. The latter
boasted of possessing principles so evident, and a theory so
well connected, that they had to fear no other obstacle than
the stupidity of their auditors or the cunning malice of their
rivals; and they are willing to offer arguments for their theory
to everybody and to maintain it against all comers. St. Paul,
on the contrary, acknowledges that his theory is obscure, and
that he knows it only imperfectly;[8] and that it cannot be com-

---

4 Luke 5:27 and 9:59.
5 Acts 16:31.
6 Matthew 11:25.
7 *Ibid.,* 16:17.
8 I Corinthians 13:12.

prehended unless God communicates a spiritual discernment, and without this, it must be considered as foolishness.[9] He admits[10] that most of the people converted by the apostles were of low condition and ignorant. He does not challenge philosophers to dispute with him, and he exhorts the faithful to be carefully on guard against philosophy,[11] and to avoid contests with philosophy, which had already destroyed the faith of some persons.[12]

The Church Fathers were governed by the same attitude. They demanded an immediate submission to the authority of God, and they regarded philosophical disputes as one of the greatest obstacles that the true faith could encounter.[13]

. . . .

This passage from St. Paul, "We walk by faith, and not by sight,"[19] alone should suffice to convince us that there is nothing to gain from one philosopher to another for the person who undertakes either to prove the mysteries of the Christian religion or to take the defensive position. For here is what the difference between the faith of a Christian and the knowledge of a philosopher consists in. This faith produces a perfect certitude, but its object will never be evident. Knowledge, on the other hand, produces together both complete evidence of the object and full certainty of conviction.* If a Christian then undertakes to maintain the mystery of the Trinity against a philosopher, he would oppose a nonevident object to evident objections. Would this not be to fight blindfolded and with

---

9 *Ibid.*, 2:14.

10 *Ibid.*, 1:26.

11 Colossians 2:8.

12 I Timothy 6:20, 21.

13 See the passages from the Church Fathers that De Launoi has compiled in the second chapter of his book *De varia Aristotelis fortuna.*

19 II Corinthians 5:7.

* [Compare this passage with what Kierkegaard says about subjective and objective certainty in the *Concluding Unscientific Postscript,* tr. David F. Swenson, completed by Walter Lowrie (Princeton: Princeton University Press, 1960), Bk. II, Pt. II, esp. chaps. 1–3.]

hands tied while having as an antagonist a man who can make use of all his faculties? If it were the case that the Christian could answer all the objections raised by the philosopher without making use of anything but the principles of the natural light, it would not be true, as St. Paul affirms, that we walk by faith and not by sight. Knowledge, and not divine faith, would be the Christian's share.

Can anyone be scandalized by an avowal that is a natural consequence of the evangelical spirit and the doctrine of St. Paul?

Maxims common to the Catholic and Protestant theologians. If these reflections on the conduct of the early centuries are not sufficient to make an impression, if, I say, such objects considered from afar do not make a sufficient impression, I request that one be willing to take the trouble to examine the maxims of modern theologians. The Roman Catholics and the Protestants agree in saying that reason must be rejected when it is a question of judging a controversy about the mysteries. This amounts to saying that one must never agree to this condition, that if the literal sense of a passage in Scripture contains some inconceivable doctrines, such as are opposed to the most evident maxims of the logicians and the metaphysicians, it shall be declared false, and that reason, philosophy, the natural light, will be the measure to be used for deciding that one given interpretation of Scripture is preferable to any other. They [the Roman Catholic and Protestant theologians] not only say that all persons should be rejected who stipulate such a thing as a preliminary condition for dispute, but they also maintain that these are persons who tread a path that can only lead to Pyrrhonism, or to deism, or to atheism; so that the most necessary barrier for preserving the religion of Jesus Christ is the obligation to submit oneself to the authority of God, and to believe humbly in the mysteries that it has pleased him to reveal to us, however inconceivable they may be, and however impossible they may appear to our reason.

. . . .

The sixth objection is that I have not refuted the Manicheans.
The difficulty that remains for me to examine will detain us
a little while. It is based on the claim that I reported at length
what objections the Manicheans could make and that I have
not taken the trouble to produce the arguments that refute
them. Here is something to satisfy all reasonable readers about
the grumbling on this matter. There were four reasons which
made me not refute Manicheanism.

The first is that in the present disposition of mankind there
is no heresy that is less to be feared than this one. People can
only be horrified by an hypothesis that allows for an eternal
and uncreated nature, distinct from God, and an enemy of God,
and essentially wicked. And, as for freethinkers or those in
general who have cultivated the study of metaphysics, and who
have a penchant for misusing it, there is nothing they dislike
more than the multiplicity of principles. Their depraved taste
leads them rather to be perfect Unitarians[68] than to declare
themselves in favor of dualism.

In the second place, all Christians, no matter how ignorant
they may be, include omnipotence and infinity so clearly in the
idea of the divine nature that they have no need for borrowed
arms in order to combat Manicheans. This idea alone makes
them strong enough in an offensive war. They find enough
there to refute solidly that hypothesis of the Manicheans. I
therefore believe that it was not necessary to point out to any of
my readers how that doctrine had to be attacked.

In the third place, the observation I made and expatiated on
sufficiently in remark D of the article "Manicheans" [p. 144]
contains all that is necessary to make those of sound judgment
dislike the doctrine of two principles. I said that the worth of
a theory consists in that it contains nothing repugnant to

---

68 It is thus for brevity that one might call those who, along with the
Spinozists, acknowledge only one substance in the universe; but note that
below I ascribe this name to those who acknowledge only one first cause of
all things.

evident ideas and it accounts for the phenomena. I added that the Manichean theory has, at the most, only the advantage of explaining several phenomena that strangely perplex the followers of the unity of principle; but for the rest, it [the Manichean theory] is based on a supposition that is repugnant to our clearest ideas, whereas the other theory [the Unitary one] is based upon such notions. By this sole remark, I attribute superiority to the Unitarians and take it away from the dualists; for all those who are acquainted with reasoning are in accord that a system is much more imperfect when it lacks the first of the two qualities mentioned above than when it lacks the second one. If it is built on an absurd, perplexed, and improbable supposition, this is not compensated for by the happy explanation of phenomena. But if it does not explain them in a completely satisfactory fashion, this is compensated for by the clearness, probability, and conformity that is found in it with the laws and ideas of order; and those who have embraced it because of this perfection have not been accustomed to be disheartened under the pretext that they cannot account for all the items of experience. They ascribe this defect to the limited nature of their understanding, and they think that with enough time an actual means will be found for resolving the difficulties. A Cartesian philosopher, finding himself harried by an objection concerning the principle given by Descartes about the ebb and flow of the sea, replied, among other things, that an opinion must not lightly be given up, "and particularly when it is well grounded in other respects. It was objected to Copernicus, when he proposed his theory, that Mars and Venus would appear of a much greater magnitude at a certain time because they approached the earth by several diameters. This consequence was necessary, and yet nothing like this was seen. Though he did not know what answers to give, he did not believe that his theory ought to be abandoned on this account. He only said that time would show this, and that perhaps the difficulty was the result of the great distance involved. This answer was taken as an admission of defeat, and with some

justice. But after the telescope was invented, it was found that
this same item that had been raised as a great objection is the
confirmation of the Copernican theory and the destruction of
the Ptolemaic one."[71]

By the way, observe here a beautiful example of what I said
about the perfections of a theory. That of Copernicus is so
easy, so simple, so mechanical that it ought to be preferred to
that of Ptolemy, even though it might be less successful in explaining some phenomena.

Finally, my fourth reason is that I pointed to a remedy so
good and so certain that it would have been superfluous to make
use of any other expedient to make up for the disadvantage. The
dualistic theory provides a better explanation of several facts
than that of the Unitarians; but on the other hand, it contains
some monstrous absurdities that are in direct opposition to our
ideas of order. The theory of the Unitarians enjoys the opposite
perfection to that defect; and thus, all things being duly considered, it is preferable to the other. This could have sufficed in
some fashion, but I was not satisfied with it. I observed further
that the theory of the Unitarians was in accord with Scripture,
and that of the dualists was invincibly refuted by the Word of
God. What could one desire that is stronger and more demonstrative in order to be sure that the theory of the Unitarians is
true, and the other false? In order to remove all scruples, was
it necessary besides this that I should refute philosophically
the Manichean theory? Would not one be of little faith if he
had need of such a discussion? God speaks, and that does not
completely convince you? You want more security, you wish
that his testimony be ratified by human reason? Is that not
unworthy of a man who has not lost his common sense? Do you
fear the objections of the Manicheans when you accept revealed
authority? Why do you not say with Scripture, "If God is with
us, who shall be against us?"[73] You cannot answer the difficulties

---

[71] Gadroys, *Lettre à M. de la Grange-Trianon, pour servir de réponse à
celle que M. Castelet a écrite.*

[73] Romans 8:21.

they pose to you about the origin of evil and the decrees of reprobation? Well then, tell them what the lesser catechism of the Reformed Churches answers to this question about the Trinity: "How can this be? It is a secret that surpasses our understanding and yet is very certain; FOR GOD DECLARED IT TO US SO BY HIS WORD."[74] Every philosophical subtlety that tends to remove the conviction of heavenly truth in you should be considered as one of those attacks that St. Paul requires to have repulsed with "the shield of faith."[75] Take it up then, and you will have sufficient good arms; and think carefully that in fearing that this would not be enough you would expose yourself to the jeering that was directed at a cardinal who pitied the popes when they had no other assistance at all save that of the Holy Ghost.[76] ...

But let us nowadays have some regard for persons of little faith.

. . . .

Conclusion of this Clarification. Those who will take the trouble to consider attentively all I have set forth in this Clarification will no doubt cease to be shocked by what has been complained about in the article "Paulicians," and others. They will see that this article and those in which the same subject has been treated can be read without giving offense, and even with edification, provided that one keeps in mind:

I. That it is the property of the Gospel mysteries to be liable to objections that the natural light cannot clear up.

II. That unbelievers cannot justly draw any advantage from the fact that the maxims of philosophy cannot furnish any

---

[74] *Petit Catechisme,* Sec. II.

[75] Ephesians 6:16.

[76] "If the popes, who have only God behind them, are pitied by Cardinal Pallavicini, a Jesuit, and appear as unhappy to the rest of mankind, how could they convert the Mohammedans? Some other aid than that of the Holy Ghost must then be needed for such conversions, and indeed it would be a great pity if the pope had no other assistance than that" (*Evangile nouveau du Cardinal Palavicin,* Chap. IV, Article I).

solution at all to the difficulties that they can set forth against
the mysteries of the Gospel.

III. That the objections of the Manicheans on the origin of
evil and predestination ought not to be considered in general
as impugning predestination, but with this particular consideration that the origin of evil, the decrees of God thereupon, and
the like, form one of the most incomprehensible mysteries of
Christianity.

IV. That it ought to suffice for every good Christian that his
faith is based on the testimony of the Word of God.

V. That the Manichean theory, considered in itself, is absurd,
indefensible, and contrary to the ideas of order; that it is subject
to being answered in kind, and that it cannot remove the
difficulties.

VI. That, in any case, no one should be scandalized by what
I said without also regarding the doctrine of the most orthodox
theologians as scandalous, since everything that I have said
is a natural and inevitable consequence of their views, and that
I have only related, in a more prolix way, what they have taught
more concisely.

There will perhaps be some people who will find my refutation of Manicheanism imperfect because I do not answer the
objections set forth by me as made by the Manicheans. I beg
those who are bothered about this to remember that as for
evident answers drawn from the natural light, I do not know of
any, and as for answers that Scripture can furnish, they are
found in innumerable controversial books.

Those who ask about the utility or the *cui bono* of the discussions which have displeased them will find my answer in the
third Clarification.

THIRD CLARIFICATION

What has been said about Pyrrhonism in this diction-ary cannot be harmful to religion.

I. As THE basis of this third Clarification I set forth at the outset this certain and incontestable maxim, *that the Christian re-ligion is of a supernatural kind, and that its basic component is the supreme authority of God proposing mysteries to us, not so that we may understand them, but so that we may believe them with all the humility that is due to the infinite being, who can neither deceive nor be deceived.* This is the polar star of all the discussions and all the disputes about the articles of religion that God has revealed to us through Jesus Christ.

From this it necessarily follows that the tribunal of philosophy is incompetent to judge controversies between Christians, since they ought to be carried only to the tribunal of revelation.

Every dispute about the question of religion's prerogatives ought to be rejected from the very first word. No one ought to be allowed to examine whether it is necessary to believe what God orders us to believe. This ought to be accepted as a first principle in matters of religion. It is up to the metaphysicians to examine whether there is a God and whether he is infallible;[1] but Christians, insofar as they are Christians, ought to suppose that this is something already decided.

Then it is only a question of fact, namely, whether God re-quires that we believe this or that. Two sorts of people can have doubts about this, some because they do not believe that Scripture is divine, others because they do not believe that the sense of Scripture is such and such.

---

[1] See above, remark L of the second article "Maldonat" [not included in these selections].

Every dispute, then, that Christians can engage in with philosophers is on this question of fact, whether Scripture was written by authors inspired by God. If the proofs offered by the Christians on this subject do not convince the philosophers, the controversy ought to be discontinued; for it would be useless to go into a detailed examination of the doctrine of the Trinity, and the like, with people who do not acknowledge the divinity of Scripture, the sole and unique means of judging who is wrong or who is right in such controversies. Revealed authority ought to be the common principle of the disputants on this matter; and thus there is no more dispute when one of the parties does not admit this principle and the other does; "It is pointless to dispute with a person who denies the principles."

If those who do not admit it stubbornly persist in scolding and disputing, they ought to be told coldly, "You depart from the question, you do not establish the thesis, you do not prove the negative." And if they laugh at this response, their derision must be pitied.

II. *The nature of the Pyrrhonists.* Now, of all the philosophers who ought not to be permitted to dispute about the mysteries of Christianity until they have accepted Revelation as the criterion, there are none as unworthy of being heard as the followers of Pyrrhonism; for they are people who profess to acknowledge no certain sign that distinguishes the true from the false; so that if, by chance, they came across the truth, they could never be sure that it was the truth. They are not satisfied with opposing the testimony of the senses, the maxims of morality, the rules of logic, and the axioms of metaphysics; they also try to overthrow the demonstrations of the geometers, and all that the mathematicians can produce of the most evident character. If they stopped at the ten modes or tropes for suspending judgment,* and if they had limited themselves to employing them against natural science, they could still be dealt

* [These are the set of arguments appearing in Sextus Empiricus, *Pyrrhoniarum hypotoposeon* I. 14, dealing mainly with sense data, relativism, etc.]

with. But they go much further; they have a kind of weapon that they call the *diallelos*,[2] which they wield at the first instant it is needed. After this is done, it is impossible to withstand them on any subject whatsoever. It is a labyrinth in which the thread of Ariadne cannot be of any help. They lose themselves in their own subtleties; and they are overjoyed at this, since this serves to show more clearly the universality of their hypothesis, that all is uncertain, not even excepting the arguments that attack uncertainty. Their method leads people so far that those who have really seen the consequences of it are forced to admit that they do not know if anything exists.[3]

Theologians should not be ashamed to admit that they cannot enter a contest with such antagonists, and that they do not want to expose the Gospel truths to such an attack. The bark of Jesus Christ is not made for sailing on this stormy sea, but for taking shelter from this tempest in the haven of faith. It has pleased the Father, the Son, and the Holy Ghost, Christians ought to say, to lead us by the path of faith, and not by the path of knowledge or disputation. They are our teachers and our directors. We cannot lose our way with such guides. And reason itself commands us to prefer them to its direction.

But is it not quite scandalous, I will be told, that you have related, without refuting it, the claim made by an *abbé* that Pyrrhonism finds several arguments in the doctrines of the Christians that make it more formidable than it ever was before? I answer that this can only offend those who have not sufficiently examined the character of Christianity. It would be a very false supposition to think that Jesus Christ has had any sort of plan of favoring, either directly or indirectly, any one sect of philosophers in their disputes with other ones. His plan was rather to confound all philosophy and to show its vanity. He wanted

---

2 See Sextus Empiricus, *Pyrrhoniarum hypotoposeon* II. 4, and I. 16. [This weapon purports to show that the adversary is involved in either circular reasoning or an infinite regress.]

3 See what Sextus Empiricus, in *Adversus mathematicos* VII. 65ff., says of Gorgias of Leontini; and see above, article "Zeno of Elea," remark E [p. 350].

his Gospel to strike against not only the religion of the pagans, but also the aphorisms of their wisdom; and notwithstanding this contrast between his principles and those of the world, the Gospel would triumph over the gentiles by the ministry of a small number of ignorant people who made use neither of eloquence, nor dialectic, nor any of the tools needed in all other revolutions. He desired that his disciples and the wise men of this world be so diametrically opposed that they should consider each other fools. He wished that, as his Gospel would appear as foolishness to the philosophers, their knowledge in turn should appear as folly to the Christians. Read carefully these words of St. Paul: "For Christ sent me not to baptize but to preach the Gospel: not with wisdom of words, lest the cross of Christ should be made of none effect. For the preaching of the cross is to them that perish foolishness; but unto us which are saved it is the power of God. For it is written, 'I will destroy the wisdom of the wise and will bring to nothing the understanding of the prudent.' Where is the wise? Where is the scribe? Where is the disputer of this world? Hath not God made foolish the wisdom of this world? For after that in the wisdom of God the world by wisdom knew not God, it pleased God by the foolishness of preaching to save them that believe. For the Jews require a sign, and the Greeks seek after wisdom. But we preach Christ crucified, unto the Jews a stumbling block, and unto the Greeks foolishness, but unto them which are called, both Jews and Greeks, Christ the power of God, and the wisdom of God. Because the foolishness of God is wiser than men; and the weakness of God is stronger than men. For ye see your calling, brethren, how that not many wise men after the flesh, not many mighty, not many noble are called. But God hath chosen the foolish things of the world to confound the wise; and God hath chosen the weak things of the world to confound the things which are mighty; and base things of the world, and things which are despised hath God chosen, yea, and things which are not, to bring to nought things that are: that no flesh should glory in his presence. But of him are ye in Christ Jesus, who of God is made

unto us wisdom, and righteousness, and sanctification, and redemption: that, according as it is written, 'He that glorieth, let
him glory in the Lord.' And I, brethren, when I came to you,
came not with excellency of speech or of wisdom, declaring
unto you the testimony of God. For I determined not to know
any thing among you, save Jesus Christ, and him crucified. And
I was with you in weakness, and in fear, and in much trembling.
And my speech and my preaching was not with enticing words
of man's wisdom, but in demonstration of the Spirit and of
power: that your faith should not stand in the wisdom of men,
but in the power of God. Howbeit we speak wisdom among
them that are perfect: yet not the wisdom of this world, nor of
the princes of this world, that come to nought. But we speak the
wisdom of God in a mystery, even the hidden wisdom, which
God ordained before the world unto our glory; which none of
the princes of this world knew; for had they known it, they
would not have crucified the Lord of glory. But as it is written,
'Eye hath not seen, nor ear heard, neither have entered into the
heart of man, the things which God hath prepared for them
that love him.' But God hath revealed them unto us by his
Spirit: for the Spirit searcheth all things, yea, the deep things
of God. For what man knoweth the things of a man, save the
spirit of man which is in him? Even so the things of God
knoweth no man, but the Spirit of God. Now we have received,
not the spirit of the world, but the Spirit which is of God; that
we might know the things that are freely given to us of God.
Which things also we speak, not in the words which man's
wisdom teacheth, but which the Holy Ghost teacheth; comparing spiritual things with spiritual. But the natural man
receiveth not the things of the Spirit of God: for they are foolishness unto him: neither can he know them, because they are
spiritually discerned."[5]

III. Do you believe that if anyone had said to the apostles

---

[5] I Corinthians 1:17–2:14. [This Scriptural text has been the favorite of
the so-called Christian skeptics. It is cited over and over again by Montaigne,
Charron, La Mothe le Vayer, and others.]

that their doctrine exposed the dogmatic philosophers to new attack from Pyrrhonists, that they would have cared about this? "Let us not trouble ourselves about disputes with those people," they would have said; "let the dead bury the dead. The more they shall fight and mangle one another, the better can the vanity of their alleged knowledge be seen. Neither the dogmatists nor the skeptics will ever be capable of entering the kingdom of heaven if they do not become like little children, if they do not change their maxims, if they do not renounce their wisdom, and if they do not make a burnt offering of their vain theories at the foot of the cross, to the alleged foolishness of our preaching. This is the old man whom they should chiefly put away* before being in the condition to receive the celestial gift and to enter upon the paths of faith, the road chosen by God for eternal salvation. If the Pyrrhonists abuse our mysteries in order to root themselves still more in uncertainty, and if they oppose us with *ad hominem* arguments, so much the worse for them, unless God makes use of their errors to make them understand better the necessity for submission to his Word." This is what St. Paul and his fellow disciples would have replied to such difficulties. One ought to be completely convinced that had the occasion presented itself for them to give their decision about the nature of pagan philosophy on the basis of whether it facilitated or made more difficult conversion to the Gospel, they would have stated positively that the method, the principles, the usages, and the disputes of the Peripatetics, Academics, and others were so great an obstacle to faith that the most necessary preliminary for entering into the kingdom of God was to forget or lay aside the entire content of false knowledge.[6] I believe that they would have stated this for the present time and for the time to come. . . .

---

* [Colossians 3:9.]

6 These words of Jesus Christ in the Gospel according to St. John (3:3), "Except a man be born again, he cannot see the kingdom of God," are chiefly true with regard to philosophers. They have more need of being reborn than other men. The require one regeneration as men, and another as philosophers.

All ages have required and will require that knowledge of the revealed truths be sought by different means than those of philosophy. Philosophy does not cure the mental wavering that ought to be cured if one hopes by prayer to obtain true wisdom for us. Let us cite an apostle on this. "If any of you lack wisdom, let him ask of God, that giveth to all men liberally and upbraideth not; and it shall be given him. But let him ask in faith, nothing wavering. For he that wavereth is like a wave of the sea driven with the wind and tossed. For let not that man think that he shall receive any thing of the Lord."[8] Judge, I beg of you, whether the Pyrrhonists, who are always much more in their element when the efforts they employ to invent reasons for doubting everything have succeeded in providing them with specious objections against certitude, are people who are susceptible of receiving grace by means of disputation. The modern missionaries of the Gospel ought to treat them as the first ones would have done. They ought to advise them to rid themselves of all spirit of contention, and to believe in God on his Word; and, in case they find them intractable, they ought especially to remember this precept of the great St. Paul and apply it to the people in question, "But avoid foolish questions, and genealogies, and contentions, and strivings about the law; for they are unprofitable and vain. A man that is a heretic after the first and second admonition reject."[9] It would be very nice to see our Thomists and our Scotists undertaking to convert the New World by maintaining theses in the European fashion. They would make very poor converters. . . . Their public disputations change nobody. Everyone departs from them with the same opinions he arrived with. If the Thomistic explanations of our mysteries were proposed to the learned Chinese, and if they asked, "How shall we believe this, when we have no idea of it at all?" one would do well to send them, not to a disputa-

---

8 James 1:5–7.
9 Titus 3:9–10.

tion, but to an answer like the one the angel Gabriel made to the Virgin.[10]

Today, as in the time of Lactantius, it can be affirmed that the search for the true religion ought to be carried on by examining the alleged and apparent foolishness under which God has hidden the treasures of his wisdom.[11] "What can be the cause why wisdom, after having been sought for during so many ages with the utmost pains and application by the greatest geniuses, should not yet be found, unless it be that philosophers have sought for it outside its own limits, that is, where it cannot be found? But since the philosophers in question, after inquiring into and searching all things, have not been able to find wisdom anywhere, and since it is absolutely necessary for it to be somewhere, it is plain that it ought to be chiefly sought after there where the characteristics of foolishness appear, under the veil whereof, God, lest the mysteries of his divine work should be discovered, concealed the treasure of wisdom and truth."[12] The same Lactantius has judiciously observed in another place that it becomes the supreme majesty of God to speak as a teacher, and to speak in a few words that are true, and not to argue and to add proofs to his declarations. . . .

From all that I have just said, it is easy to conclude that one cannot be alarmed by the Pyrrhonian objections without revealing the weakness of his faith, and without grasping on the wrong side what should be taken by the right handle.

IV. A true believer, a Christian, who knows the spirit of his religion well, does not expect to see it conform to the aphorisms of the Lyceum, or to be capable of refuting, merely by the strength of reason, the difficulties of reason. He is well aware that natural things are not proportional to supernatural ones, and that if a philosopher were asked to put on a level basis and in a perfect harmony the Gospel mysteries and the Aristotelian

---

10 " 'How shall this be, seeing I know not a man?' And the angel answered and said unto her, 'The Holy Ghost shall come upon thee, and the power of the Highest shall overshadow thee' " (Luke 1:34–35).

11 This is to be understood with regard to the infidels.

12 Lactantius, IV. 2.

axioms, one would be requesting of him what the nature of things will not permit. One must necessarily choose between philosophy and the Gospel. If you do not want to believe anything but what is evident and in conformity with the common notions, choose philosophy and leave Christianity. If you are willing to believe the incomprehensible mysteries of religion, choose Christianity and leave philosophy. For to have together self-evidence and incomprehensibility is something that cannot be. The combination of these two items is hardly more impossible than the combination of the properties of a square and a circle. A choice must necessarily be made. If the advantages of a round table do not satisfy you, have a square one made; and do not pretend that the same table could furnish you with the advantages of both a round table and a square one. Once again, a true Christian, well versed in the characteristics of supernatural truths and firm on the principles that are peculiar to the Gospel, will only laugh at the subtleties of the philosophers, and especially those of the Pyrrhonists. Faith will place him above the regions where the tempests of disputation reign. He will stand on a peak, from which he will hear below him the thunder of arguments and distinctions; and he will not be disturbed at all by this—a peak, which will be for him the real Olympus of the poets and the real temple of the sages, from which he will see in perfect tranquility the weaknesses of reason and the meanderings of mortals who only follow that guide. Every Christian who allows himself to be disconcerted by the objections of the unbelievers, and to be scandalized by them, has one foot in the same grave as they do.

V. *Answer to those who ask what need there was to mention the objections that the Gospel mysteries can furnish to the Pyrrhonists.* What I am going to say about this will be able to show us how important it is to know the right use of things. Many people have asked, What was the use of this display of the Pyrrhonian and Manichaean difficulties? They could have found the answer to this question if they had looked for it in my dictionary, where it appears in a hundred places, most notably in remark C [p. 204] of article "Pyrrho."[17] But, since they would not or could not look into this, let us examine their problem here at greater length. I do not see that they would have too much to complain about reasonably if I contented myself with asking them, What is the use of so many of the details that historians give us? Is it not certain that they present some of them whose entire utility consists in giving the reader some pleasure, and which can even do harm in the hands of those who make bad use of the best of things? Does this excuse the historians from the obligation of reporting the truth as accurately as possible? Then, is it not necessary that a historian of ideas show accurately and amply the strength and the weakness of them, though this might accidentally give rise to some disorders, and though it might only give rise to the amusement of his readers and might serve only as an example of the regard that ought to be had for the laws of history? But this is neither the sole nor the chief answer that I have to offer.

Nothing is more necessary than faith, and nothing is more important than to make people aware of the price of this theological virtue. Now, what is there that is more suitable for making us aware of this than meditating on the attitude that distinguishes it from the other acts of the understanding? Its essence consists in binding us to the revealed truths by a strong conviction, and in binding us to these solely by the motive of God's authority. Those who believe in the immortality of the soul on the basis of philosophical reasons are orthodox, but so far they have no share in the faith of which we are speaking. They only have a share in it insofar as they believe this doctrine because God has revealed it to us, and they submit humbly to the voice of God everything that philosophy presents to them that is most plausible for convincing them of the mortality of the soul. Thus, the merit of faith becomes greater in proportion as the revealed truth that is its object surpasses all the powers of our mind; for, as the incomprehensibility of this object increases by the greater number of maxims of the natural light

---

17 See also the article "Zeno of Elea," remark G [p. 359].

that oppose it, we have to sacrifice to God's authority a stronger reluctance of reason; and consequently we show ourselves more submissive to God, and we give him greater signs of our respect than if the item were only moderately difficult to believe. Why was it, I ask you, that the faith of the Father of the faithful [Abraham] was of so great a degree? Is it not because it was he "who against hope believed in hope" (Romans 4:18)? There would not have been very much merit in hoping, on the basis of God's promise, for something that was very probable naturally. The merit therefore consisted in this, that the hope of this promise was opposed by all kinds of appearances. Let us say also that the highest degree of faith is that which embraces on divine testimony truths that are the most opposed to reason.

This view has been set forth in a ridiculous light, coming from the pen of a master. "The devil take me if I believed anything," the Maréchal d'Hocquincourt is made to say, "but since that time I could bear to be crucified for religion. It is not that I see more reason in it than I did before; on the contrary, I see less than ever. But I know not what to say to you, for I would submit to be crucified without knowing why or wherefore." "So much the better, my Lord," replied the father, twanging it very devoutly through the nose, "so much the better; these are not human impulses but are inspired by heaven. Away with reason; this is the true religion, away with reason. What an extraordinary grace, my Lord, has heaven bestowed upon you! 'Be ye as little children.' Children are still in their state of innocence; and why? Because they are not endowed with reason. 'Blessed are the poor in spirit.' They commit no sin, and for this reason, because they are not endowed with reason. 'No reason; I know not why nor wherefore.' Beautiful words! They ought to be written in gold letters. 'It is not that I see more reason in it than I did before; on the contrary, I see less than ever.' This is really altogether divine to those who delight in celestial things. 'Away with reason.' What an extraordinary grace, my Lord, has heaven bestowed upon you!"[19] If one gives

---

19 "Conversation between Maréchal d'Hocquincourt and Father Canaye," in *Œuvres mêlées de St. Evremont,* Vol. IV. [St. Evremond, or Charles de

this passage a more serious and modest air, it will become reasonable.

.   .   .   .

VI . . . . I am going to cite two Protestants whose testimony ought to carry more weight because their professions are such as are not reputed to humble reason in order to exalt faith, the one being a physician and the other a mathematician. The former declares that when he meditates on the mysteries, he stops when reason come to this, *O Altitudo!*[21] He protests that if rebellious reason or Satan endeavor to perplex him, he escapes from all their traps by this single paradox of Tertullian, "It is certain because it is impossible" ("Certum est, quia impossibile"). . . . "There are people," he continues, "who find it easier to believe because they have seen the sepulcher of Jesus Christ and the Red Sea. But, as for myself, I am happy about not having seen either Jesus Christ or his apostles and about not having lived in the times of miracles. My faith would then have been involuntary, and I would have had no share in this blessing; "Blessed are they that have not seen, and yet believed." He forms for himself an exalted idea of the faith of those who lived before Jesus Christ; for although they possessed only shadows, signs, and some obscure oracles, they waited for things that seemed to be impossible. "Some believe the better for seeing Christ's sepulcher, and when they have seen the Red Sea, doubt not of the miracle. Now, contrarily, I bless myself and am thankful that I lived not in the days of miracles, that I never

---

Marguetel de St. Denis, Seigneur de Saint Evremond, was a major *libertin* writer of the seventeenth century.]

21 "I chose to lose myself in a mystery, to pursue my reason to an *O Altitudo!*" (Sir Thomas Browne, *Religio Medici*, Pt. I, sec. 8). [*O Altitudo* refers to Romans 11:33–36: "O the depth of the riches both of the wisdom and knowledge of God! How unsearchable are his judgments, and his ways past finding out! For who hath known the mind of the Lord? Or who hath been his counselor? Or who hath first given to him and it shall be recompensed unto him again? For of him, and through him, are all things: to whom be glory forever. Amen."]

saw Christ nor his disciples, that I was not one of those Israelites who passed through the Red Sea, nor one of Christ's patients on whom he wrought his wonders; then my faith would have been thrust upon me; nor should I enjoy that greatest blessing pronounced to all that believe and saw not. It is an easy and necessary belief to credit what our eye and sense hath examined; I believe he was dead and buried and rose again, and desire to see him in his glory, rather than to contemplate him in his cenotaph or sepulcher. Nor is this much to believe; in all fairness, we owe this faith unto history; they only had the advantage of a bold and noble faith who lived before his coming, who upon obscure prophecies and mystical types could raise a belief and expect apparent impossibilities."[23] . . . "Yet do I believe that all this is true which indeed my reason would persuade me to be false; and this I think is no vulgar part of faith, to believe a thing not only above, but contrary to, reason and against the arguments of our proper senses."[25]

Note that this writer speaks this way in a book entitled *Religio Medici (The Religion of the Physician)*, which according to some people, might be entitled, *The Physician of Religion*, a work, in a word, that has made some people believe that the author was a bit remote from the kingdom of heaven.[26] One could then apply to him these words of the Gospel, "I have not found so great faith, no, not in Israel" (Matthew 8:10).

VII. The mathematician I am to cite published a work of thirty-six pages in London in 1699 entitled *Theologiae christianae principia mathematica* [*Mathematical Principles of Christian Theology*].* He claims that the principles of the

---

23 *Ibid.*

25 *Ibid.*

26 "This author is a melancholic, agreeable in his thoughts, but who, in my judgment, is seeking for a teacher in religious matters, like many others; and perhaps in the end he will not find any" (Guy Patin, Letter III in Vol. I).

* [The Latin text and an English translation of a good part of this work have recently appeared in *History and Theory*, Supplement 4 (1964), entitled "Craig's Rules of Historical Evidence (1699)."]

Christian religion are only probable, and he reduces to geo-
metric calculations the degrees of their probability and those of
the decrease of this probability. He finds that it [the Christian
religion] can last 1,454 years more, from whence he concludes
that Jesus Christ will return by then. He dedicates this work to
the bishop of Salisbury and observes in his dedicatory epistle
that those who will blame him for calling the principles of
Christianity only probable will be people who have neither
carefully examined the basis of their religion nor understood
well the nature of faith. How does it happen, he says, that so
many encomiums are bestowed on this virtue in Scripture, and
so many rewards are promised to him who will embrace it? Is
it not because it leads men into the right way in spite of the
stumbling blocks and the fetters that they meet with? Let us
give his words. "I do not doubt but there will be some persons,
who, having more zeal than judgment, will absolutely condemn
my book and too rashly conclude that I rather destroy than
contribute to the advantage of religion. For the persons in
question, considering all the doctrines of the Christian religion
as most certain, will conclude that I attempted a work altogether
unworthy of the Christian profession since I therein endeavored
to show only the probability of the religion in question. To such
persons I have no more to say than this, that, being blinded by
prejudice, they have not examined with sufficient accuracy the
grounds of the religion they profess nor understood rightly the
nature of faith, which is so highly applauded in the Scriptures.
For what is faith but that persuasion of the mind whereby, by
reasons drawn from probability, we believe certain propositions
to be true. If the persuasion results from certainty, in that case
knowledge, not faith, is produced in the mind; for as probability
begets faith, so it destroys knowledge, and, on the contrary,
certainty begets knowledge and destroys faith. Thus, knowledge
removes all occasion for doubting, whereas faith never fails to
leave some hesitation in the mind. The reason why so many
encomiums are bestowed upon faith, and so many rewards are
annexed to it, is that mankind, notwithstanding the many

scruples that disturb their minds, do yet tread the straight path of virtue and piety and strive, with their utmost endeavors, to do all they think will be pleasing to their almighty Creator. They discover so great a readiness in obeying all the divine commands that they will not reject such as seem to be but probably such."[28]

VIII. *That it is of use to set forth at large reasoned lists of the difficulties of faith.* There are so many people who so little examine the nature of divine faith and who so rarely reflect on this act of their minds that they have need to be removed from their indolence by long lists of the difficulties that surround the doctrines of the Christian religion. It is through a lively awareness of these difficulties that one learns of the excellence of faith and of this blessing of heaven. In the same way one also learns of the necessity of mistrusting reason and of having recourse to grace. Those who have never been present at the mighty contests between reason and faith, and who do not know the strength of philosophical objections, do not know a considerable share of the obligation they owe to God and do not know about the method for triumphing over all the temptations of incredulous and proud reason.

The real means of taming it is to realize that if it is capable of inventing objections, it is incapable of finding any way of unraveling them, and that in a word, it is not through reason that the Gospel has been established. . . .

And here, it seems to me, is more than is necessary to dissipate the scruples to which the alleged triumphs of the Pyrrhonists had given rise in the minds of some of my readers.*

---

28 John Craig, Dedicatory Epistle.

* [Throughout this entire Clarification there are striking similarities to some of Kierkegaard's views on the relationship of faith and reason, and on the nature of faith. Compare what Bayle has said here with the views presented in Kierkegaard's *Philosophical Fragments, Concluding Unscientific Postscript, Fear and Trembling,* and *Training in Christianity.* If the reader is interested, he can find more details in Richard Popkin, "Kierkegaard and Scepticism," *Algemeen Nederlands Tijdscrift voor Wijsbegeerte en Psychologie,* 51 (1959), 123–141; and "Theological and Religious Scepticism," *Christian Scholar,* 39 (1956), 150–158.

FOURTH CLARIFICATION

If there are obscenities in this book, they are of such kind that they cannot be justly criticized.

. . . .

That the most delicate terms pollute the imagination as much as the coarsest ones. For this I have need only to prove this single proposition: "The coarsest expressions and the most decent that can be employed to designate an obscene matter paint it with equal vivacity and distinctness in the imagination of the author or the reader." This seems at first sight to be a great paradox, and yet it can be made plausible to everyone by a common argument. Let us imagine one of those adventures that sometimes serve as gossip for a whole city, such as a marriage about to be performed and put off suddenly due to the opposition of a third party. This third party is a girl who is pregnant and who demands that the marriage that her lover has contracted with another be annulled. Suppose that a very virtuous woman who has only heard in general about the opposition desires to know the girl's motives. One could answer her in hundreds of different ways without making use of the expressions that a street porter or a debauchee would employ in such cases. One could tell her: "She has **had** the misfortune to be got with child"; "He enjoyed her"; "**He** had her company"; "They have been too intimate"; "They have had commerce together"; "He has received the last favor from her"; "She has let him have the most precious thing she owned, as the consequences plainly show"; "What passed between them cannot be modestly expressed, for that would offend chaste ears"; "She is obliged to have her honor restored." One could find several other better circumlocutions in order to answer the question

436

of the virtuous woman; but they are all going to paint in her imagination, as strongly as Michelangelo could have done on a canvas, the obscene and brutal action that resulted in the girl's pregnancy. And if by chance this virtuous woman had heard the bawdy expression used by one debauchee to whisper to another to let him know what was going on, she would not have had a clearer idea of the matter. No person, no matter how chaste he or she may be, can sincerely deny what I have just now said if he or she will take the trouble to examine what goes on in his or her mind. It is certain then that the most decent and the coarsest expressions equally pollute the imagination when the item described is an obscene one.

Make use as much as you please of the most chaste expressions that are employed in Scripture to represent what is called conjugal duty: "Adam knew his wife Eve"; "Abraham went in unto Hagar"; "I went unto the prophetess"; you will never be able to weaken the image raised by this term. It imprints itself on the mind just as if you used the language of a winegrower. Let us say the same about the phrases, "to consummate the marriage"; "The marriage was consummated"; "The marriage was not consummated"; which are, as it were, consecrated and cannot be passed by in the most serious accounts and in the most majestic histories[69]—those expressions excite the same idea as the words used by a peasant would.[70]

But how does it happen then, I will be asked, that a virtuous woman is not offended by expressions that are roundabout, and she would be angry if bawdy terms were used? I answer that it is due to the accessory ideas that accompany such terms, and that do not accompany a roundabout expression. The im-

---

[69] As those in which the divorce of Henry VIII and Catherine of Aragon is treated.

[70] The expression, "the parts that shall be nameless," is considered very modest and chaste. However, it is as expressive as any other. Basically, it amounts to naming what one says is not being named. It amounts to characterizing it in such a way that no one can be in doubt about what is intended.

modesty observed in people who talk like street porters, and their lack of respect are the real reasons why one gets angry. Three ideas are found in their expression. One is direct and is the principal one. The two others are indirect and accessory. The direct idea makes the obscenity of the object known and does not make it known any more distinctly than any other word can do. But the indirect and accessory ideas make known the attitude of the person who is speaking, his brutishness, his contempt for those who hear him, the desire he has to affront a virtuous woman. This is what makes her angry. . . . Therefore she is offended . . . because of the disrespect and incivility shown her. And this is the reason why wanton women very often carry on with much more fury than a virtuous woman against those who speak obscenely to them. They take this as an insult and a shocking affront. It is not love of chastity that animates them, but pride and the desire for vengeance. . . .

That is how I prove that it would not have been possible to keep out of this dictionary all matters that pollute the imagination. One necessarily pollutes it, no matter what one does to state that Henri IV had natural children.

The impossibility of closing the door to all objects that may pollute the imagination. It is certain then that it would have sufficed for me that I stayed within the limits of ordinary civility. A person who should have so great a love for purity as not only to wish that no unchaste desire might ever be excited in his soul but likewise that no obscene idea might be imprinted in his imagination could never achieve his goal unless he were to lose both sight and hearing as well as the memory of a multitude of matters that he could not prevent having seen and heard. Such a perfection is not to be hoped for as long as one can see both men and beasts, and as long as one knows the meaning of certain words that necessarily enter into the language of a country. It does not at all depend on us whether we have certain ideas when such and such an object strikes our senses, for those imprint themselves in the imagination whether we will or no. Chastity is in no danger from them provided the heart is disen-

gaged from them and disapproves of them. If in order to be
chaste it was necessary that no impure idea strike the imagination, it would be necessary to be careful about going to church
where they censure impurity and where so many lists of marriage
banns are read. It would be necessary never to hear the liturgy
that is read before the whole congregation on wedding days.
It would be necessary never to read the Holy Scripture, which
is the most excellent of all books; and it would be necessary to
flee, as from the plague, from all conversations in which people
are speaking of pregnancies, childbirths, and baptisms. The
imagination is a gadabout that moves with extreme rapidity
from effect to causes. It finds this path so well beaten that it
gets from one end to the other before reason has had a chance
to restrain it.

. . . .

This is what I have to say on the first of the two questions
that I was to discuss. I hope that one will see clearly the full
strength of my justification, and that it will be agreed that if
there are in my dictionary any obscenities worthy of censure,
they do not result from any expressions that I employed when
I am speaking for myself. Let us see now if they consist in the
things themselves, whether I have quoted the words of other
authors, or whether I have only given the sense of them. This
is the second question that I have undertaken to discuss.

One cannot take the affirmative on this question without
establishing these hypotheses: (1) that a historian is obliged to
suppress all the impure actions that he comes across, either in
the lives of princes, or in the lives of private citizens; (2) that
a moralist who condemns lewdness should never specify anything that might offend modesty. The purists, whom I have
spoken of so much above, must necessarily adopt these hypotheses; and it is certainly the case that there have always been
people who have condemned histories and satires in which lewd
disorders have been painted in the most frightful colors.

If our purists wish to avoid blame for reasoning inconsistently and for giving up maxims today that they return to tomorrow, they have to accept both hypotheses that I have indicated. They ought to say: (1) that a historian ought simply to note that Charlemagne, the two Joannas of Naples, and Henri IV were not chaste; (2) that a preacher or spiritual director, and any other person who wants to improve moral conduct, should simply and only generally censure lewd disorders.

.   .   .   .

An answer to three objections. Let us here examine three objections that have been commonly made. It is said: (1) that a doctor or a casuist is obliged by the nature of his subject to deal in filth, but that my work does not involve such a requirement; (2) that those who write in Latin can take liberties not permitted in our language; (3) that things permitted in previous ages ought to be prohibited in ours because of its prodigious corruption.

The first of these three difficulties can only occur in the minds of those readers who have no idea of the nature of my book. It is not a book . . . in which one only puts what one wants to. This is a historical dictionary, with commentary. "Laïs" ought to have its place in it as well as "Lucretia"; and since it is a dictionary that comes into the world after several others, it ought principally to furnish what is not reported in the others. It is necessary to give in it not only a recital of the best known events, but also a detailed account of less well-known events, and a collection of what has been dispersed in various places. It is necessary to bring to bear proofs, to examine them, confirm them, and clarify them. In a word this is a work of compilation. Now, no one ought to be unaware that "a compiler who narrates and comments on things has all the privileges of a doctor, or a lawyer, and so on. He may, as the occasion requires, make use of their professional vocabulary. If he reports the divorce of Lotharius and Tetberga, he can give extracts from Hincmar, Archbishop of Rheims, who wrote down the obscenities that were given as evidence during the trial." This is what I said in my *Reflections on the Alleged Judgment of the Public* in 1697. I repeat it along with this other passage: "When anyone has let me know the secret how to gather together in a compilation everything that the ancient writers say about the courtesan Laïs, and yet not relate any lewd events, then I will plead guilty. It must at least be proven to me that a commentator does not have the right to collect all that is said of Helen. But how would one prove this? Where is the legislator who has said to the compilers, 'So far you shall go, you shall not go beyond this. You shall not quote Athenaeus, nor this scholiast, nor that philosopher?' Is it not the case that the only thing that limits their writing is their reading?" I could name a great number of theologians who, having chosen a certain subject from a cheerfulness of heart, have quoted right and left everything that seemed proper to them, although it included items that might pollute the imagination. I will name only three of them: Lydius, Saldenus, and Lomeier. They were Flemish ministers, the first at Dordrecht, the second at The Hague, and the third at Zutphen. They were much esteemed for their erudition and their virtue. Let anyone read the dialogues of the first on marriage ceremonies, the dissertations of the second on the worth of a dog, and on eunuchs, and those of the third concerning kisses. He will find frightful obscenities therein and abominable quotations.

I will be answered that these works are in Latin. This is the second problem I have to resolve, and I shall show without any trouble that it is really no difficulty at all. For an obscene object does not harm decency any less when it is portrayed in Latin in the soul of those who understand that language than when it is painted in French in the souls of those who understand French. And if painting obscene objects in the imaginations of oneself and one's readers is something to be condemned, then one cannot exonerate those three ministers. They understood what they wrote, and they made it intelligible to all their readers, and consequently they have polluted their own minds, and they are daily polluting the imaginations of those who read their works. But would it not be quite unjust to blame them on that account? It is necessary then not to blame those who write in French, for they do no more than understand what they write and make it intelligible to their readers.

I am aware that it will be claimed that there are two differences in these cases: one, that those who understand Latin are not as numerous as those who understand French; the other, that those who understand Latin are better able to resist the malign influence of obscene objects than other men can. Here are three answers to this. In the first place, I say that Latin is known to so great a number of people throughout Europe that the first difference could never suffice to exonerate those who relate or quote obscenities in that language. The evil will always be great, and in fact, very great. In the second place, I say that it is only by small degrees that study provides strength to resist such objects as pollute the imagination; and thus Latin obscenities would always be very dangerous with respect to students. Generally speaking, one rarely finds that they are more chaste and less debauched than other young men. Lastly, I say that most of my readers have studied; for those who have not studied would hardly care to take the time to read a book interspersed, as this one is, with passages in Greek and Latin. In any case, they can understand nothing of the chief obscenities since they are in Latin. I conclude that if there is anything just and solid in the differences objected to me, it will favor my side rather than that of my opponents.

Let us go on to the third difficulty, which deals with the extreme corruption of our age. We have lost, it is said, the modesty of both our manners and our words. Such expressions as were formerly modest are no longer so. It is necessary to employ others that only excite decent ideas; for otherwise, the slight amount of virtue left will be lost. I am not going to examine whether it is right to claim that the present age is more corrupt than previous ones. The same lamentations have always been made, and this ought to make us somewhat doubtful about the claim. I find it hard to believe that the corruption of our time is equal to that of the reigns of Charles IX and Henri III. But let us not argue about this. Let us employ the "I grant for the sake of the argument" of the logicians, and let us suppose what is asked of us. I shall then make the contrary conclusion to what the critics have done. For it is never as necessary to show in the strongest and liveliest of terms the deformity of vice as when it is making the greatest havoc; and it would be as poor a means of stemming the torrents of uncleanness to employ soft words against it, as not daring to brand women who prostitute themselves with an odious name. . . . Those who claim that in view of the infinite corruption of our time one has to abstain from all narrations that they consider coarse are like a traveler who, in order to prevent his cloak, already completely covered with mud, from being dirtied, takes care not to bring it into a room where smoking is going on. If the depravity of the heart is so great that the reading of a sordid historical fact could impel young people to commit adultery, you may be assured that they are like so many plague-stricken patients whose condition you are afraid of worsening by exposing them to someone with hives. A polished style and delicate circumlocutions will not cure people so corrupted nor stop them at the brinks of precipices.

Surely what is here is the sophism of finding the wrong cause of an ill. The fate of chastity does not depend on this. You are not going to the origin of the evil. It requires completely different remedies. One has already completely absorbed obscenities and has completed his course in matters lewd and filthy, in words at least, before having read Suetonius. Wicked conversations, inevitable for any young man who is not kept under constant surveillance, are a thousand times worse than histories of obscenities. . . .

There is no middle ground here. It is necessary either that books make no mention of any lewd fact, or that our censors admit that the books will always be dangerous, no matter how delicately they be written. One translation may be more polite than another; but if they are both faithful, one will always find in them the images of obscenities that the original relates.

.   .   .   .

It is time to end this long dissertation. It is a more difficult matter to deal with than one would imagine. I hope that my justification will be most clearly seen, not by those who are so blinded by presumption as to be able to recognize when they have been disabused of something, but by those who were prevailed upon to believe, either on another's testimony, or for superficial reasons. If they deserve to be excused for having been imposed upon by specious appearances before I had presented these four Clarifications, they cannot hope to be excused if they remain obstinate in their error. These persons should have followed the precept of Jesus Christ, "Judge not according to the appearance, but judge righteous judgment" [John 7:24]. They relied on the first impressions that objects made on them and did not wait until they had heard the reasons on both sides. This is always necessary, and especially when it is a question of judging a writer who does not follow the common path. The first thing that they should suspect is that he has some reasons for this and that he would not take such a step if he had not examined the matter for a long time and from all sides and with much more care and attention than is given by those who only read his work. This well-grounded suspicion should have made people very slow and cautious in coming to an opinion. But, what is done is done. One can only hope that their second thoughts will be better than their first ones.

I shall inform my readers that one will find in various parts of this dictionary some apologetical reflections[123] right next to things that can shock tender minds.

---

[123] Chiefly with regard to obscenities.

Index

NOTE: The front matter (roman numeral page numbers) has been repaged for this edition. Therefore, index references to pages vii–x now refer to pages v–viii; index references to pages xi–xxxix now refer to pages viii–xxxvi; and index references to pages xli–xliv now refer to pages xxxvii–xl.

445

St. Louis Community College
at Meramec
Library